Praise for *The 8th Habit*

"Stephen Covey continues to *wow* us with his new *The 8th Habit*. As the world's most respected leadership expert, he builds on the foundation of his bestselling 7 *Habits* and gives another pattern to follow to live a life that is passionate, makes a difference and leaves a legacy of greatness that long outlives a life."

—Larry King

"This remarkable new book, *The 8th Habit: From Effectiveness to Greatness*, provides the key to unlocking a wondrous gift—namely, the greatness within each of us. It also achieves the same substantive standards Stephen Covey provided in *The 7 Habits of Highly Effective People*."

—John R. Wooden, Coach Emeritus,
UCLA Basketball, and author of *My Personal Best*

"Stephen Covey continues to amaze. With this book, he enables readers to take another giant step toward realizing the greatness that resides within ourselves and others. His 8th Habit is really a timeless principle of leadership—one of respect for the individual, an essential truth lost in a world that increasingly regards people as little more than a means of production. In a marketplace that is global and linked by seemingly infinite networks, Stephen helps us reveal and celebrate the unique greatness of the countless people who touch our lives every day. As the leader of 120,000 talented individuals in nearly 150 countries, I appreciate the distinction—and the framework for leadership that this learned man so freely shares."

—William G. Parrett, Chief Executive Officer,
Deloitte Touche Tohmatsu

"With *The 8th Habit*, Stephen Covey has taken leadership to a new, inspiring level. A book that all who aspire to leadership positions must read."

—Arun Gandhi, President, M.K. Gandhi Institute for Nonviolence

"Great leaders know and appreciate the value of people. They don't just listen to the opinions of others, they seek them out. They make sure every member of their team has the opportunity to make a meaningful, lasting contribution. They recognize that their most important responsibility as a leader is to develop their people, give them room to grow and inspire them to realize their full potential. This has long been our philosophy at Marriott, where we believe that if we take great care of our associates, they will take great care of our customers. Stephen Covey shares this philosophy, and his book *The 8th Habit: From Effectiveness to Greatness* is an excellent guide on how to be a stronger, more effective and truly inspiring leader."

—J.W. Marriott, Jr., Chairman and CEO, Marriott International, Inc.

"As usual, Stephen R. Covey has excelled in focusing on what inspires the heart and at the same time gets the business done. The 8th Habit—to have peace of mind and intense focus—is essential."

—Ram Charan, author of *What the CEO Wants You to Know* and coauthor of *Execution: The Discipline of Getting Things Done*

"I have been waiting more than a decade for the next phase of Stephen Covey's work on *The 7 Habits of Highly Effective People*. The demands on my life have changed dramatically since I first read *The 7 Habits* and I needed another way to look at my life and my balance. I am inspired again!"

—Greg Coleman, EVP, Yahoo! Media and Sales

"*The 8th Habit* is a powerful, practical road map for progressing beyond effectiveness. Anyone who aspires to happiness and fulfillment should read this book."

—Clayton M. Christensen, Robert and Jane Cizik Professor of Business Administration, Harvard Business School

"The Godfather of Leadership has done it one better! Stephen Covey's *The 8th Habit* will provide you with the ultimate tool to discover your unmistakable *voice* in pursuit of your true *vision.*"

—Pat Croce, former President, Philadelphia 76ers (NBA), and bestselling author of *I Feel Great and You Will Too!* and *Lead or Get Off the Pot!*

"An absolute must-read for aspiring business executives who want to significantly increase their personal effectiveness in the workplace and at home. Covey has created a brilliant blueprint for both career and personal success in the new millennium."

—Douglas R. Conant, President and CEO, Campbell Soup Co.

"*The 8th Habit* is filled with timeless principles that will help both individuals and organizations in their pursuit of excellence. Stephen's latest insights are challenging and compelling. This book is a call to action for twenty-first-century leaders."

—Tim Tassopoulos, Sr. Vice President, Operations, Chick-fil-A

"Stephen Covey's new work resonates strongly with my belief that every individual and every organization has the potential to achieve and sustain greatness. He understands that greatness requires passion and passion must be driven by core business practices that foster and reward collaboration, growth and commitment."

—Ann Livermore, Executive Vice President, Technology Solutions Group, HP

"I believe Stephen Covey has really captured the essence of what leadership is all about. *The 8th Habit* will turn out to be the most important one for successful executives."

—Michael H. Jordan, Chairman and CEO, EDS

SIMON &
SCHUSTER

ALSO BY STEPHEN R. COVEY

The 7 Habits of Highly Effective People
The 7 Habits of Highly Effective People Personal Workbook
The 7 Habits of Highly Effective People Journal
The 7 Habits of Highly Effective Families
Living the 7 Habits
The Nature of Leadership
First Things First
Principle-Centered Leadership

ALSO FROM FRANKLINCOVEY CO.

The 7 Habits of Highly Effective Teens
The 7 Habits of Highly Effective Teens Personal Workbook
The 7 Habits of Highly Effective Teens Journal

Life Matters
businessThink
What Matters Most
The 10 Natural Laws of Successful Time and Life Management
The Power Principle
Breakthrough Factor

THE 8th HABIT

*From Effectiveness
to Greatness*

STEPHEN R. COVEY

**SIMON &
SCHUSTER**

London · New York · Sydney · Toronto · Dublin

A VIACOM COMPANY

First published in Great Britain by
Simon & Schuster UK Ltd, 2004
A Viacom Company

Book design by Ellen R. Sasahara

1 3 5 7 9 10 8 6 4 2

Simon & Schuster UK Ltd
Africa House
64–78 Kingsway
London WC2B 6AH

www.simonsays.co.uk

Simon & Schuster Australia
Sydney

A CIP catalogue record for this book is
available from the British Library

ISBN 0-7432-0682-7

Printed & bound in Great Britain by
Mackays of Chatham plc

To the humble, courageous, "great" ones
among us who exemplify how
leadership is a choice,
not a position

ACKNOWLEDGMENTS

One of the great learnings of my life is this: If you want to make a new contribution, you've got to make a whole new preparation. Though every significant writing project I've ever undertaken has reinforced this principle, it is so easy to forget. I began working on this book five years ago thinking I could draw on my lifetime of study, teaching and consulting in the field of leadership and "whip it out" in a matter of a few months. After more than a year of teaching the material and writing, my team and I finished an initial rough draft—thrilled we had finally arrived. It was at that moment we experienced what hikers often discover when climbing mountains: We hadn't reached the summit at all, only the top of the first rise. From this new vantage point of sweat-earned insights we could see things we had never seen before—ones only made visible at the top of that hill. So we set our sights on the "real" mountain and began the new climb.

We literally went through this same experience another dozen times, each time thinking we had finally reached the "peak," each time convinced that the book was finally "there" and each time being humbled into the realization that we had only risen to yet another critical level of insight, and that there was another mountain ahead.

The greatest and most inspiring mountain climbing achievements in history are not so much stories of individual achievement, but are stories of the extraordinary power of a unified, talented, prepared *team* that stays loyally committed to one another and to their shared vision *to the end*. Most climbing teams that set out to climb Mount Everest never reach the summit—only the very, very few. For one reason or another, most people and teams, when pressed to their limits by the extreme conditions, drop out along the way and either choose to or are forced to turn back. The story behind the five-year climb to completing this book is no different. Were it not for the determination and unflagging commitment, patience, encouragement and synergistic contributions of the remarkable team that assisted me with this project, the book would not only have failed to become *what* it is, it would have never seen the light of day!

So it is with deep gratitude that I express my appreciation to the following for their contributions:

- To literally tens of thousands of people in various settings all over the world who cared enough to give honest feedback and to willingly share their real-time, real-life issues, pains and hopes, all of which put me on a "chain of mountains" learning climb that resulted in constant reinvention, precious insights and endless tests of the team's patience.
- To Boyd Craig for his extraordinary, able, five-year commitment, passion and devotion in both developmental and line editing of the book; for managing all dimensions of this massive team book project; for his leadership and synergistic partnering with our publisher, our agent and within our company; and above all for his spirituality, judgment, flexibility, patience and content expertise. My heartfelt gratitude goes likewise to Boyd's wife, Michelle Daines Craig, for her magnificent positive spirit and unfailing support and sacrifice that sustained the "marathon."
- To my office staff and extended office support team—Patti Pallat, Julie Judd Gillman, Darla Salin, Julie McAllister, Nancy Aldridge, Kara Foster Holmes, Luci Ainsworth, Diane Thompson and Christie Brzezinski—for truly uncommon devotion and loyalty, second-mile make-it-happen service and world-class professionalism.
- To my committed associates at FranklinCovey, especially to Bob Whitman and my son Sean for their thoughtful, in-depth review of the final manuscript, and their invaluable, practical feedback.
- To Edward H. Powley for his spearheading assistance on the leadership literature review, and to Richard Garcia and Mike Robins for their tireless, persistent research assistance.
- To Tessa Meyer Santiago for her editorial assistance in early drafts of the book.
- To Sherrie Hall Everett for her years of work in creating and re-creating the book's graphics.
- To Brad Anderson, Bruce Neibaur, Micah Merrill and many other talented colleagues who, over the years, have been the creative energy behind the award-winning films included on the companion DVD to this book.

- To Greg Link for his visionary marketing genius and continued commitment to our mission.
- To my son Stephen for teaching me so much about trust, both by his own personal example and by drilling down into its theoretical and practical foundations.
- To my delightful literary agent, Jan Miller, and her partner, Shannon Miser-Marven, for years of championing service and advocacy.
- To Bob Asahina, my long-time trusted editor, for once again helping me remember to get out of my own head and to always start with where the reader is.
- To our valued publishing partners at Simon & Schuster—especially Carolyn Reidy, Martha Levin, Suzanne Donahue and Dominick Anfuso—for hanging in there through the extended "labor and delivery" process, including more than a few "false labor" drills on the way to the summit.
- To my dear wife, Sandra, my children and my grandchildren who, though taken to their wits' end with this never-ending book project, chose to smile and encourage rather than wring my neck. Also to my beloved grandfather Stephen L Richards; my noble parents, Stephen G. and Louise Richards Covey; and my dear sisters and brother, Irene, Helen Jean, Marilyn and John, who from my boyhood to the present have profoundly influenced who I have become.
- To the God and Father of us all, for His plan of happiness for *all* His children.

CONTENTS

THE 8th HABIT

THE PAIN

L ISTEN TO THE VOICES:

   "I'm stuck, in a rut."

   "I have no life. I'm burned out—exhausted."

"No one really values or appreciates me. My boss doesn't have a clue of all I'm capable of."

"I don't feel especially needed—not at work, not by my teenage and grown children, not by my neighbors and community, not by my spouse—except to pay the bills."

"I'm frustrated and discouraged."

"I'm just not making enough to make ends meet. I never seem to get ahead."

"Maybe I just don't have what it takes."

"I'm not making a difference."

"I feel empty inside. My life lacks meaning; something's missing."

"I'm angry. I'm scared. I can't afford to lose my job."

"I'm lonely."

"I'm stressed out; everything's urgent."

"I'm micromanaged and suffocating."

"I'm sick of all the backstabbing politics and kissing up."

"I'm bored—just putting in my time. Most of my satisfactions come off the job."

"I'm beat up to get the numbers. The pressure to produce is unbelievable. I simply don't have the time or resources to do it all."

"With a spouse who doesn't understand and kids who don't listen or obey, home is no better than work."

"I can't change things."

• • •

THESE ARE THE VOICES of people at work and at home—voices of literally millions of parents, laborers, service providers, managers, professionals and executives all over the world who are fighting to make it in
the new reality. The pain is *personal*, and it's deep. You may relate with
many of the statements yourself. As Carl Rogers once said, "What is
most personal is most general."[1]

Of course some people *are* engaged, contributing and energized in
their work . . . but far too few. I frequently ask large audiences, "How
many agree that the vast majority of the workforce in your organization
possesses far more talent, intelligence, capability and creativity than
their present jobs require or even allow?" The overwhelming majority
of the people raise their hands, and this is with groups all over the world.
About the same percentage acknowledge that they are under immense
pressure to produce more for less. Just think about it. People face a new
and increasing expectation to produce more for less in a terribly complex world, yet they are simply not allowed to use a significant portion
of their talents and intelligence.

In no way is this pain more clearly or practically manifest in *organizations* than in their inability to *focus on* and *execute* their highest priorities.
Using what we call the xQ (Execution Quotient) Questionnaire*, Harris Interactive, the originators of the Harris Poll, recently polled 23,000
U.S. residents employed full time within *key industries*† and in *key functional areas*.‡ Consider a few of their most stunning findings:

- Only 37 percent said they have a clear understanding of what
  their organization is trying to achieve and why.
- Only 1 in 5 was enthusiastic about their team's and organization's
  goals.
- Only 1 in 5 workers said they have a clear "line of sight" between
  their tasks and their team's and organization's goals.

---

* For a more detailed summary of the results of the Harris Interactive study of 23,000
workers, managers and executives who took the xQ Questionnaire, see Appendix 6: xQ
Results.

† Key industries include: accommodation/food services, automotive, banking/finance,
communications, education, health care, military, public administration/government,
retail trade, technology services, and telecommunications.

‡ Key functional areas include: accounting, administrative assistant/secretary, advertis-
ing/marketing professional, business executive, computer specialist, education administrator, financial professional, government professional, health care professional, and
sales agent/representative.

- Only half were satisfied with the work they have accomplished at the end of the week.
- Only 15 percent felt that their organization fully enables them to execute key goals.
- Only 15 percent felt they worked in a high-trust environment.
- Only 17 percent felt their organization fosters open communication that is respectful of differing opinions and that results in new and better ideas.
- Only 10 percent felt that their organization holds people accountable for results.
- Only 20 percent fully trusted the organization they work for.
- Only 13 percent have high-trust, highly cooperative working relationships with other groups or departments.

If, say, a soccer team had these same scores, only four of the eleven players on the field would know which goal is theirs. Only two of the eleven would care. Only two of the eleven would know what position they play and know exactly what they are supposed to do. And all but two players would, in some way, be competing against their own team members rather than the opponent.

The data is sobering. It matches my own experience with people in organizations of every kind all around the world. Despite all our gains in technology, product innovation and world markets, most people are not thriving in the organizations they work for. They are neither fulfilled nor excited. They are frustrated. They are not clear about where the organization is headed or what its highest priorities are. They are bogged down and distracted. Most of all, they don't feel they can change much. Can you imagine the personal and organizational cost of failing to fully engage the passion, talent and intelligence of the workforce? It is far greater than all taxes, interest charges and labor costs put together!

WHY AN 8TH HABIT?

The world has profoundly changed since *The 7 Habits of Highly Effective People* was published in 1989. The challenges and complexity we face in our personal lives and relationships, in our families, in our professional lives, and in our organizations are of a different order of magnitude. In fact, many mark 1989—the year we witnessed the fall of the Berlin

Wall—as the beginning of the Information Age, the birth of a new reality, a sea change of incredible significance—truly a new era.

Many have asked whether the 7 Habits are still relevant in today's new reality. My answer is always the same: The greater the change and more difficult the challenges, the *more* relevant they become. You see, the 7 Habits are about becoming *highly* effective. They represent a *complete* framework of universal, *timeless* principles of character and human effectiveness.

Being *effective* as individuals and organizations is no longer optional in today's world—it's the price of entry to the playing field. But surviving, thriving, innovating, excelling and leading in this new reality will require us to build on and reach beyond effectiveness. The call and need of a new era is for *greatness*. It's for *fulfillment, passionate execution*, and *significant contribution*. These are on a different plane or *dimension*. They are different in kind—just as *significance* is different in *kind*, not in *degree*, from success. Tapping into the higher reaches of human genius and motivation—what we could call *voice*—requires a new mind-set, a new skill-set, a new tool-set . . . a new habit.

The 8th Habit, then, is not about adding one more habit to the 7—one that somehow got forgotten. It's about seeing and harnessing the

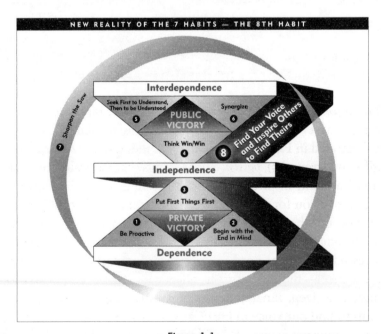

Figure 1.1

power of *a third dimension* to the 7 Habits that meets *the* central challenge of the new Knowledge Worker Age. This 8th Habit is to *Find Your Voice and Inspire Others to Find Theirs*.

The 8th Habit represents the pathway to the enormously promising side of today's reality. It stands in stark contrast to the pain and frustration I've been describing. In fact, it is a timeless reality. It is the voice of the human spirit—full of hope and intelligence, resilient by nature, boundless in its potential to serve the common good. This voice also encompasses the soul of organizations that will survive, thrive and profoundly impact the future of the world.

Figure 1.2

Voice is *unique personal significance*—significance that is revealed as we face our greatest challenges and which makes us equal to them.

As illustrated in Figure 1.2, voice lies at the nexus of *talent* (your natural gifts and strengths), *passion* (those things that naturally energize, excite, motivate and inspire you), *need* (including what the world needs enough to pay you for), and *conscience* (that still, small voice within that assures you of what is right and that prompts you to actually do it). When you engage in work that taps your talent and fuels your passion—that rises out of a great need in the world that you feel drawn by conscience to meet—therein lies your voice, your calling, your soul's code.

There is a deep, innate, almost inexpressible yearning within each one of us to find our voice in life. The exponential, revolutionary explosion of the internet is one of the most powerful modern manifestations of this truth. The internet is perhaps the perfect symbol of the new world, of the Information/Knowledge Worker economy, and of the dramatic changes that have occurred. In their 1999 book, *Cluetrain Manifesto*, authors Locke, Levine, Searls and Weinberger put it this way:

> All of us are finding our voices again. Learning how to talk to one another. . . . Inside, outside, there's a conversation going on today that wasn't happening at all five years ago and hasn't been very much in evidence since the Industrial Revolution began. Now, spanning the planet via Internet and Worldwide Web, this conversation is so vast, so multifaceted, that trying to figure out what it is about is futile. It's about a billion years of pent up hopes and fears and dreams coded in serpentine double helixes, the collective flashback déjà vu of our strange perplexing species. Something ancient, elemental, sacred, something very, very funny that's broken loose in the pipes and wires of the twenty-first century.
>
> . . . there are millions and millions of threads in this conversation, but at the beginning and end of each one is a human being. . . .
>
> This fervid desire for the Web bespeaks a longing so intense that it can only be understood as spiritual. A longing indicates something is missing in our lives. What is missing is the sound of the human voice. The spiritual lure of the Web is the promise of the return of voice.[2]

Rather than further describe *voice*, let me illustrate it through the true story of one man. When I met Muhammad Yunus, founder of the Grameen Bank—a unique organization established for the sole purpose of extending microcredit to the poorest of the poor in Bangladesh—I asked him when and how he had gained his vision. He said he didn't have any vision to begin with. He simply saw someone in need, tried to fill it, and the vision evolved. Muhammad Yunus's vision of a poverty-free world was set in motion with an event on the streets of Bangladesh. While interviewing him for my syndicated column* on Leadership, he shared his story with me:

It all started twenty-five years ago. I was teaching economics at a university in Bangladesh. The country was in the middle of a famine. I felt terrible. Here I was, teaching the elegant theories of economics in the classroom with all the en-

---

* *New York Times Syndicate.*

thusiasm of a brand-new Ph.D. from the United States. But I would walk out of the classroom and see skeletons all around me, people waiting to die.

I felt that whatever I had learned, whatever I was teaching, was all make-believe stories, with no meaning for people's lives. So I started trying to find out how people lived in the village next door to the university campus. I wanted to find out whether there was anything I could do as a human being to delay or stop the death, even for one single person. I abandoned the bird's-eye view that lets you see everything from above, from the sky. I assumed a worm's-eye view, trying to find whatever comes right in front of you—smell it, touch it, see if you can do something about it.

One particular incident took me in a new direction. I met a woman who was making bamboo stools. After a long discussion, I found out that she made only two U.S. pennies each day. I couldn't believe anybody could work so hard and make such beautiful bamboo stools yet make such a tiny amount of profit. She explained to me that because she didn't have the money to buy the bamboo to make the stools, she had to borrow from the trader—and the trader imposed the condition that she had to sell the product to him alone, at a price that he decided.

And that explains the two pennies—she was virtually in bonded labor to this person. And how much did the bamboo cost? She said, "Oh, about twenty cents. For a very good one twenty-five cents." I thought, "People suffer for twenty cents and there is nothing anyone can do about it?" I debated whether I should give her twenty cents, but then I came up with another idea—let me make a list of people who needed that kind of money. I took a student of mine and we went around the village for several days and came up with a list of forty-two such people. When I added up the total amount they needed, I got the biggest shock of my life: It added up to twenty-seven dollars! I felt ashamed of myself for being part of a society which could not provide even twenty-seven dollars to forty-two hard-working, skilled human beings.

To escape that shame, I took the money out of my pocket and gave it to my student. I said, "You take this money and give it to those forty-two people that we met and tell them this is a loan, but they can pay me back whenever they are able to. In the meantime, they can sell their products wherever they can get a good price."

> *All that is necessary for the triumph*
> *of evil is that good men do nothing.*[3]
> EDMUND BURKE

After receiving the money, they were very excited. And seeing that excitement made me think, "What do I do now?" I thought of the bank branch which was located on the campus of the university, and I went to the manager and suggested that he lend money to the poor people that I had met in the village. He fell from the sky! He said, "You are crazy. It's impossible. How could we lend money to poor people? They are not creditworthy." I pleaded with him and said, "At least give it a try, find out—it's only a small amount of money." He said, "No. Our rules don't permit it. They cannot offer collateral, and such a tiny amount is not worth lending." He suggested that I see the high officials in the banking hierarchy in Bangladesh.

I took his advice and went to the people who matter in the banking section. Everybody told me the same thing. Finally, after several days of running around, I offered myself as a guarantor. "I'll guarantee the loan, I'll sign whatever they want me to sign, and they can give me the money and I'll give it to the people that I want to."

So that was the beginning. They warned me repeatedly that the poor people who receive the money will never pay it back. I said, "I'll take a chance." And the surprising thing was, they repaid me every penny. I got very excited and came to the manager and said, "Look, they pay back, there's no problem." But he said, "Oh, no, they're just fooling you. Soon they will take more money and never pay you back." So I gave them more money, and they paid me back. I told this to him, but he said, "Well, maybe you can do it in one village, but if you do it in two villages it won't work." And I hurriedly did it in two villages—and it worked.

So it became a kind of struggle between me and the bank manager and his colleagues in the highest positions. They kept saying that a larger number, five villages probably, will show it. So I did it in five villages, and it only showed that everybody paid back. Still they didn't give up. They said, "Ten villages. Fifty villages. One hundred villages." And so it became a kind of contest between them and me. I came up with results they could not deny because it was their money I was giving, but they would not accept it because they are trained to believe that poor people are not reliable. Luckily, I was not trained that way so I could believe whatever I was seeing, as it revealed itself. But the bankers' minds, their eyes were blinded by the knowledge they had.

Finally, I had the thought, Why am I trying to convince them? I am totally convinced that poor people can take money and pay it back. Why don't we set up a separate bank? That excited me, and I wrote down the proposal and went to the government to get the permission to set up a bank. It took me two years to convince the government.

On October 2nd 1983, we became a bank—a formal, independent bank. And what excitement for all of us, now that we had our own bank and we could expand as we wished. And expand we did.

> *When you are inspired by some great purpose, some extraordinary project, all your thoughts break their bounds. Your mind transcends limitations, your consciousness expands in every direction, and you find yourself in a new, great and wonderful world.*
>
> THE YOGA SUTRAS OF PATANJALI

Grameen Bank now works in more than 46,000 villages in Bangladesh, through 1,267 branches and over 12,000 staff members. They have lent more than $4.5 billion, in loans of twelve to fifteen dollars, averaging under $200. Each year they lend about half a billion dollars. They even lend to beggars to help them come out of begging and start selling. A housing loan is three hundred dollars. These are small numbers to those of us in business. But think in terms of the individual impact: To lend $500 million annually required 3.7 million people, 96 percent of whom are women, to make a decision that they could and would take steps to change their lives and the lives of their families; 3.7 million people had to decide that they were capable of creating change; 3.7 million people survived the sleepless night to show up trembling but committed at the Grameen office the next morning. At the heart of this empowerment lies individual women who chose individually and in synergistic norm-producing groups to become self-reliant, independent entrepreneurs producing goods out of their own homes or neighborhoods or backyards to become economically viable and successful. They *found* their voices.

As I have studied and interviewed some of the world's great leaders, I noticed that their sense of vision and voice has usually evolved slowly. I am sure there are exceptions. Some may have a vision of what is possible suddenly burst upon their consciousness. But generally speaking, I find that vision comes as people sense human need and respond to their conscience in trying to meet that need. And when they meet that need, they see another, and meet that, and on and on. Little by little, they begin to generalize this sense of need and start thinking of ways to institutionalize their efforts so they can be sustained.

Muhammad Yunus is an example of a man who did exactly that—sensed human *need* and responded to *conscience* by applying his *talent* and *passion* to meet that need—first personally, then in building trust and searching for creative solutions to problems, and finally by institutionalizing the capacity to fill the needs of society through an organization. He found his voice in inspiring others to find theirs. The microcredit movement is now spreading across the world.

> *Few of us can do great things, but all of us can do small things with great love.*
> MOTHER TERESA

THE PAIN—THE PROBLEM—THE SOLUTION

I've begun by describing the pain of the workforce. It is felt by people at every level of every kind of organization. It is felt in families, in communities and in society generally.

The purpose of this book is to give you a road map that will lead you from such pain and frustration to true fulfillment, relevance, significance and contribution in today's new landscape—not only in your work and organization, but also in your whole life. In short, it will lead you to *find your voice.* If you so choose, it will also lead you to greatly expand your influence regardless of your position—inspiring others you care about, your team and your organization to find their voices and increase *manyfold* their effectiveness, growth and impact. You will discover that such influence and leadership comes by *choice*, not from position or rank.

The best and often only way to break through pain to a lasting *solution* is to first understand the fundamental *problem* causing the pain. In this case, much of the problem lies in behavior that flows out of an incomplete or deeply flawed paradigm or view of human nature—one that undermines people's sense of worth and straitjackets their talents and potential.

The *solution* to the problem is like most significant breakthroughs in human history—it comes from a fundamental *break with* old ways of thinking. The promise of this book is that if you will be patient and pay the price of understanding the root problem and then set a course of living the timeless, universal principles embodied in the solution outlined in this book, your influence will steadily grow from the inside-out; you will find your voice and will inspire your team and organization to find theirs in a dramatically changed world.

Chapter 1 has briefly touched on the painful reality.

Chapter 2 identifies the core problem. Understanding this deeply entrenched problem will shed a profound light on the challenges we face personally, in our family and work relationships and in the organizations in which we spend much of our lives. It will require some mental effort—twelve pages' worth. But the investment of delving into the *human* side of what has happened in *organizations* over the last century will give you the key paradigm for the rest of the book and will begin to give you wisdom, guidance and power in dealing with many of the most significant *personal* and *relationship* challenges and opportunities you face. So hang in there; it will be worth it.

Chapter 3 provides an overview of the 8th Habit solution that unfolds in the remainder of the book and a brief section on how to get the most out of this book.

FILM: *Legacy*

Before moving on to the next chapter, I would like to invite you to first view a little three-minute film called *Legacy*. It has been shown in movie theaters across the United States. It will give you a few moments to reflect on the core elements of your voice and four corresponding universal human needs—living, loving, learning and leaving a legacy. It will subtly communicate the book's one basic model or paradigm discussed in the next chapter—the WHOLE PERSON model.

In most of the chapters of this book I will refer to *a short film* like this one, which attempts to teach the essence of the content of that chapter. *You will find these films—many of which have won prestigious national and international film awards—on the DVD included with the book.* The films, some true to life and others fictionalized, are powerful and charged with emotion. I'm convinced that they will enable you to better *see, feel* and *understand* this material. I also believe you'll enjoy, and find tremendous value in, them. If you're not interested in the films, that's fine. Just skip the references to them and read on.

Now simply insert the DVD into your DVD player and select *Legacy* from the menu. Enjoy.

Chapter 2

THE PROBLEM

When the infrastructure shifts, everything rumbles.[1]
STAN DAVIS

WE ARE WITNESSES TO one of the most significant shifts in human history. Peter Drucker, one of the greatest management thinkers of our time, puts it this way:

"In a few hundred years, when the history of our time is written from a long-term perspective, it is likely that the most important event those historians will see is not technology, not the Internet, not e-commerce. It is an unprecedented change in the human condition. For the first time—literally—substantial and rapidly growing numbers of people have choices. For the first time, they will have to manage themselves.

"And society is totally unprepared for it."[2]

TO UNDERSTAND THE CORE problem and the profound implications of Drucker's prophetic statement, we must look first at the context of history—namely, the five ages of civilization's voice: first, the Hunter and Gatherer Age; second, the Agricultural Age; third, the Industrial Age; fourth, the Information/Knowledge Worker Age; and finally, an emerging Age of Wisdom.

Imagine for a moment that you take a step back in time and are a hunter and a gatherer of food. Each day you go out with a bow and arrow or stones and sticks to gather food for your family. That's all you've ever known, seen and done to survive. Now imagine someone

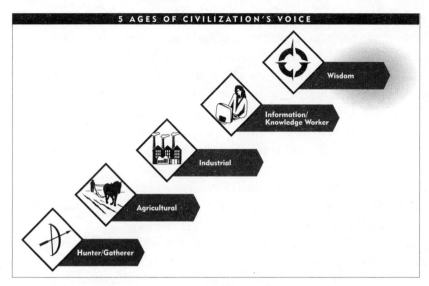

Figure 2.1

comes up to you and tries to persuade you to become what he calls a "farmer." What do you think your response would be?

You see him go out and scratch the earth and throw little seeds into the ground and you see nothing; you see him watering the soil and removing weeds and still you see nothing. But eventually you see a great harvest. You notice his yield as a "farmer" is fifty times greater than yours as a hunter and gatherer, and you are considered one of the best. What would you do? You would likely say to yourself, "Even if I wanted to, I couldn't do that. I don't have the skills and I don't have the tools." You just wouldn't know how to work that way.

Now the farmer is so productive that you see him making enough money to send his kids to school and give them great opportunities. You are barely surviving. Little by little, you're drawn to go through the intense learning process of becoming a farmer. You raise your children and grandchildren as farmers. That's exactly what happened in our early history. There was a downsizing of hunters and gatherers of over 90 percent; they lost their jobs.

Several generations pass, and along comes the Industrial Age. People build factories and learn specialization, delegation and scalability. They learn how to take raw materials through an assembly line with very high levels of efficiency. The productivity of the Industrial Age goes up fifty times over the family farm. Now if you were a farmer producing fifty times more than hunters and gatherers and all of a sudden you see an industrial factory rise up and start outproducing the family farm by fifty times, what would you say? You might be jealous, even threatened. But what would you need to be a player in the Industrial Age? You would need a completely new skill-set and tool-set. More importantly, you'd need a new mind-set—a new way of thinking. The fact is that the factory of the Industrial Age produced fifty times more than the family farm, and over time, 90 percent of the farmers were downsized. Those who survived in farming took the Industrial Age concept and created the industrialized farm. Today, only 3 percent of the people in the United States are farmers, who produce most of the food for the entire country and much of the world.

Do you believe that the Information/Knowledge Worker Age we're moving into will outproduce the Industrial Age fifty times? I believe it will. We're just barely beginning to see it. It will outproduce it fifty times—not twice, not three or ten times, but fifty. Nathan Myhrvold, former chief technology officer at Microsoft, puts it this way: "The top software developers are more productive than average software developers not by a factor of 10X or 100X or even 1000X but by 10,000X."

Quality knowledge work is so valuable that unleashing its potential offers organizations an extraordinary opportunity for value creation. If that is true, just think of the value of unleashing the potential of your children. Knowledge work leverages all of the other investments that an organization or a family has already made. In fact, knowledge workers are the link to all of the organization's other investments. They provide focus, creativity, and leverage in utilizing those investments to better achieve the organization's objectives.

Do you believe the Knowledge Worker Age will eventually bring about a downsizing of up to 90 percent of the Industrial Age workforce? I believe it. Current outsourcing and unemployment trends are just the tip of the iceberg. In fact, these trends have become a very hot political issue. But the reality is that much of our losses in Industrial Age jobs have less to do with government policy and free trade agreements than they do with the dramatic shift in our economy to the Knowledge Worker Age. Do you think it will be threatening to today's workforce to learn the new mind-set, the new skill-set, and the new tool-set of this new age? Imagine what it will take. Imagine what it will take for *you*— what it will take to be a player in this new era. Imagine what it will require of your organization!

Drucker compares the Industrial—Manual Worker Age with today's Knowledge Worker Age this way:

> The most important, and indeed the truly unique, contribution of management in the 20th century was the fifty-fold increase in the productivity of the MANUAL WORKER in manufacturing.
>
> The most important contribution management needs to make in the 21st century is similarly to increase the productivity of KNOWLEDGE WORK and the KNOWLEDGE WORKER.
>
> The most valuable assets of a 20th-century company were its *production equipment.* The most valuable asset of a 21st-century institution, whether business or non-business, will be its *knowledge workers* and their *productivity.*[3]

The great historian Arnold Toynbee said that you could pretty well summarize the history of society and the institutions in it in four words: *Nothing fails like success.* In other words, when you have a challenge and the response is equal to the challenge, that's called success. But once you have a new challenge, the old, once-successful response no longer works. That's why it's called a failure. We live in a Knowledge Worker Age but operate our organizations in a controlling Industrial Age model that absolutely suppresses the release of human potential. Voice is essentially irrelevant. This is an astounding finding. The mind-set of the Industrial Age that still dominates today's workplace will simply not work in the Knowledge Worker Age and new economy. And the fact is, people have taken this same controlling mind-set home. So often it dominates the way we communicate and deal with our spouses and the way we try to manage, motivate and discipline our children.

THE THING MIND-SET OF THE INDUSTRIAL AGE

The main assets and primary drivers of economic prosperity in the Industrial Age were machines and capital—*things.* People were necessary but replaceable. You could control and churn through manual workers with little consequence—supply exceeded demand. You just got more able bodies that would comply with strict procedures. People were like things—you could be efficient with them. When all you want is a person's body and you don't really want their mind, heart or spirit (all inhibitors to the free-flowing processes of the machine age), you have reduced a person to a thing.

So many of our modern management practices come from the Industrial Age.

It gave us the belief that you have to control and manage people.

It gave us our view of accounting, which makes people an expense and machines assets. Think about it. People are put on the P&L statement as an expense; equipment is put on the balance sheet as an investment.

It gave us our carrot-and-stick motivational philosophy—the Great Jackass technique that motivates with a carrot in front (reward) and drives with a stick from behind (fear and punishment).

It gave us centralized budgeting—where trends are extrapolated into the future and hierarchies and bureaucracies are formed to drive "getting the numbers"—an obsolete reactive process that produces "kiss-up" cultures bent on "spending it so we won't lose it next year" and protecting the backside of your department.

All these practices and many, many more came from the Industrial Age—working with manual workers.

The problem is, managers today are still applying the Industrial Age control model to knowledge workers. Because many in positions of authority do not see the true worth and potential of their people and do not possess a complete, accurate understanding of human nature, *they manage people as they do things*. This lack of understanding also prevents them from tapping into the highest motivations, talents and genius of people. What happens when you treat people like things today? It insults and alienates them, depersonalizes work, and creates low-trust, unionized, litigious cultures. What happens when you treat your teenage children like things? It, too, insults and alienates, depersonalizes precious family relationships and creates low trust, contention and rebellion.

THE DOWNWARD SPIRAL OF CODEPENDENCY

What happens when you manage people like things? They stop believing that leadership can become a choice. Most people think of leadership as a position and therefore don't see themselves as leaders. Making personal leadership (influence) a choice is like having the freedom to play the piano. It is a freedom that has to be earned—only then can leadership become a choice.

Until then, people think that only those in positions of authority should decide what must be done. They have consented, perhaps unconsciously, to being controlled like a thing. Even if they perceive a need, they don't take the initiative to act. They wait to be told what to do by the person with the formal title, and then they respond as directed. Consequently, they blame the formal leader when things go wrong and give him or her the credit when things go well. And they are thanked for their "cooperation and support."

This widespread reluctance to take initiative, to act independently, only fuels formal leaders' imperative to direct or manage their subordinates. This, they believe, is what they must do in order to get followers to act. And this cycle quickly escalates into codependency. Each party's weakness reinforces and ultimately justifies the other's behavior. The more a manager controls, the more he/she evokes behaviors that necessitate greater control or managing. The codependent culture that develops is eventually institutionalized to the point that no one takes responsibility. Over time, both leaders and followers confirm their roles in an unconscious pact. They disempower themselves by believing that others must change before their own circumstances can improve. The same cycle reappears in families between parents and children.

This silent conspiracy is everywhere. Not many people are brave enough to even recognize it in themselves. Whenever they hear the idea, they instinctively look *outside* themselves. When I teach this material to large audiences, I often pause after a couple of hours and ask the question, "How many like this material, but feel that the people who *really* need it aren't here?" They usually explode in laughter, but most hands go up.

Perhaps you, too, are thinking that the people who really need a book like this aren't reading it. That very thought reveals codependency. If you look at this material through the weaknesses of another, you disempower yourself and empower their weakness to continue to suck initiative, energy and excitement from your life.

FILM: *Max & Max*

Before moving deeper, I would like to illustrate the nature of the *problem* we've been discussing with a great little film called *Max & Max*. It's the fictional story of Max the hunting dog and Max the customer service rep. It's also a story about a boss by the name of Mr. Harold, who manages his employees, including his new hire Max, like he does his dog Max.

The setting of this short movie is the workplace. But remember, *everyone* has a workplace. For students, teachers and administrators, it is a school. For many it is a place of business, community or government service. For families it is the home. For yet others it is in the community, church, synagogue or mosque. So this is not just about work, it is about human relationships and interactions between people united in a common purpose. I challenge you to translate the setting of this film into every other area you give your life to with others.

People so relate and resonate with this film both organizationally and personally. I invite you to watch *Max & Max* now by inserting the companion DVD to the book into your DVD player and selecting *Max & Max*.

NOW THINK ABOUT the film you just watched. Max, like most of us when we begin a new job, is full of passion, enthusiasm and fire. When he takes initiative to get and keep customers, Mr. Harold takes a piece of hide off him. Max is micromanaged and controlled to the point that his spirit is broken, he becomes gun-shy, and he loses his vision of his purpose, potential and freedom to choose. He's lost his *voice*. He swears never to take initiative again. Max the person gets into a codependent mind-set with Mr. Harold, and you can see him gradually becoming like Max the dog—just waiting for his next command. You might be tempted to blame the problem on Mr. Harold, but notice that *his* boss treats him just the same way he treats Max. Such insulting micromanaging is endemic throughout the whole company. The whole culture is codependent. No one is exercising leadership (initiative and influence) because everyone assumes leadership is a function of position.

The truth is, most organizations are not too unlike Max and Mr. Harold's. Even the best organizations I've worked with over the last forty years are absolutely filled with problems. The pain from these problems and challenges is becoming much more acute because of the changes taking place in the world. Just like with *Max & Max*, such challenges generally fall into three categories: *organizational, relationship* and *personal.*

At the *organizational* level, a controlling management philosophy drives performance, communication, compensation/reward, training, information and other core systems that suppress human talent and voice. This control philosophy has its roots in the Industrial Age and has become the dominant management mind-set of those in positions of authority across all industries and professions. Again, I call it the *"Thing" Mind-set of the Industrial Age*.

At the *relationship* level, again, most organizations are filled with *codependency*. There is a fundamental lack of trust, and many lack the skill and mind-set to work out their differences in authentic, creative ways. Though organizational systems and controlling management practices do much to foster this codependency, the problem is compounded by the fact that so many people have been raised being compared to others at home and competing against others in school, in athletics and in the workplace. These powerful influences cultivate a scarcity mentality, so that many people have a hard time being genuinely happy for the successes of others.

At the *personal* level, these organizations are filled with bright, talented, creative people at every level who feel straitjacketed, undervalued and uninspired. They are frustrated and don't believe they have the power to change things.

THE POWER OF A PARADIGM

Author John Gardner once said, "Most ailing organizations have developed a functional blindness to their own defects. They are not suffering because they cannot resolve their problems, but because they cannot *see* their problems." Einstein put it this way: "The significant problems we face cannot be solved at the same level of thinking we were at when we created them."

These statements underscore one of the most profound learnings of my life: If you want to make *minor*, incremental changes and improvements, work on practices, behavior or attitude. But if you want to make significant, quantum improvement, work on *paradigms*. The word *paradigm* stems from the Greek word *paradeigma*, originally a scientific term but commonly used today to mean a perception, assumption, theory, frame of reference or lens through which you view the world. It's like a map of a territory or city. If inaccurate, it will make no difference how hard you try to find your destination or how positively you think—you'll stay lost. If accurate, then diligence and attitude matter. But not until.

For instance, how did they attempt to heal people in the Middle Ages? *Bloodletting*. What was the paradigm? The bad stuff is in the blood; get it out. Now if you did not question this paradigm, what would you do? Do more. Do it faster. Do it more painlessly. Go into TQM or Six Sigma on bloodletting. Do statistical quality controls, variance analysis. Do strategic feasibility studies and organize around brilliant marketing plans so that you can advertise, "We have *the* highest-quality, world-class bloodletting unit in the world!" Or you might take people into the mountains and let them do free falls off cliffs into each other's arms so when they return to the bloodletting unit of the hospital they'll work with more love and trust. Or you might let members of the bloodletting unit sit around in hot tubs and explore their psyches with each other so that they develop authenticity in their communication. You might even teach positive thinking to your patients, as well as your employees, so the positive energy is optimized when bloodletting takes place.

Can you imagine what happened when the germ theory was discovered—when Semmelweis of Hungary, Pasteur of France, and other empirical scientists discovered that germs are a primary cause of disease? It immediately explained why women wanted to be delivered by midwives. The midwives were cleaner. They washed. It explained why more men on war's battlefields were dying from staph infections than bullets. The disease was spread behind the front ranks through germs. The germ theory opened whole new fields of research. It guides health care practices to the present day.

That's the power of an accurate paradigm. It *explains*, and then it *guides*. But the problem is that paradigms, like traditions, die hard. Flawed paradigms go on for centuries after a better one is discovered. For instance, though history books talk about George Washington dying of a throat infection, he probably died of bloodletting. The throat infection was the symptom of something else. Since the paradigm was that the bad stuff was in the blood, they took from him several pints of blood in a twenty-four-hour period. You and I are counseled not to give more than one pint every two months if we're well.

The new Knowledge Worker Age is based on a new paradigm, one entirely different than the *thing* paradigm of the Industrial Age. Let's call it the Whole-Person Paradigm.

THE WHOLE-PERSON PARADIGM

At the core, there is one simple, overarching reason why so many people remain unsatisfied in their work and why most organizations fail to draw out the greatest talent, ingenuity and creativity of their people and never become truly great, enduring organizations. It stems from *an incomplete paradigm of who we are—our fundamental view of human nature.*

The fundamental reality is, human beings are not *things* needing to be motivated and controlled; they are four dimensional—body, mind, heart and spirit.

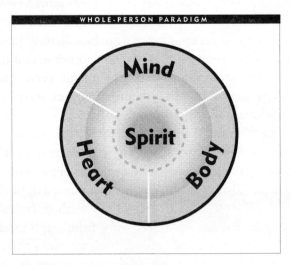

Figure 2.2

If you study all philosophy and religion, both Western and Eastern, from the beginning of recorded history, you'll basically find the same four dimensions: the physical/economic, the mental, the social/emo-

Figure 2.3

tional and the spiritual. Different words are often used, but they reflect the same four universal dimensions of life. They also represent *the four basic needs and motivations of all people* illustrated in the film in the first chapter: to live (survival), to love (relationships), to learn (growth and development) and to leave a legacy (meaning and contribution)—see figure 2.3.

PEOPLE HAVE CHOICES

So what's the direct connection between the controlling "thing" (part-person) paradigm that dominates today's workplace and the inability of managers and organizations to inspire their people to volunteer their highest talents and contributions? The answer is simple. People make choices. Consciously or subconsciously, people decide how much of

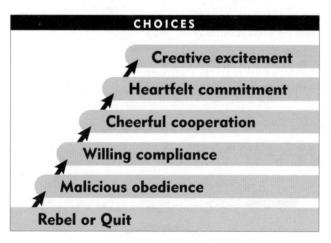

Figure 2.4

themselves they will give to their work depending on how they are treated and on their opportunities to use *all* four parts of their nature. These choices range from rebelling or quitting to creative excitement:

Now consider for a moment which of these six choices listed in figure 2.4—rebel or quit, malicious obedience, willing compliance, cheerful cooperation, heartfelt commitment or creative excitement—you would make under the following five scenarios:

First, you are not treated fairly. That is, there are a lot of politics at play in your organization; there is nepotism; the pay system doesn't seem fair and just; your own pay does not accurately reflect the level of your contribution. What would your choice be?

Second, let's say that you are treated fairly in terms of your pay, but you are not treated kindly. That is, you are not respected; your treatment is inconsistent, arbitrary, capricious, perhaps largely dictated by the mood of your boss. What would your choice be?

Third, let's say that you are paid fairly and treated kindly, but when your opinion is wanted, it is given to you. In other words, your body and heart are valued, but not your mind. What would your choice be?

Fourth, now let's say that you are paid fairly (body), treated kindly (heart), involved creatively (mind), but you are asked to dig a hole and fill it again, or to fill out reports that no one ever sees or uses. In other words, the work is meaningless (spirit). What would your choice be?

Fifth, now let's say that you are paid fairly, treated kindly, and involved creatively in meaningful work, but that there is a lot of lying and cheating going on with customers and suppliers, including other employees (spirit). What would your choice be?

Now notice we went through all four parts of the whole-person paradigm—body, mind, heart and finally spirit (spirit being divided in two parts—the meaninglessness of the work and the unprincipled way that it was done). The point is, if you neglect any one of the four parts of human nature, you turn a person into a thing, and what do you do with things? You have to control, manage and carrot-and-stick them in order to motivate them.

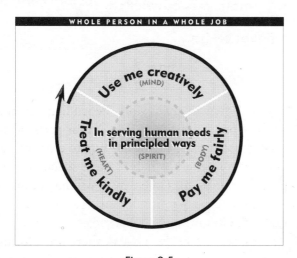

Figure 2.5

I have asked these five questions all around the world in different settings, and almost inevitably, the answer falls into the bottom three categories—people would rebel or quit, maliciously obey (meaning they'll
do it but hope it doesn't work), or at best willingly comply. But in today's
Information/Knowledge Worker Age, only one who is respected as
a whole person in a whole job—one who is *paid fairly, treated kindly,
used creatively* and given opportunities to *serve human needs in principled
ways* (see figure 2.5)—makes one of the upper three choices of cheerful
cooperation, heartfelt commitment or creative excitement (see again
figure 2.4).

Identity is destiny.

Can you begin to see the how the core problems in the workplace today and the core solution to those problems lie in our paradigm of human nature? Can you see how many of the solutions to the problems in
our homes and communities lie in this same paradigm? This Industrial
Age "thing" paradigm and all the practices that flow from it are the
modern-day equivalent of bloodletting. A comprehensive description of
four chronic problems in organizations caused by neglecting the four parts
of human nature and the solution involving *four roles of leadership* influence will follow, beginning with chapter 6. We move first, however, to
the *individual* response and solution to the pain and problems we've discussed.

Chapter 3

THE SOLUTION

There is nothing so powerful as an idea whose time has come.
VICTOR HUGO

H ENRY DAVID THOREAU once wrote, "There are a thousand hacking at the branches of evil to one who is striking at the root."[1] This book is dedicated to striking at the root of the significant problems we face.

We've started with the *pain;* we've explored the underlying *problem*—one that has personal roots and that involves a deeply imbedded paradigm and set of traditions in the workplace. Now let's set the context for the *solution* and give an overview of how it will be unfolded in the remainder of the book.

I'VE WORKED WITH ORGANIZATIONS around the world for over forty years and have been a student of the findings of the great minds who have studied organizations. Most of the great cultural shifts—ones that have built great organizations that *sustain* long-term growth, prosperity and contribution to the world—started with the choice of *one* person. Sometimes that one person was the formal leader—the CEO or president. Very often it *started* with someone else—a professional, a line manager, someone's assistant. Regardless of their position, these people first changed themselves from the *inside out.* Their character, competence, initiative and positive energy—in short, their moral authority—inspired and lifted others. They possessed an anchored sense of identity, discovered their strengths and talents, and used them to meet needs and

25

produce results. People noticed. They were given more responsibility. They magnified the new responsibility and again produced results. More and more people sat up and noticed. Top people wanted to learn of their ideas—how they accomplished *so much*. The culture was drawn to their vision and to them.

People like this just don't get sucked into or pulled down for long by all the negative, demoralizing, insulting forces in the organization. And interestingly, their organizations are no better than most organizations. To some degree, they're *all* a mess. These people just realize that they can't wait for their boss or the organization to change. They become an island of excellence in a sea of mediocrity. And it's contagious.

Where does a person get such internal strength to swim against the current and to withstand negative cultural provocations, subordinate selfish interests and develop and sustain such vision and determination?

They learn of their true nature and gifts. They use them to develop a vision of great things they want to accomplish. With wisdom they take initiative and cultivate great understanding of the needs and opportunities around them. They meet those needs that match their unique talents, that tap their higher motivations and that make a difference. In short, *they find and use their voice*. They serve and inspire others. They apply PRINCIPLES that govern growth and prosperity in human beings AND in organizations—principles that draw the highest and best from a "whole person"—body, mind, heart and spirit. Equally significant, they also choose to influence and *inspire others to find their voice* through these principles as well.

This two-part solution—*Find Your Voice* and *Inspire Others to Find Theirs*—is a road map for individuals at ANY level of an organization to maximize their fulfillment and influence, become an irreplaceable contributor,* and inspire their team and the broader organization to do the same. Accordingly, the book is organized into two main sections:

1. Find Your Voice
2. Inspire Others to Find Their Voice

Let's briefly introduce each.

---

* For a free report that compares your assessment of your team's or organization's ability to execute its top priorities with those of others around the world, go to www .The8thHabit.com/offers.

FIND YOUR VOICE

> *Two roads diverged in a wood, and I—*
> *I took the one less traveled by,*
> *And that has made all the difference.*[2]
>
> ROBERT FROST

Figure 3.1 illustrates two dramatically different roads of life and is the simple outline or map of the 8th Habit: Find Your Voice and Inspire Others to Find Theirs. This Two Roads diagram will appear at the beginning of the remaining chapters through chapter 14. *Each new version of the developing diagram will highlight the focus of that chapter.* In this way you will see where you are, where you've been and where you are headed.

EVERYONE *CHOOSES* ONE of two roads in life—the old and the young, the rich and the poor, men and women alike. One is the broad, well-traveled road to mediocrity, the other the road to greatness and meaning. The range of possibilities that exists within each of these two destinations is as

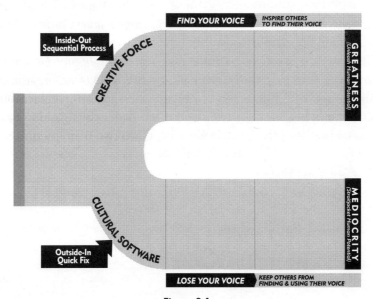

Figure 3.1

wide as the diversity of gifts and personalities in the human family. But the contrast between the two destinations is as the night is to the day.

The path to mediocrity straitjackets human potential. The path to greatness unleashes and realizes human potential. The path to mediocrity is the quick-fix, short-cut approach to life. The path to greatness is a process of sequential growth from the inside out. Travelers on the lower path to mediocrity live out the *cultural "software"* of ego, indulgence, scarcity, comparison, competitiveness and victimism. Travelers on the upper path to greatness rise above negative cultural influences and *choose* to become the creative force of their lives. One word expresses the pathway to greatness. Voice. Those on this path find their voice and inspire others to find theirs. The rest never do.

THE SOUL'S SEARCH FOR MEANING

Deep within each one of us there is an inner longing to live a life of *greatness* and contribution—to really matter, to really make a difference. We may doubt ourselves and our ability to do so, but I want you to know of my deep conviction that *you can* live such a life. You have the potential within you. We all do. It is the birthright of the human family.

I once visited with the commander of a military base who was truly on fire with his commitment to undertake a significant cultural change inside his organization. He had been in the service for over thirty years, was a full colonel, and was eligible for retirement that very year. After he had been teaching and training his organization for many months I asked him why he planned to stay on and undertake such a major initiative—one that would require swimming upstream against the tremendous resisting forces of tradition, lethargy, indifference and low trust. I even said to him, "You could relax. You'd have a good retirement. Award banquets would be held in your honor. Loved ones and associates would celebrate you."

He became very sober, paused for a long time and then decided to share with me a very personal, almost sacred, experience. He said that his father had recently passed away. When the father was on his deathbed, he called his wife and son (the colonel) to him to say good-bye. He could barely speak. His wife wept during the entire visit; the son drew down close to his father, and his father whispered into his ear, "Son, don't do life like I did. I didn't do right by you or by your mother and never really made a difference. Son, promise me you won't do life like I did."

Those were the last words the colonel heard from his father, who passed away shortly thereafter. But he regarded them as the greatest gift and legacy his father could have ever given him. He made his mind up then and there that he was going to make a difference—in every area of his life.

LATER THE COLONEL told me privately that he *had* been planning to retire and relax. In fact, he had secretly hoped that his successor would not do as well as he had and that this would be obvious and apparent to all. But when he had this epiphany with his father, he determined not only to become a change catalyst in building principles of enduring leadership into the culture of his command but also to see to it that his successor would be *more* successful than he had been. By striving to institutionalize these leadership principles into the structures, systems and processes of his organization, he would increase the likelihood of passing on his legacy one leader-generation to another.

He said further, that up until that experience with his father, he had knowingly taken the easier road, acting basically in a custodial role in the traditions of the past, and that he had chosen a life of mediocrity. But with his father, he resolved, as never before, to live a life of greatness, a life of real contribution, a life of significance—one that really made a difference.

All of us can consciously decide to leave behind a life of mediocrity and to live a life of greatness—at home, at work and in the community. No matter what our circumstances may be, such a decision can be made by every one of us—whether that greatness is manifest by choosing to have a magnificent spirit in facing an incurable disease, by simply making a difference in the life of a child, giving that child a sense of worth and potential, by becoming a change-catalyst inside an organization, or by becoming an initiator of a great cause in society. We all have the power to decide to live a *great* life, or even simpler, to have not only a good day but a *great* day. No matter how long we've walked life's pathway to mediocrity, we can always choose to switch paths. Always. It's never too late. We can find our voice.

• • •

ONCE YOU MAKE the *choice* to follow this "road less traveled," the pathway to finding your own voice is to:

1. **Discover Your Voice** by coming to understand your true nature—what I call *three magnificent birth-gifts* (chapter 4) and by developing and using with integrity the *intelligence* tied to each of the four parts of your nature.

2. **Express Your Voice** by cultivating the highest manifestations of these human intelligences—*vision, discipline, passion* and *conscience* (chapter 5).

FILM: *Discovery of a Character*

I would like to share with you a powerful, true story that embodies this process of finding your voice. Several years ago, our firm participated with our local PBS station in broadcasting a video dramatization we developed and filmed in England. The central figure in this remarkable story is an Englishman who transcended a childhood spent as a street urchin to become a reasonably successful writer with a nice home and a loving family. At the time of the story, however, he had developed "writer's block." It seemed his creativity had turned off. His debts were mounting. He was under tremendous deadline pressure from the publisher. He was becoming more and more depressed. He began to fear that his own children would end up on the streets like so many he saw around, like he, himself, had as a youth—particularly when his father was in debtor's prison.

He was discouraged. He couldn't sleep. He began to spend his nights walking the streets of London. He saw the poverty, the inhumane conditions of children working nights in the factories, the terrible struggle of parents trying to eke out a living for their families. Gradually, the full reality of what he was seeing began to hit him—the impact of selfishness and greed and those who would take advantage of others. An idea touched his heart and began to grow in his mind. There was something he could do that would make a difference!

He returned to his writing with an energy and enthusiasm he had never known. The vision of contribution impassioned and consumed him. He no longer felt doubt or discouragement. He didn't worry about his own financial concerns. He wanted to get this story out, to make it as inexpensive as possible, to make it available to as many people as possible. His whole life had changed. He'd truly found his voice.

I invite you now to watch a brief film that dramatizes this remarkable man's true experience. You can view it by inserting the companion DVD into your DVD player and selecting *Discovery of a Character.* I believe you'll be inspired by the rest of his story.

INSPIRE OTHERS TO FIND THEIR VOICE

Once you've found your own voice, the *choice* to expand your influence, to increase your contribution, is the choice to inspire others to find *their* voice. Inspire (from the Latin *inspirare*) means to breathe life into another. As we recognize, respect and create ways for others to give voice to *all four parts of their nature*—physically, mentally, emotionally/socially and spiritually—latent human genius, creativity, passion, talent and motivation are unleashed. It will be those organizations that reach a critical mass of people and teams expressing their full voice that will achieve next-level breakthrough in productivity, innovation and leadership in the marketplace and society.

Part 2 of *The 8th Habit* begins with chapter 6. It is to Inspire Others to Find Their Voice. Since most of the world's work is done in organizations, the focus is on principles you can apply to positively influence others in any organization (business, education, government, military, community, even family).

Most likely, you will also have many practical "yeah, but" questions come to your mind. To assist you, *you will find a brief section of commonly asked questions and my responses at the end of each remaining chapter.* I hope they are helpful to you, but feel free to skip them if you are not interested. Following the last chapter of the book you will also find a "chapter" dedicated to questions and answers that are more general and comprehensive in nature.

GETTING THE MOST OUT OF THIS BOOK:
LEARNING BY TEACHING AND DOING

If you would like to get the most out of this book and initiate powerful change and growth in your life and organization, I recommend two simple ideas to you. If you will do these two things, I guarantee dramatic results. The first is to *teach* others what you learn; the second is to systematically *apply* what you learn—to do it!

Teach and Share As You Go

Almost everyone acknowledges *you learn best when you teach another* and that your learning is internalized when you *live* it.

While teaching at the university years ago, I met a visiting professor, Dr. Walter Gong, from San Jose, California. He taught a one-semester class for faculty entitled How to Improve Your Teaching. The essence of his program was this great principle: *The best way to get people to learn is to turn them into teachers.* In other words, you learn the material best when you teach it.

I immediately started to apply that principle in my work and at home. When I first started university teaching, my classes only had about fifteen to thirty students. When I started applying Dr. Gong's principle, I found that I could effectively teach many more students; in fact, some of my classes were packed with nearly a thousand students, and yet the students' performance and test scores actually went up. Why? When you teach you simply learn better. Every student becomes a teacher, and every teacher a student.

Now, the common paradigm is that the teacher-student ratio is critical—fewer students means higher-quality teaching. But if you turn your students into teachers, you gain leverage. You move the fulcrum over.

Also when you teach or share what you're learning with others, you implicitly commit socially to live what you teach. You will naturally be more motivated to live what you're learning. This sharing will be a basis for deepening learning, commitment and motivation, making change legitimate, and enrolling a support team. You will also find that sharing creates bonding with people—especially with your children. Have them regularly teach you what they are learning in school. My wife, Sandra, and I have found that doing this simple thing essentially eliminates any need for external motivation with their studies. Those who teach what they are learning are, by far, the greatest students.

Integrate What You Learn into Your Life

To know and not to do, is really not to know. To learn and not to do is not to learn. In other words, to understand something but not apply it is really not to understand it. It is only in the *doing*, the *applying*, that knowledge and understanding are internalized. For instance, you could study tennis as a sport by reading books and hearing lectures, but until you've actually played it, you wouldn't really know the sport. To know and not to do is not to know.

> *Self-knowledge is best learned, not by contemplation,*
> *but by action. Strive to do your duty and you will soon*
> *discover of what stuff you are made.*
>
> JOHANN GOETHE

There are at least four approaches you could take in applying what you learn in this book:

1. The first would be to simply read the book straight through. Then decide what you want to apply in your life and work. This is the way most people approach a book. It reflects the desire many of us have to get emotionally or mentally connected with a flow of ideas in a book and then run with it.

2. The second approach would be to read through the entire book and then use the comprehensive understanding and cumulative motivation to go back and read the book a second time—this time with the intent to apply as you go. This could work very well for many.

3. A third approach—one that I personally believe will yield the greatest results—would be to adopt it as a *yearlong personal growth and development program*. Take a month for each of the remaining twelve chapters. Start by reading the next chapter, teach it and then apply it the rest of the month. You will find that if you will actually seek to apply what you learn in each chapter for a month, the insight you gain in the chapters that follow will profoundly increase.

4. The fourth approach is simply to adapt the third approach to your own timeline. Some readers might want to go faster or slower than one chapter a month. Read and apply a new chapter every week, every two weeks, every two months, or in whatever time frame you choose. This retains the power of the third approach yet allows you the flexibility to adapt it to your own desires and circumstances.

To assist you in applying the principles in each chapter of the book, regardless of which approach you choose, I have put together a number of application ideas and exercises to get you started. Simply go to www.The8thHabit.com/offers and the exercises will be emailed to you at your request. I've also included on the last two-page spread of the book a chart that will assist you in completing what we could call "The 8th Habit Challenge." The Challenge involves accomplishing Development/Action Steps for each chapter:

1. Read the chapter.
2. Teach the chapter to at least two people, including work colleagues, family members, friends, etc.
3. Make a sincere, concerted effort to live the principles included in the chapter for one month.
4. Report the results and your learnings from seeking to live the ideas in the chapter to a trusted colleague, family member or friend.

Once you have completed the entire "8th Habit Challenge" chart, you can certify you have done so at www.The8thHabit.com/challenge and you will receive a special recognition for your accomplishment.

AS WE MOVE now to Part 1: Find Your Voice, consider the words of Abraham Lincoln: "The dogmas of the quiet past are inadequate to the stormy present." We must think anew. We must develop not only a new mind-set but also a new skill-set and a new tool-set that flows from it. This is difficult to do; it throws everyone out of their comfort zones. But a new reality has emerged, a new economy, a new challenge. This new challenge—not only surviving but truly thriving in this new reality—requires a new response, a new habit. Remember, habits lie at the intersection of knowledge, attitude and skill. As you develop these three dimensions of the 8th Habit, you'll increasingly become equal to the new challenge and to your unlimited possibilities.

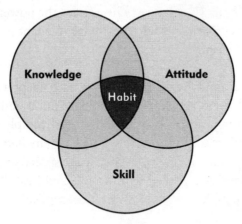

Figure 3.2

Part 1

FIND YOUR VOICE

Chapter 4

DISCOVER YOUR VOICE—
UNOPENED BIRTH-GIFTS

There are so many gifts
Still unopened from your birthday,
There are so many hand-crafted presents
That have been sent to you by God.
The Beloved does not mind repeating,
"Everything I have is also yours."
There are so many gifts, my dear,
Still unopened from your birthday.[1]

HAFIZ

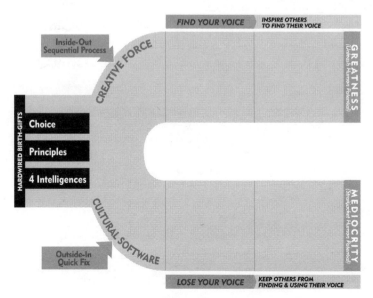

Figure 4.1

THE POWER TO *discover* our voice lies in the potential that was bequeathed us at birth. Latent and undeveloped, the seeds of greatness were planted. We were given magnificent "birth-gifts"—talents, capacities, privileges, intelligences, opportunities—that would remain largely unopened except through our own decision and effort. Because of these gifts, the potential within an individual is tremendous, even infinite. We really have no idea what a person is capable of. A baby may be the most dependent creation in the universe, and yet within a few short years, it becomes the most powerful. The more we use and magnify our present talents, the more talents we are given and the greater our capacity becomes.

> *All children are born geniuses; 9,999 out of*
> *every 10,000 are swiftly, inadvertently*
> *degeniusized by grownups.*
>
> BUCKMINSTER FULLER

Let's examine our three most important gifts (figure 4.2):

First, *our freedom and power to choose;*

Second, *natural laws or principles,* which are universal and never change; and

Third, *our four intelligences/capacities*—physical/economic, emotional/social, mental and spiritual. These four intelligences/capacities correspond to the four parts of our human nature—symbolized by body, heart, mind and spirit.

```
"HARDWIRED" BIRTH-GIFTS
           (Mostly unopened)

■ Freedom and Power to Choose

■ Principles (Natural Laws)
      ▪ Universal
      ▪ Timeless
      ▪ Self-Evident

■ The 4 Intelligences/Capacities
   (IQ) MENTAL              (EQ) EMOTIONAL/SOCIAL
   (PQ) PHYSICAL/ECONOMIC   (SQ) SPIRITUAL
```

Figure 4.2

Author Marianne Williamson beautifully expressed how oftentimes we are awed, even fearful, of our native endowments—largely, I believe, because of the sense of responsibility they lay upon us:

> Our deepest fear is not that we are inadequate. Our deepest fear is that we are powerful beyond measure. It is our light, not our darkness, that most frightens us. We ask ourselves, Who am I to be brilliant, gorgeous, talented, fabulous? Actually, who are you not to be? You are a child of God. Your playing small doesn't serve the world. There is nothing enlightened about shrinking so that other people won't feel insecure around you. We are all meant to shine, as children do. We were born to make manifest the glory of God that is within us. It's not just in some of us; it's in everyone. And as we let our own light shine, we unconsciously give other people permission to do the same. As we're liberated from our own fear, our presence automatically liberates others.[2]

OUR FIRST BIRTH-GIFT: THE FREEDOM TO CHOOSE

For half a century I've been involved in the subject of this book in many different contexts all around the world. If you were to ask me what one subject, one theme, one point, seemed to have the greatest impact upon people—what one great idea resonated deeper in the soul than any other—if you were to ask what one ideal was most practical, most relevant, most timely, regardless of circumstances, I would answer quickly, without any reservation, and with the deepest conviction of my heart and soul, that *we are free to choose.* Next to life itself, the power to choose is your greatest gift. This power and freedom stand in stark contrast to the mind-set of *victimism* and culture of *blame* so prevalent in society today.

Fundamentally, we are a product of choice, not nature (genes) or nurture (upbringing, environment). Certainly genes and culture often influence very powerfully, but they do not determine.

> *The history of free man is never written by chance but by choice—their choice.*[3]
> DWIGHT D. EISENHOWER

The essence of being human is being able to direct your own life. Humans act, animals and human "robots" react. Humans can make choices based on their values. Your power to choose the direction of your life allows you to reinvent yourself, to change your future, and to powerfully influence the rest of creation. It is the one gift that enables all the gifts to be used; it is the one gift that enables us to elevate our life to higher and higher levels.

Over the years in speaking to various groups, time and again I have had people come to me and basically say, "Please tell me more of my freedom and power to choose. Please tell me again of my worth and potential, that I have no need to compare myself with others." Many also comment that as interesting (or boring) as the speech may have been, the thing that literally electrified their souls was the internal sense of their own freedom to choose. This was so delicious to them, so exhilarating, that they could hardly ponder it long or deep enough.

This power of choice means that we are *not* merely a product of our past or of our genes; we are *not* a product of how other people treat us. They unquestionably influence us, but they do *not* determine us. We are self-determining through our choices. If we have given away our *present* to the *past*, do we need to give away our *future* also?

One of the most profound and truly life-changing experiences of my life—one conceptually fundamental to my work on the 7 Habits—took place while I was on a sabbatical in Hawaii. One day I was wandering leisurely around the stacks in a library. Being in a very meditative and reflective state of mind, I pulled down a book. In it I read three sentences that staggered me to the core:

Between stimulus and response there is a space.
In that space lies our freedom and power to choose our response.
In those choices lie our growth and our happiness.

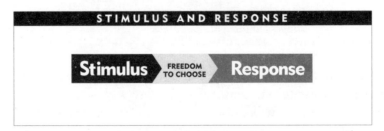

Figure 4.3

Intellectually, I had learned from many sources about our freedom to choose our response to whatever happens to us. But on that particular day, in that reflective mood, and in those relaxed circumstances, the idea of the space between whatever happens to us and our response to it hit me like a ton of bricks. Since then I have come to understand and believe that the *size* of the space is largely determined by our genetic or biological inheritance and by our upbringing and present circumstances.

With many who have grown up with unconditional love in supportive circumstances, the space may be very large. With others, due to various genetic and environmental influences, it may be very small. But the key point is, there is still a space there and it is in the *use* of that space that the opportunity to enlarge it exists. Some with a very large space, when facing adverse circumstances, may choose to cave in, thereby reducing the size of the space between stimulus and response. Others with a small space may swim upstream against powerful genetic, social and cultural currents and find their freedom expanding, their growth accelerating, and their happiness deepening. The former simply do not open this most priceless of all birthday gifts. Gradually, they become a function more of their conditions than their decisions. The latter, perhaps stumblingly and with great, sustained effort, open this priceless gift of freedom to choose and discover the force that releases almost all of the other gifts given at birth.

The maverick psychiatrist R.D. Laing captured in the words below how failing to notice that we have this space kills our ability to change. Humans alone have self-awareness. Read, think about, and then reread this quotation:

> *The range of what we think and do is limited by what we fail to notice. And because we fail to notice that we fail to notice, there is little we can do to change; until we notice how failing to notice shapes our thoughts and deeds.*

An awareness of our freedom and power to choose is affirming because it can excite our sense of possibility and potential. It can also threaten, even terrify, because suddenly we're responsible, that is, "response-able." We become accountable. If we've taken shelter over the years in explaining our situation and problems in the name of past or present circumstances, it is truly terrifying to think otherwise. Suddenly, there is no excuse.

No matter what has happened, is now happening, or will happen, there is a space between those things and our responses to them. If there is even a fraction of a second between stimulus and response, that space represents our power to choose our response to any situation.

Certainly there are things that happen to us over which we have no choice. One such thing would be our genetic makeup. Though we do not choose our genes, we do have the power to choose how we respond to them. If you have a genetic predisposition to a particular disease, that doesn't mean that you'll necessarily get the disease. By using that self-awareness and your willpower to follow a regimen of proper exercise and nutrition and the most advanced medical wisdom, you may avoid the very illnesses or cancers that have taken your ancestors.

Those who develop increasing inner power and freedom to choose can also become what I call a *transition person*—one who stops unworthy tendencies from being passed on from prior generations to those that follow (your children and grandchildren).

I was recently privileged to receive the Fatherhood Award from the National Fatherhood Initiative. I was deeply moved by what one of my fellow award recipients said upon receiving the award. His first comment was that this award was a greater honor and more important to him than any award he had ever received. Although other awards were evidence of a successful career, he viewed the National Fatherhood Award he was accepting as a far greater indicator of "success." He said, and I'm paraphrasing, "I never knew my father; my father never knew his father; but my son knows his father." His statement truly represents one of the finest and most worthy successes in life. It indicates true greatness and success; but, more importantly, his role as a transition person will profoundly impact generation after generation in immeasurably positive ways.

You can also be a transition person in the organization you work for. For instance, you may have an absolutely awful boss. Your working circumstances may be not only unpleasant but also unjust. However, by the wise exercise of your freedom to choose, you may change those circumstances and profoundly influence your boss for good, or at least insulate yourself from obsessing or being emotionally taken over by others' weaknesses. Remember, any time your emotional life is a function of someone else's weaknesses, you disempower yourself and empower those weaknesses to continue to mess your life up. Again, yesterday holds tomorrow hostage.

Here's a true story that powerfully illustrates our ability to choose. It is told firsthand by one courageous, inspiring person who learned to influence, even lead, a "bad" boss:

When I came on board as director of human resources, I heard horror stories about what my boss was like. I was actually in his office when he lost his temper with an employee. I vowed then and there never to get on my boss's bad side. I made good on that promise. I spoke nicely to him in the hallways. I had all my reports in on·time to his secretary. I made sure I wasn't one of the last people out of the office for lunch so he wouldn't single me out. I didn't even want to play golf with him in case I beat him.

A short time later, I started seeing myself in all my cowardly glory. I was consumed with things on the job that I had no control over. I'd spend precious creative energy devising solutions to problems that hadn't even happened yet. Because I was scared, I wasn't giving the company my best effort. I wasn't an agent of change. In fact, the only change I felt comfortable instituting was me changing to another company. I even had an interview scheduled.

Ashamed of myself, I canceled that interview and committed to focus only on those things I could truly influence for just ninety days. I began by deciding I wanted above all to create a sound relationship with my boss. We didn't have to be best buddies, but we did have to interact like colleagues.

One day my boss came into my office. After some discussion and after swallowing and practicing the words in my head a few times, I said: "By the way, what can I be doing to help you be more effective here?"

He was perplexed. "What do you mean?"

I bravely forged on. "What can I do to alleviate some of the pressure that you have in your job? It's my job to make sure your job gets easier." I gave him a big sort of nervous, please-don't-think-I'm-weird smile. I'll never forget the look on his face. That was really the beginning point of our relationship.

At first, I was asked to do just little things, things I couldn't really screw up, like "Type this memo up for me" or "Do you mind making this call for me?" After six weeks of doing that, he came to me and said, "I understand with your background you know workers comp pretty well. Do you mind working on this aspect of insurance? Our rates are high; see what you can do." It was the first time he had asked me to do anything that had a significant impact on the organization. I took a $250,000-a-year premium and got it reduced to $198,000. Plus I got them to waive the fee for terminating midstream on our contract by negotiating over some mishandled claims. This was an additional savings of $13,000.

Once when we had a disagreement I proved to him that it stayed behind

*closed doors. He didn't hear about it later from the marketing department. I soon
discovered that my ninety-day test was paying off. My relationship and influence
did grow by focusing on what I could do to change the environment in which I
worked. Today, the trust between my boss and me is very high, and I feel I am
making a contribution here.*

> One ship drives east and another drives west
> With the self same winds that blow.
> 'Tis the set of the sails,
> And not the gales,
> That tells us the way to go.
> Like the winds of the sea are the ways of fate;
> As we voyage along through life,
> 'Tis the set of a soul
> That decides its goal,
> And not the calm, or the strife.[4]
>
> ELLA WHEELER WILCOX

I challenge you to think deeply about this first gift—to reflect on that
space that exists between stimulus and response, and to use it wisely in
enlarging your freedoms and keeping yourself constantly growing,
learning and contributing. Eventually, your exercise of that power will
enlarge the response until the very nature of your responses will begin
to shape the stimuli. You literally create the world in which you live.
The great American philosopher-psychologist William James consistently taught that when we change our thinking we change our lives.

OUR SECOND BIRTH-GIFT: NATURAL LAWS OR PRINCIPLES

We've been discussing the wise use of the space between stimulus and
response, our freedom to choose. What does this "wise use" mean?
Where is wisdom? Basically, it means to live by *principles* or *natural laws*
rather than going along with today's culture of *quick fix*.

Once Einstein saw the needle of a compass at the age of four, he always understood that there had to be "something behind things, something deeply hidden." This also pertains to every other realm of life.
Principles are *universal*—that is, they transcend culture and geography.

They're also *timeless*, they never change—principles such as fairness, kindness, respect, honesty, integrity, service, contribution. Different cultures may translate these principles into different practices and over time may even totally obscure these principles through the wrongful use of freedom. Nevertheless, they are present. Like the law of gravity, they operate constantly.

Another thing I've discovered is that these principles are *inarguable*. That is, they are self-evident. For example, you can never have enduring trust without trustworthiness. Think about it; that is a natural law.

I once served as the assistant survival instructor to a group of about thirty people. After going about twenty-four hours without any food, water or sleep, we climbed down a mountain and needed to cross a raging river to get to our food and water on the other side. There was a rope stretched from a tree on one bank to a tree on the other bank, where breakfast was available. I volunteered to go first. Thinking I was much stronger than I actually was, I started bouncing and fooling around in the middle of the rope rather than utilizing all my strength to get to the other side. When I felt my strength starting to ebb, I immediately tried to get to the other side—but the strength kept ebbing from my body. I used every technique I knew of, including visualization and willpower, but to no avail. I eventually fell into the raging waters. As I reached the shore about twenty-five yards downstream and lay there exhausted on the banks, all my students could do was cheer and laugh— beautifully illustrating how "pride goeth before the fall." The body is a natural system. It's governed by natural law. No amount of positive mental attitude could get around the literal limits of my muscle conditioning.

I like how C.S. Lewis speaks of those who say there are no such things as universal principles:

> Whenever you find a man who says he does not believe in a real Right and Wrong, you will find the same man going back on this a moment later. He may break his promise to you, but if you try breaking one to him he will be complaining "It's not fair" before you can say Jack Robinson. A nation may say treaties do not matter; but then, the next minute, they spoil their case by saying that the particular treaty they want to break was an unfair one. But if treaties do not matter, and if there is no such thing as Right and Wrong—in other words if there is no Law of Nature—what is the difference between a fair treaty and an

unfair one? Have they not let the cat out of the bag and shown that whatever they say, they really know the Law of Nature just like anyone else?

It seems, then, we are forced to believe in a real Right or Wrong. People may be sometimes mistaken about them, just as people sometimes get their sums wrong, but they are not a matter of mere taste and opinion any more than the multiplication table. . . . These, then, are the two points I wanted to make. First, that human beings, all over the earth, have this curious idea that they ought to behave in a certain way, and cannot really get rid of it. Secondly, that they do not in fact behave in that way. They know the Law of Nature: they break it. These two facts are the foundation of all clear thinking about ourselves and the universe we live in.[5]

Natural and Moral Authority

Natural authority is the dominion of natural laws. You can't ignore natural laws, and you have no choice but to operate by them. All actions have consequences. Like it or not, when we pick up one end of the stick we pick up the other. If you jump off a ten-story building, you can't change your mind at the fifth story. Gravity controls. That is the stamp of nature. Nature has also stamped people with the freedom and power to choose, and, therefore, they have natural authority or dominion over all of the rest of creation. Endangered species survive only by our consent. They don't have freedom and power to choose. They lack self-awareness. They can't reinvent themselves. They're totally subject to humans, who, because they are self-aware, alone have freedom and power to choose and to reinvent themselves. This is natural authority.

What is *moral authority*? It is the principled use of our freedom and power to choose. In other words, if we follow principles in our relationships with each other, we tap into the permission of nature. Natural laws (like gravity) and principles (like respect, honesty, kindness, integrity, service and fairness) control the consequences of our choices. Just as you get bad air and bad water when you consistently violate the environment, so also is trust (the glue of relationships) destroyed when you're consistently unkind and dishonest to people. By the principled, humble use of freedom and power, the humble person obtains moral authority with people, cultures, organizations and entire societies.

Values are social norms—they're personal, emotional, subjective and arguable. All of us have values. Even criminals have values. The question you must ask yourself is, *Are your values based upon principles?* In the last analysis, principles are natural laws—they're impersonal, factual, objective and self-evident. Consequences are governed by principles, and behavior is governed by values; therefore, value principles!

People who are "star-struck" (celebrity obsessed) are an example of those whose values may not be anchored in principles. Popularity shapes their moral center. They don't know who they are and don't know which way "north" is. They don't know what principles to follow because their lives are based on social values. They are torn between social awareness and self-awareness on the one hand and natural law and principles on the other. In an airplane, that's called vertigo, where you lose all sense of reference to the ground (principles) and you become completely lost. Many people walk through life with vertigo or moral mushiness. We all see people like this. You see them in your life and in popular culture. They've never paid the price of getting deeply centered or of anchoring their values in changeless principles.

The key task, then, is to determine where "true north" is and then to align everything toward that. Otherwise, you'll live with the inevitable negative consequences that follow. Again, they are inevitable because even though values control behavior, principles control the consequences of behavior. Moral authority requires the sacrifice of short-term selfish interests and the exercise of courage in subordinating social values to principles. And our conscience is the repository of those principles.

FILM: *Law of the Harvest*

I invite you now to view a film entitled *The Law of the Harvest*. You will find it on the companion DVD to the book. In this film you will see a simple, yet powerful, illustration of how Mother Nature teaches the inescapable law of the harvest. All lasting results are produced in a sequence, are governed by principles and are grown from the inside out. As you watch the film, remember that the same is true of *human* nature. There is a "law of the harvest" that governs human character, human greatness and all human relationships. And it stands in stark contrast to our culture of quick-fix, victimism and blame.

OUR THIRD BIRTH-GIFT:
THE FOUR INTELLIGENCES/CAPACITIES OF OUR NATURE

As expressed earlier, the four magnificent parts of our nature consist of body, mind, heart and spirit. Corresponding to these four parts are four capacities, or *intelligences*, that all of us possess: our physical or body intelligence (PQ), our mental intelligence (IQ), our emotional intelligence (EQ) and our spiritual intelligence (SQ). These four intelligences represent our third birth-gift.

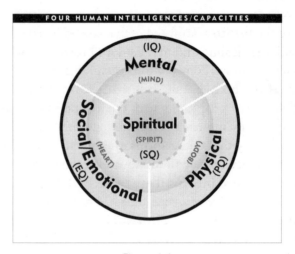

Figure 4.4

Mental Intelligence (IQ)

When we speak of intelligence, we usually think in terms of *Mental Intelligence (IQ)*, that is, our ability to analyze, reason, think abstractly, use language, visualize and comprehend. But this is far too narrow an interpretation of intelligence.

Physical Intelligence (PQ)

The *Physical Intelligence (PQ)* of the *body* is another kind of intelligence we are all implicitly aware of but often discount. Just think about what your body does without any conscious effort. It runs your respiratory, circulatory, nervous and other vital systems. It is constantly scanning its environment, destroying diseased cells and fighting for survival.

The human body is an incredible system—roughly 7 trillion cells with a mind-boggling level of physical and biochemical coordination necessary just to turn a page, cough, or drive a car. When you consider how little of it you have to think about, it becomes even more amazing. When was the last time you reminded your heart to beat, your lungs to expand and contract, or your digestive organs to secrete just the right chemicals at just the right time? These and a myriad of other processes are handled unconsciously for us every moment we live. Intelligence manages the whole system, much of it unconscious.[6]

DOE CHILDRE AND BRUCE CRYER

Doctors are the first to acknowledge that the body heals itself. Medicine simply facilitates healing and may remove obstacles, but it can also create obstacles if it works contrary to body intelligence.

How does the body balance and harmonize the functioning of the brain, which contains the mind, with the functioning of the heart, which symbolically represents emotional intelligence? Our body is a brilliant piece of machinery that outperforms even the most advanced computer. Our capacity to act on our thoughts and feelings, and to make things happen, is unmatched by any other species in the world.

Controlled double-blind scientific laboratory studies are producing increasing evidence of the close relationship between body (physical), mind (thinking) and heart (feeling).

> Plaque seen in a rural store in North Carolina:
> *The brain said, "I'm the smartest organ in the body."*
> *The heart said, "Who told you?"*[7]

Emotional Intelligence (EQ)

Emotional Intelligence (EQ) is one's self-knowledge, self-awareness, social sensitivity, empathy and ability to communicate successfully with others. It is a sense of timing and social appropriateness, and having the courage to acknowledge weaknesses and express and respect differences. Prior to the nineties, when EQ became a hot topic, it was sometimes described as right-brain capacity, as distinguished from left-brain capacity. The left brain was considered the more analytic, the site of linear thinking,

language, reasoning and logic; the right brain, the more creative, the
site of intuition, sensing and holistics. The key is respecting both sides
and exercising choice in developing and using their unique capacities.
Combining thinking and feeling creates better balance, judgment and
wisdom.

> *Intuition will tell the thinking mind where to look next.*
> DR. JONAS SALK, DISCOVERER OF THE POLIO VACCINE

There has been a great deal of research suggesting that in the long
run, emotional intelligence is a more accurate determinant of successful
communications, relationships and leadership than is mental intelligence. Author and EQ authority Daniel Goleman says this:

> For star performance in all jobs, in every field, emotional competence is
> twice as important as purely cognitive abilities. For success at the high-
> est levels, in leadership positions, emotional competence accounts for
> virtually the entire advantage. . . . Given that emotional competencies
> make up two-thirds or more of the ingredients of a standout perfor-
> mance, the data suggests that finding people who have these abilities, or
> nurturing them in existing employees, adds tremendous value to an or-
> ganization's bottom line. How much? In simple jobs like machine oper-
> ators or clerks, those in the top 1 percent with emotional competency
> were three times more productive (by value). For jobs of medium com-
> plexity, like sales clerks, or mechanics, a single top emotional competent
> person was twelve times more productive (by value).[8]

The theory of emotional intelligence is destabilizing to people who have
anchored their strategy for success on sheer mental intelligence. A person, for example, may be a ten on a ten-point IQ scale but emotionally
score only a two, and not know how to relate well with others. They
may compensate for this deficiency by over-relying on their intellect
and borrowing strength from their formal position. But in so doing,
they often exacerbate their own weaknesses and, in their interactions,
the weaknesses of others as well. Then they try to intellectually rational-
ize their behavior.

> Borrowing strength builds weakness—
> in self, in others and in relationships.

Developing stronger emotional intelligence is one of the greatest challenges faced by parents and leaders at all levels of organizations.

Spiritual Intelligence (SQ)

The fourth intelligence is *Spiritual Intelligence (SQ)*. Like EQ, SQ is becoming more mainstream in scientific inquiry and philosophical/ psychological discussion. Spiritual Intelligence is the central and most fundamental of all the intelligences because it becomes the source of *guidance* of the other three. Spiritual intelligence represents our drive for meaning and connection with the infinite.

Richard Wolman, author of *Thinking with Your Soul*, writes of the "spiritual" in this way:

> By spiritual I mean the ancient and abiding human quest for connected-ness with something larger and more trustworthy than our egos—with our own souls, with one another, with the worlds of history and nature, with the indivisible winds of the spirit, with the mystery of being alive.[9]

Spiritual intelligence also helps us discern true principles that are part of our conscience, which are symbolized by the compass. The compass is an excellent physical metaphor for principles, because it always points north. The key to maintaining high moral authority is to continually follow "true north" principles.

> *The spirit of man is the candle of the Lord.*[10]
>
> PROVERBS 20:27

Consider this quotation by authors Danah Zohar and Ian Marshall in *SQ: Connecting with Our Spiritual Intelligence:*

Unlike IQ, which computers have, and EQ, which exists in higher mammals, SQ is uniquely human and the most fundamental of the three. It is linked to humanity's need for meaning, an issue very much at the forefront of people's minds. . . . SQ is what we use to develop our longing and capacity for meaning, vision, and value. It allows us to dream and to strive. It underlies the things we believe in and the role our beliefs and values play in the actions we take. It is, in essence, what makes us human.[11]

Semantics and the Superior Nature of Spiritual Intelligence

There has been an enormous amount of study, observation and research in the area of intelligence, particularly over the last twenty years. There are numerous books and an entire body of literature. Different words are sometimes used to describe the same things. Part of what I call spiritual intelligence some people may call emotional intelligence, and vice versa. I fully acknowledge this semantics difficulty. Again, I encourage you, the reader, to not get hung up on word definitions but to search continuously for the underlying meaning.

Howard Gardner's book on the theory of multiple intelligences, *Frames of Mind*, is a brilliant treatment of the concept of separate, yet overlapping, intelligences. I've also gained greatly from both Robert Cooper's and Daniel Goleman's work on emotional intelligence. I have heard their presentations in different settings and know that their approaches are research-based and comprehensive, and include some of the elements I've spoken about under spiritual intelligence.

Some books separate out visual intelligence from verbal, analytical, artistic, logical, creative, economic and other intelligences. I appreciate their contributions but again believe you can put them all under the four areas of body, mind, heart and spirit—the four dimensions of life.

I'll never forget an experience in Hawaii with the Young Presidents' Organization. A small group of corporate presidents gathered for breakfast with some of the leading authorities in the field of management and leadership, each of whom had written notable bestsellers and were widely respected and quoted. In a forum where no one was being quoted and where there was a great deal of mutual respect, one of the presidents asked, with a real sense of humility, "Aren't you guys basically saying the same thing?" To a person, they acknowledged that they were. Each had his or her own semantics and definitions and often had some unique in-

> *In moments of powerful beauty, emotions move that can melt even the thickest and most cynical of skins. Endorphins flow. There is a release of tension. Energies, internal and external, flow and connect. The experience is not only soft and calm, but it also contains the power and creativity of nature and the Universe. To create and to work consciously with these moments of connection is to exercise what we might call our spiritual muscles and our spiritual intelligence. What do I mean by spiritual? I simply mean that whole reality and dimension which is bigger, more creative, more loving, more powerful, more visionary, more wise, more mysterious—than materialistic daily human existence.*
>
> *There is no theology or belief system that relates to this meaning of spiritual.*[12]
>
> WILLIAM BLOOM

sight not voiced by the others, but in terms of the most basic elements, they were the same. They talked more in terms of underlying principles than practices.

I've really had to work hard to avoid the semantics problem myself and do so by always trying to look for underlying meanings. But I do believe there is another dimension of intelligence that has not been treated in great depth elsewhere. And that is the role of spiritual intelligence in guiding and directing the other intelligences. In that sense, it is superior to the other intelligences.

Let me share an experience that may help make the point of spiritual intelligence being the highest of our capacities. I am enormously impressed with the work of the late Anwar Sadat, president of Egypt, in his efforts with former U.S. president Jimmy Carter and former Israeli prime minister Menachem Begin to bring about the Camp David Peace Accord between Israel and Egypt.

While being given a tour of the grounds of Camp David in a golf cart a few years ago, I was shown, by the president of the United States, the exact location where that accord was signed. It was a very emotional experience for me. I've come to see Sadat as a person that knew about the

> When the history of the world and of institutions, societies, communities, families and individuals is finally written, the dominant theme will be the degree to which people have lived not by their socialized conscience but by their divine conscience. That is the innate, intuitive wisdom contained in the principles or natural laws that are taught in all the major religions and enduring philosophies of the world. It won't be geopolitics, economics, government, wars, social culture, art, education or churches. The moral or spiritual dimension—how true people and institutions are to universal, timeless principles of right and wrong—will be the overarching and underlying supreme governing force.

space between stimulus and response. He developed enormous space as a young man while in solitary confinement in cell 54 of the Cairo central prison. Just sense the depth of that understanding reflected in his words:

> He who cannot change the very fabric of his thought will never be able to change reality, and will never, therefore, make any progress.[13]

Before his shift in perspective concerning Israel, Sadat had become an enormously popular president, deeply devoted to the Arab cause. He went around Egypt giving political speeches about how he would never shake the hand of an Israeli as long as they occupied one inch of Arab soil, shouting "Never! Never! Never!" The enormous crowds of people would shout back, "Never! Never! Never!"

We invited Sadat's wife, Madame Jehan Sadat, to be the keynote speaker at our International Symposium. I had the privilege of having lunch with her. I asked her what it was like living with Anwar Sadat—particularly at the time he made the bold peace initiative of going to the Knesset in Jerusalem, a move that culminated in the Camp David Accord.

She said she had a hard time believing his change of heart, particularly after all he'd been doing and saying. Here's my paraphrasing of what she recounted:

Confronting him directly in their living quarters of the palace, she asked him, "I understand you are thinking about going to Israel. Is this correct?"

"Yes."

"How could you possibly do this after all you have been saying?"

"I was wrong, and this is the right thing to do."

"You will lose the leadership and support of the Arab world."

"I suppose that could happen; but I don't think it will."

"You will lose the presidency of your country."

"That, too, could happen."

"You'll lose your life." (And, as we know, he did, to an assassin's bullet.)

He responded, "My life is ordained. It will not be one minute longer or one minute shorter than it was ordained to be."

She embraced him and said he was the greatest person she had ever known.

Then I asked her what it was like when he returned from Israel. She said it normally takes thirty minutes to travel from the airport to the palace. That day it took over three hours. The highways and streets were thronged with hundreds of thousands of people, cheering Sadat in enthusiastic support of what he was doing—the same people who just one week earlier had been cheering for the exact opposite approach. He was doing what was right, and they knew it. Spiritual intelligence is a higher endowment than emotional intelligence. They recognized that you cannot think and live independently in an *inter*dependent world.

Sadat had subordinated his ego and EQ (social sensitivity, empathy and social skills) to his SQ (conscience), and the results resonated through the whole world. The leadership of his spiritual intelligence elevated his other intelligences, and he became a person of tremendous moral authority.

This pathway to moral authority, personal fulfillment and influence for good is not the realm of great world leaders alone. The potential for simple, great, quiet moral authority lies within each one of us.

DEVELOPING THE 4 INTELLIGENCES/CAPACITIES

Because these four dimensions of life obviously overlap, you really can't work exclusively on any one without touching directly or indirectly on the others. Developing and using these intelligences will instill within you quiet confidence, internal strength and security, the ability to be simultaneously courageous and considerate, and personal moral authority. In many ways, your efforts to develop these intelligences will

profoundly impact your ability to influence others and inspire them to
find their voice.

To assist you in further developing your four native intelligences, I
have prepared an action guide in the back of the book that will provide
you with several well-founded, practical ways to develop each of the intelligences. It is called Appendix 1: Developing the 4 Intelligences/
Capacities—A Practical Guide to Action and can be found on page 331.
Though you may find some of it to be simple common sense, remember, common sense is not common practice, and I guarantee that if you
will focus your efforts in these areas, you will find that great peace and
power will come into your life.

> *Back of every noble life there are*
> *principles that have fashioned it.*[14]
> GEORGE H. LORIMER

I have also found that by making four simple assumptions in our lives
we can immediately begin leading a more balanced, integrated, powerful life. They are simple—one for each part of our nature—but I promise you that if you do them consistently, you will find a new wellspring of
strength and integrity to draw on when you need it most.

1. For the *body*—assume you've had a heart attack; now live accordingly.
2. For the *mind*—assume the half-life of your profession is two
   years; now prepare accordingly.
3. For the *heart*—assume everything you say about another, they
   can overhear; now speak accordingly.
4. For the *spirit*—assume you have a one-on-one visit with your
   Creator every quarter; now live accordingly.

FILM: *A.B. Combs Elementary*

When in life can we start developing the moral authority and inner
strength that flow from the four human intelligences? I'll illustrate with
a film that you've got to see. It is the story of a woman who is principal
of A.B. Combs Elementary School (K–5) in Raleigh, North Carolina—a
magnet school with a mission to produce leaders for society. It shows

her in, perhaps, her finest hour, but I suspect there will be many more in the future.

But before you watch it, let me first ask this one question: When is the best time to learn the software that enables you to find your voice? When in one's lifetime is the best time to get the cultural overlay, the software, to be completely in harmony with our "hardwired" gifts? I think we would all agree it is in our childhood—primarily, in our early home life. But what if people have bad early home lives and learn the software of victimism, scarcity, and the metastasizing cancers of competing, complaining, contending, comparing and criticizing. Could one's early home life take place at school? Could a teacher or a school administrator become a surrogate parent to perhaps compensate for the dysfunctionality of the home when the children are very young and impressionable and innocent and uncorrupted?

> *Scientific evidence—largely from the field of neuroscience, which concerns our basic biology and how our brains develop—shows that the human child is "hardwired to connect." We are hardwired to connect to other people, to moral and spiritual meaning, and to openness to the transcendent. Meeting these basic needs for connection is essential to health and human flourishing.*[15]
>
> A REPORT TO THE NATION FROM THE COMMISSION ON CHILDREN AT RISK: YMCA OF THE USA, DARTMOUTH MEDICAL SCHOOL, INSTITUTE FOR AMERICAN VALUES

Better still, what if you could get a partnership between home and school so that there is continual reinforcement and alignment from both sides at all times with the child? Can you imagine the result if the software and the hardware were aligned during those first few years of childhood—the kinds of people it would produce and the kind of achievements that would flow from their characters and competencies?

In its very low production quality, the film you are about to see is more like a home movie than a professionally produced film. It is about a great partnership between a school and the homes of its students, fashioned largely by the leadership of the principal, Mrs. Muriel Thomas Summers.

Mrs. Summers got a vision of the possibilities of introducing principle-based character education into the curriculum of a K–5 school (little children ranging from ages five through ten), and of involving fellow administrators, faculty and families in the preparation. She chose *The 7 Habits of Highly Effective People* as their curriculum. You will see in the Action Guide at the back of the book how 7 *Habits* is a powerful framework for developing our human intelligences, particularly EQ.

Frankly, I'm a little embarrassed by this film and hesitate to even share it because it talks about the "Covey" Habits. So when I visited the school, I reinforced to the people that the Habits are nothing more than universal, timeless principles belonging to all humanity that I organized into an actionable, sequential framework of thinking. I quoted T.S. Eliot, who said, "We must never cease from exploring. At the end of all of our exploring will be to arrive at where we began and know the place for the first time."

You'll notice in the video of this school celebration assembly that it's the little children who conducted this assembly and gave the speeches. You can't see the families in front, but they are there—you can hear babies crying, so you sense their presence. There was a true partnership formed, and the principles of responsibility, purpose, integrity, win-win, seeking first to understand, synergy and sharpen the saw became integrated into their total curriculum.

Many people feel there is no real connection between academic performance and character; many people also feel there is no connection between subject learning and principles. But the whole concept behind Finding Your Voice and Inspiring Others to Find Theirs is a synergistic concept. It is the integration of our intelligences and capacities, which unleashes human potential. I directly asked the principal what impact introducing principle-centered character training into the curriculum had on academic performance. She said the impact was profound. I asked if she had any numbers. She answered, "Yes. Eighteen months ago, sixty-seven percent of our students performed at or above grade level in national academic standards; today ninety-four percent are at or above grade level." Just consider the significance of what she said—the same families, the same facilities, the same core curricula and learning materials, the same buildings—only one variable: Character principles were introduced and integrated into the classes and lives of these students. Eighteen months!

Talk about overlaying principle-centered software and the freedom to choose with hardwired gifts! How marvelous this would be if this could happen in the homes and the schools of young people throughout the world; the people who are the future. It's an answer to the dilemma expressed by author and founder/CEO emeritus of Visa International, Dee Hock: "The problem is never how to get new, innovative thoughts into your mind, but how to get the old ones out."[16]

One more word before you watch the film. The "Wall of Wonder" they talk about and that they asked me to help unveil is somewhat blurred and difficult to discern, but it's basically made up of 560 ceramic panels, each painted by a child, all blended into a montage of beautiful colors. At the center it talks about the four parts of our nature, as manifested in the four needs—to live, to love, to learn, to leave a legacy. This whole film was not prepared or staged—everything was authentic, spontaneous and real-time, as I'm sure you'll be able to tell at the outset. This is a school of fifty-six different nationalities. When I arrived at the school, many of these children had on their native costumes and carried their native flags. I've never seen a level of diversity in one location that even compares to this.

A.B. Combs has received numerous awards, including the following:

- National Blue Ribbon School of Excellence (given by the U.S. Department of Education)
- National Magnet Schools of Excellence Award, three years running (the highest award given by the National Magnet Schools of America). Named one of the top five magnet schools (out of thousands) in the U.S. in academic performance, with 98 percent of their students performing at or above grade level.
- North Carolina School of Excellence (based on academic achievement)
- North Carolina Governor's Entrepreneurial Award (awarded for leadership and risk-taking in education)
- Winner, National Schools of Character
- Invited to present at the Model Schools Conference, 2004
- Finalist for the 21st Century Award for Educational Excellence, 2004

Enjoy the film.

QUESTION & ANSWER

Q: Are we basically a product of nature (our genes) or of nurture (our upbringing and environmental conditions)?

A: The very question itself is based on a false dichotomy. It is based on a false paradigm or map of human nature, that of determinism. We are a product of neither nature nor nurture; we are a product of choice, because there is always a space between stimulus and response. As we wisely exercise our power to choose based on principles, the space will become larger. Little children and people who are mentally handicapped may not have that space, but the overwhelming majority of adults do. Determinism is deeply imbedded into present-day culture and is reinforced by the terrifying sense that if I do have choice, then I am also responsible for my present situation. Until a person can honestly say "I am what I am" and "I am where I am because I so choose to be there," that person cannot say with conviction, "I choose otherwise."

Q: Are leaders born or made, meaning environmentally conditioned and trained?

A: Again, this question is based on a false dichotomy, a flawed paradigm of determinism. Because of the space between stimulus and response, people have the power of choice; therefore, leaders are neither born nor made—meaning environmentally trained and nurtured. They are self-made through chosen responses, and if they choose based on principles and develop increasingly greater discipline, their freedom to choose increases. In the book *Geeks and Geezers: How Era, Values, and Defining Moments Shape Leaders*, authors Warren G. Bennis and Robert J. Thomas make the case that leaders are made, not born.[17] The basic concept is that because of one intense transformational experience, they make those choices that enable them to become a leader. Dr. Noel Tichy also basically says that leaders aren't born, they are taught. Again, the implication is that people make the *choice* to be taught and to follow the teachings. In both instances, the authors are really saying that leaders aren't made or born, they are self-made—leadership is a function of choices.

Q: Must you develop *all* four capacities or intelligences?

A: Yes, because you won't really be able to develop any one of them to its mature, sustainable level without working on all four. This is what integrity means. It means the *whole* of our life is integrated around principles. Our capacity for production and enjoyment is a function, in the last analysis, of our character, our integrity. This takes constant effort to develop the physical muscle fiber, the emotional/social muscle fiber, the mental muscle fiber and the spiritual muscle fiber by getting us out of our comfort zones and doing those exercises that cause the fiber to break (pain); then it is repaired and enlarged and strengthened after a proper period of rest and relaxation. See *The Power of Full Engagement* by authors Jim Loehr and Tony Schwartz.[18]

Q: What about retirement?

A: Retire from your job but never from meaningful projects. If you want to live a long life, you need *eustress*, that is, a deep sense of meaning and of contribution to worthy projects and causes, particularly, your intergenerational family. If you want to die early, retire to golf and fishing and sit around swallowing prescriptions and occasionally seeing your grandkids. Want evidence for this? Study Hans Selye's book, *Stress Without Distress*.

Chapter 5

EXPRESS YOUR VOICE— VISION, DISCIPLINE, PASSION AND CONSCIENCE

Most powerful is he who has himself in his power.

LUCIUS AMAEUS SENECA

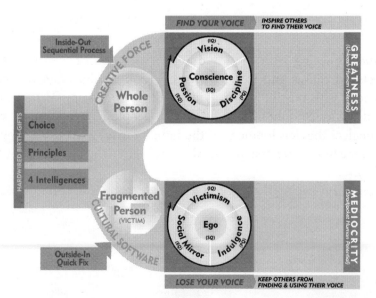

Figure 5.1

W HEN YOU STUDY the lives of *all* great achievers—those who have had the greatest influence on others, those who have made significant contributions, those who have simply made things happen—you will find a pattern. Through their persistent efforts and inner struggle, they have greatly expanded their four native human intelligence or capacities. The highest manifestations of these four intelligences are: for the mental, *vision;* for the physical, *discipline;* for the emotional, *passion;* for the spiritual, *conscience.* These manifestations also represent our highest means of *expressing our voice.*

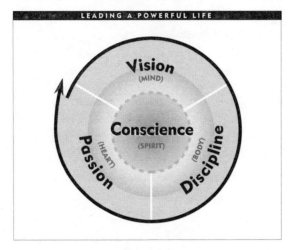

Figure 5.2

Vision is seeing with the mind's eye what is possible in people, in projects, in causes and in enterprises. Vision results when our mind joins need with possibility. As William Blake once said, "What is now proved was once only imagined." When people have no vision, when they neglect the development of the mind's capacity to create, they fall prey to the human tendency toward *victimism* (see the lower road of Figure 5.1).

Discipline is paying the price to bring that vision into reality. It's deal-

> *He that would govern others*
> *first should be master of himself.* [1]
>
> PHILIP MASSINGER

ing with the hard, pragmatic, brutal facts of reality and doing what it takes to make things happen. Discipline arises when vision joins with commitment. The opposite of discipline and the commitment that inspires sacrifice is *indulgence*—sacrificing what matters most in life for the pleasure or thrill of the moment.

Passion is the fire, the desire, the strength of conviction and the drive that sustains the discipline to achieve the vision. Passion arises when human need overlaps unique human talent. When one does not have the passion that flows from finding and using one's voice to serve great purposes, the void is filled with insecurity and the empty chatter of a thousand voices that drive the *social mirror.* In relationship and organizational settings, passion includes compassion.

Conscience is the inward moral sense of what is right and what is wrong, the drive toward meaning and contribution. It is the guiding force to vision, discipline and passion. It stands in stark contrast to the life dominated by *ego.*

> *Whatever weakens your reason, impairs the tenderness*
> *of your conscience, obscures your sense of God,*
> *takes off your relish for spiritual things, whatever*
> *increases the authority of the body over the mind,*
> *that thing is sin to you, however innocent*
> *it may seem in itself.* [2]
>
> SUSANA WESLEY (JOHN WESLEY'S MOTHER)

These four words—vision, discipline, passion and conscience—essentially embody many, many other characteristics used to describe those traits we associate with people whose influence is great, whether known to many or few.

Most differences in the words we use to describe people we admire—whether in the home, in the community, in a business or in government—are simply a matter of semantics. See in figure 5.3 many such traits listed on the underwater mass of the icebergs labeled vision, discipline, passion and conscience.

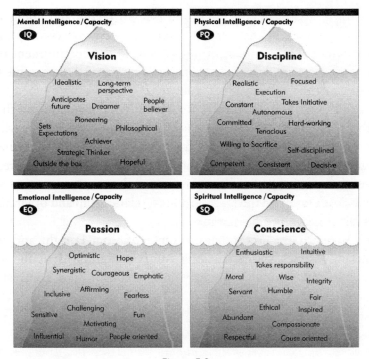

Figure 5.3

The best leaders operate in four dimensions: vision, reality, ethics, and courage. These are the four intelligences, the four forms of perceiving, the languages for communicating that are required to achieve meaningful, sustained results.

The visionary leader thinks big, thinks new, thinks ahead—and most important, is in touch with the deep structure of human consciousness and creative potential.

You must gain control over the patterns that govern your mind: your worldview, your beliefs about what you deserve and about what's possible. That's the zone of fundamental change, strength, and energy—and the true meaning of courage.[3]

PETER KOESTENBAUM, MANAGEMENT PHILOSOPHER

VISION, DISCIPLINE AND PASSION RULE THE WORLD

Any individual who has had profound influence on others, on institutions or on society, any parents whose influence has been intergenerational, anyone who has really made a difference for good or ill, possessed three common attributes: vision, discipline and passion. I suggest that these three attributes have ruled the world from its beginning. They represent leadership that works.

Consider just a few notable leaders from modern history:

George Washington had the vision of building a new nation, united and free from foreign interference. He disciplined himself to learn how to recruit, supply and keep people from deserting the Revolutionary Army. Angered by discrimination against colonial military officers, British land policies, and restriction on U.S. expansion, Washington was passionate about the cause of liberty.

Florence Nightingale, the founder of modern nursing, worked her entire adult life to improve the quality of nursing in military hospitals. Her vision and passion overcame her personal reticence.

Mohandas K. Gandhi was instrumental in establishing India as an independent state though he never held an elected or appointed office. He had no formal position from which to lead people. Gandhi's moral authority created such strong social and cultural norms that it ultimately shaped political will. He governed his life by an awareness of a universal conscience that resided within the people, the international community, and the British themselves.

Margaret Thatcher was the first female leader of a major industrial nation. She served three terms as prime minister of Great Britain, the longest continuous premiership in the twentieth century. Her critics are not few, but she was passionate about urging people to assume the discipline of personal responsibility and to build self-reliance, and she was passionate about bolstering free enterprise in her country. During her tenure in British politics, she helped lift Britain out of economic recession.

> *Being powerful is like being a lady;*
> *if you have to tell people you are, you aren't.*
>
> MARGARET THATCHER

Nelson Mandela, former president of South Africa, spent almost twenty-seven years in prison for fighting against the apartheid regime. Mandela was impelled by his imagination rather than by his memory. He could envision a world far beyond the confines of his experience and memory, which included imprisonment, injustice, tribal warfare and disunity. Deep within his soul resonated a belief in the worth of every South African citizen.

Mother Teresa dedicated herself wholeheartedly, freely and unconditionally to the service of the poor. She bequeathed her highly disciplined upholding of the vows of poverty, purity and obedience upon her organization, which has both grown and strengthened even since her passing.

> *The fruit of silence is PRAYER. The fruit of prayer is FAITH. The fruit of faith is LOVE. The fruit of love is SERVICE. The fruit of service is PEACE.*[4]
>
> MOTHER TERESA

You'll remember that I mentioned that anyone who has really made a difference for good *or ill* in the world possessed three common attributes: vision, discipline and passion. Now consider another leader who possessed all three but produced shockingly different results. *Adolf Hitler* passionately communicated his vision of a thousand-year reign of the Third Reich and of a superior Aryan race. He built one of the most disciplined military-industrial machines that the world has ever seen. And he evidenced brilliant emotional intelligence in his impassioned oratory, inspiring in the masses almost fanatical dedication and fear, which he channeled into hate and destruction.

There is, however, a huge difference between leadership that works and leadership that endures; every one of the aforementioned leaders laid a foundation and provided a contribution that endured, except for one—the last.

> *Once I really am in power, my first and foremost task will be the annihilation of the Jews.*[5]
>
> ADOLF HITLER

When conscience governs vision, discipline and passion, leadership endures and changes the world for good. In other words, *moral authority makes formal authority work*. When conscience does not govern vision, discipline and passion, leadership does not endure, nor do the institutions created by that leadership endure. In other words, formal authority without moral authority fails.

The words "for good" means that it "lifts" and also that it "lasts." Hitler had vision, discipline and passion but was driven by ego. Lack of conscience was his downfall. Gandhi's vision, discipline and passion were driven by conscience, and he became a servant to the cause and the people. Again, he had only moral authority, no formal authority, and he was the father and founder of the second largest country in the world.

When vision, discipline and passion are governed by formal authority void of conscience or moral authority, it also changes the world, but not for good, rather for evil. Instead of lifting, it destroys; rather than lasting, it is eventually extinguished.

Let's take a closer look at each of these four attributes: vision, discipline, passion and conscience.

VISION

Vision is seeing a future state with the mind's eye. Vision is applied imagination. All things are created twice: first, a mental creation; second, a physical creation. The first creation, vision, is the beginning of the process of reinventing oneself or of an organization reinventing itself. It represents desire, dreams, hopes, goals and plans. But these dreams or visions are not just fantasies. They are reality not yet brought into the physical sphere, like the blueprint of a house before it's built or musical notes in a score just waiting to be played.

Most of us don't envision or realize our own potential. William James said, "Most people live in a very restricted circle of their potential being. We all have reservoirs of energy and genius to draw upon of which we do not dream."

Each of us has immeasurable power and capacity to reinvent our lives. In the following story, notice how one grief-stricken woman was able to create a new vision of her life:

I was forty-six years old when my husband, Gordon, was diagnosed with cancer. Without hesitation, I took early retirement to be with him. Although his death eighteen months later was expected, my grief consumed me. I sorrowed over our dreams unfulfilled. I was only forty-eight and had no reason to live.

My overarching question through my sorrow was, Why did God take Gordon and not me? I felt Gordon had so much more to offer the world than I had. With my body, mind and spirit fatigued beyond measure, I was motivated to find new meaning in my life.

I grabbed on to the idea that all things are created twice, first mentally and then physically. I had to ask myself what talents I had. An aptitude assessment test clarified for me what my strongest abilities were. To create a sense of balance in my life, I focused on the four parts of my nature. On an intellectual level, I realized that I loved to teach; spiritually and socially, I wanted to continue to support the racial harmony we had endeavored to create in our biracial marriage; emotionally, I knew I needed to give love. When my mother was alive she would rock critically ill babies in the hospital. I wanted to give comfort as she had and continue her legacy of unconditional love.

I was afraid to fail, but I told myself it would be okay to try different things, like trying on hats. If I didn't like teaching after a semester, I didn't have to go back. I began by going to graduate school so I could teach on the college level. Graduate school is hard, but at age forty-eight, it was especially tough! I was so used to passing documents off to my secretary to type, it took me a semester just to learn how to type my own papers. Turning off the TV and returning the cable box were acts of sheer will.

I completed graduate school and began teaching at a historically black college in Little Rock, Arkansas. I was appointed by the governor to serve on the Martin Luther King Commission to improve racial relations. I rock crack babies and AIDS infants who are hooked up to ventilators, for however short a period of time they have. I know I'm giving comfort, and that gives me a sense of peace.

Now my life is good. I can feel Gordon smiling at me. He told me time and time again before he died that he wanted me to have a life full of laughter, happy memories and good things. How could I waste my life, with that directive on my conscience? I don't think I could. I have an obligation to live my life the best I can for the people I love the most—whether they are here or on the other side.

Albert Einstein said, "Imagination is more important than knowledge." Memory is past. It is finite. Vision is future. It is infinite. Vision is greater than history, greater than baggage, greater than the emotional scars of the past.

When somebody asked Einstein what question he would ask God if he could ask one, he replied, "How did the universe start? Because everything after that is just math." And after thinking for a while, he changed his mind. He said, "Instead I would ask, 'Why was the universe created?' Because then I would know the meaning of my own life."

Perhaps the most important vision of all is to develop a sense of self, a sense of your own destiny, a sense of your unique mission and role in life, a sense of purpose and meaning. When testing your own personal vision first ask yourself: Does the vision tap into my voice, my energy, my unique talent? Does it give me a sense of "calling," a cause worthy of my commitment? Acquiring such meaning requires profound personal reflection, asking deep questions and envisioning.

The author, filmmaker and world-renowned storyteller Sir Laurens van der Post said, "Without vision we all suffer from an insufficiency of data. We look at life myopically, that is, through our own lens, our own world. Vision enables us to transcend our autobiography, our past to rise above our memory. This is particularly practical in human relationships and creates a magnanimity of spirit toward others."

When we talk about vision, it's important to consider not only the vision of what's possible "out there" but also the vision of what we see in other people, their unseen potential. Vision is about more than just getting things done, accomplishing some task, achieving something; it is about discovering and expanding our view of others, affirming them, believing in them, and helping them discover and realize the potential within them—helping them find their own voice.

In many Eastern cultures, people greet others by putting their arms in an inverted V shape at their chest and bowing to the other person. In so doing they are saying, "I salute the greatness in you," or "I salute the divinity within you." I know another person who, when she encounters a person, says audibly or in her heart, "I love you. What is your name?" Seeing people through the lens of their potential and their best actions, rather than through the lens of their current behavior or weaknesses, generates positive energy and reaches out and embraces others. This affirming action is also one of the keys to rebuilding broken relationships. It is also the key to successful parenting.

There is great power in viewing people separately from their behav-

> *Thee lift me and I'll lift thee and we'll ascend together.*
> QUAKER PROVERB

ior, for as we do, we affirm their fundamental, unconditional worth. When we perceive and acknowledge the potential of others, it is as if we hold up a mirror to them reflecting the best within them. This affirming vision not only frees them to become their best but we too are freed from reacting to unwanted behavior. When people behave far below their potential, our affirming attitude and words become "that's not like you."

While on an international trip many years ago I remember being introduced to a young man about eighteen years old. He had had some great challenges in his youth, including drug and alcohol abuse. Though he was turning his life around, as the two of us visited alone I could tell that he was struggling for a sense of direction and doubted himself. I also discerned that he was a special young man, full of greatness and real potential. It beamed from his countenance and spirit. Before we parted, I looked him right in the eye and told him that I believed he would be a person of great influence in the world throughout his life, and that he had unusual gifts and potential.

Almost twenty years later, he has become one of the most promising, able young men I know. He has a beautiful family and is a professional of real accomplishment. A friend of mine was recently visiting with him. During their conversation, this young man spontaneously recounted the experience I described above. Of it, he said, "You have no idea how that one hour impacted my life. I was told I was someone with potential that far surpassed what I had ever imagined. That thought caught hold inside me. It has made all the difference in the world."

Cultivating the habit of affirming people, of frequently and sincerely communicating your belief in them—particularly teenagers who are going through their second identity crisis—is supremely important. It's a relatively small investment with incalculable, unbelievable results. Again, remember the incredible effect it has upon us when someone communicates his or her belief in us (our potential) when we don't believe in ourselves (our history).

DISCIPLINE

Discipline is just as important as vision, though it is second in the chain. Discipline represents the second creation. It's the executing, the making it happen, the sacrifice entailed in doing whatever it takes to realize that vision. Discipline is willpower embodied. Peter Drucker once observed

> *When the morning's freshness has been replaced by the weariness*
> *of midday, when the leg muscles quiver under the strain, the climb*
> *seems endless, and, suddenly, nothing will go quite as you wish—*
> *it is then that you must not hesitate.*[6]
>
> DAG HAMMARSKJÖLD

that the first duty of a manager is to define reality. Discipline defines reality and accepts it; it is the willingness to get totally immersed in it, rather than deny it. It acknowledges the stubborn, brute facts of things as they are.

> *Leadership is the capacity to*
> *translate vision into reality.*
>
> WARREN BENNIS

Without vision and a sense of hope, accepting reality may be depressing or discouraging. Happiness is sometimes defined as the ability to subordinate what you want now for what you want eventually. This personal sacrifice, the process of subordinating today's pleasure for a greater longer-term good, is exactly what discipline is all about.

Most people equate discipline with an absence of freedom. "Shoulds kill spontaneity." "There's no freedom in 'have to.' " "I want to do what I want to do. That's freedom, not duty."

In fact, the opposite is true. Only the disciplined are truly free. The undisciplined are slaves to moods, appetites and passions.

Can you play the piano? I can't. I don't have the freedom to play the piano. I never disciplined myself. I preferred playing with my friends to practicing, as my parents and piano teacher wanted me to do. I don't think I ever envisioned myself as a piano player. I never had a sense of what it might mean, a kind of freedom to create magnificent art that might be valuable to myself and to others throughout my entire life.

What about the freedom to forgive, to ask forgiveness? What about the freedom to love unconditionally, to be a light, not a judge—a model, not a critic? Think of the discipline involved in these. Discipline comes from being "discipled" to a person or a cause.

The great educator Horace Mann once said, "In vain do they talk of happiness who never subdue an impulse in obedience to a principle. He who never sacrificed a present for future good, or a personal to a general one, can speak of happiness only as the blind speak of color."

I remember the internal struggle I faced as a fifty-year-old university professor in deciding to leave the safe haven and comfort zone of university professorship to set up my own business. If it weren't for the vision of the greater good I might do, we never would have had the discipline to make the sacrifice and begin the self-denying processes of establishing a new business, taking out a second mortgage, and going deeply into debt. We even acquired a new tongue-in-cheek motto, "Happiness is a positive cash flow," and sweated through each payroll for years. We could never have endured this difficult period if we hadn't had the vision of what was possible and the discipline to hang in there.

I truly believe that discipline is the trait common to all successful people. I admire the work of insurance executive Albert E. N. Gray, who spent a lifetime trying to discover the common denominator of success. Finally, he came to the simple but profound realization that although hard work, good luck and astute human relations are all important the successful person has "formed the habit of doing things that failures don't like to do."[7] Successful people don't like doing them either, necessarily. But their dislike is subordinated by the strength of their purpose.

People who lack discipline and are unable to subordinate and sacrifice simply play at working. In a sense, every workday becomes like a long masked ball. They spend the day creating smoke screens, emails detailing what they're working on, phone messages reporting on the status of projects, long meetings to discuss how to do things. Generally, people who spend their time making excuses are those who lack focus and discipline. Setbacks are inevitable; misery is a choice. There are always reasons, never an excuse.

PASSION

Passion comes from the heart and is manifest as optimism, excitement, emotional connection, determination. It fires unrelenting drive. Enthusiasm is deeply rooted in the power of choice rather than circumstance. Enthusiasts believe that the best way to predict the future is to create it. In fact, enthusiasm becomes a moral imperative, making the person part of the solution rather than part of the problem of feeling essentially hopeless and helpless.

Aristotle said, "Where talents and the needs of the world cross, therein lies your vocation." We could say, "Therein lies your passion, your voice"—that which energizes your life and gives you your drive. It is the fuel at the heart of vision and discipline. It keeps you at it when everything else may say quit. When asked by his doctor how many hours a week he spent working, one man replied, "I don't know. How many hours a week do you breathe?" When life, work, play and love all revolve around the same thing, you've got passion!

The key to creating passion in your life is to find your unique talents and your special role and purpose in the world. It is essential to know yourself before you decide what work you want to do.* The Greek philosophy, "Know yourself, control yourself, give yourself" is exquisitely sequenced and wise. One's talent, one's mission or role in life is usually detected more than it is invented. Author, filmmaker and world-renowned storyteller Sir Laurens van der Post wrote:

> We have to look inwards to look into ourselves, look into this container, which is our soul; look and listen to it. Until you have listened in to that thing which is dreaming through you, in other words—answered the knock on the door in the dark, you will not be able to lift this moment in time in which we are imprisoned, back again into the level where the great act of creation is going on.

The great contributors in life are those who, though afraid of the knock at the door, still answer it. Courage is the essence of passion, and is, as Harold B. Lee once said, "the quality of every virtue acting at its highest testing point."[8]

There's a common misconception that a person's skill is their talent. Skills, however, are not talents. Talents, on the other hand, require skills. People can have skills and knowledge in areas where their talents do not lie. If they have a job that requires their skills but not their talents, organizations will never tap into their passion or voice. They'll go through the motions, but this will only make them appear to need external supervision and motivation.

If you can hire people whose passion intersects with the job, they won't require any supervision at all. They will manage themselves better

---

* For a free e-booklet and mp3 audio on critical career-building principles, including topics like "How to Get Any Job You Want," go to www.The8thHabit.com/offers.

than anyone could ever manage them. Their fire comes from within, not from without. Their motivation is internal, not external. Just think about the times when you were passionate about a project, something that was so compelling and absorbing that you could hardly think of anything else. Did you need to be managed or supervised? Of course not; the thought of being told when and how to do it would have been insulting.

WHEN YOU CAN give yourself to work that brings together a need, your talent, and your passion, power will be unlocked.

CONSCIENCE

> *Labour to keep alive . . . that little*
> *spark of celestial fire, conscience.*[9]
> GEORGE WASHINGTON

Much has been said from the outset of this book about the singular importance of conscience. There is a mass of evidence that shows that conscience, this moral sense, this inner light, is a universal phenomenon. The spiritual or moral nature of people is also independent of religion or of any particular religious approach, culture, geography, nationality or race. Yet all of the enduring major religious traditions of the world are unified when it comes to certain basic underlying principles or values.

Immanuel Kant said, "I am constantly amazed by two things; the starry heavens above and the moral law within." Conscience is the moral law within. It is the overlapping of moral law and behavior. Many believe, as do I, that it is the voice of God to his children. Others may not share this belief but recognize that there is an innate sense of fairness and justice, an innate sense of right and wrong, of what is kind and what is unkind, of what contributes and what detracts, of what beautifies and what destroys, of what is true and what is false. Admittedly, culture translates this basic moral sense into different kinds of practices and words, but this translation does not negate the underlying sense of right and wrong.

As I work in nations of different religions and different cultures, I have seen this universal conscience revealed time and again. There really is a set of values, a sense of *fairness, honesty, respect* and *contribution* that transcends culture—something that is timeless, which transcends the ages and is also self-evident. Again, it is as self-evident as the fact that trust requires trustworthiness.

Conscience and Ego

Conscience is the still, small voice within. It is quiet. It is peaceful. Ego is tyrannical, despotic and dictatorial.

Ego focuses on one's own survival, pleasure and enhancement to the exclusion of others and is selfishly ambitious. It sees relationships in terms of threat or no threat, like little children who classify all people as "He's nice" or "He's mean." Conscience, on the other hand, both democratizes and elevates ego to a larger sense of the group, the whole, the community, the greater good. It sees life in terms of service and contribution, in terms of others' security and fulfillment.

Ego works in the face of genuine crisis but has no discernment in deciding how severe a crisis or threat is. Conscience is filled with discernment and senses the degree of threat. It has a large repertoire of responses. It has the patience and wisdom to decide what to do when. Conscience sees life on a continuum. It's capable of complex adaptation.

Ego can't sleep. It micromanages. It disempowers. It reduces one's capacity. It excels in control. Conscience deeply reveres people and sees their potential for self-control. Conscience empowers. It reflects the worth and value of all people and affirms their power and freedom to choose. Then natural self-control emerges, imposed neither from above nor from the outside.

Ego is threatened by negative feedback and punishes the messenger. It interprets all data in terms of self-preservation. It constantly censors information. It denies much of reality. Conscience values feedback and attempts to discern whatever truth it contains. It isn't afraid of information and can accurately interpret what's going on. It has no need to censor information and is open to an awareness of reality from every direction.

Ego is myopic and interprets all of life through its own agenda. Conscience is a social ecologist listening to and sensing the entire system and environment. It fills the body with light, is able to democratize ego to reflect more accurately the entire world.

Further Insights into Conscience

Conscience is sacrifice—the subordinating of one's self or one's ego to a higher purpose, cause or principle. Again, sacrifice really means giving up something good for something better. But in the mind of the person sacrificing, there really is no sacrifice—only to the observer is it sacrifice.

Sacrifice can take many forms as it manifests itself in the four dimensions of our lives: making physical and economic sacrifices (the body); cultivating an open, inquisitive mind and purging oneself of prejudices (the mind); showing deep respect and love to others (the heart); and subordinating one's own will to a higher will for the greater good (the spirit).

> *A new philosophy, a new way of life, is not given for nothing. It has to be paid dearly for and only acquired with much patience and great effort.*
>
> FYODOR DOSTOEVSKY

Conscience teaches us that ends and means are inseparable, that ends actually preexist in the means. Immanuel Kant taught that the means used to accomplish the ends are as important as those ends. Machiavelli taught the opposite, that the ends justify the means.

Consider the seven things that, according to Gandhi's teaching, will destroy us. If you study them slowly and carefully, you will see in a powerful way how each represents an *end* being accomplished through an unprincipled or unworthy *means:*

- Wealth without work
- Pleasure without conscience
- Knowledge without character
- Commerce without morality
- Science without humanity
- Worship without sacrifice
- Politics without principle

Isn't it interesting how each one of these admirable ends can be falsely attained? But if you reach an admirable end through the wrong means, the ends ultimately turn to dust in your hands.

In your business dealings, you know those who are honest with you and who keep their promises and commitments. You also know exactly those who are duplicitous, deceitful and dishonest. Even when you reach a legal contract agreement with those who are dishonest, do you really trust they'll come through and keep their word?

> *People are often unreasonable, illogical, and self-centered;*
> *forgive them anyway.*
> *If you are kind, people may accuse you of selfish,*
> *ulterior motives; be kind anyway.*
> *If you are successful, you will win some false friends and*
> *some true friends; succeed anyway.*
> *If you are honest and frank, people may cheat you;*
> *be honest and frank anyway.*
> *What you spend years building,*
> *someone could destroy overnight; build anyway.*
> *If you find serenity and happiness, they may be jealous;*
> *be happy anyway.*
> *The good you do today, people will often forget tomorrow;*
> *do good anyway.*
> *Give the world your best anyway.*
> *You see, in the final analysis, it is between you and God;*
> *it was never between you and them anyway.*
>
> MOTHER TERESA

It's conscience that constantly tells us the value of both ends and means and how they are inseparable. But it's ego that tells us that the end justifies the means, unaware that a worthy end can never be accomplished with an unworthy means. It may appear that you can, but there are unintended consequences that are not seen or evident at first that will eventually destroy the end. For instance, you can yell at your kids to clean their rooms, and if your end is to have a clean room, you'll accomplish just that. But I guarantee you that not only will the means negatively affect the relationships but the room won't stay clean when you leave town for a few days.

> *Wisdom denotes the pursuing of the best ends by the best means.*[10]
> FRANCES HUTCHESON

Conscience profoundly alters vision, discipline and passion by introducing us into the world of relationships. It moves us from an independent to an interdependent state. When this happens, everything is altered. You realize that vision and values must be shared before people will be willing to accept the institutionalized discipline of structures and systems that embody those shared values. Such shared vision creates discipline and order without demanding them. Conscience often provides the *why*, vision identifies *what* you're trying to accomplish, discipline represents *how* you're going to accomplish it, and passion represents the strength of feelings behind the why, the what, and the how.

CONSCIENCE TRANSFORMS *passion into compassion.* It engenders sincere caring for others, a combination of both sympathy and empathy, where one's pain is shared and received. Compassion is the interdependent expression of passion. *Guideposts* contributor JoAnn C. Jones related an experience in which her university professor taught her to live and learn by the guidance of her conscience:

> *During my second month of nursing school, our professor gave us a pop quiz. I was a conscientious student and had breezed through the questions, until I read the last one: What is the first name of the woman who cleans the school?*
>
> *Surely this was some kind of joke. I had seen the cleaning woman several times. She was tall, dark-haired and in her fifties, but how would I know her name? I handed in my paper, leaving the last question blank.*
>
> *Before the class ended, one student asked if the last question would count toward our quiz grade. "Absolutely," said the professor. "In your careers you will meet many people. All are significant. They deserve your attention and care, even if all you do is smile and say hello."*
>
> *I've never forgotten that lesson. I also learned her name was Dorothy.*[11]

When people strive to live by their conscience, it produces integrity and peace of mind. German-born Presbyterian minister and motivational speaker/

author William J. H. Boetcker said earlier in the twentieth century, "That you may retain your self-respect, it is better to displease the people by doing what you know is right, than to temporarily please them by doing what you know is wrong." This self-respect and integrity, in turn, produce in those who possess them the ability to be both kind and courageous with other people: *kind* in that they show a great respect and reverence for other people, their view, feelings, experiences and convictions; *courageous* in that they express their own convictions without personal threat. The interplay between differing opinions can produce those third alternatives that are better than what either person had initially proposed. This is true synergy, where the whole is greater than the sum of the parts.

People who do not live by their conscience will not experience this internal integrity and peace of mind. They will find their ego attempting to control relationships. Even though they might pretend or feign kindness and empathy from time to time, they will use subtle forms of manipulation and will even go so far as to engage in kind but dictatorial behavior.

The private victory of integrity is the foundation for the public victories of establishing a common vision, discipline and passion. Leadership becomes an interdependent work rather than an immature interplay between strong, independent, ego-driven rulers and compliant, dependent followers.

FILM: *Stone*

There is a man in Uganda who beautifully illustrates the power of allowing conscience to wisely direct our vision, discipline and passion. His name is Stone, and he was a great soccer player. The dream of every kid in Uganda is to become good enough at soccer that the European clubs will sign him or her as a player. The big, serious money from Europe was looking at Stone, when, during a game, somebody purposely hit him in a way that "blew out" his knee. His professional career was over.

Stone could have become vindictive or revengeful. He could have wallowed in self-pity or lived in his celebrity for the rest of his life. But he didn't. Instead he chose his response. He used his imagination (vision) and his conscience to inspire and influence young "problem" Ugandan boys and teenagers who would otherwise be lost in life with no marketable skills, no role models, and no hope.

I would like to invite you to see Stone in action. I want you to feel his spirit, and to sense his heart and vision. You can see Stone's story in a short, powerful, award-winning film that's included on the companion DVD to this book. I know you will enjoy the experience.

As you watch the film, notice how Stone overcame his cultural overlay toward revenge by tapping into his birth-gifts. Notice how he personally paid the price in sacrifice and discipline. Notice also how, with unrelenting passion, he reached out to the young men in his country so that they, too, could learn to govern their own lives by their conscience, as well as gain a vision of becoming first a good soccer player, then economically self-reliant, and then responsible adults, fathers and contributing citizens. Notice how they gradually became more and more independent of Stone so that they themselves were governed by the principles (conscience) of self-mastery, training and contribution. Notice, finally, how Stone communicated the worth and potential of these young men so clearly that they were inspired to see it in themselves.

You might be interested to know that a long-time colleague of mine visited Stone in Uganda several years after this film was made. He offered this update on Stone: "I was so impressed with his *balance* of body, mind, heart and spirit. He is very physically active, relentlessly teaching his boys soccer—six different teams a day! His mind is alert—always looking for new ways to achieve his mission of guiding the youth to new horizons. He is a Christian but lives in a Muslim neighborhood, with a Muslim landlord. His daily actions engender peace and harmony in his neighborhood. Socially he cares for each child, parent and person he meets. His character and deep integrity moved me well beyond even what is portrayed in this film."

PART 1: FIND YOUR VOICE—
SUMMARY AND A FINAL CHALLENGE

As we approach the end of this section on Finding Your Voice, let's go back and reconnect with our main purposes.

We know there is a painful gap between possessing great potential and actually realizing a life of greatness and contribution—between being aware of tremendous problems and challenges in the workplace and developing the internal power and moral authority to break out of those problems and become a significant force in solving them.

I commend to you again this simple way of thinking about life: a whole person (body, mind, heart and spirit) with four basic needs (to live, to learn, to love, to leave a legacy), and four intelligences or capacities (physical, mental, emotional and spiritual) and their highest manifestations (discipline, vision, passion, conscience), all of which represent the four dimensions of voice (need, talent, passion and conscience).

WHOLE PERSON	4 NEEDS	4 INTELLIGENCES / CAPACITIES	4 ATTRIBUTES	VOICE
BODY	To Live	Physical Intelligence (PQ)	Discipline	Need ("See" meeting needs)
MIND	To Learn	Mental Intelligence (IQ)	Vision	Talent (Disciplined focus)
HEART	To Love	Emotional Intelligence (EQ)	Passion	Passion (Love to do)
SPIRIT	To Leave a Legacy	Spiritual Intelligence (SQ)	Conscience	Conscience (Do what's right)

Table 1

As we respect, develop, integrate and balance these intelligences and their highest manifestations, the synergy between them lights *the fire within* us and we find our voice. You may be interested to know that I first introduced the idea and language of "The Fire Within" in the book *First Things First*, coauthored with Roger and Rebecca Merrill. Years later, the Salt Lake Organizing Committee for the 2002 Winter Olympics called me requesting permission to use as the central theme of the 2002 Games "Light the Fire Within." Without hesitation I said, "Of course—we would be honored." I was inspired and thrilled to see how they used the "Light the Fire Within" theme to portray the magnificent potential of the human spirit. Several weeks after the Games, SLOC president Mitt Romney told me that it's the first time he knows of in the history of the Olympic Games that the organizers were successfully able to create a lasting, identifying theme that actually "took hold" in the hearts and minds of the athletes, volunteers and worldwide viewers.

In chapter 1, I suggested that *voice* (see figure 5.4) lies at the nexus of *talent* (your natural gifts and strengths), *passion* (those things that naturally energize, excite, motivate and inspire you), *need* (including what the world needs enough to pay you for), and *conscience* (that still, small voice within that assures you of what is right and that prompts you to actually do it). I also said that when you engage in work (professional, community, family) that taps your *talent* and fuels your *passion*—that rises out of a great *need* in the world that you feel drawn by *conscience* to meet—therein lies your voice, your calling, your soul's code.

Figure 5.4

Perhaps you have noticed the similarity between these four dimensions of voice and the four personal leadership attributes of vision, discipline, passion and conscience (see Figure 5.5). Two of the terms, passion and conscience, are identical. The other two, *talent* and *need*, are paral-

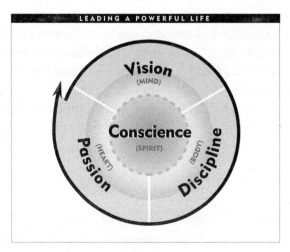

Figure 5.5

lels to *discipline* and *vision*. In fact, if you were to move the "conscience" circle (shaded to indicate its central, preeminent rate) on Figure 5.4 up to the center, you would essentially have the same model.

These four dimensions of *voice* are beautifully illustrated in the story of Muhammad Yunus. How did he find his voice? First he sensed a *need*. The voice of *conscience* inspired him to take action. Since his talent matched the need, he *disciplined* his *talent* to provide a solution. The work involved in the solution not only drew upon his talent but it also tapped his *passion*. Out of *need* grew *vision*—vision to multiply the capacity of people and institutions to meet similar needs around the world, and thereby inspire them to find *their* voice.

With the end to Part 1: Find Your Voice I extend to you a promise and a challenge. My promise: if you will apply these four capacities— talent (discipline), need (vision), passion and conscience—to any role of your life, you can find your voice in that role. My simple challenge: Take two or three of the primary roles in your life, and in each role, ask yourself the following four questions:

1. What *need* do I sense (in my family, in my community, in the organization I work for)?
2. Do I possess a true *talent* that, if disciplined and applied, can meet the need?
3. Does the opportunity to meet the need tap into my *passion?*
4. Does my *conscience* inspire me to take action and become involved?

If you can answer all four questions in the affirmative and will make a *habit* of developing a plan of action and then going to work on it, I guarantee you will begin to find your true voice in life—a life of deep meaning, satisfaction and greatness.

Let's move now to Part 2: Inspire Others to Find Their Voice.

QUESTION & ANSWER

Q: Could this approach to personal leadership help me solve one of my lifelong challenges—losing weight and staying in shape?

A: If you're like most people, you've resolved from time to time to get into shape, and, in most cases, this usually involves losing some weight. Oftentimes, getting into shape merely means replacing fat with muscle, which may actually increase your weight since muscle weighs about twice as much as fat. Nevertheless, our fundamental task is to get into shape and become physically healthy, strong and fit. That is the vision. What is the discipline? Usually it involves a strict regimen of exercise, proper nutrition, rest and stress management. Passion represents the depth of feeling, the emotional commitment, and the drive. Conscience provides the why, the reason, the worthy causes of being healthier so that you can live longer, provide for your family properly, help raise your grandchildren, or simply feel better. You'll also find that if the motivation is only external—looking better, vanity, a change of season, New Year's resolution time, etc.—such motivation will often lose its power and fail to sustain itself because the cause is not worthy of such total commitment. Before making a bad food choice, train yourself to inwardly say: "My temptation is emotional, and resisting will further my needed weight loss and strengthen my character. Furthermore, nothing tastes as good as thin feels."

It is very common to become discouraged by the cycle of setting a goal to lose weight, and then abandoning it within days or even hours. Many complain, "I'm just not disciplined." My experience is that the biggest problem is not the discipline; it's that we have not yet paid the price with vision—we're also not yet connected with our deepest values and motivations (conscience), with those things most important to us. Let me illustrate with the experience of a friend of mine:

> I had been working very hard on my career. By the time I turned forty-five, I was quite successful. I was also about sixty pounds overweight, a compulsive eater during times of stress, and one who didn't have time to exercise regularly because of work. On his fifth birthday, my son, Logan, gave me a book on healthy living. Inside, his mother had helped him write the following words: "Daddy, for my birthday this year, I want you to be healthy. I want you to be around a while." Talk about a punch in the gut. Ouch.
>
> That plea from my son changed my perspective on my lifestyle completely. The eating and the lack of regular physical exercise weren't just my individual choice anymore. I saw suddenly that I was creating a very unhealthy legacy for my children. I was modeling for them that one's body was unimportant, that self-control was unimportant, that the only thing worth

working hard for in this life was money and prestige. I realized that my stewardship to my children involved more than just providing for their physical, financial and emotional needs. It also involved providing healthy role models on which they could pattern their lives. I had not been doing that.

So I committed myself to being healthy for my children. Not to losing weight, but to being healthy. That's the key for me. My commitment had to be to something that held real value for me. I had tried so many diets and exercise programs before. Normally I would be fine until stresses happened in my life. To have losing weight as my inspiring motivation was simply not enough. But my children are significant enough. I care enough about them that I can choose to make healthy decisions. I established as a goal for myself that I wanted to be healthy. I wanted to be vital, to have energy to play with my kids after work, to be able to play in the company softball tournament without getting winded on the way to first base. As a way to reach that goal, I implemented a diet and exercise program. The key here is that the diet and exercise program was not the goal. Being healthy for my children was. I decided to share my goal with somebody else who wanted to be healthy. We now work together on an exercise program. I made sure I set aside time for me to accomplish my goals. I learned to know when to stop working and to pay attention to the needs of my body.

It's been two years since I changed my way of thinking. I don't struggle anymore to get out of bed. Exercising has almost become second nature. I don't talk myself out of my exercise program like I did at the beginning. Sure, there are still days that I don't do too well. I think I'm tired, I think my hamstring is strained, I have a headache, it's too hot. Some days, I plain talk myself out of running. But it's so much easier now for me to get back on track. Because I have this larger goal, this greater commitment to somebody I love more than myself, I can get right back on track.

Q: What about getting a job?

A: Getting into shape is primarily an independent effort. Getting the job you want is clearly a highly interdependent one and relies on effective development of influence with other people.

Now, let's think through how to get the job you want by looking at the same four attributes of personal influence: vision, discipline, passion and conscience. The key is all four. Neglect any one of them and you'll find it much more difficult to get the job you want, and if you do get it, you will likely not be able to sustain what you committed to and what it requires of you.

Let's assume there's a very soft job market and that most employers are letting people go, not hiring—particularly in the industry and city where you want to live and work. How do you get the job that you want?

First of all, to even get a vision, you need to know what this job is. Use discipline to figure out what the job actually entails. Use discipline to understand the job, to understand the organization you want to be employed by, to understand the unique requirements of the job, and to understand the marketplace so that you understand the forces that are in place, including competition, customers' wants and needs, and the characteristics and trends in that industry. In other words, pay the price to understand the challenges and problems faced by the organization you want to join.

Next, identify where your passion is, e.g., does this job uniquely reflect your talent, gifts, interests, capacities and skills? If so, does your conscience tell you this is a job worthy of being committed to? If so, can you envision yourself working in this manner?

After you've done all this preliminary work you are ready to go to the job interview—not as another problem for the interviewer to deal with but as a solution to the problems decision-makers are facing.

Show an understanding of their most significant problems better than most of the people in their present employ. Show a level of passion and commitment to meet their situation better than most of the people in their employ. Suggest, if necessary, a trial period, even at your expense, until they become convinced that you are a better solution to their problem than anyone else they're looking at or than many they may already employ, simply because you're a leader. You take initiative to make good things happen. You don't wait to be told. You're not always being acted upon. You act, but you're not foolish in your action. You are very aware. You're very sensitive. You're very empathic and respectful.

You also engage in this job-finding process in a principled way. There is no exaggeration for effect, no deceit, no manipulation, no lying, no cheating, no duplicity or putting other people down. You become very focused on the organization's needs, their concerns, their problems, and on their customers' needs, concerns and problems. You talk that language.

Anyone that will take such an approach with a decision-maker will get attention, and in most cases, will blow them away with the depth of their preparation and discipline and willingness to pay the price and sacrifice.

I have given this counsel over and over and over again to many people through the years. A small percentage took it, and in almost every case, they succeeded in getting the job they wanted. I also usually recommend that they study the latest edition of the book *What Color Is Your Parachute?* by Richard Bolles, to help them better understand this process.

Q: What about achieving life balance?

A: Survey after survey indicates that one of the greatest challenges faced by most people is life balance. People tend to focus so much on work and other pressing activities that the relationships and activities they really treasure most end up getting squeezed and pushed aside. They end up becoming addicted to urgency.

Let me illustrate a solution with the story of a man who got caught up in this whirlpool of urgency. Notice that he took time to think about what mattered most to him (conscience, vision and passion), and then used those criteria to creatively decide how to organize his life to be in harmony with his priorities (discipline) and create the life balance he desired. Notice also how the solution came through synergy with his wife. Here is his true story told in his own words:

> *I have always had a special friendship with my mother. Together we endured a series of life events, which has created a wonderful relationship. At one time in my life, even though I loved my mother and really enjoyed spending time with her, I got caught up in my commitments to work, the community, and to my own family. My life got so busy, weeks would go by before I would make even a quick phone call just to check in. And when I did manage to squeeze in a visit, we would have just sat down to talk, and it would be time for me to leave. Another meeting to go to, another deadline to meet. My contact with this wonderful woman became mostly hit-and-miss.*
>
> *My mother never put any pressure on me to visit more often, but I wasn't happy with the situation. I knew my life was out of control if I couldn't consistently spend time with my mother. So, my wife and I brainstormed for a solution. She suggested scheduling a time each week or so that would work*

for both our family and my mother. When we looked at the calendar, we saw my wife has choir practice every Wednesday evening. That night became my night to spend with my mom.

Now my mom knows that every week or two I will be coming on a specific night, at a specific time. I won't be running off within the first ten minutes, and there are few interruptions. If she wants to get some exercise, we go for a walk together. Other times she'll cook a meal for me. Sometimes I take her shopping at the mall, which is further away than she feels comfortable driving to. No matter what we do, we always talk—about family, about current events, about memories.

Every evening I spend with my mother is a peaceful oasis in my busy life. I tell my wife it's one of the best suggestions she's ever given me.

This beautiful little story is just one illustration of what can be done when we focus our hearts and minds upon what truly matters and then live with integrity to do it. When my own father died, I decided I was going to maintain and even increase my very special relationship with my mother because of the new void in her life. I resolved that despite a very heavy travel schedule and no matter where I was, I would phone her every day for the rest of her life. Though we lived fifty miles apart, I would also make special efforts to visit her at least every two weeks. She lived for another ten years and I cannot begin to express the depth of my gratitude for her life and for the preciousness of our time together.

I learned that when you regularly communicate with another person, you reach a new level of understanding that almost runs by nuance. I found that the daily phone call was not too unlike our semiweekly visit; we felt as close to each other and as open and authentic with each other as we did when we were together. It was like one continuous conversation. It really didn't make much difference whether it was on the phone or face-to-face, which surprised me, because I'd always thought nothing could replace face-to-face contact. I am sure in another sense that is correct. Because each conversation contains the cumulative effect of the previous conversations, there is hardly anything to catch up on. Instead, you can share deep insights and feelings rather than just experiences. Intimate communication means in-to-me-see.

Just like the gentleman in the previous story, I, too, have had the tremendous benefit of having a very supportive and understanding wife who has the "abundance mentality." My wife, Sandra, doesn't see life as a fixed piece of pie where there is only so much time, where time with my mother would mean time away from her. She saw that time with my mother would actually increase the depth of our own relationship.

When Mother passed away, we put on her tombstone a line from Shakespeare's 29th Sonnet: "For thy sweet love remembered, such wealth brings . . ." I would encourage you to read this sonnet slowly and carefully. Let your imagination fill in the richness and meaning of each phrase:

> When in disgrace with fortune and men's eyes,
>   I all alone beweep my outcast state,
> And trouble deaf Heaven with my bootless cries,
>   And look upon myself, and curse my fate,
> Wishing me like to one more rich in hope,
>   Featur'd like him, like him with friends possess'd,
> Desiring this man's art, and that man's scope,
>   With what I most enjoy contented least:
> Yet in these thoughts myself almost despising,
>   Haply I think on thee,—and then my state
> (Like to the lark at break of day arising
>   From sullen earth) sings hymns at heaven's gate;
> For thy sweet love remember'd such wealth brings
>   That then I scorn to change my state with kings'.

Perhaps the highest way to bring balance to life is the family. The first and most demanding form of personal growth also takes place in the family and provides the greatest contribution to society.

I believe, as a wise leader once said, that the most important work you do in the world will be within the walls of your own home. David O. McKay taught, "No other success can compensate for failure in the home."[12] My convictions about the importance of family are so deep and strong that they led me several years ago to write the book *The 7 Habits of Highly Effective Families.*

Parenthood is the most important leadership responsibility in life and will provide the greatest levels of happiness and joy. And when true leadership—i.e., vision, discipline, passion and conscience—is not manifested in parenthood, it will provide the greatest source of sorrow and disappointment.

It's amazing to me how small adjustments in one's life along the lines of vision, discipline, passion and conscience can have such huge conse-

quences. I believe all of us at a future date will be both amazed and sad-
dened by the realization of how such small changes could have brought
about such big results.

For parents to instill a sense of vision and possibility into a family, to
exercise the discipline and sacrifice to pull that vision off, and to endure
through the difficult times with a deep sense of passion, drive and commitment, all in a conscience-driven way, I suggest, is the ultimate and
best test of leadership. If part of the vision is to see this family culture
transmitted from generation to generation, perhaps in that alone will
our lives be fulfilled and joyful, even if we accomplish nothing else. But
if we fail in that, we may find that success in other things will not adequately compensate. I often think about the poignant words of John
Greenleaf Whittier: "For all sad words of tongue and pen, The saddest
are these: It might have been!"[13] But someone else taught, "It is never
too late for us to become what we might have been."

Part 2

INSPIRE OTHERS TO FIND THEIR VOICE

Chapter 6

INSPIRING OTHERS TO
FIND THEIR VOICE—
THE LEADERSHIP CHALLENGE

In everyone's life, at some time, our inner fire goes out.
It is then burst into flame by an encounter with another human being.
We should all be thankful for those people who rekindle the inner
*   spirit.*

ALBERT SCHWEITZER

WHEN I WAS A YOUNG MAN, I had an experience with a leader that profoundly shaped the rest of my life. I had decided to take a break in my education to give some extended volunteer service. The invitation came to go to England. Just four and one-half months after my arrival, the president of the organization came to me and said, "I have a new assignment for you. I want you to travel around the country and train local leaders." I was shocked. *Who was I* to train leaders two and three times my age? Sensing my doubt, he simply looked me in the eye and said, "I have great confidence in you. You can do this. I will give you materials to help you prepare to teach these leaders and to facilitate their sharing best practices with one another."

His confidence, his ability to see more in me than I saw in myself, his willingness to entrust me with responsibility that would stretch me to my potential unlocked something inside me. I accepted the assignment and gave my best. It tapped me physically, mentally, emotionally, spiritually. I grew. I saw others grow. I saw patterns in basic leadership principles. By the time I returned home, I had begun to detect the work I wanted to devote my life to: unleashing human potential. I found my "voice." And it was my leader that inspired me to find it.

I realized in time that I wasn't the only one he treated this way. His affirmation of others, his ability to unite us in vision toward our work that inspired and motivated us, his pattern of providing us with enabling resources and empowering us as true leaders with accountability and stewardship became the norm in our entire organization. We began to lead and serve others in the same way, and the results were remarkable.

I've realized since then that the principles that guided his leadership are common to great leadership in any organization, regardless of the level or formal position of the person. My teaching, consulting and leadership experience in business, university, volunteer and church organizations—and especially in my own family—have taught me that leadership influence is governed by principles. When you live by them, your influence and moral authority increase and you are often given even greater formal authority. The biblical parables of the pounds and the talents illustrate that the more you use and magnify the gifts or talents you have been given, the more gifts and talents you are given. But if they are ignored or buried and remain undeveloped and unused, the very talents or gifts that you have been given will be lost and often given to another. So you end up not only losing talents but also losing influence and opportunities.

LEADERSHIP DEFINED

Simply put—at its most elemental and practical level—*leadership is communicating to people their worth and potential so clearly that they come to see it in themselves.* Think about this definition. Isn't this the essence of the kind of leadership that influences and truly endures?! To communicate the worth and potential of others so clearly, so powerfully and so consistently that they really come to see it in themselves is to set in motion the process of *seeing, doing* and *becoming*.

> Leadership is communicating to people their worth and potential so clearly that they come to see it in themselves.

What a way to think about and to define the irreplaceable role of *grandparenting*! The most essential role of grandparents is to communicate, in as many ways as possible, the worth and potential of their children, grandchildren and great grandchildren clearly that they really believe it and act on that belief. If this spirit suffused our culture and society, the impact on the civilization of the world would be unimaginably magnificent and endless.

Let's explore in depth perhaps—next to relationships—the most common and continuous means of communicating to people their worth and potential: the *organization*.

Organization Defined

As we move now to Part 2 of the 8th Habit—Inspire Others to Find Their Voice—we enter into the domain of leadership. Again, this is not leadership as a formal position but leadership as a choice to deal with people in a way that will communicate to them their worth and potential so clearly they will come to see it in themselves. Regarding our focus on this kind of leadership in the *organization*, I would like to emphasize four simple points:

1. At the most elemental level, an organization is nothing more or less than *a relationship with a purpose (its voice)*. That purpose is aimed at meeting the needs of one or more persons or stakeholders. The simplest organization would be two people who share a purpose, such as in a simple business partnership or a marriage.
2. Almost *all* people belong to an organization of one kind or another.
3. *Most* of the world's work is done in and through organizations.
4. The highest challenge inside organizations, including families, is to set them up and run them in a way that enables each person to inwardly sense his or her innate worth and potential for greatness and to contribute his or her unique talents and passion—in other words, voice—to accomplish the organization's purpose and highest priorities in a principle-centered way. We could call this the *Leadership Challenge*.

In short, an organization is made up of individuals who have a *relationship* and a *shared purpose*. You can see, then, how this organizational application applies to each one of us.

MANAGEMENT AND/OR LEADERSHIP?

Literally hundreds of books and thousands of articles have come out in the last few years on leadership. This points out how vital the subject is. Leadership really is the *enabling* art. The purpose of schools is educating kids, but if you have bad leadership, you have bad education. The purpose of medicine is helping people get well, but if you have bad leadership, you'll have bad medicine. We could give illustration after illustration to show that leadership is the highest of the arts, simply because it *enables* all the other arts and professions to work. This is particularly true for a family.

I've spent a lifetime studying, teaching and writing on both leadership and management. In fact, as a part of my preparation for writing this book, I initiated a literature review of leadership theories of the twentieth century. I've included it in the back of the book as Appendix 2: Literature Review of Leadership Theories, which can be found on page 352.

As a part of the literature review of leadership theories, we gathered statements from leading authors who described the differences between leadership and management. Here is a small sampling (Table 2). The full collection can be found in the back of the book as Appendix 3, Representative Statements on Leadership and Management, on page 360.

Leadership	Management
"Leaders are people who do the right thing; —WARREN BENNIS	Managers are people who do things right."
"Leadership is about coping with change." —JOHN KOTTER	"Management is about coping with complexity."
"Leadership has about it a kinesthetic feel, a sense of movement... —KOUZES AND POSNER	Managing is about 'handling' things, about maintaining order, about organization and control."
"...Leaders are concerned with what things mean to people." —ABRAHAM ZALEZNIK	"Managers are concerned about how things get done."
"Leaders are the architects... —JOHN MARIOTTI	Managers are the builders."
"Leadership focuses on the creation of a common vision... —GEORGE WEATHERSBY	Management is the design of work...it's about controlling..."

Table 2

This literature review has reinforced to me that *both* management *and* leadership are vital—and that either one without the other is insufficient. At times in my life, I've fallen into the trap of overemphasizing leadership and neglecting the importance of management. I'm sure this is because it's become so evident to me that most organizations, families included, are vastly overmanaged and desperately underled. This gap has been a major motivating force in my professional work and has led me to focus on principles of leadership. Nevertheless, I've been powerfully reminded of the vital part that management plays.

I learned (painfully) that you can't "lead" things. In fact, it wasn't until I turned over the management of my company to my son, Stephen, and a team of people with strengths that compensated for my weaknesses that it really became profitable. You can't lead inventories and cash flow and costs. You have to manage them. Why? Because things don't have the power and freedom to choose. Only people do. So you *lead* (empower) people. You *manage and control* things. Here's a list of the kinds of things that need managing (see figure 6.1):

WHAT THINGS NEED MANAGING (CONTROLLING)?

THINGS WITHOUT FREEDOM TO CHOOSE

Money	Structures	Physical resources
Costs	Systems	Facilities
Information	Processes	Tools
Time	Inventory	

SOMETIMES...

"People" choose to be managed under their own leadership (many professionals and other producers).

Figure 6.1

This literature review has also reminded me how profoundly I've been influenced by many of these great minds and teachers over the years. To them, I owe a debt of gratitude. My experiences and teaching have also led me to conclude that the key to understanding organizational behavior is not to study organizational behavior, per se. It is to study and understand *human nature*. For once you understand the fundamental elements of human nature, you possess the key to unlock the potential inside of people and organizations. This is exactly why the Whole-Person Paradigm—symbolized by body, mind, heart and spirit—is supremely relevant to understanding organizations, as well as individuals. In a very real sense there is no such thing as organizational behavior. There is only *individual* behavior collectivized in organizations.

"So what?" you may ask. What does all this theory have to do with the challenges I face day in and day out? Why is it so necessary to understand organizations to better understand and solve my problems?

The simple, almost obvious, answer is that they are so interrelated. We all live in and work in one organization or another, including that of the family. We need *context* to understand ourselves.

As mentioned earlier, all organizations, even the best of them, are absolutely filled with problems. I've worked with thousands. Even the organizations I admire most struggle to some degree. And the interesting thing is that most of the problems are about the same. Certainly, there are unique personalities and circumstances connected to the problems. But when it comes right down to it, at the core, most problems have common roots. Peter Drucker put it this way:

> There are of course differences in management between different organizations—missions define strategy after all and strategy defines structure. But the differences between managing a chain of retail stores and managing a Roman Catholic Diocese are amazingly fewer than retail executives or bishops realize. The differences are mainly in the application rather than principles. The executives of all these organizations spend for instance about the same amount of time on people problems—and the people problems are almost always the same.
>
> Whether you are managing a software company, a hospital, a bank, or a Boy Scout organization, the differences apply to only about 10 percent of your work. This 10 percent is determined by the organization's specific mission, its specific culture, its specific history, and its specific vocabulary. The rest is pretty much interchangeable.[1]

My goal in Part 2: Inspire Others to Find Their Voice is to help you discover how, by working and struggling to solve your personal challenges and problems, you can greatly increase *your* own influence and the influence of your organization—whether it be your team, department, division or entire organization, including your family.

Let's begin by looking first at the dual nature of the problems we face. Before we do, I invite you to gear up your mind for the energy it will take to really get your arms around our complex organizational challenges. I do so with two quotes. The first is again the observation by Albert Einstein: "The significant challenges we face cannot be solved at the same level of thinking we were at when we created them." You have been given a new paradigm of human nature—the whole-person paradigm—body, mind, heart and spirit. You have learned that it stands in great contrast to today's Industrial Age "thing" paradigm of control. You will need this "whole-person" view to understand and solve the problems you face in your organization.

The second quote is by Oliver Wendell Holmes. He said, "I wouldn't give a fig for the simplicity on the near side of complexity; but I would give my right arm for the simplicity on the far side of complexity." What this means is that our significant challenges cannot be solved with simplistic little quick-fix programs-of-the-month or psyche-up slogans and formulas. We must *earn* a comprehension of the *nature* and root of the problems we face in organizations and likewise earn our learnings about the *principles* that govern the solutions by incorporating the new mind-set and skill-set they represent into our character. This will require some real effort. But I promise you if you will hang in there, you will be empowered with a powerfully *simple* and clear combination of KNOWLEDGE, ATTITUDE, and SKILL—the three elements of HABIT—that will make you equal to the new challenges of the new world. You will have developed the 8th Habit that unleashes human potential.

GLOBAL SEISMIC SHIFTS

As we move now to seek a deeper understanding of the organizational challenge, I invite you to consider seven seismic shifts that characterize the new Knowledge Worker Age. In them you find the context of today's workplace and of your *personal* challenges.

- *The Globalization of Markets and Technologies:* New technologies are transforming most local, regional and national markets into global markets without borders.

- *The Emergence of Universal Connectivity:* In the book *Blown to Bits,* Evans and Wurster state, "The narrow, hard-wired, and proprietary communication channels that bound people or companies together have become obsolete almost overnight. And with them, the very business structures that created or exploited those channels have also become obsolete. In short, the glue that has traditionally held all of our economic activities together is rapidly melting in the heat of universal connectivity. And this will separate the *flow* of information from the *flow* of things for the first time in history.[2]

- *The Democratization of Information/Expectations:* No one manages the internet. It is a sea change of global proportion. For the first time in history the pure voice of the human spirit rings out in millions of unedited conversations unfettered by borders. Real-time information drives expectations and social will, which ultimately drive the political will that impacts every person.

- *An Exponential Increase in Competition:* The internet and satellite technologies make anybody who is hooked up a potential competitor. Organizations must constantly develop better ways of competing against lower labor prices, lower material costs, faster innovation, greater efficiency and higher quality. The forces of free enterprise and competition are driving quality up, driving cost down and driving increased speed and flexibility in order to do the job the customer has hired us to do. No one can afford to simply benchmark against competitors or even so-called excellence; we must benchmark against "world class."

- *The Movement of Wealth Creation from Financial Capital to Intellectual and Social Capital:* The wealth-creation movement has gone from money to people—from financial capital to the summary notion of human capital (both intellectual and social), which includes all dimensions. More than two-thirds of the value added to today's products comes from knowledge work; twenty years ago it was less than one-third.

- *Free Agency:* People are becoming more and more informed, aware and conscious of options and alternatives than ever before. The employment market is turning into a free agent market and people have more and more awareness of choices. Knowledge workers will resist management efforts to label them, and they are increasingly determined to brand themselves.

- *Permanent White Water:* We live in a constant, churning, changing environment. In turbulent white water, every single person must have something inside them that guides their decisions. They must independently understand the purpose and guiding principles of the team or organization. If you try to manage them, they won't even hear you. The noise, the roar, the immediacy and urgency of all the dynamic challenges they face will simply be too great.

FILM: *Permanent Whitewater*

We've developed a short, engaging video that describes the white-water conditions and complexity we now live in. It contrasts the past and the present and points to three constants we can rely on in dealing with the challenges you'll learn more of in this chapter.

I invite you to view the film now by inserting the DVD into your DVD player and selecting *Permanent Whitewater.*

CHRONIC AND ACUTE PROBLEMS

There are two kinds of problems in both the physical body and in organizations: chronic and acute. *Chronic* means underlying, causal, continuing. *Acute* means painful, symptomatic, debilitating. Organizations, like people, can have chronic problems that are not yet acute. Treating these acute problems may mask the underlying chronic condition.

Several years ago I had a fascinating experience that illustrates this point. A friend of mine was head of surgery at a hospital in Detroit and specialized in cardiovascular medicine. I asked him if I could spend a day observing surgeons perform surgeries. The experience was absolutely mind-boggling. During one particular surgery that my friend performed, he replaced three vessels. When he finished, I asked, "Why did you have to *replace* the vessels? Why didn't you just clean them out?"

He explained in layman's language, "In the earlier stages you can do that, but over time, the plaque builds up until it eventually becomes part of the content of the wall itself."

"Now that you've corrected these three places," I asked, "is the man clear?" My friend replied, "Stephen, it's chronic. It's all the way through him." He guided my gloved hand to feel the vessels. You could feel the brittleness of the cholesterol material. "But notice," said my friend, "this man is an exerciser; he's developed *some* supplemental circulation that provides oxygen to muscles, but there's no supplementation to these three occluded vessels. He could still have a heart attack or stroke if a blood clot were to form. He has extensive *chronic* heart disease."

Not all chronic conditions have acute symptoms. Before the first acute symptoms ever appear, diseases such as cancer can spread until it's too late.* Just because you can't see surface symptoms doesn't mean the underlying problems are not there. Sometimes people suffer heart attacks when they suddenly stress their bodies—like shoveling heavy snow after the first winter storm of the season. They don't realize they have a heart condition until the stress conditions reveal the acute symptoms.

The same is true in organizations. You can have serious chronic problems in an organization that shows no acute signs because some organizations do not compete in a tough, global marketplace; they compete locally or in a protected market. They may be financially successful— sometimes very successful. But, as you know, success is relative. The competition's problems may be worse. So why change?

PREDICTING FOUR CHRONIC PROBLEMS
AND THEIR ACUTE SYMPTOMS

The power of an accurate paradigm lies in its ability to explain and predict. If, then, this Whole-Person Paradigm of human nature is accurate, it should give you an uncommon ability to explain, predict and diagnose the greatest problems in your life and in your organization. It should not only help you recognize the more obvious acute symptoms of the problems but it should also help you see the underlying chronic "root" causes. Then you will be able to use this paradigm to start resolving your problems, expanding your influence to create a high-performance, high-trust organization or team—an organization that is able to consistently *focus on* and *execute* its highest priorities.

This is why you will continue to see the same diagram in every part of the book (see figure 6.2). I simply add new words or phrases to reflect a new application of the four areas of choice—body, mind, heart and spirit. In this case, you'll be able to see that this Whole-Person Para-

---

* For a free, brief mp3 audio on principles of preventative health, go to www.The 8thHabit.com/offers.

digm gives you the developing capacity to see both the chronic and acute problems that arise when an organization neglects the mind, body, heart or spirit of its people.

Let's just test it in an organizational setting. The same thinking would apply to a team, a family, a community or any relationship. Try to specifically identify the problem in each case before reading on.

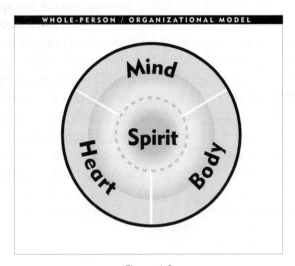

Figure 6.2

Let's start *first* at the center of the diagram with *spirit*. If the spirit, or conscience, is consistently neglected throughout an organization, what problem will result? Think about it. What happens in relationships when people are treated or act in ways contrary to their conscience? Won't an obvious loss of trust result? *Low trust* is the first chronic problem that all organizations face. What would its acute manifestations be? Low-trust organizations that operate in tough market conditions are filled with the acute, painful symptoms of backbiting, in-fighting, victimism, defensiveness, information hoarding, and defensive, protective communication.*

Second, what chronic problem results when you neglect the *mind* or vision in an organization? You will have *no shared vision or common value system*. Under these conditions, what symptomatic behavior would you expect to see? You would see people acting with hidden agendas, playing

---

* To see how you can actually measure the tremendous financial costs of problems like low trust in your organization, see Appendix 4: The High Cost of Low Trust.

political games, and using different criteria in decision making. You would see an ambiguous, chaotic culture.

Third, what problem results in an organization when there is widespread neglect of discipline in the *body* politic (skeletal structure, systems, processes)? In other words, what condition would you expect to see when there is no execution or systemic support behind the priorities of the organization? There will simply be *no alignment* or discipline built into the organization's structures, systems, processes and culture. When managers possess inaccurate and incomplete paradigms of human nature, they design systems—including communication, recruiting, selecting, placing, accountability, reward and compensation, promotion, training and development and information systems—that fail to draw out the full potential of people. Neither individuals, teams, departments, nor the whole organization will be aligned with a core mission, set of values and strategy. This will create profound misalignment with the marketplace and with customers and suppliers outside the organization.

> *All organizations are perfectly*
> *aligned to get the results they get.*
> ARTHUR W. JONES

This misalignment will manifest itself in a thousand ways, contributing to even lower trust and more politicized behavior and interdepartmental rivalries. *Rules* will take the place of human judgment because as things get out of hand, managers will feel the need for increased control. Bureaucracy, hierarchies, rules and regulations will become like *prostheses* for trust. Any talk of people or leadership development will be considered soft, "touchy-feely," unrealistic, wasteful and costly. People, like things, will become an expense, not an investment. The need for more management and more control will become increasingly evident, producing the codependent condition of "wait until told" in the vast majority of the people, as we discussed earlier. This will serve as further evidence to the so-called formal leaders that nothing is going to happen until they externally carrot-and-stick, motivate, control, and even bring down the iron fist when necessary—passivity justifying external motivation and control justifying more passivity. It is a self-fulfilling prophecy. Managing (controlling) people never inspires them to their greatest work and contributions around their true voice or passion. These are volunteered.

Fourth, what happens when you neglect the *heart?* What happens when there is no passion, no emotional connection to the goals or work, no internal volunteer enthusiasm or commitment inside the organization? The result is a profound *disempowerment* of the people. The whole culture is in a funk. What acute symptoms would you expect to see? Pause and predict it. You will find a great deal of moonlighting, daydreaming, boredom, escapism, anger, fear, apathy and malicious obedience.

Can you see the predictive, explanatory power of this model or paradigm? Neglect body, mind, heart or spirit, and you get four chronic problems in an organization—*low trust, no shared vision and values, misalignment* and *disempowerment*—and all their acute symptoms (see figure 6.3).

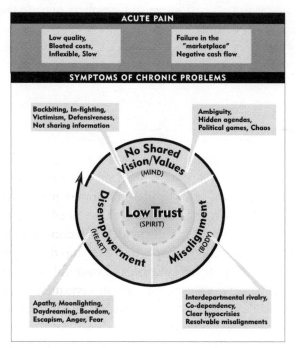

Figure 6.3

The collective result of these chronic problems and their symptoms is the acute pain of failure in the marketplace, negative cash flow, low quality, bloated costs, inflexibility, slowness, and a lot of finger pointing: a culture of blame instead of a culture of responsibility.

If you think back on the film *Max & Max*, you will be able to identify every one of these four chronic problems.

THE PARADIGM IN PRACTICE

Let me illustrate the explanatory power of this paradigm.

I remember once having an initial visit with the top executives of a large organization and asking them about their mission statement. Hesitatingly they pulled it out. It basically said, "Our goal is to increase the assets of the owners." I asked them if they put that on the wall to inspire their employees and customers. They all smiled and said, "Well, no, we have another statement that's hanging on the wall, but this is what we're really aiming for."

Even though I was just becoming acquainted with their industry and company, I said, "Why don't I tell you what your corporate culture is like. You're split apart. If your industry is unionized, you're plagued with labor disputes. You're hovering over, checking up, and carrot-n-sticking your employees to do their jobs. There's an enormous amount of negative energy spent in interpersonal conflict, interdepartmental rivalries, hidden agendas and political games."

Amazed at my fortune-telling skills, they asked, "How could you know so much? How could you describe us so accurately?"

I said, "I don't have to know much about your industry or you. All I have to know about is human nature. Your real purpose focuses on only one of the four parts of our nature—the body (economic)—and on only one stakeholder—the owners. You completely neglect the other three parts—mind, heart and spirit—and all other stakeholders. You can't do that without suffering dire consequences." I went on to predict, "When this meeting breaks up, half of you will talk about the other half. There's no trust here. The duplicity is evident." They were sadly amazed by the accuracy of the observations, and they were considered a "successful" organization. The truth is you can never succeed with stockholders until you first succeed in the marketplace, and you can never succeed in the marketplace until you first succeed in the workplace.

"Well, what can we do to change?" they asked.

I said, "You have to seriously go to work on all four parts. Involve everybody's mind so that people get on the same song sheet. Live by the universal principles of fair play, honesty, integrity and truth so that you can develop a bedrock of trust on which to build that song sheet. Use the criteria embodied in your vision and values to guide all strategic, structural and operational decisions. You must create the conditions of both personal and organizational trust before you'll get any true empowerment or release of human potential." I suggested that they might even begin by developing a mission statement for their own executive team.

They asked me how long these things would take.

I said, "How bad are you hurting?"

They said, "Not very bad."

I replied, "Then you probably won't be able to accomplish it. There isn't enough pain, enough force of circumstance, enough humility." I suggested they forget the whole project.

They said, "Yes, but we hear good things about what's happened in other places you've worked. We also have a sense that because the marketplace is changing and competition is going to become fierce, we may have some real struggles on the horizon. We probably do need the help. We want to make changes."

I suggested that if they were truly sincere and would really work together, they could make these changes; but it would probably take two or three years or more.

One remarked, "You don't know how fast and efficient we are." Referring to the idea of producing an improved mission statement, he continued, "We'll whip this baby out this weekend." In other words, he was thinking they could go offsite for some kind of vision workshop and develop a mission statement with new purple phrases that would be more appealing to the people.

Gradually these executives came to see that short-term thinking and short-cut techniques would never produce the long-term results they desired. Slowly they came to grips with the underlying chronic issues, starting with themselves, and developed great respect for all four parts of human nature. They eventually came to see that leadership was everybody's business, and that each person needed to take an inside-out approach.

The organization strengthened itself from the roots. It took three to four years. In the end, they had such strength, such levels of empowerment and trust that they were able to deal with the vigorous new competition that emerged and also maintain their successful patterns in the marketplace. Many of the top executives took CEO positions outside the company, but the organization's culture and bench strength were so deep that the company continued growing profitably.

THE INDUSTRIAL AGE RESPONSE

Now what would the Industrial Age response to the four chronic problems be?

If *trust* is low and there is no moral authority, then the *boss* is at the center—the leader knows best and makes all the decisions—"It's MY way or the highway."

As for a lack of shared vision and values, *rules* will take the place of vision and mission. "Don't worry about anything but your job. Just do what you're told, follow the rules and leave the thinking to me."

Misalignment? Just make things more efficient—machines, policies, people, everything. *Efficiency* is the name of the game.

Disempowerment? You've got to keep *control.* You can't trust people. The only way to get much out of people is to use the carrot and stick—dangle the carrot (rewards) for performance out in front of them to motivate them, and keep a healthy amount of fear going with the stick (punishments or loss of your job) if you fail to perform.

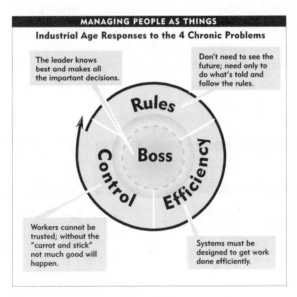

Figure 6.4

THE LEADERSHIP SOLUTION IN ORGANIZATIONS

The decision to inspire others to find their voice takes you right into the thick of the four chronic organizational problems that result from today's Industrial Age control model.

Every one of us who has found his or her voice possesses the power to rewrite the bad Industrial Age "boss, rules, efficiency, control" software in their organization. The process involves *four roles* that become the antidote to the four chronic organizational problems (see figure 6.6). They are the positive manifestations of body, heart, mind and spirit in an organization, whereas the four chronic problems are the negative manifestations of neglecting them. Realistically, how do you solve these four chronic problems? Where there is low trust, we focus on *modeling* trustworthiness to create trust. Where there is no common vision or values, we focus on *pathfinding* to build a common vision and set of values. Where there is misalignment, we focus on *aligning* goals, structures, systems and processes to encourage and nurture the empowerment of people and culture to serve the vision and the values. Where there is disempowerment, we focus on *empowering* individuals and teams at the project or job level.

I call these four roles the *4 Roles of Leadership*—again, not leadership as a position but leadership as a proactive intention to affirm the worth and potential of those around us and to unite them as a complementary team in an effort to increase the influence and impact of the organizations and important causes we are part of. Remember, in a complementary team, individual strengths (voices) become productive and their weaknesses become irrelevant because they are compensated for by the strengths of others.

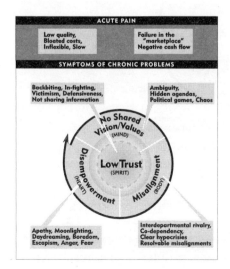

Figure 6.5

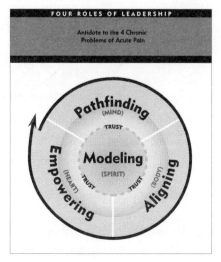

Figure 6.6

The 4 Roles of Leadership are simply four qualities of personal leadership—vision, discipline, passion and conscience—*writ large* in an organization (see figure 6.7):

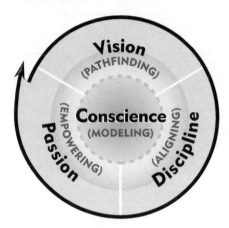

Figure 6.7

- *Modeling* (conscience): Set a good example.
- *Pathfinding* (vision): Jointly determine the course.
- *Aligning* (discipline): Set up and manage systems to stay on course.
- *Empowering* (passion): Focus talent on results, not methods, then get out of people's way and give help as requested.

Those in formal positions of authority in an organization may see these four roles as a challenging but natural way to fulfill their stewardships. But seeing them as roles for senior executives *only* would perpetuate the prevailing codependent mind-set that says, "the boss does all the important thinking and decision making." These four roles are for everyone, regardless of position. They are simply the pathway to increasing your influence and the influence of your team and organization.

My colleagues at FranklinCovey and I have been teaching the 4 Roles of Leadership model since 1995, but many other experts in the field of leadership have independently come to models that are grounded in the same principles. For instance, in the insightful book *Results-Based Leadership* (1999), authors Dave Ulrich (University of Michigan), Jack Zenger and Norm Smallwood developed, after years of research, observation and consultation, a four-box leadership model that

Figure 6.8

is almost identical to the 4 Roles model.[3] The main difference is the words used, but you can see that the meaning is essentially the same.

Further validation of this leadership model can be found in a recently published five-year study conducted by Nitin Nohria, William Joyce, and Bruce Robertson (see "What Really Works," *Harvard Business Review*, July 2003). In what they call The Evergreen Project, they "examined more than 200 well-established management practices as they were employed over a ten-year period by 160 companies." This research enabled them to distill which management practices truly produce superior results. Their compelling conclusion is that without exception, companies that outperformed their industry peers *excelled at four primary management practices:*

1. **Strategy**—Devise and maintain a clearly stated, focused strategy.
2. **Execution**—Develop and maintain flawless operation execution.
3. **Culture**—Develop and maintain a performance-oriented culture.
4. **Structure**—Build and maintain a fast, flexible, flat organization.

Figure 6.9

The Evergreen Project concluded that these companies also *embraced two of four secondary practices*—talent, innovation, leadership, and mergers and acquisitions. But just think about the first four *primary* management practices they identified. Aren't these practices that enabled companies to dramatically outperform their competitors essentially another way of describing the 4 Roles of Leadership? Again, different words for the same underlying principles.

THE SIGNIFICANCE OF SEQUENCE: *A Sports Metaphor*

These four roles are also highly interdependent. In a sense, they are *sequential*. But in another sense, they are *simultaneous*. Both senses are correct. They are sequential because you must have trust from trustworthiness before you can really move into the other roles that will release human potential. They are simultaneous in the sense that once the culture based on this leadership has been established, one must pay constant attention to all four processes, all four roles.

I would like to illustrate the significance of sequence in these four roles by comparing it to professional sports, where, like the business world, competition is very intense. When a player goes to professional training camp out of shape—lacking *muscle* strength and cardiovascular endurance—he is simply unable to develop the intended *skills*. And if he can't develop the skills, there is no way he can become a useful member of a *team* and part of a winning system.

In other words, muscle development precedes skill development, and skill development precedes team and system development. The body is a natural system and is governed by natural laws. The sports metaphor is a very apt and powerful image that we can relate to the broader area of enlarging capacity and finding our voice. Personal development precedes the building of trusting relationships, and trusting relationships are an absolute prerequisite to developing an organization characterized by teamwork, cooperation and contribution to the wider community.

For instance, let's say that a person is unable to even keep the promises he makes to himself—his life is inconsistent, flaky and mood-based. Is there any way that he'd be able to develop healthy, trusting relationships with others? The answer is obvious. And if there was a lack of trust in his relationships with others, would he have any foundation for an effective family or team organization that makes significant contributions? Again, the answer is obvious: no.

Just like a child can't run before it can walk or walk before it can crawl, just like you can't do calculus until you understand algebra, and you can't do algebra until you understand basic math, some things of necessity come ahead of others. Once you understand the importance of this sequence, you will see why, even though the two are interdependent, it is vital to first pay the price of striving to find your voice *personally* before even *attempting* to develop the skills of building high-trust relationships and creative problem solving. The synergistic work of high-trust relationships then becomes the foundation for creating a team or organization of cooperative people—teams that are on the same page regarding purpose and values and are willing to play their role inside that context. Ultimately, individuals, teams and organizations are then able to spread their influence by serving and meeting the needs of those in their stewardship. To put *service above self* gives meaning to all three levels and leads us into the *Age of Wisdom*, the fifth age of civilization.

Perhaps the best way to illustrate the tremendous importance and power of this sequence would be to share the experience I frequently give audiences I'm teaching. I invite a man who looks very strong and healthy to come up in front and do twenty straight-back push-ups. If he is truly strong and practiced, he can do it fairly easily. But very few can; even many who appear strong and healthy hardly make it past five or six.

Using this physical analogy, I suggest that until people can do twenty emotional push-ups at the personal level, they won't have the power or freedom to do the thirty emotional push-ups required to meet the challenges and demands of relationships. And until they can do the fifty push-ups at both the personal and relationship levels, there is no way they can build a team and produce a high-trust, high-performance organizational culture.

Keeping this sequence in mind, we move now from the *character development* involved in finding your *own* voice, to the *skill development* and the *team and system development* required to inspire others to find their voice in *organizations*.

FOCUS AND EXECUTION:
AN OUTLINE FOR THE REST OF THE BOOK

As the new extended diagram that follows shows, the 4 Roles also represent the upper road to "Inspire Others to Find Their Voice" and achieving organizational greatness, whereas the four chronic organizational problems represent the lower road to keeping others from finding their voice, which results in organizational straitjacketing and mediocrity.

The process of Inspiring Others to Find Their Voice could be summarized in two words: FOCUS and EXECUTION. *Focus* embodies the modeling and pathfinding roles; *execution*, the aligning and empowering roles. In the remainder of the book you will learn to make Inspiring Others to Find Their Voice a HABIT by developing the ATTITUDE, SKILL and KNOWLEDGE of the following principles.

FOCUS—Modeling and Pathfinding

1. **The Voice of Influence.** Being a *model* involves finding your own voice first (Part 1) and then choosing the ATTITUDE of initiative—being what I call a *trim-tab*, or taking initiative to expand your influence in every opportunity around you **(chapter 7).**

2. **The Voice of Trustworthiness.** *Modeling* character and competence lays the foundation for trust in every relationship and organization. You cannot have trust without trustworthiness. KNOWLEDGE of this principle and of the principles underlying the pathfinding, aligning and empowering roles are the doorway to influence **(chapter 8).**

3. **The Voice and Speed of Trust.** *Modeling* also involves developing strong relationship SKILLS that Build Trust **(chapter 9)**

and **Blending Voices**—creating Third-Alternative Solutions to your challenges and differences with others **(chapter 10).**

4. **One Voice.** *Pathfinding* involves creating with others a common vision about your highest priorities and the values by which you will achieve your priorities **(chapter 11).**

EXECUTION—Aligning and Empowering

5. **The Voice of Execution.** *Aligning* goals and enabling systems for results **(chapter 12).**

6. **The Empowering Voice.** Releasing passion and talent, clearing the way before them and then getting out of the way **(chapter 13).** *Empowerment* is where the rubber meets the road in a team and is the culminating fruit of the 4 Roles of Leadership.

Chapter 14—The 8th Habit and The Sweet Spot will show how the approach outlined in this book fosters three dimensions of *greatness*—personal, leadership and organizational. You will learn how they combine and can be translated into *4 Disciplines of Execution* that can enable your organization to achieve breakthrough performance in the Knowledge Worker Age.

Chapter 15—Using Our Voices Wisely to Serve Others, pulls it all together by showing how the 8th Habit (Finding Your Voice and Inspiring Others to Find Theirs) will lead us into the next age of mankind's voice—the Age of Wisdom. Again, this final section is concluded with a section of Questions & Answers—the most commonly asked questions I've dealt with over the years that deal with the issues we cover in the book.

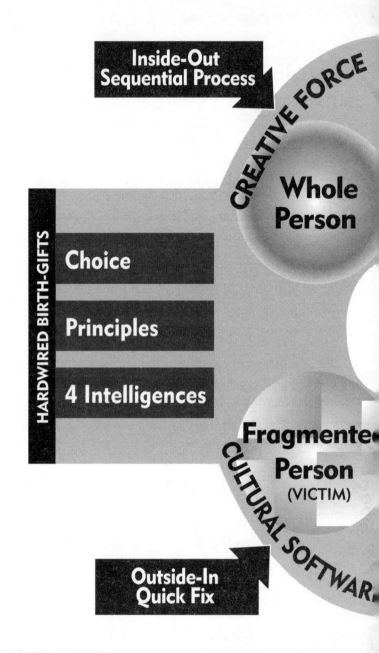

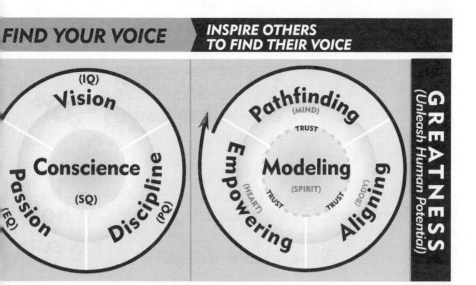

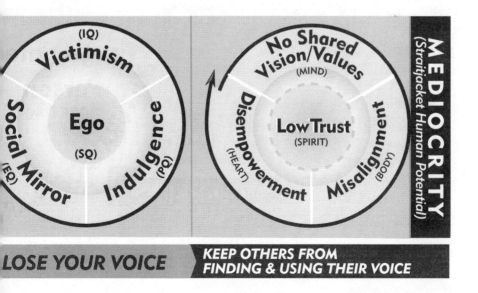

Figure 6.10

QUESTION & ANSWER

Q: How would you define leadership?

A: Again, leadership is communicating people's worth and potential so clearly that they come to see it in themselves. Notice the words *worth* and *potential*. People must feel an intrinsic sense of *worth*—that is, that they have intrinsic value—totally apart from being compared to others, and that they are worthy of unconditional love, regardless of behavior or performance. Then when you communicate their potential and create opportunities to develop and use it, you are building on a solid foundation. To communicate people's potential and to give them a sense of *extrinsic* worth is a flawed foundation, and their potential will never be optimized.

Q: There are so many leadership books out today—what in your material is truly unique that adds value?

A: What is unique about this leadership material that adds real value? I would say five things: First—the *sequential development*. I know of no book that focuses on the absolute necessity of personal development and integration before trust can be built at the relationship level and insists that both of these are necessary before you can build effective, sustainable organizations, including families. Second—it takes a *whole-person* approach. I know of no material out there that deals with all four intelligences, giving the highest emphasis to spiritual intelligence, or conscience, in guiding the other three. Third—it is based entirely upon *principles* that are timeless, universal and self-evident, as differentiated from values that all people and organizations have but which may not be based upon principles. As you know, values control our behavior, but principles control the consequences of our behavior. When you pick up one end of the stick, you pick up the other. Fourth—it teaches that leadership through the developmental principle-centered process can become a *choice* (moral authority) rather than only being a position (formal authority) and that the key to the new age of knowledge workers is to think in terms of release, not control; in terms of transformation, not just transaction. In other words, you manage things but you lead people. Fifth—the whole-person approach is "written large" for an organization, including a family, in terms of the *4 Roles of Leadership*—modeling, pathfinding, aligning and empowering. This is an amazingly powerful explanatory paradigm which can be used to diagnose most any problem or challenge and to identify the high leverage steps in resolving them.

Q: Can leadership be taught?

A: No, but it can be learned. Again, the key is the exercise of the space between stimulus, that is the teaching, and response, that is the learning, and if people will exercise their freedom of choice to learn the knowledge, skills and character traits associated with leadership (vision, discipline, passion and conscience), they will learn to be leaders that others will happily choose to follow. In a very real sense they are both followers of principles. Ultimately a good leadership team is a complementary team where people's strengths are made productive and their weaknesses made irrelevant by the strengths of others.

Focus—

Modeling and Pathfinding

Chapter 7

THE VOICE OF INFLUENCE—
BE A TRIM-TAB

We must become the change we seek in the world.

GANDHI

M ODELING is the spirit and center of any leadership effort. It begins with Finding Your Voice—developing the four intelligences and expressing your voice in vision, discipline, passion and conscience. Modeling these characteristics of personal

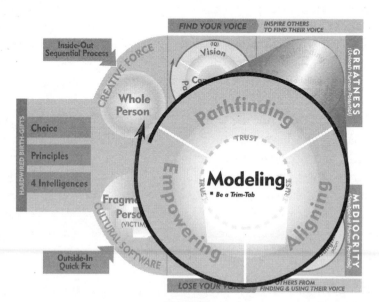

Figure 7.1

leadership alters and changes the other three roles at their very core.

Modeling is primarily done *during* the other three roles. It is also done *before*, which brings a sense of confidence and trust in the leader. But it is only when people actually experience for themselves how a conscience-driven person models pathfinding, aligning and empowering that leadership actually takes place. People then come to know for themselves how respected, appreciated and valued they are. Why? Because their opinions are sought. Their input is respected. Their unique experience is valued. They are genuinely involved in the pathfinding process. They are participants. They don't just hear about the mission statement and the strategic plan. They help develop them. They own them. Or if the mission statement and strategic plan were developed beforehand, they identify with them either because they made a conscious choice to do so before they came on board, or because of their admiration for the model leader.

Sometimes mental and emotional *identification* is a more powerful force than involvement. You see this with the followers of a Gandhi, a Martin Luther King, or a Nelson Mandela. Perhaps you, yourself, have so admired someone that you buy deeply into their vision, even though you were not involved in creating that vision. This is identification. It is a very powerful psychological force, sometimes even more powerful than actual participation. This is particularly the case with vision and strategic planning, more than with values. Brilliant visionaries and strategists are often in a class by themselves, and this is often recognized by the culture itself—but again only if trust and personal trustworthiness are there. Ultimately, however, identification is based on *involvement* of some sort, directly or indirectly.

Modeling is also not the work of just an individual; it's the work of a *team*. When you have a team of people that builds on each individual's strengths and organizes to make individual weaknesses irrelevant, you have true power in an organization. So when you think of modeling, think of an individual *and* a *complementary team*. The spirit of a complementary team is that you are there to play a unique role that compensates for the weaknesses of others. You're not there to find and focus on their weaknesses or to bad-mouth them behind their backs. You're there to make up for their weaknesses as they make up for yours. No one has all strengths, and very few people can be excellent in all roles. Mutual respect becomes the moral imperative.

THE ATTITUDE OF INFLUENCE

The habit of responding to the inner desire to make a difference, to matter, to extend our influence to the people and causes we most value all begins with a mind-set or ATTITUDE, a choice—the choice to use the *voice of influence*.

WHEN I TEACH the principles you find in this book, I like to open up for questions either privately or from the audience throughout the day. Inevitably, someone will raise their hand and say something like this: "Dr. Covey, these principles are great. I believe them. How I want to live them! But you have no idea what it's like to work in an organization like mine. If you had a boss like my boss you would understand that there's no way I could ever pull off what you're talking about. What do I do?" You can just see their thinking. They see only two alternatives. "My boss is a jerk and he's never going to change. I can either quit (which I can't afford to do) or I do the best I can and just live with it."

When I teach how these principles apply to marriage and family, I have women come up to me and essentially say the same thing about their husbands, and husbands say the same about their wives: "If you only knew what my husband is like you'd know what I mean. There's no way this will work." Again, two alternatives: leave or just bear with it as long as I can.

How easy it is for people to think and feel, "I'm a victim; I've tried everything; there's nothing more I can do; I'm stuck." They're frustrated and miserable but don't see any other option.

> Victimism gives your future away.

My response to their question usually shocks them a little. I can see by their widening eyes that some are even offended to begin with. This is what I say:

"Any time you think the problem is *out there*, that very thought *is* the problem."

"So you're implying that this is *my* problem?" some reply.

"What I'm trying to say is that any time you wrap your emotional life around the weaknesses of another person, you give away your emotional freedom to that person and give them permission to continue to mess up your life." Your past holds your future hostage.

Obviously, this is a relationship problem, but until people have found their own voice, there is no way they will have the maturity, inner security or character strength to apply the principle-centered solution with the "jerk" boss. Or it could be that they have the inner strength but haven't yet developed the skills that come from patience and persistent practice.

The continued interaction during teaching is usually very sobering to them, but eventually we come to the point that they recognize they are not a victim—that they can choose their response to the other person's behavior. Society so manufactures and reinforces the mind-set of victimism and blame. But you and I have the power to use our birth-gifts to become the creative force of our own lives and to choose an approach that will increase our influence in an organization. We can become the leader of our own boss.

THE GREEK PHILOSOPHY OF INFLUENCE

The Greek philosophy of influence called *ethos, pathos, logos,* is an excellent summary of the process of increasing your influence (see figure 7.2).

Ethos basically means your ethical nature, your personal credibility, the amount of trust or confidence others have in your integrity and competency. When people consistently come through in a principle-

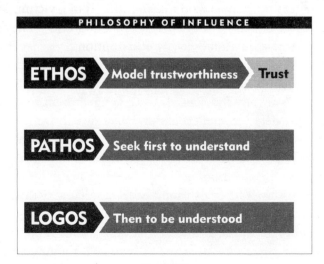

PHILOSOPHY OF INFLUENCE

ETHOS > Model trustworthiness > **Trust**

PATHOS > Seek first to understand

LOGOS > Then to be understood

Figure 7.2

centered way on those things they have promised and what is expected
of them, they have ethos. *SQ.*

Pathos is empathy—it's the feeling side. It means that you understand
how another person feels, what his needs are, how she sees things, and
what he is trying to communicate—and she feels it. *EQ.*

Logos basically stands for logic. It has to do with the power and persuasion of your own presentation, your own thinking. *IQ.*

The sequence, of course, is supremely important. To move to logos
before people feel understood is futile; to try to create understanding
when there is no faith in your character is likewise futile.

ONE TIME I was teaching a Twenty Group—a group of twenty professional insurance general agents who gather together every quarter in
a learning forum for an idea exchange. For two years I was their resource person. One January in our meeting they were all complaining
and murmuring about the lousy training and development program in
the company. And the straw that broke the camel's back took place just
before Christmas at the big international awards ceremony held in
Hawaii, where part of the time was spent in training. The training involved no idea exchange or learning from one another. At best it was an
expensive and impressive laser show. They complained that this was typical of the training they received and that it was essentially short-lived
and useless.

I asked them why they didn't change it. They responded, "Well,
that's not our role; we're not in charge of that." I told them they were
copping out, that they could change the training program if they had
the mind to. They were among the top general agents in the entire
company and had enormous credibility, or *ethos.* They could visit with
anyone in the company they chose. I encouraged them to make a presentation to the decision-makers and to make sure to begin by describing the decision-makers' point of view *(pathos)* as well as or better than
they could themselves—including all their potential concerns about
making changes to the training program and beautifully orchestrated
annual celebrations. The goals would be to describe these concerns until the executives felt so deeply understood that they would then be open
to the *logos,* or logic, of the agents' recommendations.

So they sent two representatives to see not only the president and
CEO but also the person in charge of training and development. They

allowed for whatever time they needed to describe the company's approach and the reasons for it, as well as the economic, political and cultural struggles of making a change. They continued this description until it was obvious that the decision-makers felt deeply understood. As soon as they felt understood, they became very open to influence (the key to influence is always to first be influenced, that is to first be open and seek understanding). They literally asked for the recommendations of these two general agents, who gave not only the recommendations but also a plan of action that dealt with all the economic, political and cultural realities they had described before.

The decision-makers were blown away. Even though the recommendation was to start off by designing a pilot program, the decision-makers instantly made it a company-wide program.

When we had our next quarterly meeting, they told me what happened. So I said, "Now what do you want to take on—what other stupid thing is going on in the company that you'd like to see changed?" This Twenty Group was literally amazed at how they had empowered themselves—how their initiative and courage and empathy had paid off. They ceased moaning, complaining and murmuring, and started taking more and more responsibility. While continuing to plow their own small fields, they surveyed large fields and saw things in a larger context. They saw the top decision-makers as human beings who were struggling just as they were, who needed models rather than critics, needed sources of light rather than sources of judgment.

This story clearly illustrates the inside-out approach and its power. Remember that every time you think the problem is out there, *that very thought* is the problem.

Hopefully you can clearly see how, by exercising initiative and empathy, by building ethos, by focusing and working on those things that are within your ability to influence, you can become a change catalyst in any situation. Again, by doing so, you literally become the leader of your boss. That is, while the boss may have formal authority, you have moral authority and power to influence.

A TRIM-TAB

I understand that the amazing paradigm shifter Buckminster Fuller chose to put this epitaph on his tombstone: "Just A Trim-Tab." A trim-tab on a boat or plane is the small rudder that turns the big rudder that

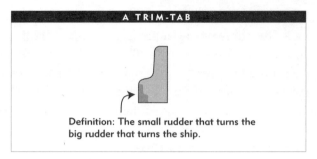

Figure 7.3

turns the entire ship (see figure 7.3). This Twenty Group was a trim-tab; Gandhi was a trim-tab.

I believe there are numerous potential trim-tabbers in every organization—businesses, government, schools, families, nonprofit and community organizations—who can lead and spread their influence no matter what position they hold. They can move themselves and their team or department in such a way that it positively affects the entire organization. The trim-tab leader exercises *initiative* within his or her own Circle of Influence (see figure 7.4), however small it may be.

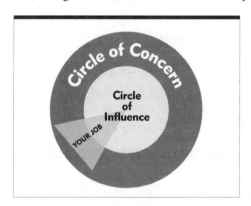

Figure 7.4

To illustrate, observe the diagram, which is comprised of two circles, the larger circle being the Circle of Concern (those things which concern and interest you) and the smaller circle, the Circle of Influence (those things over which you have control or influence). It also indicates that a person's job is largely outside one's Circle of Influence.

In chapter 1, I began by citing some absolutely stunning data resulting from a study conducted by Harris Interactive using our xQ (Execution Quotient) Questionnaire. Because the implications of this research are so insightful, I will refer to additional findings through the remainder of the book. Touching on the topic of influence, you may be interested to know that only 31 percent of xQ respondents say they focus on things they can directly impact rather than things they can't. Trim-tab leaders—regardless of formal position—apply vision, discipline, passion and conscience to the outside edge of their Circle of Influence, which causes it to expand. In many cases, these are people without significant positions or formal decision-making power.

Taking initiative is a form of self-empowerment. No formal leader has empowered you. The organizational structure hasn't empowered you. Your job description hasn't empowered you. You empower yourself based on the issue or the problem or the challenge at hand. You exercise the appropriate level of initiative or self-empowerment.

> The key question is always, What is the best thing I can do under these circumstances?

7 LEVELS OF INITIATIVE OR SELF-EMPOWERMENT

In the following diagram (see figure 7.5), you will see a continuum of 7 Levels of Initiative—from "Wait until told" at the lowest level of initiative, to "Ask," to "Make a recommendation" and "I intend to," to "Do it and report immediately" and "Do it and report periodically," and finally

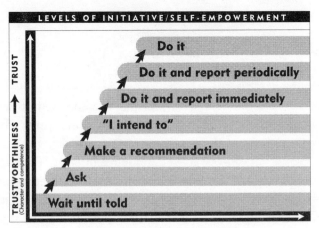

Figure 7.5

just "Do it," which is right at the center of your ability to control and influence.

You choose which level of initiative to use based on how far the task lies within or without your Circle of Influence. This takes situational sensitivity and judgment, but little by little your Circle of Influence will expand.

Choosing our level of initiative widens our definition of "voice," so that we can find our voice in any set of circumstances. It may be in a job that we don't enjoy at all. By exercising a level of initiative, we can change the nature of that job, or we can influence others that are in our Circle of Influence but outside our job.

In our present job, we can strive for excellence. We can benchmark against world-class, rather than national/regional/local, standards. A lawyer could be more of a peacemaker. An educator could be more of a caring shepherd and coach and mentor. A doctor could focus more on education and prevention and deal with the whole person instead of just body parts, technology and chemistry. A parent could strive to have 80 percent of all interactions positive, with only 20 percent involved with chastening, correcting or disciplining. The salesperson could listen more for needs and adapt with integrity. The marketing person could guarantee the integrity of merchandising and advertising. The business executive would be careful to underpromise and overdeliver. In short, we can teach principles always and everywhere, and sometimes we may need to use words.

LET'S EXPLORE EACH of the levels of initiative.

1. Wait until told.

This would involve a concern that obviously lies *outside* of not only your Circle of Influence but also your job. On this one, you just wait. You don't want to be doing someone else's job. You don't want to be making recommendations about things that are way outside of your Circle of Influence. People would not have confidence in your recommendation for a number of reasons. They would see your recommendation as being entirely inappropriate and perhaps see you as being entirely out of line. Acting in areas far outside of your Circle of Influence will actually cause your Circle of Influence to become smaller.

So what do you do? You smile—just like the Serenity Prayer used by Alcoholics Anonymous:

God, grant me the serenity
To accept the things I cannot change,
Courage to change the things I can,
And wisdom to know the difference.

You no longer waste your energy on something you can do nothing about. Now, if you have influence with someone who can do something about it, that's different. You can then move higher up the levels of initiative and self-empowerment.

But it's not easy to smile and do nothing about the issue for now. Many people obsess about stupid things that they can't change at the present time. They swap war stories with coworkers and massage one another's hearts about the things they can do nothing about. But that just weakens their ability to make things happen on the issues and concerns that they *can* do something about. Again, their past holds their future hostage.

They then fall into the trap of codependency that spawns what, again, I call the five metastasizing emotional cancers: criticizing, complaining, comparing, competing and contending. People who don't have their own deep internal act together seek their security from sources outside themselves. Because they're codependent with their environment, they engage in these destructive, cancerous behaviors.

These five emotional cancers literally metastasize their cancerous cells into relationships, and sometimes through an entire culture. Then you've got an organization that's so polarized, so divided, that it's almost impossible to consistently deliver high quality to customers.

FIVE CANCEROUS BEHAVIORS

▶ **Criticizing**

▶ **Complaining**

▶ **Comparing**

▶ **Competing**

▶ **Contending**

Figure 7.6

One note on competing: Although competition for a sense of worth within relationships, families, and work teams and cultures is damaging, I believe that it can be very healthy in settings such as athletics and the marketplace. It can stretch and draw out the best in people and organizations. In the marketplace, you can look upon your competitors as your teachers against whom you can benchmark yourselves. While you may be trying to beat out your competitors, what you're really trying to do is win better for your customers and to learn from those who are doing it better and faster than you are. That's the power of the free enterprise system: competition inside the marketplace, cooperation inside the workplace. Remember we must be "bilingual" and avoid the single-minded danger Abraham Maslow observed: "He that is good with the hammer tends to think everything is a nail."

2. Ask.

It would be reasonable and logical to ask a question about something *within* your job description but *outside* your Circle of Influence. Because it's outside your Circle of Influence, you can't do much about it; but since it affects your job, most people would still consider it legitimate to at least ask. If the question is intelligent and is the result of thorough analysis and careful thinking, it could be very impressive and may increase your Circle of Influence.

3. Make a Recommendation.

Where would you put "Make a Recommendation"? Right at the outside edge of your Circle of Influence. It's not even in your job. You're making a recommendation that is outside of your job and at the outside edge of your Circle of Influence.

A beautiful illustration of the third level of initiative and self-empowerment is found in the military doctrine of Completed Staff Work. The five basic steps of this doctrine are:

1. Analyze the problem.
2. Come up with alternative and recommended solutions.
3. Develop recommended steps to execute the solution.
4. Incorporate an awareness of all realities (political, social, economic competencies, etc.).

5. Make a recommendation in a way that only requires approval by a single signature.

Completed Staff Work requires the effective executive to wait for the best work. First, she asks people to think through problems and issues. Then, when they have done their best thinking, they are to bring a final recommendation. She looks only at that final recommendation.

When using Completed Staff Work, upper-level management does not rescue people with quick and easy answers, even though they might plead for them. If the executive doesn't wait until the work is done, she cheats people of growth—and they cheat her and the company of time. Moreover, people cannot be held responsible for results if they are given the methods.

> *Once in Sicily, I told a general who was somewhat reluctant to attack that I had perfect confidence in him. To show it, I went home.*
>
> *Never tell people what to do, and they will surprise you with their ingenuity.*[1]
>
> GENERAL GEORGE S. PATTON

You can see how much time and work this saves the executive and how much more initiative it requires from the staff person. I've seen this work marvelously in many, many situations. It also immediately enlarges one's Circle of Influence.*

4. "I intend to."

"I intend to" is actually one notch of initiative higher than making a recommendation and is an extension of it. I first learned this principle while sailing in the Hawaiian Islands on the USS *Santa Fe*, a multibillion-dollar nuclear submarine, in simulated war games. What a

---

* To receive a free copy of a complete article on Completed Staff Work go to www.The 8thHabit.com/offers.

magnificent sight it was to stand on the bridge with the commanding officer, Captain David Marquett, as we pulled out of the Lahaina Sea Port, and to see that massive, black tube one hundred yards in front of you (about the length of an American football field) and about a hundred feet behind, plowing through the water.

While the two of us were engaged in a conversation, an officer approached us and said, "Captain, I intend to take this boat down four hundred feet." The captain asked, "What is the sounding (depth of the ocean floor)?" He answered, "About eight hundred." "What does the sonar (the electronic device that senses other ships, boats, subs, and other objects) say?" The officer replied, "Nothing, only fish." The captain answered, "Give us another twenty minutes—then carry out your intention."

Throughout the day people would come up to the captain and say "I intend to do this," or "I intend to do that." The captain would often ask questions and then say "Very well." Sometimes he would ask no questions and simply reply, "Very well." The captain reserved only the tip-of-the-iceberg-type decisions for his own confirmation. The great mass of the iceberg—the other 95 percent of the decisions—were being made without any involvement or confirmation by the captain whatsoever.

I asked the captain about his leadership style. He said that he wanted to empower his people as far as he possibly could within the confines of the naval context. He thought that if he required them to own not only the problem but also the solution to the problem, they would begin to view themselves as a vitally important link in the chain of command. He matured the culture to the point where the officers and sailors declared their own intentions regarding the captain's decision authority.

"I intend to" is different in kind than "I recommend." The person has done more analytical work, to the point that he is totally prepared to carry out the action once it is approved. She has owned not only the problem but the solution as well, and she is ready to implement it.

Those sailors had a real sense of adding value—something, they indicated to me, that they had not had with other skippers when they'd been merely in a "Wait until told" mode. This is why "I intend to" is on the outside edge of one's Circle of Influence and one's job. Meaningful empowerment significantly reduces turnover—that is, losing top people to much higher paying work.

Months after my sub ride I was thrilled to receive a letter from Captain Marquett informing me that the USS *Santa Fe* was awarded the

Arleigh Burke Trophy for most improved submarine, ship, or aviation squadron in the Pacific. Such is the fruit of trim-tabbing empowerment!

5. Do it and report immediately.

"Do it and report immediately" would be on the outside edge of one's Circle of Influence but within one's job. You report immediately because other people need to know. This enables others to see if everything was done correctly and to allow for timely corrections if necessary. It also provides information needed by others before they can make consequent decisions and take follow-up actions.

6. Do it and report periodically.

This level of initiative pertains to actions that could be part of normal self-evaluation in a performance evaluation visit or on a formal report, so that the information can be communicated and used by others. When you report periodically, you find yourself clearly within your job description and within your Circle of Influence.

7. Do it.

When something is right at the center of your Circle of Influence and the core of your job description, you just do it. Sometimes, in some cultures, it's easier to get forgiveness than to get permission, so if you're convinced you're right and that the action is not that far outside your Circle of Influence, it may be best to "do it."

There is great power in the idea of taking responsibility and just doing it—making it happen. This highest level of initiative reminds me of a true story called "A Message to Garcia."

> When the war broke out between Spain and the United States at the turn of the century, the American president needed to get a message to a Cuban revolutionary named Garcia. He was hiding somewhere on the island of Cuba out of reach of mail or telegraph. Nobody knew how to reach him. But an officer suggested that if anybody could do it, it would be an officer by the name of Rowan.
>
> When McKinley gave the letter to Rowan in Washington, D.C., the officer didn't ask, "Where is he at? How do I get there? What do you want me to do when I'm there? How will I get back?" He just took the

message and figured out how to get to Garcia. He took a train to New York. A ship to Jamaica. Broke the Spanish blockade to get to Cuba in a sailboat. Then wild carriage rides, marching and riding through the Cuban jungle. Nine days of traveling later, Rowan got the message to Garcia at nine in the morning. That same afternoon at five, he started his return journey to the United States.

Giving further insight, author Elbert Hubbard wrote:

My heart goes out to the man who does his work when the "boss" is away as well as when he is at home, . . . the man who, when given a letter for Garcia, quietly takes the missive, without asking any idiotic questions, and with no lurking intention of chucking it into the nearest sewer, or of doing ought else but deliver it. . . . Civilization is one long, anxious search for just such individuals. Anything such a man asks will be granted; his kind is so rare that no employer can afford to let him go. He is wanted in every city, town, and village—in every office, shop, store and factory. The world cries out for such: he is needed, and needed badly—the man who can "Carry a Message to Garcia."*

THE TRIM-TAB SPIRIT

You can see that no matter what issue, problem or concern you have, you can empower yourself by taking initiative in some way. Be sensitive, be wise, be careful regarding timing, but do *something* about the situation. Avoid complaining, criticizing or being negative; be especially wary of absolving yourself from responsibility and simply blaming "them" for failures. We live in a culture of blame—a full 70 percent of xQ respondents say that people in their organization tend to blame others when things go wrong. So taking responsibility will mean swimming against the current.

Taking initiative requires some *vision*, some standard to be met, or some improvement to be achieved. It requires some *discipline* in the doing. It requires getting your heart and your *passion* into it and doing it in a *conscience*-directed or principled way toward a worthy end.

Tom Peters describes the trim-tab attitude and spirit this way:

---

* For a free public-domain copy of the complete text of "A Message to Garcia," go to www.The8thHabit.com/offers.

Winners, no kidding, adore crummy jobs. Why? Because those jobs allow lots and lots of space. Nobody cares! Nobody is watching! You're on your own! You are king! You can get your hands dirty, make mistakes, take risks, perform miracles! The most common lament of the "unempowered" is that they don't have "the space" to do anything cool. To which I unfailingly reply: Rubbish!

Bottom line: Relish the "little" assignment or "chore" that no one else wants! SEEK IT OUT! It's a license for self-empowerment, whether it's the redesign of a form or planning a weekend client retreat . . . you can turn it into something grand and glorious and Wow.[2]

Once, I served as the administrative assistant to the president of a university. In many ways, he was dictatorial, controlling, always assumed he knew what was best and would make all the important decisions. On the other hand, he was a visionary—a brilliant, talented person. But he treated everyone like a gofer—"go for this, go for that"—as if they didn't have a mind. These highly educated, motivated men and women gradually became disenchanted, and then disempowered. They would stand around the executive corridors complaining about the president.

"I can't believe what he did. . . ."

"You know, let me tell you the latest. . . ."

"You think that's bad. You ought to see what he did when he came into our department. . . ."

"Really, I had never heard that."

"Yeah, I've never been in a job where I felt so constricted and straitjacketed by all these foolish rules and this bureaucracy. It's bogging me down."

They spent hours massaging each other's hearts.

Then there was Ben. He simply took another approach: He went straight to the third level of self-empowerment and initiative. Even though he, too, was treated like a gofer, he decided to start at the *make a recommendation* level.

He decided to be the best gofer around. This earned him credibility—ethos. He would then anticipate the president's needs and the reasons behind his gofer requests. "Now, let's see. Why does the president want this information? He's preparing for a board meeting and he wants me to gather data on how many university campus securities across the country carry sidearms because he's getting criticized about our approach. I think I'll help him prepare for that board meeting."

> Complement, don't criticize, your boss.

Ben came to a preliminary meeting, presented his gofer data, then went the second mile in analysis and recommendations. The president turned to me, speechless. Then he turned back to Ben and said, "I want you to come to the board meeting and make the recommendation. Your analysis is brilliant. You anticipated exactly what the need is."

Everybody else on the staff had bought into the silent conspiracy of "wait until told." But not Ben. He'd exercised leadership by empathizing with the president, by determining what it was he really wanted and needed. Ben started out with a relatively low position. But pretty soon he was regularly making presentations to the board.

I worked in that role for four years. By the end of the fourth year, Ben was the second most influential person on the campus even though he hadn't risen through the academic ranks. The president would not make any significant moves without Ben's blessing. When Ben retired, there was a special recognition award put in his name. Why? Because he modeled trustworthiness, loyalty to the university, and willingness to do whatever it took.

I think Ben understood the futility of wishing for something to be different. Can you see in this story how leadership can become a choice? Can you see how you, too, can become the leader of your boss, as Ben did?

> When we say that leadership is a choice, it basically means you can choose the level of initiative you want to exercise in response to the question What is the best I can do under the circumstances?

You will always need to make a judgment call regarding these 7 Levels of Initiative. It takes judgment and wisdom to know what level of initiative to exercise—*what* you should do, *how* you should do it, *when* you should do it, and perhaps most importantly, *why* you should do it. This will take all four intelligences. The "why" question usually taps into spiritual intelligence because it gets at your value system, the source of motivation. The "what to do" question usually taps into your intellectual intelligence as you think analytically, strategically and conceptually. The "when to do it" and "how to do it" questions usually tap into your emotional intelligence as you read the environment, sense the cultural and political operating norms, and discern your own strengths and weaknesses. The doing intelligence will also come into play as you carry out your intentions and tactically implement the "how."

When you wisely use initiative through all 7 Levels of Initiative, you'll find that your Circle of Influence will get larger and larger until it encompasses your entire job. Interestingly, and this almost always happens, as your Circle of Influence enlarges, so too does your Circle of Concern.

A trim-tab leader is constant—like a lighthouse, not a weather vane—a constant, dependable source of light, not someone who twists and turns with every social wind.

> *Give the world the best you have and you may*
> *get hurt. Give the world your best anyway.*
> MOTHER TERESA

As you take this inside-out, initiative-seizing approach, people in formal positions will have increasing confidence in your character and competence. Trust will increase. It is almost inevitable that they will want to build higher and higher levels of initiative and empowerment into your job. You will find yourself becoming the leader of your boss ... and your boss will naturally become part of a complementary team as servant leader.

FILM: *Mauritius*

I invite you now to watch a film entitled *Mauritius*. You will find it on the companion DVD to the book. Not only organizations or individuals can be trim-tabs; this film illustrates how an entire country or society could trim-tab its own success and culture—in spite of profound ethnic, racial, cultural and other differences. In fact, it is not in spite of, but simply *because* of, the differences that they have produced such remarkable cultural strength.

The statements shown at the beginning of the film were accurate as of the time of its production. Some conditions in Mauritius have changed since, including increased pockets of social strife. The real point of the story, however, is not that Mauritius is a perfect society; it is that *whatever* challenges we may face—whether individually, as families, as organizations or even as nations—we can work within our Circle of Influence and creatively "trim-tab" our way through them.

QUESTION & ANSWER

Q: All this sounds good, but you don't know my boss. He is a control freak and is threatened by competent people around him. My situation is so different.

A: Yes, every situation is unique and different in some way. But in another sense, at bottom, challenges and problems are very similar. The key does not lie in the circumstance; it lies in the space between stimulus and response—that is, in the circumstance and your response to it. This is where your freedom to choose belongs. If you use this freedom wisely and base your choices on principles, not only will your freedom to choose increase in size but you will also develop an internal source of personal security so that your life will not be a function of the weaknesses of others. You will no longer disempower yourself and empower the weaknesses of others to continue to mess your life up. You may do a cost-benefit analysis and decide to do something different or go somewhere else. Or you may simply decide to rely on the pragmatics of the marketplace and trim-tab a larger circle of influence until you become indispensable to, and ultimately even the leader of, your boss. You have to use all four intelligences so you can be both creative and inspired. You also need to work inside your own Circle of Influence but outside your job. You also need to exercise a great deal of initiative and volunteerism in understanding unmet needs and unsolved problems so that you can exercise the appropriate level of initiative. You also need to do your own job superbly, so as to merit the confidence of others, surveying other fields while cultivating well your own. Remember, ethos (credibility) first, pathos (empathy) second, and logos (logic) third.

Q: Realistically, how can a person become the leader of their boss?

A: Become a light, not a judge. Become a model, not a critic. Go to work inside your own Circle of Influence so that your moral authority is developed and expanded and you have credibility. Courageously take initiative to make good things happen. Empathize with your boss's world, concerns, purposes and mind-set. Empathize, also, with the culture and the market, and then take these initiatives. Remember, again, no bad-mouthing. Be patient and persistent, and you will grow in influence. The pragmatics of results will convert the cynic. This is leadership—a choice, remember, not a position.

Q: You often say it is easier to get forgiveness than permission, but then sometimes if you do take a little initiative based on that idea, you get reprimanded severely or even fired.

A: Keep investing in your personal and professional development and in your power to produce solutions to problems, and you will always have a source of economic security. Your security does not come from your job or from the patronage of other people; it comes from your ability to meet needs and solve problems. Keep investing in those abilities, and you will have endless opportunities. Also, pick your battles very carefully—don't take initiative that is way outside your Circle of Influence. Instead, work outside your job but inside your Circle of Influence. Then take initiative in the form of well thought through analysis and recommendations, and you will inevitably find your Circle of Influence getting larger and larger.

Chapter 8

THE VOICE OF TRUSTWORTHINESS— MODELING CHARACTER AND COMPETENCE

The supreme quality for leadership is unquestionably integrity. Without it, no real success is possible no matter whether it is on a section gang, a football field, in an army, or in an office.

DWIGHT DAVID EISENHOWER

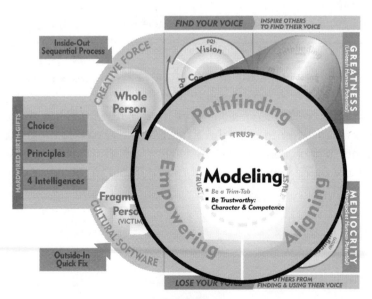

Figure 8.1

S OME TIME AGO I was asked to consult for a bank that was having a problem with employee morale. "I don't know what's wrong," bemoaned their young president. Bright and charismatic, he'd risen through the ranks only to see his institution faltering. Productivity and profits were down. He blamed his employees. "No matter what incentives I provide," he said, "they won't shake off this gloom and doom."

He was right. The atmosphere seemed poisoned with suspicion and lack of trust. For two months I ran workshops, but nothing helped. I was stumped.

"How can anyone trust what's happening here?" was a typical employee refrain. But no one would tell me the source of the distrust.

Finally, in more casual conversations, the truth emerged. The boss, who was married, was having an affair with an employee. And everyone knew it.

It was obvious now that the company's poor performance was caused by his conduct. But the greatest damage this man was doing was to himself. He was thinking only of his own gratification, disregarding long-term consequences. Moreover, he had violated a sacred trust with his wife.

In a word, his failing was one of *character.*

---

90 percent of all leadership failures are character failures.

Just as trust is the key to all relationships, so also is trust the glue of organizations. It is the cement that holds the bricks together. I have also learned that *trust is the fruit of the trustworthiness of both people and organizations.* Trust comes from three sources: the personal, the institutional, and one person consciously choosing to *give* it to another—an act that leads me to *feel* your belief that I can add value. You give me trust and I return it. *Trust* is a verb AND a noun. When it's both a verb and a noun, it's something shared and reciprocated between people. That is the essence of how a person becomes the leader of their boss. They merit trust by giving it. *Trust* the verb comes from the potential trustworthiness of the one receiving the trust and the clear trustworthiness of the one giving the trust. The fourth role—Empowering—embodies making *trust* a verb.

We've surveyed over 54,000 people and asked them to identify the essential qualities of a leader; integrity was, by far, the number one response (see figure 8.2).

Figure 8.2

In many settings today it is out of vogue to speak in terms of character. It's become equated with soft, touchy-feely stuff or with someone's religion. Some people wonder if our inner values matter anymore. After all, hasn't our noted bank executive succeeded in every visible way, despite his transgressions?

This question demonstrates a quandary of our modern life. Many have come to believe that the only things we need for success are talent, energy and personality. But history has taught us that over the long haul, who we *are* is more important than who we appear to be.

As I did a review of leadership and success literature going back to the founding of the United States, in preparation for writing *The 7 Habits*, I found that during the first 150 years, the focus was almost exclusively on the importance of character and principles. As we moved into the Industrial Age and after World War I, the focus began to shift to personality, techniques, and technologies—what we could call the Personality Ethic.

This trend is continuing, but I sense a countertrend emerging as people experience the fruits of valueless organizational culture. More and more organizations are recognizing the need for trustworthiness, for character, for producing trust in the culture. More and more people are seeing the need to look deeply into their own souls, to sense how they, themselves, contribute to the problems, and to figure out exactly what they can do to contribute to the solution and serve human needs.

> *Character, in the long run, is the decisive factor*
> *in the life of an individual and of nations alike.*[1]
> THEODORE ROOSEVELT

What became of the bank president who was intimately involved with an employee? When I confided to him what I knew of his affair and the effect it was having on his staff, he ran his fingers through his hair. "I don't know where to begin," he said.

"Is it over?" I asked.

He looked me squarely in the eye. "Yes. Absolutely."

"Then begin by talking with your wife," I answered.

He told his wife, who forgave him. Then he called a meeting of his staff and addressed their morale problem. "I have found the cause of the problem," he said. "It is me. I am asking you to give me another chance."

It took time, but eventually employee morale—a sense of openness, optimism and trust—improved. In the end, however, the executive was doing himself the greatest favor. He was finding his own path to character.

PERSONAL TRUSTWORTHINESS

Wherever you find lasting trust, you will find trustworthiness. It is always so. It is a principle. Just as trust comes from trustworthiness, trustworthiness comes from *character* and *competence*. When you develop both strong character and competence, the fruit is wisdom and judgment—the foundation of all great and lasting achievement and trust. The following diagram (see figure 8.3) helps to identify the main factors dealing with the production of trust.

Let's begin with the three facets of personal *character:* integrity, maturity and the Abundance Mentality.

Integrity means you are integrated around principles and natural laws

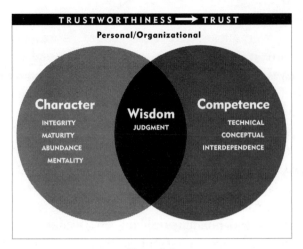

Figure 8.3

that ultimately govern the consequences of our behavior. Honesty is the principle of telling the truth. Integrity is keeping promises made to self and/or others.

> *One man cannot do right in one department of life whilst he is occupied in doing wrong in any other department. Life is one indivisible whole.*[2]
>
> MAHATMA GANDHI

Maturity develops when a person pays the price of integrity and winning the private victory over self, allowing him or her to be simultaneously courageous and kind. In other words, such a person can deal with tough issues compassionately. The combination of courage and kindness is both the source and the product of integrity.

Abundance Mentality means that rather than seeing life as a competition with only one winner, you see it as a cornucopia of ever enlarging opportunity, resources and wealth. You don't compare yourself to others and are genuinely happy for their successes. Scarcity-minded people come out of a comparison-based identity and are threatened by the successes of others. Even though they might pretend and say otherwise, they know that it's eating their hearts out. Those with the Abundance Mentality see their competitors as some of their most valued and important teachers. These same three attributes—integrity, maturity and Abundance Mentality—perfectly describe a complementary team.

• • •

NOW LET'S LOOK at the *competence* side of personal trustworthiness.

Technical competence is the skill and knowledge necessary to accomplish a particular task.

Conceptual knowledge is being able to see the big picture, how all parts relate to one another. It's being able to think strategically, and systematically, not just tactically.

Interdependency is an awareness of the reality that all of life is connected, particularly with organizations and complementary teams that are attempting to win and keep the loyalty of customers, associates, suppliers and owners. Independent thinking in an interdependent reality would again be analogous to playing tennis with a golf club or thinking analog ideas in a digital world.

As my son-in-law Matt was being interviewed for medical school, he was asked whom he would prefer: an honest surgeon who was incompetent, or a competent surgeon who was dishonest. He reflected and gave a very good answer. He said, "It all depends on the issue. If I needed the surgery, I'd go for the competent one. If it was a question of whether to have the surgery or not, I'd go for the honest one."

Both character and competence are, of course, necessary, but they are also individually insufficient. General H. Norman Schwarzkopf put it this way:

> I've met a lot of leaders in the army who were very, very competent. But they didn't have character. For every job they did well in the Army, they sought reward in the form of promotions, in the form of awards and decorations, in the form of getting ahead at the expense of somebody else, in the form of another piece of paper that awarded them another degree . . . a sure road to the top. You see, these were competent people, but they lacked character. I've also met a lot of leaders who had superb character but who lacked competence. They weren't willing to pay the price of leadership, to go the extra mile because that's what it took to be a great leader. To lead in the twenty-first century . . . you will be required to have both character and competence.[3]

You will clearly discover, if it's not already obvious to you, why there is no way you can make significant progress in your relationships with other people if your own life is a mess or if you're basically untrustworthy. That's why, in the last analysis, to improve any relationship, you must start with yourself; you must improve yourself.

MODELING IS LIVING THE 7 HABITS OF HIGHLY EFFECTIVE PEOPLE

The 7 Habits of Highly Effective People embody the essence of becoming a balanced, integrated, powerful person and creating a complementary team based on mutual respect. They are the principles of personal *character*. The Habits cannot be adequately covered here in a way that truly impacts—that is best experienced in the book. But below you'll find a brief summary of the 7 Habits:

The 7 Habits of Highly Effective People

Habit 1—Be Proactive

Being proactive is more than taking initiative. It is recognizing that we are responsible for our own choices and have the freedom to choose based on principles and values rather than on moods or conditions. Proactive people are agents of change and choose not to be victims, to be reactive, or to blame others.

Habit 2—Begin with the End in Mind

Individuals, families, teams and organizations shape their own future by first creating a mental vision for any project, large or small, personal or interpersonal. They don't just live day-to-day with no clear purpose in mind. They identify and commit themselves to the principles, relationships and purposes that matter most to them.

Habit 3—Put First Things First

Putting first things first means organizing and executing around your most important priorities. Whatever the circumstance, it is living and being driven by the principles you value most, not by the urgent agendas and forces surrounding you.

Habit 4—Think Win-Win

Thinking win-win is a frame of mind and heart that seeks mutual benefit and mutual respect in all interactions. It's thinking in terms of abundance and opportunity rather than scarcity and adversarial competition. It's not thinking selfishly (win-lose) or like a martyr (lose-win). It's thinking in terms of "we," not "me."

Habit 5—Seek First to Understand, Then to be Understood

When we listen with the intent to understand others, rather than with the intent to reply, we begin true communication and relationship building. Opportunities to then speak openly and to be understood come much more naturally and easily. Seeking to understand takes consideration; seeking to be understood takes courage. Effectiveness lies in balancing or blending the two.

Habit 6—Synergize

Synergy is the third alternative—not my way, not your way, but a third way that is better than either of us would come up with individually. It's the fruit of respecting, valuing, and even celebrating one another's differences. It's about solving problems, seizing opportunities, and working out differences. It's the kind of creative cooperation of 1+1=3, 11, 111 . . . or more. Synergy is also the key to any effective team or relationship. A synergistic team is a complementary team—where the team is organized so that the strengths of some compensate for the weaknesses of others. In this way you optimize and run with strengths and make individual weaknesses irrelevant.

Habit 7—Sharpen the Saw

Sharpening the saw is about constantly renewing ourselves in the four basic areas of life: physical, social/emotional, mental and spiritual. It's the habit that increases our capacity to live all other habits of effectiveness.

THE FIRST THREE HABITS can be summarized in a very simple four-word expression: *Make and keep promises.* The ability to make a promise is proactivity (Habit 1). The content of the promise is Habit 2, and keeping the promise is Habit 3.

> Only 57 percent of workers surveyed agree that their organizations consistently do what they say they will do.

The next three complementary-team Habits can be summarized in a short phrase: *Involve people in the problem and work out the solution together.* This necessitates mutual respect (Habit 4), mutual understanding (Habit 5), and creative cooperation (Habit 6). Habit 7, Sharpen the Saw, is increasing your competency in the four areas of life: body, mind, heart and spirit. It's renewing one's personal integrity and security (Habits 1, 2 and 3) and renewing the spirit and character of the complementary team.

Here is a chart that describes the principles and paradigms of each of the 7 Habits (see table 3):

Habit	Principle	Paradigm
❶ Be Proactive	Responsibility/Initiative	Self-determination
❷ Begin with the End in Mind	Vision/Values	Two Creations / Focus
❸ Put First Things First	Integrity/Execution	Priority / Action
❹ Think Win-Win	Mutual Respect/Benefit	Abundance
❺ Seek First to Understand, Then to be Understood	Mutual Understanding	Consideration Courage
❻ Synergize	Creative Cooperation	Value Differences
❼ Sharpen the Saw	Renewal	Whole Person

Table 3

PRINCIPLES EMBODIED IN THE 7 HABITS

Look carefully at each of these principles. As mentioned earlier, you'll notice three things: First, they are *universal*—that means they transcend culture and are embodied in all major world religions and enduring philosophies; second, they are *timeless*—they never change; and third, they are *self-evident.* How do we know when something is self-evident? As mentioned before, by trying to argue against it. You simply can't do it. In the case of the principles underlying the 7 Habits, you can't argue against the importance of responsibility or initiative, of having a purpose, of integrity, of mutual respect, of mutual understanding, of creative cooperation, or of the importance of continuous renewal. The 7 Habits are character principles that shape *who and what you are.*

They provide the credibility, moral authority and skill base for your influence in an organization, including your family, community and society; they are at the core of the first of the 4 Roles of Leadership—modeling. The 4 Roles of Leadership are then *what you do* as a leader to inspire others to find their voice (see 8.4).

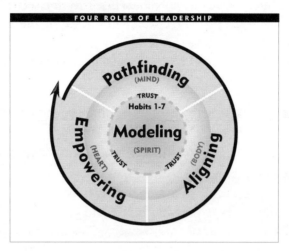

Figure 8.4

Many organizations have trained their employees in the 7 Habits. Many of those people have found the 7 Habits to be very useful at *work* if the structures and systems support them. But because, in many cases, low-trust cultures and misaligned structures and systems have not been supportive, many have concluded that the 7 Habits don't really work at *work*. This 4 Roles model creates a compatible and supportive context for the 7 Habits so that they can really be lived both at work and at home. In fact, we have found that this is the way people really learn the 7 Habits—not as an intellectual exercise but as an experiential exercise. It is only when people apply the 7 Habits—that is, actually live them—that they come to really know them. To know them intellectually but not do them is to really not know them. The 4 Roles context will create an entirely new life for the 7 Habits, and they will be perceived as strategically vital to an organization instead of just a nice sideshow training program. The 4 Roles mainstream the 7 Habits.

I remember once training a very large group of top public and private sector executives in Egypt. They thought I came to sell the 7 Habits. My opening comment was, "You think I've come here to sell the 7 Habits. I'm telling you *not* to buy the 7 Habits, because all you'll do is see it as a training program for others of lesser rank—you won't fundamentally alter your leadership style and reinvent the structures, systems and processes that reinforce the principles in the 7 Habits. Such changes require a new paradigm of leadership. *That's* what I've come to teach. If you want to be the leader of the Arab world and to become current with the new economic global marketplace, you need a larger and supportive context for the 7 Habits. Then you will be totally astonished at the results you can achieve." Apparently, it intrigued them. At the break they got on their cell phones, and the audience doubled for the later sessions.

7 HABITS PARADIGMS

Each one of the 7 Habits not only represents a principle, but also a paradigm, a way of thinking (see again table 3).

When we more deeply consider that Habits 1, 2 and 3 are represented in the four-word expression "make and keep promises," we come to understand the accompanying paradigm of each habit. Habit 1, Be Proactive, is a paradigm of self-determination rather than genetic, social, psychic or environmental determination—I can and will make a promise. It's the power of *choice*. Habit 2, Begin with the End in Mind, is the paradigm that all things are created twice, the mental, then the physical; it is the content of the promise—I can consider both the substance of a promise I want to make and what I hope to accomplish from it. It's the power of *focus*. Habit 3 is the paradigm of *priority*, *action* and *execution*—I have the ability and responsibility to carry out that promise.

Habits 4, 5 and 6—Think Win-Win, Seek First to Understand, Then to be Understood, and Synergize—are the paradigms of *abundance* in dealing with others—abundance of respect, of mutual understanding (balancing *consideration* and *courage*), and of *valuing differences*. It's at the heart of a complementary team.

Habit 7 is the paradigm of continuous improvement of the *whole person*; it stands for education, learning and recommitment—what the Japanese call Kaizen. This is why the circular diagram used throughout the book uses an arrow that does not complete the circle but rather creates an upward spiral that represents constant improvement in each of the four areas of choice.

THE MODELING TOOL—THE PERSONAL PLANNING SYSTEM

Because modeling always comes first and is manifest primarily in the other three roles, your first job is to get your act together—to create FOCUS in your life. You simply have to decide what matters most to you. What are your highest values? What vision do you have for your life? What about your work at home as a father, mother, grandfather, grandmother, aunt, uncle, sister, brother, cousin, son or daughter? What kind of service would you like to give your community, your church, your neighborhood and others in need? How important is your health? How are you going to maintain and enhance your health? Some have said that health is wealth and that without it, no other wealth matters. What about your mind, your growth and development? How important is that to you? What about your work? What are your true talents? Where does your passion lie? Where are the greatest needs in your organization and in the marketplace? On what projects and initiatives does your conscience inspire you to take action? How will you truly make a difference in your work? What will your legacy be?

The focusing tool of the first role is a *personal planning system*. You begin by writing down, either in your paper planner or your electronic planning device, what matters most to you and then building those governing priorities into your planning system so that you can effectively balance the need for structure and discipline with the need for spontaneity. In short, focus and execution.

Even more powerful than visualization, writing bridges the conscious and the subconscious mind. Writing is a psycho-neuromuscular activity and literally imprints the brain. To test this, before you go to bed, write down three things you want to do or think about first thing in the morning and just see what happens. In almost all cases, you will have a consciousness of those three things when you first wake up in the morning.

> Only one-third of xQ respondents have a personal planning system.

There are many different approaches to developing and keeping a personal planning system. The key thing is that the method should work to keep the individual focused on his or her highest priorities.

Some, like myself, find that this kind of structure gives freedom, where others find it stifling. A powerful planning and organizing tool contains the following three criteria: it is *integrated* into your life/lifestyle; it is *mobile*, to always be accessible; it is *personalized*, so it exactly suits your needs.*

There is a simple process for evaluating whether or not those things upon which you are focused are clearly aligned with what matters most to you. Consider the productivity pyramid that follows.

Figure 8.5

At the base, we must first *identify* our *mission* and *governing values*—standards, ideals. Elvis Presley said, "Values are like fingerprints. Nobody's are the same, but you leave 'em all over everything you do." As we discussed earlier, these values should be anchored in *principles* so that your life will have a changeless core and inner source of security, guidance, wisdom and power. The key to this is, perhaps, writing a personal mission statement that describes what matters most to you, including your vision and values. Having this mission statement up front enables

---

* You may download a free sixty-day trial version of the premier productivity software PlanPlus for Microsoft Outlook or PlanPlus for Windows at www.The8thHabit.com/offers.

you to prioritize your life. A woman once came to me and said, "I witnessed the process of my father dying. We were very close and it was very emotional. I remember that you wrote in the *7 Habits* book that one of the most effective ways to practice Habit 2, Begin With the End in Mind, is to write four eulogies that you'd like to have given at your own funeral—one by a loved one, one by a friend, one by a work associate and one by someone you served with in your church or community. For the first time, as I watched my father pass from this world and as we prepared his funeral, I took seriously the writing of a personal mission statement where I would clarify in a deep sense what matters most to me."

If you would like some help getting a start on your personal mission statement, we have developed a complementary personal mission statement formulator that walks you through the process step-by-step.*

Next, it is important that you identify your most important *roles* (e.g., family member, church/community volunteer, friend, mother/father, team leader), and *set goals* for the week that are aligned with those values and associated with the roles you have identified. The personal planning tool will help you set goals that are attainable, that you will be accountable to yourself for, and that you can break down into smaller goals. Your level of commitment to those goals will be directly correlated to how connected they are to your values. A clear awareness of your roles and goals enables you to balance your life.

The third level of the pyramid is *weekly planning*. During this planning time, you have the chance to reflect on your roles, choose the "big rocks" and plan those in first as you begin to schedule your week. This leads you into *daily planning*, wherein you make realistic task lists, prioritize tasks, and review scheduled appointments for the day.

The book I coauthored with Rebecca and Roger Merrill, entitled *First Things First*, goes deeply into these areas of personal mission statements and planning systems, for those who are interested.

If you only do *daily* planning—outside the larger context of your values and your goals for each of your roles in life and outside of weekly planning—you'll spend your time in firefighting and crisis management. Urgency will define importance and will become addictive. You'll spend your stressed life in the thick of thin things.

---

* You may access the free personal mission statement formulator online at www.The8thHabit.com/offers.

FILM: *Big Rocks*

In the book *First Things First*, we introduced a perfect metaphor for achieving life balance and accomplishing those things that matter most to you. We captured a live, unrehearsed demonstration of this metaphor on video at one of my seminars. It is entitled *Big Rocks*, and in its own way it communicates how we can use our three birth-gifts—choice, principles, and the four human intelligences—to create positive change in our lives. You may now watch the video on the book's companion DVD.

There are many lessons to be learned from this exercise. The most important is very simple: *Put the big rocks in first.* If you fill your bowl or your life with pebbles first, and then you have a major crisis with one of your children, a financial or health setback, or a significant new creative opportunity, what are you going to do? Those things are big rocks, and there is no room left for them in your life. Always think in terms of big rocks first. Determine what is most important in your life and make your decisions based on those very important criteria. The big rocks are simply those things that matter most in your life. The main thing is to keep the main thing the main thing. Your three supernal birth-gifts give you the power to make such choices and truly become the creative force of your own life. With a burning "yes" around your high priorities, you can easily say "no" to things that are urgent but not important—smilingly, cheerfully, guilt-free, "No!"

QUESTION & ANSWER

Q: It makes sense that you've got to have trustworthy people in your organization to have trust, but what do you do if you have customers that abuse and mishandle your trustworthy employees?

A: Fire the customers! I know of an extremely prominent organization that actually writes letters to customers who, when it becomes evident to everybody, persist in mistreating employees. They've actually said to the customers they did not want their business. However, the better and higher solution is to seek some third-alternative solution with good communication—always, of course, listening first.

Chapter 9

THE VOICE AND SPEED OF TRUST

It is a greater compliment to be trusted than to be loved.

GEORGE MACDONALD

W HEN WE SEEK to expand our influence and *Inspire Others to Find Their Voice* (remember *inspire* means to breathe life into another), we move into the world of relationships. Building strong relationships not only requires a character foundation of inner security, abundance and personal moral authority, as embodied

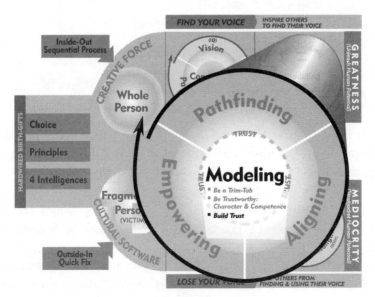

Figure 9.1

in the first part of this book, but it also involves stretching ourselves in developing vital new interpersonal SKILLS that will make us equal to the challenges we will face with others. The next two chapters on modeling are focused on developing these skills.

Almost all the work of the world is done through relationships with people and in organizations. But what is communication like when there is no trust? It's impossible. It's like walking through a minefield. What if your communication is clear and precise, yet there is no trust? You'll always be looking for hidden meanings and the hidden agenda. A lack of trust is the very definition of a bad relationship. In the words of my son, Stephen, "Low trust is the great hidden tax." In fact, this hidden tax is greater than all taxes and interest combined—hidden and unhidden!

THE SPEED OF TRUST

Now, what is communication like when there is high trust? It's easy, it's effortless, it's instantaneous. What about when there's high trust and you make mistakes? They hardly matter. People know you. "Don't worry about it, I understand." "Forget it. I know what you mean. I know you." No technology ever devised can do that. Perhaps, in a sense, this is why the heart is more important than the brain. Someone may be brain dead, but if their heart is still pumping, they live on; when your heart is dead, you're dead.

As my son, Stephen, says, "There is nothing as fast as the speed of trust." It's faster than anything you can think about. It's faster than the internet, for when trust is present, mistakes are forgiven and forgotten. Trust is the glue of life. It is the glue that holds organizations, cultures and relationships together. Ironically it comes from the speed of going slow. With people, fast is slow and slow is fast.

SEVERAL YEARS AGO I was visiting with a friend who had recently completed a major business project. I was well acquainted with his work and congratulated him on the tremendous positive impact it was having on the lives of thousands. I asked him what he had learned. He said, "You know, Stephen, I'm sure I will look back on this two-year project as one of the most important contributions of my life." Then, pausing, he slightly smiled, and with deep feeling, continued, "But my real learning was that without a unified, close relationship with my wife, it means nothing."

"Really," I replied. Sensing my interest, he then opened up and shared the following experience:

When I was first asked to take leadership of this project, I was thrilled with the opportunity. My wife and children were supportive, so I threw myself into it wholeheartedly. I felt a great weight of responsibility and was driven and energized by a sense of purpose. In the second year of the project, I worked literally day and night. The importance of the work consumed me. I felt I was doing well in staying involved in the kids' lives, including ball games and dance recitals. I usually had dinner each evening with the family. I thought I was managing pretty well. The last six months were the most intense, and it was during this time that I noticed how often my wife was becoming frustrated with me— usually over the smallest things (at least they seemed so to me). I became increasingly irritated at her lack of understanding and support of the work I was doing—especially at such a critical time. Communication became more strained—even over minor issues. When the project was finally completed, she didn't even want to go to the celebration dinner. She went, but obviously didn't enjoy herself. I knew we had to talk, really talk. So we did. And the floodgates opened.

She started to share what it was like to be "alone" all this time. Even when I was home, she felt I was somewhere else. Because our tradition of having weekly dates became much less frequent and because I usually stayed up long after she retired each night, we didn't talk and share like we used to, and she felt more and more isolated, unappreciated, and disconnected. I wasn't communicating much of anything. My nearly single-minded focus on my work and other commitments became a constant reminder of where my thoughts and feelings were not focused. She reminded me that I had even forgotten her birthday until the day was half over. And it wasn't the forgetting that was so bad, as it was a symbol of what the whole year had seemed like.

When I asked her why she hadn't opened up and shared her concerns earlier, she said she didn't want to upset me and distract me from the project. I looked in her eyes and saw deep pain and loneliness. I felt horrible. I was amazed and embarrassed that I had been so clueless. Her openness about her loneliness helped me realize how empty I had been for so long. We had both become less effective—both personally and together. I apologized and reassured her that there was no person or thing on earth more important to me than her. But my words didn't seem to get through. I realized that too many other things had communicated something different for too long. My apology and commitment to reprioritize my life helped, but it didn't make things all better overnight. It took days and weeks and months of consistent effort—talking, sharing, being there, making and keeping promises, putting aside work at the end of the day for the family, and apologizing and regrouping when I got a little off track—before the full feeling of trust and emotional connection was restored and exceeded what it had been before.

Since I visited with my friend, he has completed two more multiyear projects just as demanding and significant as the first. Yet his relationship with his wife has grown stronger through each one. His painful first experience and his increased understanding of and commitment to his wife has brought lasting change. Looking back on the contrast in his experiences, he recently shared these additional insights with me:

My real learning was that you could be deeply committed to a marriage, love your spouse, live in fidelity and loyalty toward one another, be committed to raising your children, and still have your relationship and trust deteriorate. You don't have to speak harsh, unkind words or be disrespectful to hurt someone. With one who is very close to you, all it takes is neglecting the heart, mind and spirit. Relationships and trust do not remain constant. They are maintained and deepened only as you actively nurture and build them with regular acts of kindness, consideration, appreciation and service. I learned that both the quality of our marriage and my own happiness had very little to do with what she was doing for me, and everything to do with what I was trying to do every day to foster her happiness, share her burdens, and partner with her in the things we care most about. I've learned that unity in my relationship with my wife is one of the greatest, enabling sources of power of my life—not only in our most significant work in the family and community together, but in every area of my life, including professionally. It creates a well of strength, peace, joy, belonging and energy that fuels my best work, creativity and drive to contribute.

Finally, I'm learning that strong relationships require real effort and sacrifice. They require putting someone else's well-being, growth and happiness before your own. And oh, how it's worth it! For such effort is the door to our own happiness. What would we do without the pull of such relationships that help us get outside ourselves and become equal to our potential?

MORAL AUTHORITY AND THE SPEED OF TRUST

My friend's experience is a tremendous illustration of the reality that relationships are governed by natural laws. Enduring trust in a relationship cannot be faked, and it is rarely produced by a dramatic, onetime effort. It is the fruit of regular actions inspired by the conscience and heart. In *The 7 Habits of Highly Effective People*, I introduced a metaphor for trust called the Emotional Bank Account. It is like a financial bank account into which you make deposits and take out withdrawals—only in this case, you make emotional deposits and withdrawals in your relationships that either build or destroy them. Like any metaphor, if you push it far enough, it has its limitations. But generally it is a powerful and simple way of communicating the quality of a relationship.

The diagram below lists ten key deposits and withdrawals we can make with others that, in my experience, have a profound impact on the level of trust in our relationships. It also lists the *sacrifices* required and *principles* embodied in each deposit (table 4):

MORAL AUTHORITY AND THE SPEED OF TRUST			
DEPOSITS	**WITHDRAWALS**	**SACRIFICE REQUIRED**	**INTERNALIZED PRINCIPLES**
Seek first to understand	*Seek first to be understood*	Impatience, Ego, Your agenda	Mutual Understanding
Keeping promises	*Breaking promises*	Moods, Feelings, Emotions, Time	Integrity/Execution
Honesty, openness	*Smooth manipulation*	Ego, Arrogance, Control	Vision/Values, Integrity/Execution Mutual Understanding
Kindnesses, courtesies	*Unkindnesses, discourtesies*	Self, Time, Perceptions, Stereotypes, Prejudices	Vision/Values Integrity/Execution
Win-Win or No Deal thinking	*Win-Lose or Lose-Win thinking*	"Winning means to beat," Competitiveness	Mutual Respect/Benefit
Clarifying expectations	*Violating expectations*	Kiss-up style communication	Mutual Respect/Benefit Mutual Understanding, Creative Cooperation, Renewal
Loyalty to the absent	*Disloyalty, duplicity*	Some social acceptance, Heart Massage	Vision/Values, Integrity/Execution
Apologies	*Pride, conceit, arrogance*	Ego, Arrogance, Pride, Time	Vision/Values, Integrity/Execution
Receiving feedback and giving "I" messages	*Not receiving feedback and giving "You" messages*	Ego, Arrogance, Pride Reactive Communication	Mutual Understanding
Forgiveness	*Holding grudges*	Pride, Self-Centeredness	Vision/Values, Integrity/Execution

Table 4

It's important to recognize that the reason the ten deposits build trust is that they embody principles central to human relationships. When you study each of those ten deposits, what would you say are the common elements? I suggest that *one* common denominator of the deposits is *initiative*, which is made up of willpower and determination. You'll notice that every one of them lies within your own power to do. Every one of them lies within your own ability to influence. Because they are based on principles, they produce moral authority or trust. You can see how there is no way you can make those deposits, exercise that courage, that initiative, that determination, without the ability to do the "twenty emotional personal push-ups" at the personal level.

What is the second common characteristic of the deposits? I suggest it's the absence of selfishness and the presence of *humility*. It's the willingness to subordinate oneself to another person, to a principle, or to a higher cause. It's realizing that life is not just about me and mine; using the words of the philosopher Martin Buber, it's about "I and Thou"—feeling profound reverence for the worth and potential of every person.

Moral authority, trust and bonding can evaporate over time in the absence of making continual deposits, particularly with people we work and live around all of the time. This is so because their expectations are so much higher. With people we haven't seen for years, we can often pick up where we left off. The trust and bonding and love are restored immediately because there are simply no expectations of continual depositing.

> Moral Authority: The principled exercise of free choice, which almost always involves some form of sacrifice.

A third common characteristic is that, like most worthwhile things in life, they require a *sacrifice*. (Remember, a good definition of sacrifice is giving up something—even something good—for something better.)

If you are already familiar with the Emotional Bank Account, I encourage you to see it here with new eyes and open yourself to new, added insights that will enable you to find your voice and inspire others to find theirs. You'll notice that each deposit represents a choice to use your birth-gifts in an effort to sacrifice an ineffective personal habit and replace it with an action that builds moral authority in relationships with others.

No system can long command the loyalties of men and women which does not expect of them certain measures of discipline, and particularly self-discipline. The cost in comfort may be great. The sacrifice may be real. But this very demanding reality is the substance of which comes character and strength and nobility. Permissiveness never produced greatness. Integrity, loyalty, and strength are virtues whose sinews are developed through the struggles that go on within as we practice self-discipline under the demands of divinely spoken truth.[1]

GORDON B. HINCKLEY

SEEKING FIRST TO UNDERSTAND

Why would *Seek First to Understand* be the first deposit? One simple reason. You do not know what a deposit is to another person until you understand them from their frame of reference. What may be a high-level deposit to you may be a low-level deposit to another, or even a withdrawal. What may be an important promise to you may be unimportant to another. How you express your honesty, openness, kindness and courtesy may be perceived completely differently when seen by others through their unique cultural or personal filters. While the underlying principles of each deposit hold true in every situation, it requires an understanding of others within *their* frame of reference to know how to specifically implement the practice.

After learning of the idea of making deposits into the Emotional Bank Account, one woman decided she was going to try it out. This is what she shared with me about her experience:

I decided I would do something special for my husband to improve our relationship. I figured that having the kids in clean clothes when he got home and getting the laundry done quicker would really make him happier.

After about two weeks of being Miss Superwasherwoman with no feedback from him—I mean nothing, I don't even think he had a clue—I started getting a little ticked. "This stuff ain't worth nothin'," I thought. Then, suddenly, one night when he'd gone thoughtlessly to sleep between clean sheets, I saw the light-bulb click on above my head.

"Oh my gosh. He doesn't give a hoot about Zac's clean face or his clean jeans. That's what makes me *happy. He'd rather have me scratch his back or organize a date for Friday night."* I could have kicked myself. Here I was killing myself over laundry and making all these deposits that didn't mean a thing to him.

I learned a simple truth in a very laborious way: A deposit must mean some- thing to the other person.

I've had countless experiences of my own with the enabling power of seeking to understand another. I will never forget being invited by a very prestigious, high-level executive to give my analysis and recommenda- tions regarding the selection of a new university president. It was one of the most profound communication experiences I've ever had. He left his office to come into the outer office, where I was awaiting my appoint- ment. After greeting me, he graciously ushered me into his office and had me sit right next to him, in front of his desk, where we could talk eye-to-eye without any physical structure between us. He basically said, "Stephen, thank you so much for coming in. I'm anxious to understand whatever you want me to understand."

I had prepared for this visit for a considerable period of time and had developed an outline of my presentation. I gave him a copy of the out- line and covered it slowly, point by point. Except for a few clarifying questions, he never interrupted. He listened so intently and completely that when my thirty-minute presentation was over, I felt completely understood. He made absolutely no comment—neither agreeing, dis- agreeing, or committing. But at the end he simply stood up, looked me in the eye, and, as he shook my hand, expressed how much he appreci- ated and admired me. That was it. I was profoundly moved by his open- ness, humility, graciousness and deep listening, and overwhelmed with a sense of gratitude and loyalty. Because I felt so completely understood and knew that my input had been genuinely listened to and respected, I was fully prepared to support whatever decision was made.

Even though I had been with this gentleman many times before, that face-to-face, one-on-one genuine communication experience conferred upon him such moral authority in my eyes that I never needed another visit or experience with him to renew it or to restore it. It is amazing to me even at this writing to feel the impact of such a precious conversa- tion.

MAKING AND KEEPING PROMISES

Nothing destroys trust faster than making and breaking a promise. Conversely, nothing builds and strengthens trust more than *keeping a promise* you make.

It's easy to make a promise. It usually satisfies another quickly—particularly when they're stressed or anxious about something they need you to fix. When they're happy with the promise, they like you. And we like to be liked.

That which we desire most earnestly we believe most easily. All kinds of people are suckered into deals and agreements because they want something so badly they'll believe most any explanation, story or promise of getting it. They turn a blind eye to negative information and go on in their believing.

But *promise keeping is hard.* It usually involves a painful sacrificial process—especially when the pleasant promise-making mood passes or when hard realities descend or circumstances change.

I've trained myself to never ("never say never") use the word *promise* unless I'm totally prepared to pay whatever the price is to keep it, especially with my children. They've often begged me to say "promise." Then they would feel at peace knowing I would come through—almost as if they had whatever they wanted *now.* But many times I was sorely tempted to say "I promise" just to quickly satisfy them and keep the peace at the moment. "I'll try" or "it's my goal" or "I hope to" wouldn't satisfy. Only "I promise."

Occasionally when circumstances outside my control changed, I would ask my children to understand and relieve me of the promise. In most cases they understood and relieved me. But my younger children usually didn't understand. Even though they *said* they did and freed me of the promise intellectually, they really didn't emotionally. So I kept the promise unless it was very unwise to do so. In such cases I would have to temporarily live with the diminished trust and try to rebuild it slowly in other ways.

HONESTY AND INTEGRITY

Basketball coach legend Rick Pitino captured the principle of honesty simply and profoundly: "Lying makes a problem part of the future; truth makes a problem part of the past."[2]

I remember working once with a building contractor who was unbelievably upfront and open about the challenges he was facing, even the mistakes he had made on our project. He took responsibility for the mistakes. He gave such consistent, complete financial accounting, along with all the options we could take at various stages of construction, that I absolutely and instinctively trusted the man and relied on his word from then on. I knew that if anything, he would put our interests ahead of his own. His willingness to put his integrity and our relationship above his pride and natural desire to both hide his mistakes and avoid embarrassment formed an unusual bond of trust between us. That trust earned him a great deal of business. I've also had the opposite experience several times with the same kinds of construction challenges.

> *No man for any considerable period can*
> *wear one face to himself, and another to*
> *the multitude without finally getting*
> *bewildered as to which may be true.*[3]
> NATHANIEL HAWTHORNE

Another time when I was working at a university, I had the privilege of hosting a prominent psychologist who was the former president of a national psychological association. This man was considered the father of "integrity therapy," a method of psychological treatment based on the idea that peace of mind, true happiness and balance are a function of living a life of integrity to conscience. He believed that conscience tapped into the universal sense of right and wrong common to all enduring cultures, religions and societies throughout time.

One afternoon between lectures, I drove him into the mountains to see the breathtaking views. I took the opportunity to ask him how he'd come to believe in integrity therapy.

He said, "It was very personal. I was a manic-depressive, and most of my whole life had been a series of highs and lows. Over time, as I counseled people, I would begin to feel stressed and very vulnerable. I would start slipping into depression—almost to the point where I wanted to take my life. I had enough awareness of what was happening, because of my professional education and work, to know that I was dangerous. At this point, I would institutionalize myself to preclude taking my life. After a month or two, I would come out and go back into my work. Then, after a year or so, I would slip back into it, hospitalize myself, and gradually come back to go on with my research and writing."

He continued, "At one point when I was president of the association, I became so ill, so depressed, that I was unable to go to the meetings and take up the gavel of my office. At that point, I asked myself, 'Is it possible I'm working out of the wrong framework in my life and profession?' I knew deep inside that I had been living a lie for many years. There was a dark part of my life that I had not owned up to."

As we were driving along and he began to share these things, I became very sobered and humbled. I was also a little scared of what he might say. He continued, "I decided to make a major break. I gave up my mistress. I came clean with my wife. And for the first time in many years, I had peace—a kind of peace that was different from what I had experienced when I came out of my depressions and went back into productive work. It was an inner peace of mind, a kind of self-honesty, a kind of self-unity, an integrity.

"That's when I began to explore the theory that perhaps many of the problems I had were the result of the natural conscience being ignored, denied, violated, creating a loss of personal integrity. So I began to work with this idea. I researched it. I involved other clinicians, who began working from this paradigm with their patients. I became convinced from the data that this was the case. And that's what got me into integrity therapy."

This man's openness and the depth of his conviction powerfully impressed me, as it did hundreds of students the following day in a university forum where, to my surprise, he related the same story. Modeling and openness were central to his therapeutic approach. I am also impressed with how clear it became to him that personal integrity is central not only to all our relationships but also to our psychological health and our power to be effective in our chosen life pursuits.

KINDNESSES AND COURTESIES

With people, little things are the big things. I once had a student come to me at the end of the semester and essentially say after praising the class, "Dr. Covey, you are an expert in human relations, but you don't even know my name."

He was right. I was chagrined, embarrassed and properly chastened. I have to deal with my tendency to submerge myself in intellectual conceptualization, task orientation and efficiency all the time. You see, until relationships are strong and purposes are shared, that efficiency is ineffective, particularly with insecure, "high-maintenance" people. Not so with things. Things have no feelings. People do, even so-called big people, VIPs. Small courtesies and kindnesses given consistently yield huge dividends. This is the realm of EQ.

On the other hand, people see through superficial, "kind" techniques and know when they are being manipulated. Genuine kindness, courtesy and respect come from a deep character reservoir of SQ and even obviate the necessity for a lot of social niceties and ceremonial-type courtesies.

Often when I speak to children at home or school, I tell them that if they will learn and use four expressions (totaling only ten words) sincerely and consistently, they can get what they want in most cases.

One word—"please."

Two words—"thank you."

Three words—"I love you."

Four words—"How may I help?"

Adults are big children.

THINKING WIN-WIN OR NO DEAL

Win-lose thinking is *the* underlying assumption of almost all negotiations and problem solving. It comes from society's scarcity mind-set, which says the more the other guy wins or gets, the less there is for me. The goal is to get what *you* want—which usually means figuring out how to manipulate or gain the advantage over the other guy to get him to concede as much as possible. Many try to work out differences with others, even family members, in the same way. Both parties battle it out until one concedes or they settle on a compromise.

I remember making a presentation in which I taught the idea that the key to breaking out of this win-lose mind-set is to become emotionally and mentally settled on championing the other party's "win" as much as your own. It requires courage, abundant thinking, and great creativity to not settle on anything that is a compromise for either party. I taught that a further key was to begin with a No Deal option. In fact, until No Deal is a viable option in your own mind, that is, until you are totally prepared to go for No Deal, to walk away, to agree to disagree agreeably unless both parties actually feel it is a win for them, you'll find yourself manipulating and often pressuring or intimidating others to go along with your win. But when No Deal is truly a viable option, you can honestly say to the other, "Unless this is a true win for you and you deeply and sincerely feel it, and unless it's a true win for me and I deeply and sincerely feel it, let's agree right now to go for No Deal." That process is so liberating, so freeing, and it requires such a combination of humility and kindness with strength and courage that once it is truly hammered out, both parties are transformed; such intense bonding takes place that afterwards they will always be loyal to each other in each other's absence.

After the presentation, a man who had been sitting on the front row came up to me to thank me for this very timely idea. He represented Disney-Epcot and said he intended to practice it the very next day in a situation regarding the showcasing of a particular country at the Epcot Center. He explained that the people who were willing to supply much of the financing wanted a country exhibit that Disney felt would not hold enough general interest. They were feeling pressure to compromise in order to get the funding and development moving on time. But now he saw a new option.

He later reported to me that he respectfully said to the funding source, "We really want to go for a win-win agreement and relationship with you. We certainly need the financing you're offering. But given our fundamental differences, we've concluded that if our agreement and joint project isn't genuinely going to be a *big* win for both of us, it would be better to go for a 'no deal.' " As soon as the funding source sensed his sincerity, openness and honesty of expression, they themselves stopped manipulating and pressuring. They backed up, regrouped, and then began genuine communication until a truly synergistic win-win arrangement was made.

You'll notice that the power of this Think Win-Win or No Deal deposit lies in the initial willingness to sacrifice—to suspend your own interests long enough to understand what the other person wants most, and why, so that you can then go to work together on a new, creative solution that encompasses *both* of your interests.

CLARIFYING EXPECTATIONS

Clarifying expectations is really a combination of all the other deposits mentioned because of the amount of mutual understanding and respect required to drive such communication, particularly when it is about clarifying expectations about *roles* and *goals*. If you study the underlying roots of almost all communication breakdowns, or broken, sick cultures, you'll find they come from either ambiguous or broken expectations around *roles* and *goals:* in other words, who is to do what role and what are the high-priority goals of those roles.

Once I remember doing some team building with the top executives of a large restaurant association. It became so obvious that there were conflicting priorities and goals that could no longer be ignored or tolerated without terrible consequences for the entire organization. I simply took two flipcharts and at the top of each put, "How you see MY roles and goals," and "How you see YOUR roles and goals." No judgments, no agreements or disagreements were expressed until both charts were filled out to the satisfaction of those filling them out. Just as soon as everyone could see with their own eyes that these seemingly irreconcilable differences were totally a function of differing expectations about roles and goals, humility and respect were restored. They were able to begin sincere communication in clarifying expectations.

BEING LOYAL TO THOSE NOT PRESENT

Being loyal to those not present is one of the most difficult of all the deposits. It is one of the highest tests of both character and the depth of bonding that has taken place in a relationship. This is particularly the case when everyone seems to be joining in on bad-mouthing and piling on someone who is not present. You can, in an unself-righteous way, just speak up and say, "I see it differently," or "My experience is different," or "You may have a point; let's go talk to him or her about it." By doing so, you instantly communicate that integrity is loyalty—not just to those absent but also to those who are present. Whether they acknowledge it or not, all the people present will inwardly admire and respect you. They will know that their name is precious with you when they're not there. On the other hand, when loyalty is a higher value than integrity in that you give in, go along, and join in the bad-mouthing, so, too, will everyone present know that under pressure and stress, you would do the same regarding them.

I remember heading up a meeting in a large organization where the formal leaders were discussing various personnel issues. They seemed to be in complete agreement regarding the weaknesses of a particular individual. They even began to tell jokes and funny stories about this individual in ways they would never do to the person's face. Later the same day one of the executives came to me and said that for the first time he could now trust my expressions of appreciation and affection for him. "Why so?" I asked. He replied, "Because when we were cutting that person in our earlier meeting, you went against the current and showed genuine concern, care and regard for them." I asked why that had impacted him. He said, "Because I have similar weaknesses, only they're worse. No one knows about them, not even you. So every time you've expressed your appreciation and regard for me, inwardly I've said, 'But you don't understand.' Today I feel you would. I feel you would be true and loyal to me even in my absence and that I can trust you and believe your kind expressions."

The key to the many is often the one; it is how you regard and talk about the one in that one's absence or presence that communicates to the many how you would regard and talk about them in their presence or absence.

APOLOGIZING

To learn to say "I was wrong, I'm sorry," or "I was on an ego trip, I overreacted, I ignored you, and I temporarily put loyalty above integrity"—and then to live accordingly is one of the most powerful forms of *apology* you can make. I have seen relationships that have been broken for years redeemed in a relatively short period of time with the depth and sincerity of such an apology. If you said something under the heat of the moment but did not really mean it, when you apologize explain how you were driven by your pride and what you really meant. If you said it in the heat of the moment and did mean it, then the nature of the apology will require you to actually change your heart, to privately repent until you can sincerely say, "I'm sorry; I was wrong in word and deed, and I'm working to correct both."

I remember once having an unpleasant confrontation with an individual on a very jugular issue. The feelings affected the genuineness of our communication from then on, even though on the surface it seemed polite and pleasant. Then one day he came to me and said he felt sad about the strain in our relationship and wanted to restore it to its former unity and harmony. He said it was one of the most difficult things for him to do—to look into his own heart and see where he had gone wrong. He really wanted to apologize. His apology was so humble and sincere without any form of self-justification that it caused me to look into my own heart and take responsibility for my part. We were knitted together again.

A former colleague told me once of an experience she had working with a high-level executive team at a weeklong retreat. The president began one morning by encouraging the group to really seek to listen to and understand others in their discussions before making their own points. Before moving on in the meeting, he shared a powerful personal experience illustrating his point.

What follows is her brief account (the names have been changed, as they have been in many of the stories included in this book) of what happened later that afternoon:

In the middle of our discussions, a rather obnoxious exec started to say something about a business approach he was struggling with. The group verbally pounced on him. To be honest, I would have liked to pounce on him myself, but knew it wasn't my place. Then I heard Jack, the president, laughing out loud, right in this guy's face. He was actually making fun of him in front of the whole group. Of course, the group jumped on the bandwagon.

I was stunned. Only a few hours before, the president had shared this moving experience about the value of waiting your turn, trying to understand a person's actions. Now he was doing the very opposite. I couldn't very well reprimand him in front of the whole group. So, I just glared at him. He read me loud and clear. "That was ugly. If you don't do something to rectify this right now, I'll walk out!" Really. I was so angry, I was ready to walk out on the whole group. They had just reverted to their old, combative behavior and poisonous group dynamics.

He stared back at me. I pulled myself up taller in my seat and glared, "Back at you, pal." He shrunk back in his seat. I kept on looking right at him. This went on for about five minutes, during which his team members were still crucifying the poor guy. Then all of a sudden, the president stopped the meeting. He said, "Stop, I did something wrong. David, I want to ask your forgiveness."

"For what?" David was a bit baffled. Things were normal as far as he knew.

"That was inappropriate of me. I shouldn't have laughed. We didn't listen at all. We just jumped right on you. Will you forgive me?"

I thought that David, this senior VP, would say something like, "No problem. Don't worry about it." But his response was amazing: "Jack, I forgive you. Thank you." Do you realize how much more courage it takes to actively forgive rather than trying to forget something happened?

I sat there. I was overwhelmed with emotion by Jack's behavior. He didn't have to apologize. He didn't have to seek forgiveness in front of the whole group. He's the head of an eighty-thousand-person division. He doesn't have to do anything he doesn't want to. After the meeting, I went up to him, with emotion still in my voice, and said, "Thank you for doing that." He replied, "It was the right thing to do. Thank you for glaring at me." We didn't speak about that incident again. But we both know that we had risen to our best that day.

GIVING AND RECEIVING FEEDBACK

The students I am closest to from my years as a teacher are those I gave strong feedback to. "You're better than that. I won't let you off the hook. There are no excuses. You can pay the price." Many have told me that holding them to the responsible course—having them live with the full consequences of their actions—was a life-changing, defining moment, though hard for both of us at the time.

Giving negative *feedback* is one of the most difficult communications there is. It is also one of the most needed. So many people have serious blind spots they never come to grips with because no one knows how to give them feedback. People are too fearful of rupturing a relationship or of having their personal future compromised by "taking on" their boss.

The hypocrisy in the belittling situation in Jack's story became so evident to the offender that it wasn't an issue of having a blind spot: it was one of ego. The courage and integrity of the woman who gave the feedback were more powerful than status and position. That's why it worked. Sometimes it isn't more powerful and won't work, which may necessitate going to the person privately and making a reconciliation. The best way to give feedback in a private circumstance is to describe *yourself*, not the person. Describe your feelings, your concerns or your perceptions of what was happening rather than accusing, judging and labeling the person. This approach often causes the other person to become open to information about his or her blind spot without being so personally threatened.

People in authority should make pushing back and *giving feedback* legitimate. When you do receive feedback, you need to speak explicitly about it and express gratitude for it, however much it may hurt. If you don't do this explicitly, a norm will develop which basically says that giving negative feedback and pushing back is a form of disloyalty and insubordination. Making "pushing back" legitimate, even a social norm, also frees the person with formal authority so that he or she can also "push back" without fearing it will hurt feelings, rupture a relationship or be taken as "the final word."

We all need feedback, particularly about our blind spots—those tender areas of weakness that we defend. This is why personal growth is so vital, because blind spots are not so tender. One's sense of worth is intrinsic and doesn't come from a particular weakness, known or blind.

I remember once having a strain with one of my neighbors because of how difficult it was for him to live so close to our large, noisy, sometimes disrespectful family—complete with a barking dog and glaring lights early in the morning and late at night, etc. I went to him and basically said that I wanted us to be good neighbors and would appreciate his giving me feedback about what we could do to improve things. He hesitated to speak, so I primed the pump a little by describing what it must be like to live next door to us. He then opened up with a gush of feelings, complaints and concerns that he and his wife had. But the more I listened, the more he seemed almost overwhelmed by my seeking this feedback, respecting it and trying to involve my family in an effort to improve. He also acknowledged that he had overreacted to many things and had blown the whole thing out of proportion—that much of what he was talking about was the inevitable chatter, complexity and confusion of a large family's comings and goings. As we parted he said how grateful he was for the visit and how relieved he was.

FORGIVING

> *Anger is an acid that can do more harm to the vessel in which it stands than to anything on which it is poured.*
>
> MAHATMA GANDHI

True *forgiveness* involves forgetting, letting it go, and moving on. While I was away on a business trip once I received a call from one of my managers, who wanted to resign because of how he was being criticized by his immediate superior. I asked him to hold off from making such a rash decision until we could get together. He said, "I'm not calling to counsel with you; I'm calling to inform you. I'm resigning." I realized then that I had not listened to him, which I then proceeded to do. He then opened up a Pandora's box of experiences, complaints and feelings, including even stronger ones from his wife. As I genuinely listened, the negative energy in his expression was dissipated, and on his own he agreed to visit with me as soon as I returned.

When I returned he brought his wife to my office, and they were pleasant on the surface. But as soon as we began to discuss the real issues, the deep anger and resentment gushed forth. I continued to listen until they felt understood, and then they became very open. I then taught them about the space between stimulus and response and how the greatest harm is not in what people do to us but in our response to what they do to us. They initially thought I was manipulating to get him to stay on. So I continued listening until other issues were expressed and understood, including how these issues at work had affected their own marriage and family life. It was truly like peeling off the layers of an onion until you reach the soft inner core.

By this time they were extremely open and teachable, so I emphasized again their power of choice and that they might consider asking his superior's forgiveness for the resentment and anger the manager held for his superior. His response was, "What do you mean? You've turned this whole thing about. It's not for *us* to seek forgiveness—it's for *him* to seek *our* forgiveness."

More negative energy was released until they were extremely open to the whole idea that no one can do us any harm without our consent and that our chosen response is the key determiner of our life—that we are a product of our decisions, not our conditions. They were very humbled and agreed to think about it. He later called me on the phone and said that he had come to see the wisdom of the principle we'd discussed and accepted it, that he had gone to his boss and asked for forgiveness, that his boss was literally overwhelmed by this expression, that he in turn had asked his forgiveness, and that it had restored their relationship. My friend said to me that he and his wife had reached such a point of accepting the space between stimulus and response and the power of choice

> *Forgiveness breaks the chain of causality, because*
> *he who "forgives" you—out of love—takes upon*
> *himself the consequences of what you have done.*
> *Forgiveness, therefore, always entails a sacrifice.*[4]
>
> DAG HAMMARSKJÖLD

that even if they had been rebuffed in their sincere seeking of forgiveness, he was determined to stay on and make a success of things as best he could.

It isn't the poisonous snake bite that does the serious harm. It's chasing that snake that drives the venom to the heart. Because we all make mistakes, we all need to forgive and be forgiven. It is better to focus on our own mistakes and ask forgiveness than to focus on other people's mistakes, wait for them to ask for forgiveness first, or give it begrudgingly if they do. It is better to have the spirit of the one who prayed, "Oh Lord, please help me to forgive those who sin differently than I." In this same spirit, C.S. Lewis said:

> When I come to my evening prayers and try to reckon up the sins of the day, nine times out of ten the most obvious one is some sin against charity; I have sulked or snapped or sneered or snubbed or stormed. And the excuse that immediately springs to mind is that the provocation was so sudden or unexpected. I was caught off my guard, I had not time to collect myself. . . . Surely what a man does when he is taken off guard is the best evidence for what sort of man he is. Surely what pops out before the man has time to put on a disguise is the truth. If there are rats in the cellar you are most likely to see them if you go in very suddenly. But the suddenness does not create the rats; it only prevents them from hiding. In the same way the suddenness of the provocation does not make me an ill-tempered man: it only shows me what an ill-tempered man I am. . . . Now that cellar is out of reach of my conscious will . . . I cannot, by direct moral effort, give myself new motives. After the first few steps . . . we realize that everything which really needs to be done in our souls can be done only by God.[5]

A FINAL WORD ON TRUST

Much of my focus in this chapter on Building Trust has been on things we can consciously do to build relationships of trust with others—on creating *trust*, the noun.

But remember, *trust* is also a *verb*. I started Part 2 of this book with a story of how early in my adult life someone saw potential within me that far exceeded what I saw in myself. He saw beneath the surface, beyond the obvious and evident. He looked into my heart and eyes and spirit and saw the raw, undeveloped, unseen seeds of greatness that lie within each one of us.

So he en*trusted* me with a charge and responsibility far beyond my experience and perceived ability. He *gave* me his trust, without evidence, without proof. He simply believed and expected I would rise to the challenge, and he treated me accordingly. It was an act of faith. But that act of faith so affirmed my worth and potential that I was inspired to see it in myself. His faith in me increased my own faith and vision of myself. I aspired to the highest and most noble inclinations within me. I was not perfect, but how I grew! It also became a philosophy of life to me. Affirm people. Affirm your children. Believe in them, not in what you see but in what you don't see—their potential.

True and profound are the words of the poet Goethe, who said, "Treat a man as he is and he will remain as he is; treat a man as he can and should be and he will become as he can and should be."

> Trust becomes a verb when you communicate to others their worth and potential so clearly that they are inspired to see it in themselves.

Trust is not only the fruit of trustworthiness; it is also the root of motivation. It is the highest form of motivation. *Love* also becomes a verb. It is something you do; you love or serve others; you trust others; you see their worth and potential and provide opportunity and nourishment and encouragement. If they do not live true to this trust, it will deteriorate and they will not be inspired to see their own worth and potential. They won't have the ability to communicate to others their worth and potential. To them, *trust* will not be a verb. In fact, it will be very hard for an untrustworthy person to trust anybody or to believe in anybody in a sustainable way.

Allow me to illustrate, with a story I share often, how *love*, like *trust*, can become a verb. At one seminar where I was speaking a man came up and said, "Stephen, I like what you're saying. But every situation is so different. Look at my marriage. I'm really worried. My wife and I just don't have the same feelings for each other we used to have. I guess I just don't love her anymore and she doesn't love me. What can I do?"

"The feeling isn't there anymore?" I asked.

"That's right," he reaffirmed. "And we have three children we're really concerned about. What do you suggest?"

"Love her," I replied.

"I told you, the feeling just isn't there anymore."

"Love her."

"You don't understand. The feeling of love just isn't there."

"Then love her. If the feeling isn't there, that's a good reason to love her."

"But how do you love when you don't love?"

"My friend, *love* is a verb. *Love*—the feeling—is a fruit of *love* the verb. So love her. Sacrifice. Listen to her. Empathize. Appreciate. Affirm her. Are you willing to do that?"

In the great literature of all progressive societies, *love* is a verb. Reactive people make it a feeling. They're driven by feelings. Hollywood has generally scripted us to believe that we are not responsible, that love is a feeling. But the Hollywood script does not describe the reality. If our feelings control our actions, it is because we have abdicated our responsibility and empowered them to do so.

Proactive people make *love* a verb. Love is something you do: the sacrifices you make, the giving of self, like a mother bringing a newborn into the world. If you want to study love, study those who sacrifice for others, even for people who offend or do not love in return. If you are a parent, look at the love you have for the children you sacrificed for. Love is a value that is actualized through loving actions. Proactive people subordinate feelings to values. Love, the feeling, can be recaptured.

Where is the very best place to give trust, to communicate people's worth and potential? Without any question, it's the family. If the family is dysfunctional, where is the next best place? The school. The teacher becomes like a surrogate parent who begins the trusting process again.

Remember the power you hold to give your trust to others. You may open yourself to the risk of being disappointed, and you will need to be wise in the exercise of this power. But when you do, you give a priceless gift and opportunity to others. The greatest risk of all is the risk of risk-less living.

FILM: *Teacher*

I want you now to see another film that is the true story of Helen Keller and her teacher, Anne Sullivan. Helen Keller was deaf and blind; Anne Sullivan was legally blind herself and had a very neglectful and abusive childhood herself—but transcended it by finding meaning in serving one student, Helen Keller.

The life and contributions of Helen Keller are inspiring, amazing, and never ending. Tens of millions of people have been directly or indirectly influenced by her. But the key to Helen Keller was her teacher, Anne Sullivan. As you watch this film found on the DVD in this book, study it through the lens of the two roads—the upper road to greatness and the lower to mediocrity. Study how, through her choices, Anne Sullivan became a person of vision, discipline, passion, governed by conscience and the moral authority that developed within her through sacrifice and overcoming adversity. Study how Helen Keller became a balanced, integrated, powerful person after living in darkness from birth. Study how the relationship of trust between Anne and Helen was formed through constant deposits, study the speedy, subtle communication that was enabled—the patience, the persistence, the understanding—and the bonding that took place.

In short, it is a beautiful story of two magnificent persons who found their own voices and devoted their lives to inspiring others to find theirs—"breathing life into" countless numbers throughout the world.

QUESTION & ANSWER

Q: How do you improve attitude? There's nothing more cancerous to an organization than negative attitudes. How do you deal with that?

A: Let me attempt an answer at three levels:

First, at the personal level, be an example of one with a positive attitude—one who avoids the metastasizing cancers of complaining, criticizing, comparing, competing and contending. Seriously, there is nothing more powerful than to be around a person who is a light, not a judge; who is a model, not a critic.

Second, give a little personal one-on-one time to build a relationship with the person who seems to have a sour or negative attitude. Negative attitudes are really a symptom of deeper things going on. People need to feel understood. Seeking to understand another is so therapeutic, so healing and so affirming to them that oftentimes you end up working on the roots rather than just sniping about the lack of fruits.

Third, sometimes there are other forces at play stronger than your example or your relationship with a person. Sometimes you simply have to smile and not obsess about it. This keeps the negativity cancer from metastasizing. Remember, when you build your emotional life on the weaknesses of others, including their negative attitudes, you disempower yourself and empower their negative attitudes to continue to metastasize their cancer cells through the culture. You can't change all things; you can't change people; you can only change yourself. However, I have found that sometimes if people can develop a skill or competency that is in alignment with a fundamental gift or talent that they have, their attitude toward themselves, toward others and toward life significantly improves. For example, let's say you're going to try to teach someone to play tennis. Would it be best to talk to them about their attitude if they seemed a little low or discouraged and negative? Would it be best to give them more knowledge about ground strokes and volleys? Or would it simply be best to get out there on the court, take the skill route, and have them literally practice the skills until they wanted more knowledge? You would then find their attitude naturally becoming more positive as they come to enjoy the game. These are three routes to make improvements: knowledge, skill and attitude. Most people focus on the attitude and knowledge routes. I suggest the key to those two is the skill route—people simply feel better about themselves and about life when they're good at something.

Q: **What is the best advice you've ever given as it relates to motivation?**

A: First, I would say be an example and a model and then affirm the worth and potential of other people so clearly that they come to see it in themselves—not just through your words but also through aligned reinforcing systems and incentives. We need to realize that both intrinsic and extrinsic motivations are important. The fire inside people is like a match; the way to ignite that flame is initially through friction, then other matches are lit through warmth. I'm not big on giving a lot of psych-up speeches, even though I do believe in enthusiasm. I like Ken Blanchard's teaching about catching people doing things right. They need to feel valued and appreciated, but they also need to feel that the work they are engaged in is worthy of their commitment and their best effort.

Q: In the world of the internet, where you can often escape from face-to-face, how do you optimize new technologies in a way that doesn't depersonalize the workplace but still get the increased efficiencies that the new technologies can bring?

A: In my judgment high-tech works in the long run only with high touch. Once you have a relationship, you can then think efficiently and operate efficiently. Technology enables you to be efficient, but it cannot take the place of the relationship. Remember, with people fast is slow and slow is fast. Technology, like the body, is a good servant but a bad master.

Chapter 10

BLENDING VOICES— SEARCHING FOR THE THIRD ALTERNATIVE

Leaders do not avoid, repress, or deny conflict, but rather see it as an opportunity.[1]

WARREN BENNIS

I AM CONVINCED that one of the most difficult and challenging problems of life, whether at home, at work, or elsewhere, is how you deal with conflict—how you deal with human differences. Think about your challenges—is this not so? What if you had the character

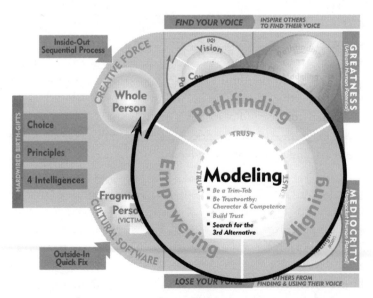

Figure 10.1

and the SKILL to resolve differences synergistically—that is, to find solutions that are better than those anyone has proposed? The capacity
and ability to produce such synergistic solutions, such creative cooperation, is built upon the foundation of *moral authority* at the personal level
and *trust* in relationships.

I ONCE HEARD Gandhi's granddaughter, Arun Gandhi, share this penetrating insight about her grandfather. All in attendance at her speech
were both humbled and electrified:

> Ironically, if it hadn't been for racism and prejudice, we may not have
> had a Gandhi. He may have been just another successful lawyer who
> had made a lot of money. But because of prejudice in South Africa, he
> was subjected to humiliation within a week of his arrival. He was
> thrown off a train because of the color of his skin, and it humiliated him
> so much that he sat on the platform of the station all night wondering
> what he could do to gain justice. His first response was one of anger. He
> was so angry that he wanted eye-for-eye justice. He wanted to respond
> violently to the people who humiliated him. But he stopped himself and
> said, "That's not right." It was not going to get him justice. It might
> have made him feel good for the moment, but it wasn't going to get him
> any justice.
>
> The second response was to want to go back to India and live among
> his own people in dignity. He ruled that out also. He said, "You can't
> run away from problems. You've got to stay and face the problems."
> And that's when the third response dawned on him—the response of
> nonviolent action. From that point onwards, he developed the philoso-
> phy of nonviolence and practiced it in his life as well as in his search for
> justice in South Africa. He ended up staying in that country for twenty-
> two years, and then he went and led the movement of India.[2]

The Third Alternative isn't my way, it isn't your way—it's *our* way.
It's not a compromise halfway between your way and my way; it's better
than a compromise. A third alternative is what the Buddhists call the
middle way—a higher middle position that is better than either of the
other two ways, like the tip of a triangle.

The Third Alternative is a better alternative than any that have been
proposed. It is a product of sheer creative effort. It emerges from the

overlapping vulnerabilities of two or more people—from their open-ness, their willingness to really listen, their desire to search. You simply don't know where it's going to end up. All you know is that it's going to end up better than where it is now. The content may change, the spirit may change, the motive may change, even two or three of these may change—and always at least one.

As with Gandhi, the Third Alternative usually *starts* within oneself. But it often takes the force of circumstance like some person opposing you before it really begins to take place within you. Did you notice from the quote by Gandhi's granddaughter the interplay between his personal inward struggle and his interpersonal relationships? Gandhi had to do considerable *personal* work before he could deal with *relationship* challenges.

IT ONLY TAKES ONE: THE MIND-SET OF SEARCHING FOR THE THIRD ALTERNATIVE

Just as doing twenty push-ups is a physical analogy or metaphor for *personal* success, I like to use the metaphor of an arm wrestle in my teaching to illustrate both the mind-set and the skill-set of searching for and achieving a true Third Alternative. I ask the audience to send a "volunteer" who is very strong and over six feet three to come up and take me on in an arm wrestle at the front of the room. As the person is being coaxed and then is walking up, I start arrogantly telling the person to prepare to lose. I brag about my prowess, skill, strength and black belt ranking. When they finally arrive up front, I tell them to repeat after me, "I am a loser," which most cooperate in doing. I tell this monster of a person that it's not a matter of size, it's a matter of technique, and that I have it, and he doesn't. I become caustic and cutting. As intended, the audience's sympathies turn to my opponent.

We get in the arm wrestle position with right foot against right foot and grab each other's hands in the middle. I then ask the table of people who "volunteered" my opponent if they would be willing to fund the contest. In other words, if he puts my arm down to the same level as our elbows, they would pay him one dollar, and if I put him down, then I would receive a dollar. They always agree. Then I ask someone nearby to be the timer. They are to tell us when to start, give us about a minute to wrestle, count the number of times he puts me down or I put him down, and then get the people at the table from which the volunteer came to fund the whole deal ($1 for each put-down). I then make sure the funding group feels their pockets are sufficiently deep to sustain this contest. They always agree.

The timer tells us to begin. I immediately go limp, and he puts me down. And usually he's very surprised and puzzled that I didn't resist. He wonders what's going on. So we go back up to the top position, and I let him put me down again. And perhaps again. And again. All of the time he's expecting resistance. He usually starts feeling a little guilty, like he's being unfair.

And then I simply say to him, "You know what would really make you feel good would be for both of us to win as much as possible." He's usually intrigued, but because I so attacked him, he doesn't know if he can trust me. Perhaps those are just nice words—what if my real plan is to flip or manipulate him in some way to my own advantage? But as I continue to let him win with no resistance, his conscience usually becomes my advocate, and he becomes open to my suggestion that if we both win, we'll both win more. Though begrudgingly, hesitatingly, and with some struggle, he is usually finally willing to let me win one.

Then we go back to the center position. And then I let him win without any resistance. And within a few more seconds, he starts going back and forth without any resistance. Occasionally some volunteers still are puzzled and wonder what's going on. They continue to resist, but eventually it becomes free-flowing, easy, and effortless for us both. Next I say, "Now why don't we really get efficient?" Then we start just moving our wrists back and forth, which is about five times faster than moving the whole arm. Then we use both arms and double the result. Finally I say, "Now let's go over to your table and do it in front of their faces so that they can count the number of dollars they'll owe us." By this time everyone is roaring and getting the message.

> Only one-third of xQ respondents agree
> that they work in a win-win environment.

I then explain to the audience that Think Win-Win—the *mind-set* of Searching for the Third Alternative—is the idea or principle of mutual respect and mutual benefit. In the arm wrestle, even though I was *pretending* to be stronger, better, and more aggressive in order to get my opponent into a win-lose mind-set, I actually brought a win-win *inten-tion* and mind-set to the arm wrestle.

Then right away I began seeking *his* interest, his win, without resistance. Once he was then sufficiently humbled, open or guilt-tripped, he then became receptive to the idea that we could both win more if we cooperated together.

Then we became creative by first moving our wrists back and forth very rapidly, and then by bringing the other two hands together, moving them back and forth as well. The end result was truly a synergistic one, where both of us won a great deal. As for the table that had to fork up the reward money, they too won a great deal . . . of learning. Of course, no real money was exchanged. But it's a very powerful, fun and physical illustration of searching for and producing a Third Alternative.

Can you see how I had to bring the inner strength and security of a "twenty-push-up" capacity at the personal level to sustain my efforts to build trust and search for a Third Alternative? Because I had created within the other person's mind a deep competitive sense of win-lose—even to the point that he was inwardly saying, "There's no way this little bald pipsqueak is going to put me down"—I had to patiently persist in the face of my opponent's understandably fierce response to my initial fake arrogance and personal attacks.

Many people believe *both* people have to think win-win. Not so. Only one has to think it. Most people also believe that the other person must cooperate, but creative cooperation that produces Third Alternatives doesn't come until later, when you synergize. One simply has to first prepare the other for it by practicing empathy or deep listening, seeking his or her interest and consistently staying with it until the other person feels trust.

I did this on the *Oprah* show one time and had to go to great lengths to persuade the producer of the show that day to let me do it. The problem was that it had to be spontaneous, and no one would know the outcome—least of all, Oprah herself. Between the loss of control and the reality of how each show has to stand up against rating standards, the producer felt very vulnerable and skeptical. But I continued to reassure her, and Oprah and I eventually went for it.

While on the air, I similarly attacked and criticized her, told her of her weakness and my strength, and that she was going *down*. It really engaged her spirit, and she made her mind up to give it all she had. So she put me down fast and held me there. I said to her, "Oprah, why don't we both win?" She said, "No way!" I said, "Why not?" She said, "I was raised on the street; anyone talk to me that way, no way I'd give in to them." "Fair enough, Oprah, let's let you win again." Again she said, "No way!" There was no trust. I said, "Look, what we'll do is gradually come up to the center; then we'll go back on your side, and you'll win another dollar . . . and I know how bad you need that." We had fun with it, and eventually, as did she, almost everyone learns the lesson.

As the Far Eastern expression goes, "one picture is worth a thousand words." I believe that one experience is worth a thousand pictures. The audience's picture of that arm wrestle is truly worth ten thousand words, and the participant's experience is worth a thousand pictures. Perhaps you, as the reader, can envision it in your own mind, and if you want to see its power, just try it with one of your children, your spouse, or one of your associates.

You see, most people won't go through the tough work of Thinking Win-Win and Seeking First to Understand to get to the Third Alternative. It does, in fact, require a private victory; it requires considerable success at the personal level to get to the point where your security lies within you rather than in people's opinions of you or in being right. The power lies in your ability to be vulnerable, because deep down, your integrity to your value system based on principles makes you invulnerable and secure. You can afford to be open to influence and flexible. You can afford to search, not knowing where you're going to end up—knowing only that it will be better than where you and the other person are starting from.

THE SKILL-SET OF SEARCHING
FOR THE THIRD ALTERNATIVE

Communication is without question *the* most important skill in life. There are basically four modes of communication: reading, writing, speaking and listening. And most people spend two-thirds to three-fourths of their waking hours doing those four things. Of those four communication modes, the one that represents 40 to 50 percent of our communication time is *listening*—the one mode we have had the least training in. Most of us have had years and years of training in reading, writing and speaking. But no more than about 5 percent of us have had more than two weeks of formal training in how to listen.

Most people think they know how to listen because they're doing it

> Only 17 percent of workers surveyed feel that communication in
> their organizations is truly open, candid and respectful.

all the time. But really they're listening from within their own frame of
reference. Of the five levels of listening you see in the Listening Continuum below—ignoring, pretend listening, selective listening, attentive
listening and empathic listening—only the highest, empathic listening,
is done within the frame of reference of the other person. To truly listen
means to transcend your own autobiography, to get out of your frame of
reference, out of your own value system, out of your own history and
judging tendencies, and to get deeply into the frame of reference or
viewpoint of another person. This is called empathic listening. It is a
very, very rare skill. But it is more than a skill. Much more.

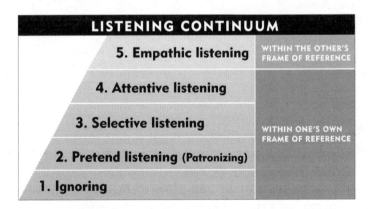

Figure 10.2

To underscore the supreme importance of communication skills, I
want you to have an experience. If you choose, you can just keep reading
and simply intellectualize this experience, but I guarantee you it won't
have anywhere near the emotional and learning impact that going
through it will have. I strongly encourage you to participate. You may
have had a similar experience through my other books, but the images
here are different. Working through the process again will reinforce
both your learning and your motivation to act upon it.

Recruit another person to do this experiment with you. First, *you, and*

> **On Listening** (an excerpt)
> *When I ask you to listen and you start giving advice, you have*
> *not done what I have asked. When I ask you to listen to me*
> *and you begin to tell me why I shouldn't feel that way, you are*
> *trampling on my feelings. When I ask you to listen and you*
> *feel you have to do something to solve my problem, you have*
> *failed me, strange as it may seem.*
> *Listen! All I asked was that you listen; not talk or do—just hear*
> *me . . . I can do for myself. I'm not helpless. Maybe discouraged*
> *and faltering, but not helpless. When you do something for me that*
> *I can and need to do for myself, you contribute to my fear and*
> *feeling of inadequacy. But when you accept as fact that I do feel*
> *what I feel, no matter how irrational, then I can quit trying to*
> *convince you and can get about the business of understanding*
> *what's behind this irrational feeling. And when that's clear, the*
> *answers are obvious and I don't need advice.*[3]
>
> RALPH ROUGHTON, M.D.

only you, look at figure 10.3 on page 194 for just one second. Then *without* looking at it yourself (it's important that you don't peek), let the other person see figure 10.4 on page 196. Finally, both of you look at figure 10.8 on page 211. Now go ahead.

What do you both see in the final picture?

Is that a picture of a young lady or a saxophone player?

Which one of you is right?

Talk to the other person to understand what they see. Listen carefully and try to see what they're seeing. Then, once you understand their point of view, explain yours to them. Help them to see what you're seeing.

What accounts for the difference in perception? Take a look at the first set of pictures that you each saw separately. What if you knew that the first picture they saw was the one on another page? Would it make more sense to you why they saw the second picture as a saxophone player? Of course it would.

When I do this little experiment with audiences, half the room is

Figure 10.3

shown the conditioning picture of the young lady for one second; the other half is shown the conditioning picture of the saxophone player. When I show the composite third picture to the whole room, half the room sees a young lady and the other half sees a saxophone player, with relatively few exceptions. They're looking at the exact same picture but with two completely different interpretations.

What follows in those training sessions is a very powerful learning experience: Both people are looking at the same object but they see different things. So I tell them to talk to their neighbor who sees it differently and to really listen to them until they understand their perspective. As soon as they see the other way to look at the picture, they're to shout out, "Ah-ha." Pretty soon, the hall is filled with triumphant *ah-ha*s. For some people, though, the learning takes a long time. I've seen people get into arguments about what the picture really stands for. They're so perturbed somebody can't see something that, to them, is so obvious, that they get upset. They get defensive, for theirs is the only way to look at the picture. On the other hand, I've seen people really drawn to each other, offering encouragement, getting really pleased when the other person sees the second aspect of the picture.

> *Creative thinking involves breaking out*
> *of established patterns in order to look at*
> *things in different ways.*
>
> EDWARD DE BONO, M.D., AUTHOR OF *LATERAL THINKING*

There are four very important things to learn about communication through this perception experience:

1. You have to be sincerely open and listen to the other person if you are to reach an understanding of *what* they see and *why* they see the world the way they do—the foundation of seeking for Third Alternatives.

2. Those things you experience *before* being presented with new information color the way you look at that information. If one second of conditioning can split a room in two, imagine what a lifetime of conditioning can do? What about in your family? How do you interpret things? People may be looking at the same exact facts, but the *meaning* of those facts is interpreted through prior personal experiences. People create meaning and act on the basis of how they perceive the world. Remember, we do not see the world as *it is*; we see the world as *we are*. Perceptions are set long before efforts to synergize. Therefore, the most significant work to be done involves communication that leads to mutual understanding.

3. There isn't just one way to interpret something. The challenge lies in creating a shared vision that accurately and honestly considers all the differing viewpoints, while still remaining true to the original vision. Who is right when challenges are interpreted differently by different people? Who is right when you and your spouse disagree? Who is right when you and your kids disagree? If you're into positional power, you'll make sure there's only one right answer. The more you invest your ego into your perception, the more rigid your mind becomes and the more frozen your responses are.

4. Most communication breakdowns are a product of semantics— how people define words. Empathy almost instantly eliminates

semantics problems. Why? Because when you really listen for understanding, you see words as symbols of meaning. The key thing is understanding meaning, not fighting over a symbol.

Going back now to the perception experience, just imagine what would happen if you were convinced that you were right regarding what you saw and that the other was wrong regarding what he or she claimed to see. Any attempt to tell the meaning of the picture would result in pure contention. Both of you would be emotionally invested in your perception, and with that skewed, emotionally driven focus, you simply could not act on the perception of the other person with any kind of integrity.

Now, compound that problem of emotional investment with positional power. Imagine what would happen if positional leaders in high places unilaterally decided how to deal with a significant challenge facing the organization and then announced that direction to the company at large. Those in top positions give their smooth presentations on how the changes will drive new structural and compensation arrangements, how the organization will work together, and the very nature of their work. The silent audience resents the heavy-handed treatment and resists the announcement. The codependent conspiracy of "wait until

Figure 10.4

told" forms; the disagreement is denied and ignored. You can just imagine the chaos.

When you borrow strength from position power but lack moral authority, you build weakness into yourself, in others, and in the relationship. You create codependency.

THE INDIAN TALKING STICK

After I trained Indian chiefs who head up Indian nations in the United States and Canada, the chiefs gave me a beautiful gift—an intricately carved, five-foot-tall Talking Stick with the name Bald Eagle inscribed on it. The Talking Stick has played an integral part in Native American government for centuries. In fact, some of the Founding Fathers of the American Republic (particularly Benjamin Franklin) were educated in the ideas behind the Talking Stick by Indian chiefs of the Iroquois Federation. It is one of the most powerful communication tools I've ever seen, because, while it is tangible and physical, it embodies a concept that is powerfully synergistic. This Talking Stick represents how people with differences can come to understand one another through mutual respect, which then enables them to solve their differences and problems synergistically, or at the very least through compromise.

Here's the theory behind it. Whenever people meet together, the Talking Stick is present. Only the person holding the Talking Stick is permitted to speak. As long as you have the Talking Stick, you alone may speak, until you are satisfied that you are understood. Others are not permitted to make their own points, argue, agree or disagree. All they may do is attempt to understand you and then articulate that understanding. They may need to restate your point to make sure you feel understood, or you may just simply feel that they understand.

As soon as you feel understood, it is your obligation to pass the Talking Stick to the next person and then to work to make him feel understood. As he makes his points, you have to listen, restate and empathize until he feels truly understood. This way, all of the parties involved take responsibility for one hundred percent of the communication, both speaking and listening. Once each of the parties feels understood, an amazing thing usually happens. Negative energy dissipates, contention evaporates, mutual respect grows, and people become creative. New ideas emerge. Third alternatives appear.

Remember, *to understand does not mean to agree with*. It just means to be able to see with the other person's eyes, heart, mind and spirit. One of the deepest needs of the human soul is to be understood. Once that need is met, the personal focus can shift to interdependent problem solving. But if that very intense need for understanding is not met, ego battles take place. Turf issues arise. Defensive and protective communication is the order of the day. Sometimes contention, even violence, can erupt.

The human need to feel understood is like the lungs' need for air. If all the air were suddenly sucked out of the room you are in, how motivated would you be to get air? Would you be interested in having a discussion or working out some difference between you and everyone else? Of course not. You'd want just *one* thing. You'd be open to other things only after you got air. Feeling understood is the equivalent of psychological air.

THIS SAME PROCESS we've been discussing can take place in people's minds without a Talking Stick, though it doesn't provide the same tangible discipline of clearly transferring the responsibility to speak with courage and then listening with empathy. There's a tremendous focus of attention and personal interest when you actually have a physical stick. You don't need an actual Talking Stick. You could use a pencil, a spoon or a piece of chalk—any tangible thing that physically places the responsibility upon the speaker to pass it only when he feels understood, and not until he does.

Haven't you ever sat in a meeting where you could just feel the hidden agendas operating? Think of the power of inserting the idea of the Talking Stick into such a meeting. If using the actual stick or pencil seems inappropriate, then express the basic underlying concept or idea. Simply speak up at the beginning of the meeting before people become emotionally invested in the jugular issues, and even if you're not the chair of the meeting, say something like this: "We're going to be talking about a lot of important things today that people have strong feelings about. To help us in our communication, why don't we agree that no one can make their point until they restate the last person's point to his or her satisfaction." (Even though this statement doesn't introduce the physical Talking Stick, it does introduce the essence of the idea, because no one can make his or her point until the other can say, "I feel understood.")

Many may hesitate to buy into this process because it seems a little pedestrian, even childish and inefficient, but I'll guarantee you, it's just the opposite. It requires such self-control and draws such maturity into the communication that even though it may seem inefficient at first, it becomes highly effective—that is, it achieves the desired results in terms of both synergistic decisions and synergistic relationships, bonding and trust.

Here's how a meeting might go with you as the facilitator of the Indian Talking Stick concept:

Sylvia and Roger are in a meeting. Right in the middle of Sylvia's effort to explain her point, Roger says something like, "I disagree with Sylvia. I think what we should do is—"

You interrupt and say, "Excuse me, Roger, remember what we agreed upon to help us in our communication?"

Roger replies, "Oh, yeah, I'm supposed to make Sylvia's point first, then I can make mine."

You answer, "No, Roger. You don't make Sylvia's point. You make Sylvia's point to *her satisfaction*. Then you can make your own."

"Oh, yeah, that's right," he responds.

"What was Sylvia's point, Roger?"

He attempts to make it.

"Is that correct, Sylvia?"

"No, not at all. What I'm trying to say is—"

Roger interrupts again.

"Again, what's our ground rule, Roger?"

"Oh, yeah, I'm supposed to make Sylvia's point to her satisfaction."

So for the first time he struggles to listen more deeply and essentially mimics her.

"How was that, Sylvia?" you ask.

She responds, "Well, he mimicked me, but he didn't get the spirit of my point at all."

"Sorry, Roger, try again."

"When's it my time? When's it my turn? I've been up with my staff for two nights preparing for this meeting."

"Remember the ground rule, Roger? There's no admission into this arena without the ticket of the other person saying that you understand their point."

So he is torn between his ego needs, hidden agendas, desire to speak, and the realization that he is not a player until he first understands to the other's satisfaction. For the first time he really listens empathetically.

Sylvia says, "Thank you, Roger. I do feel understood."

"Okay, Roger, your turn."
Roger looks and says, "I agree with Sylvia."

MY EXPERIENCE is that if people really try to understand each other, they will, in most, but not all, cases come to agree with each other. Why? Because over 90 percent of all communication problems are caused by differences in either semantics or perceptions. Again, semantics means the way you define words or terms. Perception means how you interpret data. Whenever people listen to each other with true empathy, that is, within the other's frame of reference, both semantic and perceptual problems dissolve—just as they do with the saxophone player/woman exercise. This is because they're listening from within the other's frame of reference. They're sensing how the other defines words and terms, or how the other interprets meaning and data. This puts them on the same song sheet, using the same language, which then enables them to get on with problem solving on the other 10 percent of the genuine disagreements. The spirit of this mutual understanding is so affirming, so healing, so bonding that when people do discuss their disagreements, they do it in agreeable ways and usually are able to solve them either through synergy or a form of compromise.

SILENCE IS ALSO a key to Indian Talking Stick communication with others. We must be quiet, even silent, to begin to deeply empathize with others. Of the power of this silence, Robert Greenleaf commented, "One must not be afraid of a little silence. Some find silence awkward or oppressive. But a relaxed approach to dialogue will include the welcoming of some silence. It is often a devastating question to ask oneself, but it is sometimes important to ask it. In saying what I have in mind, will I really improve on the silence?"

ON A LIGHTER NOTE, let me share a story I heard recently that shows the effects of a person who does not understand or practice the Indian Talking Stick concept.

A farmer went into his attorney's office wanting to file for divorce from his wife. The attorney asked, "May I help you?" to which the farmer replied, "Yeah, I want to get one of those dayvorces." The attorney said, "Well, do you have any grounds?" and the farmer said, "Yeah, I got about 140 acres." The attorney said, "No, you don't understand. Do you have a case?" and the farmer replied, "No, I don't have a Case, but I have a John Deere." And the attorney said, "No, you really don't understand. I mean do you have a grudge?" And the farmer replied to that, "Yeah, I got a grudge. That's where I park my John Deere." The attorney, still trying, asked, "No, sir, I mean do you have a suit?" The farmer replied, "Yes, sir, I got a suit. I wear it to church on Sundays." The exasperated and frustrated attorney said, "Well, sir, does your wife beat you up or anything?" The farmer replied, "No, sir. We both get up about 4:30." Finally, the attorney says, "Okay. Let me put it this way. WHY DO YOU WANT A DIVORCE?" And the farmer says, "Well, I can never have a meaningful conversation with her."

THE TWO STEPS TO SEARCHING
FOR A THIRD ALTERNATIVE

There are basically two steps in searching for a Third Alternative (see figure 10.5). In fact, the very searching process through these two steps feeds back and helps create the trust (moral authority) that encourages the search:

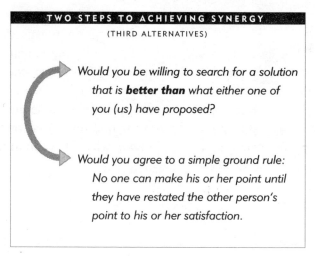

TWO STEPS TO ACHIEVING SYNERGY
(THIRD ALTERNATIVES)

*Would you be willing to search for a solution that is **better than** what either one of you (us) have proposed?*

Would you agree to a simple ground rule: No one can make his or her point until they have restated the other person's point to his or her satisfaction.

Figure 10.5

It's important to note that these two steps are not always sequential. At times you start with the first one; other times you start with the second. Sometimes you may just naturally begin interacting and genuinely trying to listen to someone else who has a totally different point of view and solution. Then you might ask the other to listen to you as you have to them, after which you might see if the other wants to search for a Third Alternative. Sometimes you find yourself going back and forth between these two steps. Every situation is different. And every relationship is very unique. Bottom line, it requires good judgment, awareness, self-control and presence to initiate these two steps.

EXPERIENCES IN SEARCHING
FOR THE THIRD ALTERNATIVE

Over the years, some of my most challenging but enjoyable professional experiences have come from acting as a third-party facilitator in taking people who are very emotionally invested in strong opposition to each other—almost to the point of irrationality—through the two steps of searching for and finding a synergistic Third Alternative. You can literally see them struggle through the modes of communication reflected in this continuum (see figure 10.6):

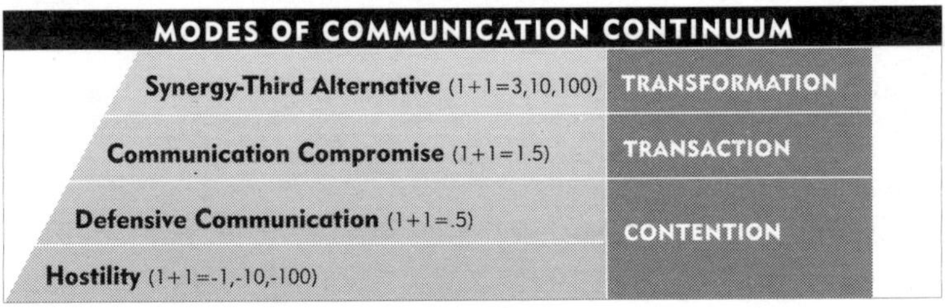

MODES OF COMMUNICATION CONTINUUM	
Synergy-Third Alternative (1+1=3,10,100)	TRANSFORMATION
Communication Compromise (1+1=1.5)	TRANSACTION
Defensive Communication (1+1=.5)	CONTENTION
Hostility (1+1=-1,-10,-100)	

Figure 10.6

One of my very first experiences took place when our firm needed to film a genuine, real-life, spontaneous experience that taught synergy for a product we were creating. So I decided to use one of my live seminars. I chose a highly charged subject—the environment—and invited two people in the audience to come up and join me on the stage: a woman who was a strong, convinced, passionate environmentalist (a real Greener), and a strong, convinced, passionate businessman who uses natural resources for economic purposes in his business. They never shook hands. (Even professional boxers touch gloves.) She even attacked him on her way up to the stage, saying, "It is your ilk that has messed up our air, our water, and our kids' futures." Then he looked at her shoes and said, "Nice shoes. Are they leather?" She looked down and then back at him and responded, "What's that got to do with it?" He retorted, "I just wonder what animal you killed." She answered, "I don't kill animals!" He responded, "Oh, you had others do the killing for you?!" That was the beginning of the communication.

Forty-five minutes later, after going through the two steps, they both were arguing for sustainable development policies at the corporate and government levels. The audience was totally amazed.

Whenever you teach the first step—would you be willing to search for a solution that is better than what either one of you have brought to the table?—people inevitably say, as did these two, "I don't know what it would be" or "I've spent years on this matter, and I have strong convictions. . . ."

So you acknowledge, "That's right. No one knows what it will be; it has to be created together. The question is, would you be willing to search for such a solution?"

They usually respond, "I *will not* compromise!"

You answer, "Of course not. Synergy is not compromise. It must be a *better* solution—you must know it, the other must know it, and you both must know that you both know it—no compromise."

"Oh, I don't know where we go from here."

"You go to step two. But no one can make their point until they restate the other person's point to his or her satisfaction." Now *that* is the test. It is tremendously challenging for people who have endlessly argued for one position to genuinely listen to another person, because unless they listen to another person and restate to his or her satisfaction, they can't make their point. It's the ticket of admission.

I DID THIS ONCE in a university setting on the subject of abortion, bringing a pro-life person and a pro-choice person up front. Both felt morally committed to their positions. I took them through the two steps in front of over four hundred people, including an entire MBA class, and many faculty and invited guests. Again, after about forty minutes of going through the two steps slowly, they both began to talk about prevention, adoption and education. The whole nature of the discussion had changed. The audience was mesmerized. Tears filled the two participants' eyes.

I asked them why this was so emotional. It wasn't because of the issue

at all. It was simply because they were ashamed of the way they had cat-
egorically judged and condemned and stereotyped, even demonized,
everyone who thought differently on this issue. By listening genuinely
and deeply they came to realize, "This is a good person. I like this person; I respect this person. I don't agree with this person's opinions, but I
am willing to listen; I am open." To watch minds become open and
hearts become softened and positions melt into a higher, synergistic
Third Alternative is a thrilling experience.

THESE TWO STEPS don't *always* work simply because people won't always apply them. I was once in Washington with the Young Presidents
Organization teaching this material, and I invited the president of the
National Education Association (NEA) and the head person behind the
voucher movement in California to come up and go through the two
steps. Begrudgingly, they went through the first one, both saying they
had no idea what they would find in the search and that they would not
compromise.

When it came to the second step of having to restate to the other's
satisfaction, they attempted, then caved in. They were very defensive
and then even became hostile, calling one another names, including describing each other's parents. The audience literally dismissed them.
They were their invited guests, and they were dismissed because they
failed to serve the purpose of the conference. Then the audience became synergistic. These were parents who genuinely cared, who were
aware that it was a very complex issue, that you couldn't make sweeping generalizations and that you needed to have deeper understanding.
The audience became more and more creative about how to strengthen
the education system—including the degree to which the market could
be brought into education in some settings and what to do in those settings where it would be very difficult and even counterproductive.

I HAVE DONE this many, many times on business issues. I ask my clients,
"What issue seems to divide your culture—one that's almost a non-
discussible?" Usually they are hesitant, but eventually they come forth
with it. I ask them, "Well, could we use that as an example in producing
synergy, a third alternative?" They usually say, "Oh, it's too tender, too
difficult—I don't know how it could be done." I explain the process and

the two steps. Then I assure them that if there is enough sincerity and moral authority in the group, which expects sincerity and genuine effort toward practicing the two points, it would give them one of the most powerful experiences their organization could ever have—not only in solving the issue but also, more importantly, in developing an immune system inside the culture that would enable them to do the same thing on any issue that comes along.

I WAS WITH a group of health care professionals once that included trustees, executives, administrators and many of the physicians. The issue to be debated—one that had been fought over for many months— was the use of outside physicians. The medical director was the spokesman for one side, the CEO for the other. In front of about a hundred people, I took them slowly through the two steps. They produced a Third Alternative that both were absolutely enthusiastic about—not just because they liked it better than the present arrangement or what either had proposed but also because it was so healing and bonding to their relationship.

I WAS WORKING with a group of insurance people in Cancun, Mexico, at one of their big international conferences. I was asked to speak on cultural transformation through principle-centered leadership. After sensing the mood of the groups—how artificial their communication on substantive issues was, how polarized the front office was from the general managers in the field and the general managers were from the producing agents, I decided to bag my prepared speech. Instead, I decided to help them see how serious this cultural malaise was and the impact it was having on their business and their customers.

So I took the one question, Who owns the customer? and had two people from each of the three groups—headquarters people, general managers and producing agents—come up in front of the entire assembly. Each in turn gave the reasons why *they* own the customer. The producing agents claimed that they found the customer, had the relationship, and sold the customer. The general managers looked with disdain on that reasoning and said, "*We* are the ones that have to service these people over time. You can walk. We can't. We have to stay and represent our products and the fulfillment of our promises." The headquarters executives looked with disdain upon both groups, saying essentially, "You people are clueless. Who developed the products? Who fulfills on the products? Who has set up the whole institutionalized system to make our business run?" Thereafter it became obvious to everybody how sick the culture had become—no *one* group owned the customer but the customer owned himself or herself—and that unless they got their act together, they would not be able to get and keep customers. The experience was humbling to them and made them very open to going through the two steps of producing a synergistic Third Alternative.

ONE TIME I RECEIVED a phone call from the president of a company to ask if I would help resolve a very costly, protracted lawsuit with a major client customer. The client was suing the company for lack of performance against their understanding of agreed-upon criteria. I knew this president well. He had been trained in the material I teach but felt a lack of confidence in his ability to apply it. I told him he didn't need me; he could do it by himself. So I retaught the material to him over the phone and got him to read the material I had given him earlier. He was very hesitant and fearful. But after my reaffirming him very strongly, he agreed to do it on his own.

He called up the president of the suing company and suggested they meet for lunch. The other president said, "There's no need. Let's let the legal process carry itself out," probably thinking that the calling president was ready to settle, compromise or play softball. He decided to stick to his hardball tactics and turned down the luncheon invitation.

So my friend told him what he was trying to do and why. He told him about the two steps and also told him that, though he would not have his own attorney come, he, the other president, could bring his attorney and say nothing if the attorney counseled him not to. This way he would avoid the risk of compromising himself in some way in the court of law. He again said, "What have you got to lose—an hour or two? It has already cost our two companies many tens of thousands of dollars, and we're just beginning the process." On that basis, the other president agreed to meet and to bring his attorney.

With the three of them in the room and two flipcharts, my friend said, "First I want to see if I understand your position in this suit," and he restated it as completely and fully as he possibly could. After a few minutes he said, "Do you feel I have a correct understanding? Has this been correct and fair?" The other president said, "Yes, except for two points." His attorney interrupted him and suggested he say no more. But this president, sensing there was genuine movement here and true sincerity in the effort, basically told his attorney to shut up, and he opened up those two points. My friend wrote them down on the flipchart. And again he asked, "Do you feel like I understand? Is there anything else you want me to understand? Has anything been omitted?" The other president said, "No, I feel you understand." And then my friend said, "Could I ask you to listen to me as I have attempted to listen to you? Would that be fair?"

What essentially happened was that the first point—that is, searching for the Third Alternative—emerged through their attempting to understand each other. The motivation to solve the problem emerged. And not only did they settle in a way that deeply satisfied both of them but they also continued their relationship. Their remaining struggle was to figure out how they were going to communicate their desire to continue this business relationship to two cultures that had coalesced around their fight and opposition with one another.

The main point is that people can do this on their own; they don't need a third-party facilitator. It takes the ability to be a participant and an observer or third-party facilitator at the same time. This takes a lot of mental and emotional discipline, but if you have faith in the principles and sufficient internal courage and integrity, you can do it.

Sometimes the nature of a Third Alternative may appear to be a compromise—that one or both gave in a little. But this isn't necessarily so. It could be that the key thing had not been the issue at all: what became the most important element was the quality of the relationship, the depth of the understanding, or the alteration of the motivation. I remember a colleague once sharing with me the story of his father and mother. It beautifully illustrates this point:

My father had been a superb dentist for thirty years when he was diagnosed with amyloidosis, a rare disease similar to cancer. The doctors gave him six months to live. Because of the effects of the disease, he had to give up his practice. So, here sits this man who had always been extremely active, with nothing to do all day except think about his fatal disease.

He decided he wanted to take his mind off things by putting a greenhouse in the backyard, where he could grow his favorite plants. This wouldn't be a fancy glass greenhouse that you see behind Victorian mansions. This would be one of those kit greenhouses complete with corrugated plastic for a roof and black plastic sides. My mother didn't want that monstrosity in her yard. She said she would die if the neighbors saw it. The g-word topic got to the point where they couldn't speak civilly to each other about it. I think the issue became the site of all their redirected anger about the disease.

One day my mom told me she was thinking about really trying to understand my father's point of view. She wanted to resolve this situation so that both could be happy. She knew she didn't want a greenhouse in her backyard. She'd rather have morning glory in all her perennial flowerbeds than that greenhouse. But she also knew she wanted my father to be happy and productive. She decided to step back and let him do it. She decided that my dad's happiness meant more to her than either the backyard or the neighbors.

As it turns out, that greenhouse kept my dad going long after the doctors had given up on him. He lived for two and a half more years. At night, when he couldn't sleep because of the chemotherapy, he went out to the greenhouse to see how his plants were doing. In the morning, watering those plants gave him a reason to get up. His greenhouse gave him work to do, something else to concentrate on while his body collapsed on him. I remember my mom commenting that supporting my dad's desire to build the greenhouse was one of the wisest things she had ever done.

Initially, the greenhouse was a "lose" to my colleague's mother until she subordinated her *initial* desires to her greater desire for her husband's happiness and welfare. This teaches that when you understand someone, you redefine what win-win is. Nevertheless, had she not initially felt enough respect to want to understand what was important to her husband, she wouldn't have made the shift.

Interestingly, the synergy that resulted was not a Third Alternative *solution*, it was a Third Alternative *attitude*. The first alternative was to not have the greenhouse. The second alternative was to let him have the greenhouse grudgingly. The Third Alternative was to truly understand him, to cheerfully and lovingly find her happiness in his satisfaction at having the greenhouse. This is often the way synergy works. An outside observer might say it was a compromise, but if you were to talk to this woman she would surely deny that she was compromising herself. She fulfilled herself in her husband's happiness and well-being. Such attitudinal synergy is a magnificent expression of mature love.

• • •

MOST TRANSACTIONS BETWEEN people end in compromise, win-lose, or lose-win. But Third Alternative solutions—whether they be in substance, in spirit, or in simply achieving mutual respect and understanding without any agreement at all—are illustrations of transformation. That is, people have been changed, they have become more open in their hearts and minds, they have learned and listened, they see things in new, fresh ways—they have been transformed. The following diagram illustrates the contrast between transactional and transformational solutions (see figure 10.7):

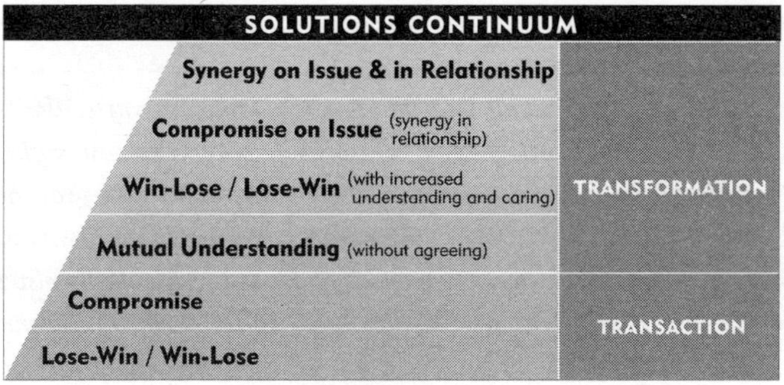

Figure 10.7

I am convinced that most disputes could be prevented and solved through synergistic Third Alternative communication. Suing and "the law" should be used as the court of last resort, not the first. A litigious culture is unhealthy for society, destroys trust, gives terrible modeling, and at best results in compromise. I hope someday to join with a corporate general counsel and a federal judge, both of whom practice these ideas with astounding results, in writing a book for attorneys and those who educate and hire attorneys, and also for those who want to solve seemingly intractable problems without hiring attorneys. The title would be *Blessed Are the Peacemakers*, subtitled *Synergy in the Prevention and Settlement of Disputes*.

BUILDING A COMPLEMENTARY TEAM THROUGH
THIRD ALTERNATIVE COMMUNICATION

Modeling open, Third Alternative communication is also absolutely necessary in efforts to build the complementary teams we've discussed. Of all the places this kind of modeling should take place, it's with the executive team. Because formal leaders have *formal* authority, they, above all, need to manifest the *moral* authority inherent in this kind of communication. A second reason is that executives are so visible, constantly building complementary teams between departments, inside departments, and throughout the entire organization.

This kind of Third Alternative communication that produces complementary teams can, however, begin at any level. The pragmatic results produced by those at lower levels will convert the cynics at higher levels of the organization—again illustrating that leadership, not just by an individual but by an entire team, is a choice, not a position.

Where do you start? Begin by having open communication between everyone on your team, in your department, and between interdependent teams and departments. As you practice the skills of Third Alternative communication, people will gradually get to know and like one another and will become more open, authentic and real. Mutual respect will develop, and people will increasingly seek to acknowledge the strengths of others and will actively strive to compensate for their weaknesses to make their strengths productive. This produces harmony, like in a musical group or an athletic team.

> When we look through the lens of each other's weaknesses, we make others' strengths irrelevant and their weaknesses more evident.

FILM: *Street Hawkers*

Several years ago, a South African company was opening up a brand-new retail-clothing store in an old part of town. The day they opened the store, the fruit and vegetable vendors, commonly called street hawkers, flooded back to that central location. They used to occupy that land before the store was built, and they had been selling there for years. Psychologically they felt that they owned it. They came right back in front of the store on the very day of opening and set up their fruit and vegetable stands. It made a mess, and made it slightly difficult for people to even get into the store.

What would you do if fruit vendors crowded around, messed up the sidewalk, and partially blocked your doorway on the day you opened your new store? What would you do?

You have two options: You can try to control the street hawkers like "things"—call the police, make them move, enforce your position as the legal owners of the property. Or you can treat them like people. You can synergize and come up with a better solution for both of you.

The manager of the store could have called the police on these hawkers. Instead, he decided to seek a Third Alternative. He first listened to their objectives and needs, then he talked about the store's needs. Together this most unlikely team of retail managers and street hawkers developed a synergistic plan that worked for both of them.

We produced a film on this experience between the new retail store and the fruit and vegetable street vendors. It's called *Street Hawkers*. I invite you now to watch this video. You can find it on the companion DVD to your book. In it you will see the kind of synergistic solutions that are developed by people who are empowered.

YOU CAN SEE from this film how the key to their creative solution was first achieving mutual understanding. You'll also notice the serendipi-

Figure 10.8

tous benefit that came from this creativity. *Serendipity* means "happy accident." Something happened that no one initially anticipated. It emerged from trust and relationship: The street hawkers essentially became the security force for the store. Street people know who the thieves are, and the thieves know this. Because pilferage of inventory is a major problem in South Africa, this became a huge benefit. You literally see the building of trust and communication. Trust is turned into a verb by entrusting a group of people, and then those people live true to that trust and reciprocate it. This is always bonding. It also creates an immune system that has the power to deal with issues or problems that may come down the pike in the future.

QUESTION & ANSWER

Q: How important are the life cycles of organizations, and is there a Third Alternative to their eventual decay and death?

A: I suggest there are four "Bermuda Triangles" which lead to decay, disaster and death. The *first* occurs at the idea stage, where a good idea is simply squelched by negative energy, self-doubt and fear. The *second* occurs at the production stage, where the great idea is not properly executed. This is where most new organizations fail—upwards of 90 percent within two years. There is just so much slip between cup and lip—between the great idea and making it happen. The *third* occurs at the management stage. Production with scalability has been institutionalized so that one can replicate or duplicate the enterprise, such as expanding to build another good restaurant, but the producer either tries to do it all or he or she tries to clone himself or herself. Formal systems are never established to keep things, especially cash flow, in control. The *fourth* occurs at the change stage, where the organization needs to reinvent itself to adapt to changing market conditions or new opportunities but gets so bogged down in its own bureaucratic life, rules and regulations that it can no longer meet and anticipate the needs of targeted customers.

Good management teams should have people with qualities that match the needs at all four stages. Most importantly, the team must have a spirit of mutual respect so that the strengths of each are acknowledged and utilized, and the weaknesses are made irrelevant by the strengths of the others. You need an *entrepreneur* (the idea person), a *producer*, a *manager*, and a *teambuilder-leader*, who helps create the norm of mutual respect and who creates a complementary team with the power to reinvent itself and take it into new life cycles.

Q: What do you do when you are involved in merger and acquisition work and trying to bring together people from different companies and different cultures? Is there some magic Third Alternative button to push to achieve interdependence in a global company?

A: The reason why most mergers and acquisitions don't work is that they are forcing the process. It's like bringing about a merger of different DNAs. Have you ever seen a blended family? How hard is it to see that work successfully? It takes time, persistence, patience and Indian Talking Stick communication toward Third Alternative solutions. In the meantime you'll see the five metastasizing cancers manifest themselves (contending, comparing, competing, criticizing and complaining). Remember with people and cultures, fast is slow and slow is fast. With things this isn't the case—fast is fast. But with people, efficiency or speed is ineffective. I have learned this personally the hard way, but it has powerfully reinforced what I'm sharing with you now: There must be an open, mutual, respectful communication of the value of the different approaches if you are to produce a Third Alternative culture. This often requires new formal leadership. Once I was working with a big company up in Canada with a very mature empowered culture. Because leaders in the headquarters of the company in the States were opening up operations in all kinds of other countries, they wanted to establish some central policies. But these policies assumed cultures far less developed and mature than the Canadian one. Canadian management asked me if I could help them maintain their relative independence and empowerment and not get sucked into roles and policies that were geared to immature cultures and the weakest links in the value chain. I was happy to help. Once the American executives came to realize that they were not interdependent with Canada, that they could use Canada as a model of what was possible, that Canada's mature culture was more productive, leaner and more profitable with greater empowerment, less bureaucracy, and less red tape, they started pointing to the Canadian operation as a model organization which the less-developed cultures could emulate.

The key is, don't artificially force interdependency—it has to come naturally through people's getting to know and understand and trust each other. Then they can become creative. Until this happens, people see interdependency as dependency.

Chapter 11

ONE VOICE—
PATHFINDING SHARED VISION,
VALUES AND STRATEGY

One day Alice came to a fork in the road and saw a Cheshire cat in a tree.
"Which road do I take?" she asked.
His response was a question: "Where do you want to go?"
"I don't know," Alice answered.
"Then," said the cat, "it doesn't matter."

LEWIS CARROLL, *ALICE IN WONDERLAND*

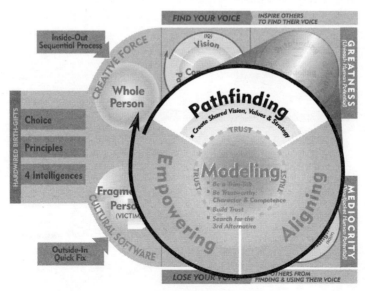

Figure 11.1

R EMEMBER, acquiring the 8th Habit is an inside-out, sequential process. Like any habit, it is a combination of ATTITUDE, SKILL and KNOWLEDGE. We've discussed the ATTI-TUDE of *trim-tabbing initiative*. We've discussed the SKILLS of *building trust* and *seeking Third Alternatives*. The 4 Roles of Leadership represent *Third Alternative* leadership and influence. They give you KNOWLEDGE of the principles of transformational leadership.

Again, this influence begins with *modeling* trustworthiness so that people will have confidence in you. But as you know, they need more than your trustworthiness. Good intentions do not compensate for bad judgment. People need a model to see how they can work and lead in a different way—different from what they are used to, different from the culture of the organization they work in, different from the controlling, transactional traditions of the Industrial Age. Your most important modeling will be to show others how a person who has found his or her voice acts inside the other three primary roles of a leader—*pathfinding*, *aligning* and *empowering*.

To help you *model* these three roles, I will begin the chapters covering the three remaining roles of leadership by 1) identifying the myth and the reality that surrounds each role, and 2) describing three contrasting alternatives for approaching each role. The key in any challenge is to always seek the higher Third Alternative.

In this chapter we take on the leadership challenge of uniting people who are diverse in their strengths and ways of seeing the world into one voice, one great purpose. It's the role of *pathfinding shared vision, values and strategic priorities*. Let's begin by looking first at the pathfinding myth, reality and alternatives.

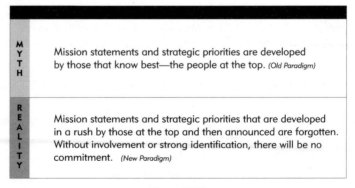

Figure 11.2

The *first alternative* to the pathfinding role of leadership would be to announce vision, values and strategy to your team or organization without any real involvement on their part.

The *second alternative* would be to get excessive involvement and get bogged down in paralysis by analysis and committee-itis; have extensive off-sites and endless discussions, almost working on the assumption that you don't need to execute strategy or empower.

The *third alternative* would be to not only reasonably involve people in the process of developing the vision, mission and strategy but also recognize that if you build a strong enough culture of trust, and are personally trustworthy yourself, the power of identification is equal to the power of involvement.

Allow me to illustrate this third alternative.

I've long been amazed at the consistent, absolutely extraordinary levels of service I've received while staying at Ritz-Carlton hotels. As I've become better acquainted over the years with Horst Schulze, the hotel chain's former longtime president and chief operating officer, I've better understood how their remarkable culture was created. Under Schulze's direction, The Ritz-Carlton Hotel Company won an unprecedented two Malcolm Baldrige National Quality Awards in the service category.

I once interviewed Horst for an internationally syndicated column I was writing. I asked him, "How would you define leadership?" Here was his response:

Leadership is creating an environment in which people want to be part of the organization and not just work for the organization. Leadership creates an environment that makes people want to, rather than have to, do. It is a business imperative to create that environment. I must give purpose, not just work and function. As a businessperson, I am obligated to create an environment where people feel part of something, feel fulfilled, and have purpose. It is purpose—it is value in their lives—that leads people to truly give of their minds. Then you are getting the maximum from them, and are giving the maximum to the person. Anything less is irresponsible to the organization and demands more handling by the individual.

When you see people only as fulfilling a function, you're treating them like a thing, like the chair you're sitting on. I don't think we as humans can assume the right to do that. None of us want to be just something standing in a corner. We found the greatest satisfaction for an employee is to feel part of something and to feel trusted to make decisions and to contribute.

Everyone is a knowledge worker in their specific area, and undoubtedly the dishwasher has more knowledge about their situation than I have. So that dishwasher can contribute to the improved environment, work conditions, productivity, lack of dish breaking, etc. They can contribute their knowledge in their area tremendously.

I had a young man from Nairobi who joined me as a dishwasher in the hotel about sixteen years ago. He couldn't speak proper English, but he was a very hardworking young man. After a while, they offered him a job in room service, then as a room service leader, then a lobby attendant, then a bartender, then he became an assistant lobby manager; he's now the food and beverage director. He's the number-two man in the hotel, and started as a dishwasher.

When I was sixteen years old, my mother took me to the hotel with my little suitcase to begin my apprenticeship. There were all these important guests and I thought they were all so above me. But I got close to a remarkable seventy-year-old headwaiter with whom I worked as an apprentice. When he moved into the room, you knew he was present, he was excellent, and there was an admiration for him. He always looked out for excellence in how he appeared, what he said, and how he did things. I saw in this maitre d' that if you do things exceptionally, you're just as important as they are. I realized I could be as important if I do what I do right, no matter what it is. In fact, that idea has become the motto of Ritz-Carlton: "We are ladies and gentlemen serving ladies and gentlemen."

Over the past twenty-two years, we have surveyed some five million people, seeking to understand the characteristics and competencies of effective leaders and managers. One of the most striking findings from this vast study was this: Managers are typically rated high on work ethic (modeling) but low on their ability to provide focus and clear direction (pathfinding). As a result, people are neither clear about, nor accountable to, key priorities, and whole organizations fail to execute. The disconnect is this—people are working harder than ever, but because they lack clarity and vision, they aren't getting very far. They, in essence, are pushing a rope . . . with all of their might.

Whereas modeling inspires trust, *pathfinding creates order without demanding it.* As soon as the people involved agree upon what matters most organizationally, they share the criteria that will drive all decisions that follow. This clarifying communication gives *focus.* It creates order. It creates stability. It also enables agility, which we will explore later in the empowering role.

Vision on a personal scale translates into *pathfinding* in an organiza-

> *The very essence of leadership is that you have to*
> *have vision; you can't blow an uncertain trumpet.*[1]
> THEODORE M. HESBURGH, PRESIDENT, NOTRE DAME

tional setting. Whereas individually you identify what *you* see to be significant, now your challenge and role is to create a *shared* view of what is important, of what matters most. Consider for a moment the following questions you might ask about your employees:

1. Do people clearly understand the organizational goals?
2. Are they committed?

Helping people clearly understand and get committed to significant goals requires you to involve them in decision making. Together you determine the destination of the organization (vision and mission). Then everybody in the organization will have ownership in the path that leads to the destination (values and strategic plan).

In determining together what is most important to an organization or team, you need to come to grips with the realities you face. Once you understand them, you work until a shared vision and value system are embodied in some kind of a mission statement and strategic plan. Speaking of the need to first become grounded in foundational realities, author Clayton M. Christensen wrote:

Every company in every industry works under certain forces—laws of organizational nature—that act powerfully to define what that company can and cannot do. Managers faced with disruptive technologies fail their companies when these forces overpower them.

By analogy, the ancients who attempted to fly by strapping feathered wings to their arms and flapping with all their might as they leaped from high places invariably failed. Despite their dreams and hard work, they were fighting against some very powerful forces of nature.

No one could be strong enough to win this fight. Flight became possible only after people came to understand the relevant natural laws and principles that defined how the world worked: the law of gravity, Bernoulli's principle, and the concepts of lift, drag, and resistance. When people designed flying systems that recognized or harnessed the power of these laws and principles, rather than fighting them, they were finally able to fly to heights and distances that were previously unimaginable.[2]

You must grapple with four realities—*market realities, core competencies, stakeholder wants and needs,* and *values*—before you will fully comprehend and be prepared to execute the pathfinding role:

- **Market Realities.** How do people in your organization or team perceive the marketplace? What is the larger political, economic and technological context? What are the competitive forces? What are the trends and characteristics of the industry? What about the possibility of disruptive technologies and disruptive business models that could make obsolete the entire industry or basic tradition?
- **Core Competencies.** What are your unique strengths? I'm very impressed with Jim Collins's approach to pathfinding. In his book *Good to Great,* he presents three overlapping circles, which represent your main strengths. He calls it the Hedgehog Concept.[3] These circles identify three questions: What are you really good at—maybe, even, what can you be best in the world at? Second, what are you deeply passionate about? And third, what will people pay for? In other words, what are the human needs and wants being met that would drive your economic engine? The nexus between these three overlapping circles represents the foundation of your value proposition.

    If we were to add one more question, What does your conscience counsel? we would have a whole-person approach (*body*—economic engine; *mind*—be best at; *heart*—passion; and *spirit*—conscience). The overlapping of all four areas is where your voice is to be found (see figure 11.3). As discussed before, this approach would apply to an individual finding his or her voice, as well as to an organization finding its voice.
- **Stakeholder Wants and Needs.** Think of all the different stakeholders—first and most importantly, the target customers. What do they really want and need? What are their issues, problems and concerns? What do *their* customers want and need? What is the market reality of the industry in which they operate? What possible technologies or business models could disrupt them or make

Figure 11.3

them obsolete? What about the owners, those that have supplied the capital or paid the taxes—what are their wants and needs? What about the associates, the employees, your coworkers—what are their wants and needs? What about all the suppliers, distributors and dealers—the entire supply chain? What about the community and the natural environment?

- **Values.** What are these people's values? What are your values? What is the central purpose of the organization? What is its central strategy in accomplishing that purpose? What job are they hiring you to do? What are the values that are to serve as guidelines? How are they prioritized in different contexts in times of stress and pressure? Most people have never even decided what matters most to them. They haven't developed the criteria that will inform and govern all other decisions, and now we're trying to do it for an entire group, team or organization. Think how complex that is, how interdependent—really, how challenging.

These are the kinds of questions and issues that must be *clarified* before you can *focus*. This is why it takes such character, competence, vision, discipline and passion governed by conscience.

Pathfinding is the toughest undertaking of all because you deal with so many diverse personalities, agendas, perceptions of reality, trust levels and egos. This underscores why modeling is the most important and central governing role. If people cannot trust the person and/or team initiating the pathfinding process, there will be no identification, and involvement will be very dysfunctional.

It took the *modeling* character and the competence of a George Washington to integrate and harmonize the brilliance and differences of a Thomas Jefferson, a John Adams, a Benjamin Franklin, an Alexander Hamilton, and other Founding Fathers of the American Republic, until finally the Declaration of Independence and the United States Constitution with its first Ten Amendments, called the Bill of Rights, were produced. Accomplishing this pathfinding work was the toughest of all tasks in founding the United States of America. But those visionary, guiding documents have enabled the United States to survive major traumas to its national life—the Civil War, the great wars, the Vietnam War, Watergate, presidential scandals, and presidential elections. And talk about empowerment, four and a half percent of the world's population produces almost a third of the world's goods!

ACHIEVING SHARED VISION AND VALUES

People frequently use the analogy of being on the same page or song sheet to describe achieving *shared* vision and values. It's an excellent analogy because it suggests there is agreement about what matters most in the organization's vision, values and strategic value proposition; and when played or sung together, the music is in harmony.

Sharing is an interesting word. When I *share* something with you, I give what I have to you. If you identify with me, believe in what I am about, and trust me, then I might simply share with you my vision. You might buy into that vision even more than if you had developed it yourself because you actually give more credence to my experience than to your own. If, on the other hand, you feel competent and desirous of getting involved and I simply share or announce to you *my* plan as *our* plan, then you have no emotional commitment. It is not shared. You would feel that the mission and value proposition were imposed upon you. We are not on the same song sheet.

In short, the mission statement and strategic plan are one thing, but the process of getting everyone on that same song sheet is another thing of *equal* importance. It is a major undertaking. The leadership work of modeling is truly manifest in the pathfinding role. Otherwise, people don't get on the same song sheet, they don't emotionally align on the strategic issues, and downstream everything goes awry. Then the only saving grace will be the sheer survival instinct inside of people. If the competition is also in disarray, you might survive. But if your main competitors synergistically unite within themselves, particularly if they are world class, you're history.

FILM: *Goal!*

If you've ever watched one of your young children or grandchildren play soccer (aka "magnet-ball") on a weekend morning, you'll get a laugh out of this great little film and will feel like you're right back on the sidelines. Notice the similarities in the challenge you face at work in trying to get everyone focused on the same big goal. Place the DVD in your DVD player now and select *Goal!* from the menu. You'll really enjoy this!

THE PATHFINDING (FOCUS) TOOLS—
THE MISSION STATEMENT AND STRATEGIC PLAN

Pathfinding is for an organization or team what modeling is for an individual. It's deciding what to *focus* on as an organization, as a team, or as a family. You ask the same kind of values-and-purposes questions that you do as an individual, only now the group does it collectively regarding their specific mission. Through an interactive process, you create a written mission statement and strategic plan (value proposition and goals). The mission statement should encompass your sense of *purpose*, your *vision* and your *values*.

The strategic plan is a crisp description of *how* you will provide value to your customers and stakeholders; it's your value proposition. It's your *focus*. It's the organization's "voice." In coming up with your strategic plan, you need to know who your customers and stakeholders are, who you want them to be, the valued service or product you are offering them, and your plan, including deadlines, to achieve certain goals in getting and keeping customers. For a family, a strategic plan is simply your action plan for realizing your vision and values in everyday life.

EMPOWERING MISSION STATEMENTS

In my experience, empowering shared mission statements are usually always produced when there are 1) enough people who are 2) fully informed, 3) interacting freely and synergistically, 4) in an environment of high trust. In fact, most mission statements created under these conditions will contain the same basic ideas and values. Words may vary, but they usually all touch on the four dimensions and needs of life—physical, mental, emotional and spiritual.

The power of the Ritz-Carlton extraordinary service culture is its foundational view of people, both of themselves and of their customers: "We are ladies and gentlemen serving ladies and gentlemen." The heart of Horst Schulze's leadership is his view of the dignity and need for meaning of the whole person. Read again and reflect on his words (p. 217).

Remember, only those people who are allowed to tap into the needs and motivations of all four parts of their nature will find their voice and volunteer their highest contributions. For the body, the need and motivation is *survival*—economic prosperity; for the mind, *growth* and *development*; for the heart, *love* and *relationships*; and for the spirit, *meaning, integrity* and *contribution*.

The organization has the same four needs:

1. *Survival*—financial health (BODY)
2. *Growth and development*—economic growth, customer growth, innovation of new products and services, increasing professional and institutional competency (MIND)
3. *Relationships*—strong synergy, strong external networks and partnering, teamwork, trust, caring, valuing differences (HEART)
4. *Meaning, integrity* and *contribution*—serving and lifting all stakeholders: customers, suppliers, employees and their families, communities, society—making a difference in the world (SPIRIT)

The key to unleashing the power of the workforce is what I call *co-missioning*. It's clarifying the mission, vision and values of the organization in a way that overlaps the four needs of the individuals with the four needs of the organization. Every person's job in the organization ought to be co-missioned to explicitly meet the four needs of both the person and the organization. An implicit Universal Mission Statement would read something like this: "To improve the economic well-being *and* quality of life of *all* stakeholders." *Your* organization's, department's, team's, or family's mission statement would not only embody the spirit of the universal mission statement but would also represent how you *uniquely* do that—your unique gift, capacity, niche—your voice.

NO MARGIN, NO MISSION

I've always been driven by a sense of mission and purpose. But it was not many years into starting my own company that I was forcefully taught the reality: no margin, no mission. In other words, unless you run your enterprise in a way that produces consistent profits over time, eventually you lose your opportunity to deliver on your mission.

Most businesses, on the other hand, are so focused on margin and meeting the quarterly numbers that they lose sight of the very vision that inspired them to get into business in the first place. They lose sight of their people and their families and the communities they operate in. They forget how interdependent they are with *all* their stakeholders. They lose their sense of mission and contribution. The problems that this latter approach has created have driven much of my professional work with organizations for the last forty years. There are significant negative consequences that follow from both the Mission/No Margin and the Margin/No Mission approaches (see figure 11.4). Neither approach is sustainable—particularly in today's global economy. The key is to go for both. The key is balance.

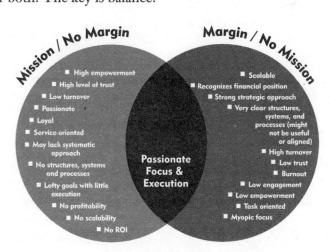

Figure 11.4

EXECUTING THE STRATEGIC PLAN

A strategic plan begins, of course, with the customer. In a very real sense, *there are only two roles in organizations: customers and suppliers.* Everybody functions simultaneously in both roles, whether inside or outside the organization. *Everybody* means all the stakeholders in the supply chain who make your organization's end product possible—those who supply the funds, those who supply the ideas and labor, those who supply the material, those families who support the employees, and the community and environment that permit and nurture the entire supply chain.

The essence of good business, therefore, is the *quality of the relationship* between customer and supplier. You, the supplier, sell more than goods and services to your many different customers. You're really selling solutions to their problems (jobs they hire in the form of your goods and services). To be able to really solve those problems in a way that is more than just a cosmetic pat on the head requires you to deeply understand these different stakeholder needs. You have to pay the price to know what matters most to these people so that you can plan strategically in a meaningful way. Values become priorities in this planning process because principle-based values don't change. Customers will change and so strategy must adapt, but if your values are tied to changeless principles, you will have a center pin to which you can anchor yourself through all the inevitable changes.

The litmus test of a good mission statement and strategic plan is being able to approach any person at any level of an organization and have them be able to describe how what they do contributes to the strategic plan and is in harmony with the governing values. To use the compass metaphor, they all know which way north is and how their part is moving the organization in the right direction.

Once a mission statement and strategic plan are deeply shared, either through identification or involvement, half the battle is won, because the mental, emotional and spiritual creation has taken place. The physical creation then follows. It's all about *executing the strategy*—"making it happen," doing, producing, aligning, empowering. This means you need to set up the structure, get the *right* people in the *right* jobs with the *right* tools and support, and then get out of their way and give help as requested.

Each sub-organization, committee, board, division, department, project and team would have to go through a similar two-creation process: the mental, then the physical; the blueprint, then the construction; the writing of the music, then the playing of the music. All things are created twice. Pathfinding is the first creation. It lays down the strategic plan for making things physical/actual/real.

You'll also find that if this process is done well and if there is deep emotional connection to it because of the identification and involvement that has preceded it, you'll be able to drive tremendous cost cutting throughout an organization when needed. Just as an individual gets swallowed up in doing things that are urgent but not important, so does an organization. The culture develops a life of its own. That's why it's necessary to constantly use the overall purpose, values and strategic plan to focus and *drive every other decision* you make. It will also give you the awareness and courage to get and stay out of "hobbies" in your business that are not central to its core purpose.

One of the greatest challenges that business leaders encounter is that of working to cascade and TRANSLATE the corporate vision from 30,000 feet into actionable line-of-sight behaviors among front-line workers to achieve critical objectives. Even if they have been involved in the development of the mission statement and strategic planning process, bringing it down to where the "rubber meets the road" is not easy. Think of how much more productive we could be if we had the right people working on the right things at the right time—the vital few projects and goals that ultimately matter most.

But that's usually the problem. Too often our strategic plans are lofty and vague, and leaders fail to translate strategy into the few crucial goals that must be accomplished in the near term. Or, just as problematic, strategies are translated into eight, eleven, or even fifteen new crucial goals, which is far too many priorities to realistically focus on. When you have too many top priorities, you effectively have no top priorities. Regarding strategic goals, it is important that they are few, prioritized, measurable and inside a *compelling scoreboard*, so everyone knows exactly what they are and how they are being achieved. Further insight on focusing your team and organization on the few "wildly important goals" and on the importance of a compelling scoreboard will be given in later chapters.

TO CREATE an environment of focus and teamwork top to bottom, employees must know what the highest priorities are, buy into them, translate them into specific actions, have the discipline to stay the course, and trust one another and collaborate effectively. Unfortunately, most people don't know where to focus their time and energy because top priorities aren't clearly identified or communicated and measured on a compelling scoreboard. If they are and workers don't feel any ownership, disagree with the strategy, are given competing priorities, or are unable to see the link between their tasks and the corporate vision, their ability to execute that vision is jeopardized. Teamwork is then threatened by low trust, backbiting, faulty systems and process, or too many barriers to action.

Organizations that are able to create a shared sense of *mission* so that each person knows and is passionate about the big WHY and WHO, as well as a clear *line of sight strategy* (the HOW and WHEN), where departments, teams, and individuals are consistently focused on their goals and people are accountable to the organization's few highest priorities, find their voice and build a powerful, principle-centered culture (see figure 11.5). Therein lies the mother lode of the pathfinding role.

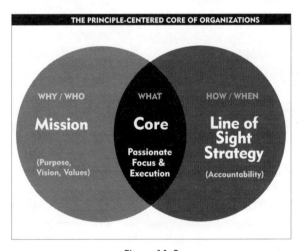

Figure 11.5

QUESTION & ANSWER

Q: I have four generations of workers. How do you unite people in shared vision and values when they are *so* different?

A: A principle-centered model is the only one that *does* apply. Whether you're dealing with old-timers, baby-boomers, Generation X or Generation Y—all of whom come from different value systems and see life through different lenses—there is one thing that unites them all: timeless, universal principles that can be the basis for developing a common vision and value system.

I know I'm making this sound a lot easier than it really is. Nevertheless, by showing respect for each generation of workers and involving them in synergistic communication, I'm convinced a Third Alternative can be achieved. Remember again the principle—involve people in the problem and work out solutions together. When you do, people become emotionally connected to the solution. When they really understand the depth of the problem and transcend looking at it only through their own generational lens, all of them become part of a social ecology.

Q: You are constantly trying to distinguish between principles and values. This is confusing to me; they seem the same.

A: The basic reason you think this way is that most well-developed values are indeed principles or natural laws. In fact, if you involve enough people in developing a value statement, and they are informed, work in an atmosphere of high trust, and communicate openly and synergistically with each other, you will find that the shared values that emerge are essentially principle-based. You will also find that any group that develops a value system in this way will be the same, even though the words may be different. The cultural practices may vary depending on where you are in the world, but my experience around the world is that regardless of the kind of organization or level within the organization, when statements of values are produced in this way, they will basically deal with the four parts of our nature—body, mind, heart and spirit—and the four basic needs: to live, to love, to learn and to leave a legacy. This pertains to both individuals and organizations. But if values are unilaterally developed and announced, they may not be principle-based. After all, even criminals have values.

Q: Is it necessary to write mission statements or do strategic planning sessions off-site?

A: It all depends. If the product of an off-site experience is mainstreamed for input throughout an entire organization, it can be very successful. But if it produces a mission statement and strategic plan that are simply announced, it will not work. The key is that there must be emotional connection; otherwise, the criteria developed will not be used to align structures, systems, processes and cultures. Mission statements that are rushed and announced are forgotten; they're nothing but PR statements. This is often the case with off-site products.

Remember, the process is as important and powerful as the product itself if you want to get emotional connection. Again, this will take a combination of involvement and identification—in other words, the trust in other people's vision is higher than their own, therefore they identify with it.

There still needs to be a process of communication, feedback, openness and participation in order to get this emotional connection. Many times I have seen technology used marvelously to produce one iteration after another. A committee of two or three people did the initial word-smithing of a straw man. Then gradually, through feedback— both sharing and listening—it became increasingly better and more deeply reflected the many different interests until there was true cultural connection.

Execution—

Aligning and Empowering

Chapter 12

THE VOICE AND DISCIPLINE
OF EXECUTION—
ALIGNING GOALS AND
SYSTEMS FOR RESULTS

No horse gets anywhere until he is harnessed.
No steam or gas ever drives anything until it is confined.
No Niagara is ever turned into light and power until it is tunneled.
No life ever grows great until it is focused, dedicated, disciplined.[1]

HENRY EMERSON FOSDICK

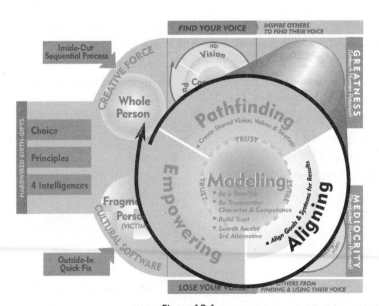

Figure 12.1

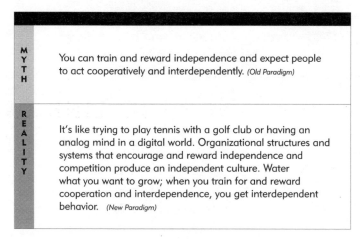

M Y T H	You can train and reward independence and expect people to act cooperatively and interdependently. *(Old Paradigm)*
R E A L I T Y	It's like trying to play tennis with a golf club or having an analog mind in a digital world. Organizational structures and systems that encourage and reward independence and competition produce an independent culture. Water what you want to grow; when you train for and reward cooperation and interdependence, you get interdependent behavior. *(New Paradigm)*

Figure 12.2

*T*HE FIRST ALTERNATIVE to the aligning role of leadership would be to believe that the personal modeling of an individual is sufficient to keep an organization on a path of healthy growth.

The second alternative would be to believe that by continuously communicating the vision and strategy you've carefully and intentionally developed, you will be able to achieve your goals as an organization. Structure and systems are of secondary importance.

The third alternative would be to 1) use both personal moral authority and formal authority to create systems that will *formalize* or *institutionalize* your strategy and the principles embodied in your shared vision and values, 2) create cascading goals throughout the organization that are aligned with your shared vision, values and strategic priorities, and 3) adjust and align yourselves to regular feedback you receive from the marketplace and organization on how well you are meeting needs and delivering value (which is one of the systems). If you say you value cooperation, you reward cooperation, not competition. If you say you value *all* stakeholders, you regularly gather information on *all* stakeholders and use it for realigning. You water what you want to grow.

Modeling principle-centered living and leadership creates and inspires trust. Pathfinding creates shared vision and order without demanding them. But now the crucial question becomes, How do we execute both values and strategy consistently without relying on the formal leader's continuing presence to keep everyone going in the right direction? The answer is alignment—*designing and executing systems and structures that reinforce* the core values and highest strategic priorities of the organization (selected in the pathfinding process).

Consider the current structures, systems and processes in your organization. Do they enable people to execute top priorities, or do they create roadblocks to doing so? Are they consistent with the organization's espoused values? It is the responsibility of leadership to remove obstacles—not create them. Yet the process of alignment requires a deep and humble examination of self and many "sacred cow" organizational systems and structure.

ORGANIZATIONAL TRUSTWORTHINESS

As mentioned earlier, the organization is the second major source of trust. When trustworthy people work within structures and systems that are not aligned with the organization's espoused values, the untrustworthy systems will dominate every time. You simply won't have trust. Through tradition and cultural expectation, these systems and processes become so deeply embedded in the organization that they are far more difficult to change than individual behavior.

> xQ data confirm that there is a serious "trust gap" within organizations. Only 48 percent of respondents agree that their organizations generally live up to the values of the organization.

For instance, almost all organizations espouse the importance of teamwork and cooperation, but they have deeply embedded systems that reward internal competition. I often tell the story of how I once worked with a company that had no spirit of cooperation. The CEO couldn't understand why his people wouldn't cooperate. He had preached it, trained for it, psyched people up about it. But still no cooperation.

While we were talking, I happened to glance up behind the CEO's desk and saw a curtain that had accidentally been left open. Behind the curtain was a mock horse race. Lined up on the left-hand side were all the horses. An oval picture of each manager's face was pasted on the front of each horse. On the right side hung a travel poster of Bermuda showing a romantic couple walking hand-in-hand down a white, sandy beach.

Now imagine the misalignment here. "Come on. Let's work together. Let's cooperate. You'll make more. You'll do better. You'll be happier. You'll enjoy it more." Then, pull the curtain . . . "Which one of you is going to win the trip to Bermuda?"

He again asked me, "Why won't they cooperate?"

Systems will override rhetoric every day of the week.

One of the great insights of Edwards Deming was that over 90 percent of all organizational problems are systemic. The problems arise because of systems or structures. They're not what he called "special caused" or people caused. However, in the last analysis, since people are the programmers and systems are the programs, people are ultimately responsible for those systems. Systems and structures are things. They are programs. They have no freedom to choose. So the leadership still comes from people. People design systems, and all organizations get the results they are designed and aligned to get.

Many honest people are incompetent when it comes to designing organizational systems. And likewise, some competent people are dishonest and duplicitous. But organizational trustworthiness requires *both* organizational character *and* organizational competence. Simply put, *alignment is institutionalized trustworthiness.* This means that the very principles that people have built into their value system are the basis for designing structures, systems and processes. Even if the environment, market conditions and people change, the principles do not. It is described well in the language of the architect: *Form follows function.* In other words, structure follows purpose. Alignment follows pathfinding. Discipline is manifest both personally and organizationally. In the organizational context, discipline is called aligning because you're creating or aligning your structures, systems, processes and culture to enable the vision to be realized.

> Beware of synergistic decision making
> and stovepipe execution.

If the value system focuses on the long term as well as the short term, then the information system should focus on both long and short term.

If the value system holds cooperation and synergy supreme, then the compensation system should reward cooperation and synergy. This doesn't mean that individual effort and performance should not be recognized and rewarded also. For instance, the size of the compensation pie may be based upon cooperation and synergy, but a particular individual's piece of that pie would be based upon individual effort within the complementary team, thus nurturing both interdependence and independence.

Many organizations fall into the trap of rewarding only individual effort at the expense of cooperative effort. Little more than lip service, the value of cooperation is not built into the recognition and reward system. Since everybody is operating on their own agenda, people go along with compensation systems that reward individual effort. Even if serving the customer at the optimal level requires teamwork, that teamwork will not happen, and the result will be failure in the marketplace. It's not that people do not want to cooperate, it's that the system rewards individual effort or internal competition. Again remember that systems will overwhelm rhetoric or good intentions "at the end of the day."

"DIDN'T YOU HIRE ALL THESE PEOPLE TO BE WINNERS?"

I came across another commonly misaligned system while speaking to a group of about eight hundred at their annual convention. In their system, only thirty of the eight hundred received rewards—thirty of eight hundred! I turned to the president and said, "Didn't you hire all of these people to be winners?"

"Yes."

"Did you hire any losers?"

"No."

"You have seven hundred seventy losers tonight."

"Well, they didn't win the contest."

"They're losers."

"Why?"

"Because of the way you're thinking? It's win-lose."

"What else could you do?"

"Make them all winners. Where did you get the concept that you have to have contests? Don't you have enough competition in the marketplace?"

"Well, that's the way life is."

"Really. How's your relationship with your wife? Who's winning?"

"Some days she wins. Some days I win."

I said, "Is that the kind of modeling you want to give to your kids for their futures? Come on."

He said, "How do I do it with compensation?"

I said, "Set up an individualized win-win performance agreement with every person and every team. If they accomplish the desired results, they win."

One year later I was invited back after a lot of pathfinding and aligning work had been done. Over one thousand people were at the annual rally. And of the one thousand, guess how many won? Eight hundred. The two hundred who didn't, chose not to. It was their choice. There was no comparison at all. And what did those eight hundred produce? They produced as much business as the previous year's thirty—*per person*. The whole culture had changed. The whole culture had moved from scarcity thinking to abundance thinking. Eight hundred people were where the last year's thirty were.

Why?

Let's answer the question by contrasting this story with the earlier Bermuda story: Instead of each one thinking, "Which *one* of us is going to Bermuda?" each was thinking, "I want you to go to Bermuda with your spouse. I want all of us to go. I'm pulling for you." Imagine how that thought process could revolutionize an internally competitive organization!

In both cases the presidents were not untrustworthy men. They had the character, even an abundance mentality; they just didn't have the mind-set or skill-set to create aligned compensation systems; they didn't have complete information systems. It's analogous to flying an airplane with only one dial working—it's disastrous! But they grasped the concept right away. Again, their problem wasn't character; their problem was competency. They had never learned the skill, and they'd been caught in a scarcity minded, traditional, duplicitous system that would remain duplicitous until they acquired the skills.

ALIGNING REQUIRES CONSTANT VIGILANCE

Aligning work is never finished. It requires constant effort and adjustment simply because you're dealing with so many changing realities. Systems, structures and processes must remain flexible so that they can adjust to those changing realities. Yet they must also be based upon unchanging *principles*. With this combination of *flexible changelessness* you create an organization that is both stable and agile.

> Principles represent the deeper well. This deeper well of principles supplies all the shallower wells and root structures of empowerment, quality, producing more for less, sustainability, scalability and agility.

One way to lubricate your organization's ability to make the constant and necessary alignment changes is, again, to be serious about benchmarking against superior performers of similar *functions* within your own organization and in all industries or professions throughout the world. This gets people involved in coming up with world-class awareness and definitions, instead of just looking to the past or extrapolating from trends in either their own industry or with their current competitors. Look for best-practice organizations that are reputed to be superior performers—not that they are perfect or will even remain superior—but look constantly for today's best and learn from them.

Observation, common sense and solid research have shown that successful organizations aren't a product of solo acts of people or of the individual traits of formal leaders. Successful organizations are a product of the organizational trait. They are not personality dependent. They are system and culture dependent. (We'll discuss culture in greater depth when we move into the empowering role.)

General Electric is one illustration of a company that made the transition from the Industrial to the Knowledge Worker Age with many of its divisions. The primary focus of the longtime CEO Jack Welch and Dr. Noel Tichy, who served as GE's manager of management education, was to embed leadership development in GE's genes and in training its leaders:

Mr. Welch's insight, which was not widely shared in business at the time, was that leadership was not the province solely of the CEO in his or her senior executive team, but had to be institutionalized throughout the company. A globalizing economy meant that a business world long characterized by stability, autocracy and strictly bounded processes would have to become more change embracing, which would require the development of nimble, adaptable leaders up and down the company hierarchies. That in turn meant building the capacity for teaching men and women not only how to manage change, but how to create it.[2]

INSTITUTIONALIZED MORAL AUTHORITY

Aligned organizations and institutions that are truly principle-centered have *institutionalized moral authority*. Institutionalized moral authority is the institutional capacity to consistently produce quality, trusting relationships with various stakeholders, and continued focus upon efficiency, speed, flexibility and market friendliness. Certain individuals may blow it from time to time, but the institution handles them appropriately and moves on.

We see institutionalized moral authority all the time in countries that have culturally sustained constitutions, written or unwritten. Individual leaders may not always act consistently with their constitutions, but these countries are able to build on the strengths of the individual leaders and rely on the rest of government to essentially make these leaders' weaknesses irrelevant. This wouldn't be the case with dictatorships or with tender, newly developing democracies that are still filled with codependent, culturally endorsed corruption.

Admittedly, corrupt, dictatorial, or ego-driven leaders can do a lot of damage for a period of time even when there's a great deal of institutionalized moral authority. But usually the organization or institution bounces back. Fundamentally, the power is in the system, not in the elected officials or appointed bureaucrats. The system is stronger than the individual weaknesses of the participants. This is why the Marriott Corporation teaches that the devil lies in the details, but *success lies in the systems*.

I visited recently with J.W. "Bill" Marriott, chairman and CEO of Marriott International, the world's largest hotel operator. Bill, and his father before him, created one of the finest organizations in the world, and they've done it in part by creating a *communication system* that taps into the genius of their people.

"The biggest lesson I've learned through the years is to listen to your people," he told me. "I find that if you have senior managers who really gather their people around them, get their ideas and listen to their input, then if you sit around a table with those managers and listen to their input, you make a lot better decisions."

His appreciation of that lesson came early in life, Marriott told me, from an encounter with one of the world's most renowned leaders, President Dwight David Eisenhower.

"I was finishing up college, had been in the navy for six months and had come home from the Supply Corps School for Christmas," he recalled. "U.S. Secretary of Agriculture Ezra Taft Benson came down to our farm with General Eisenhower. Eisenhower was president, and I was an ensign in the navy.

"It was colder than blazes outside," Marriott said, "but my dad had put up these targets for shooting. He asked President Eisenhower, 'Do you want to go out and shoot, or stay by the fire?'

"He turned around to me and asked, 'What do you think, ensign?' "

Even today, telling me the story, Marriott seemed stunned.

"I said to myself, 'You know, that's how he got by, dealing with de Gaulle, Churchill, Marshall, Roosevelt, Stalin, Montgomery, Bradley and Patton—he asked that golden question: What do you think?"

"So I said, 'Mr. President, it's too cold out there, stay inside by the fire.' "

To this day, Marriott said, that lesson has stayed with him.

"It was a real defining moment for me," he told me. "I remember thinking afterward, 'If I ever get into business, I'm going to ask that question. And if I do, I bet I'll get some pretty good information.' "

That's why Bill Marriott has structured his hotel chain the way he has, creating a culture that encourages communication both up and down the line. He realizes that simply asking "What do you think?" can turn even people who are considered "manual" workers into "knowledge" workers by listening to them and respecting their experience and wisdom.

He summarized by saying, "My son John was working up in New York with a division of a company that we had acquired. While in the kitchen, he walked up to one of the people and said, 'We've got this problem out front—what do you think we should do?'

"Tears came to the eyes of this worker as he answered, 'I've worked with this old company for twenty years, and no one has ever once asked me my opinion about anything.' "

THE ALIGNING TOOL: THE FEEDBACK SYSTEMS

Three of the leadership roles and their tools deal with one basic question: What matters most? The third role, aligning, deals with the question. Are we on target? Are we on track regarding what matters most?

The truth is, as mentioned earlier, we're *all* off track most of the time, all of us—every individual, family, organization or international flight to Rome. Just realizing this is a significant step. But, for many of us, the feeling of being off track brings with it discouragement and despair. It needn't and shouldn't be so depressing. Knowing we're off track is really an invitation to realign ourselves with true north (principles) and recommit ourselves to our destination.

Remember, our journey as an individual, team or organization is like the flight of an airplane. Before the plane takes off, the pilots file a flight plan. They know exactly where they're going. But during the course of the flight, wind, rain, turbulence, air traffic, human error and other factors act upon the plane. They move that plane slightly in different directions so that most of the time it is not even on the prescribed flight path. But barring anything too major, the plane will still arrive at its destination.

Now how does that happen? During the flight, the pilots receive constant feedback. They receive information from instruments that read the environment, control towers, other airplanes—even sometimes from the stars. And based on that feedback, they make adjustments so that time and time again, they return to the original plan.

The flight of that airplane is, I believe, the ideal metaphor for these four roles. Modeling, pathfinding, and empowering allow us to determine for our families, our organizations, our jobs and ourselves what matters most. These are our flight plans. The constant feedback that we, like pilots, receive represents our opportunity to check our progress and *realign* ourselves with the original guiding criteria. Together these roles and tools help us arrive at our envisioned destination.

ACHIEVING A BALANCE BETWEEN GETTING RESULTS AND DEVELOPING CAPABILITY

The key to the principle of alignment is to always begin with the results. What kind of results are you getting in the marketplace? Are your shareholders happy with the return on their investment? What about your employees? Are they happy with the return on their mental, physical, spiritual and emotional investment? What about suppliers? What about the community? Do you have any sense of social responsibility toward the kids, toward the schools, toward the streets, toward the air and water, toward the context in which your employees work and raise their families? What about all these results from these stakeholders? What about the customers? How is it going? What are the results? How do they benchmark against world-class standards? You have to study and examine all these stakeholder results and then examine the gap between those results and your strategy.

Effectiveness is the balance between *production of desired results* (P) and *production capability* (PC).* In other words, it's the golden eggs that people want and the goose that lays them. Sometimes we call this the P/PC Balance. The essence of effectiveness is achieving the results you want in a way that enables you to get even more of these results in the future.

Over the last ten years there have been many approaches developed to measure the P/PC Balance. I have frequently taught the importance of 360-degree feedback suggesting that the first 90 degrees represents financial accounting, and the remaining 270 degrees consists of scientifically gathered information on the perceptions of the organization's key stakeholders and the strength of their feelings around those perceptions.

There are many names for this kind of feedback. One of the strongest recent movements calls it *The Balanced Scorecard.* Sometimes I have called this approach double bottom-line accounting. Traditional accounting has always focused on the single bottom line (the golden eggs). Double bottom-line accounting also shows respect for the "goose," quantifying the health of the "goose" by summarizing the quality of the organization's relationships with all its key stakeholders— customers, suppliers, associates and their families, government, community, etc. You can imagine the power of having a two-page summary of the present and future health and strength of your organization—one page devoted to the financial statement (the present fruits of prior efforts), and the other giving you a leading indicator of your relationships with the stakeholders, which will produce all your future results.

The important thing is to come up with what we'll call a *Scoreboard*, a

---

* For more information on how to balance achieving results with building capability, see Appendix 8.

> Hardly anyone measures progress on their most important goals. Only 10 percent of xQ respondents report that they have a clear, accurate, visible scoreboard that provides genuine feedback. *Actionable intelligence for front-line decision making* is the imperative.

compelling scoreboard. The people who are involved, who will be evaluated, need to participate in establishing a compelling performance scoreboard that reflects the criteria built into the mission, values and strategy of an organization so that they can continuously stay aligned with the process and be both responsible and accountable. They need to emotionally connect to it and own it. This is *also* true of individuals, teams, departments or any person who has responsibility to complete a task or handle a project. Everyone should be involved in developing the Scoreboard, and then be accountable to it. Additional practical application suggestions on creating a compelling Scoreboard will be given in chapter 14.

Let me illustrate the importance of this idea of the Scoreboard feedback system by sharing an experience with you of an organization that came face-to-face with these diagnostic questions.

I was speaking to a national association of newspaper publishers and editors at a large conference. To prepare for the event I gathered data from cultural audits performed on various newspaper organizations. They indicated trust levels, commonality of purpose and values, systemic misalignment, and consequent disempowerment in the industry.

Before presenting the data I decided to try a different approach: walking around the large hall with a microphone and asking the questions "What is the essential role of newspapers in society? What is your central purpose?"

As I handed the microphone to person after person, they unhesitatingly spoke of the absolutely vital role that newspaper organizations play in our society. They believed the deeper analysis in the print media keeps government honest and public officials accountable and visible to the public. A cumulative expression focused around serving the country and our communities by preserving our most basic values: freedom, government being accountable to the people, the preservation of the checks and balances identified in the Constitution, helping to inform people in order to preserve the ideals of our democratic republic and free enterprise system.

Then I shifted my questions to "Do you really believe those purposes? Do you feel them in your heart?" And I walked around the room asking people to respond. The response was unanimously "yes." The next question was tougher. "How do you know if a person really believes particular values?" As different answers came forth, I posited the idea that one of the tests would be that the person tries to live his or her values. I suggested that integrity toward values indicates real belief. They agreed.

Then I got to the key question "How many of your newspaper organizations possess some function within your organizations that is similar to the function you provide to your community and to the country?" They were puzzled by my question. So I asked, "How many of you have a function inside your own organizations and/or culture to keep people honest, accountable, and aligned with your most basic ideals and values?" Only about 5 percent raised their hands. Then I shared with them the data that had been gathered from their cultural audits. I showed them the extreme levels of distrust, interpersonal conflict, interdepartmental rivalries, misalignment and profound disempowerment of people.

I then proceeded to share with them the idea of the four roles—of starting with themselves, of beginning the process of involving others in clarifying purposes, of setting up information and reinforcement and reward systems to create an optimum environment of empowerment. Many of those editors and publishers walked away from that event with a totally different paradigm of leadership. It was a very interesting and illuminating experience for all of us.

THE IMPORTANCE OF this kind of feedback applies not only to an organization, but also to individuals within an organization.

At one time I did a training program for the commanding generals of the air force in a country with a history of challenge and conflict. I was talking about the importance of getting feedback from their key stakeholders, and I noticed that the generals were nodding their heads in agreement. I turned to the general in charge and said, "Does this mean you're using such a system of feedback and measurement?"

He said, "That's the way we train these people. They're top pilots, not trained managers. Everyone gets an annual printout of the perceptions of all those they interface with, and the strength of those perceptions. They use it as the basis for their personal and professional development, and no one gets promoted unless they have high marks, including from their subordinates."

I said, "You have no idea how hard it is to get that concept bought into by many organizations in my country. What keeps it from becoming a popularity contest?"

Looking at me with disdain, he replied, "Stephen, the very survival of our country depends on these people and they know it. Do you really think we would allow ourselves to enter into popularity contests? In fact, sometimes the most unpopular people among us are given the highest marks, because they perform."

Aligning structures and systems with values and strategy is one of the toughest of all leadership and management challenges, simply because structures and systems represent the past—tradition, expectations and assumptions. Many people derive their security from the predictability and uncertainty of such structures and systems. They truly are "sacred cows" and cannot be ignored or kicked around unless there is deep buy-in and emotional connection to the strategic pathfinding criteria.

The following chart contrasts the structures and systems of the old Industrial Age control model with the new Knowledge Worker Age release/empowerment model (see table 5). While it's helpful to see the two in contrast, the real world would put these on more of a continuum than either/or. At the very least, perhaps these contrasting lists show the

ISSUE	OLD INDUSTRIAL AGE CONTROL MODEL	NEW KNOWLEDGE WORKER AGE RELEASE/EMPOWERMENT MODEL
Leadership	A position (formal authority)	A choice (moral authority)
Management	Control things and people	Control things, release (empower) people
Structure	Hierarchical, bureaucratic	Flatter, boundary-less, flexible
Motivation	External, carrot-and-sticking	Internal — whole person
Performance Appraisal	External, sandwich technique	Self-evaluation using 360° feedback
Information	Primarily short-term financial reports	Balanced Scoreboard (long-and-short term)
Communication	Primarily top-down	Open: Up / Down / Sideways
Culture	Social rules / mores of the workplace	Principle-centered values and economic rules of marketplace
Budgeting	Primarily top-down	Open, flexible, synergistic
Training & Development	Sideshow, skill-oriented, expendable	Maintenance, strategic, whole person, values
People	Expense on P & L, asset lip service	An investment with highest leverage
Voice	Generally unimportant for most	Strategic for all, complimentary, team

Table 5

extreme ends of each continuum and may serve to highlight the enormous leverage of aligning cultures, structures and systems with the pathfinding criteria.

FILM: *Berlin Wall*

The Berlin Wall was up for over forty years—over two generations. Imagine how deep the division between East and West became in the minds and hearts of the people. What a profound separation! What a profound contrast! When in 1989 it physically came down, it didn't necessarily come down in the hearts and minds of most of the people. It was like a sacred cow, like the old structures and systems of the Industrial Age. Tradition dies hard. I'll never forget a cab ride into East Berlin with no Berlin Wall, and hearing the cab driver complain about the feeling of insecurity he felt adjusting to a freer market and a more democratic society. He preferred the security and stability that the old regime and wall represented. This was a shock to me to hear him talk this way. He said most of the old-timers feel that way, and they are critical of the new generation, who prefer greater freedom to security.

As you view this film, think of how truly difficult it is for people to develop a new mind-set, a new paradigm, a new and different way of thinking—how it requires a new skill-set and a new tool-set. Think also of how futile it would be to teach people the new skills and tools with the old mind-set. It would be like putting new wine in old bottles. Please insert the companion DVD into your DVD player and select *Berlin Wall*.

We move now to the final and culminating role of leadership: empowering.

QUESTION & ANSWER

Q: What if you're in the middle of an organization with systems that are so focused on the short term, internal competition and force ranking systems, and numbers that it has produced a culture that feeds upon itself? What can you realistically do in such a situation?

A: If such an organization is tied to the competitive forces of the marketplace, you can use your freedom of choice and trim-tab yourself into a larger circle of influence. If it is not tied to the competitive forces of the marketplace, you may use the Greek philosophy—Ethos, Pathos and Logos, until others come to realize that their purposes will be better served by accepting your recommendations. Or, if you have paid the price in personal and professional development on a continuous basis to the point where your security lies in your power to produce solutions to problems and to meet human needs, you will have endless opportunities to do other things. In such a case you may do exactly that—choose to go elsewhere and do those other things.

Q: What is the most crucial activity of any management or leadership team, next to setting up the process of doing strategic pathfinding work?

A: I would say recruiting, selecting and positioning people. To use Jim Collins's language, to make sure that you have the *right* people in the *right* seats on the *right* bus. I would even say that recruiting, selecting and positioning are more important than training and development. The problem is that most organizations in a fast-moving economy need people so fast and the problems are so urgent that they go into crisis hiring practices. Remember, that which you desire most earnestly, you believe most easily. Then downstream you often have to live with real disasters. Instead, you should do strategic hiring so that you have carefully thought through the criteria, communicated them and paid the price to look in-depth at the track record of different people. Pay the price to really build a relationship with possible candidates to the point that they are authentic and transparent and have the time to decide whether their own vision, value and voice are in alignment with the strategic criteria of their future work. After this, the key is execution.

Q: In your experience, what is the best question to ask people when you hire them?

A: In my experience the best question is to say, "Starting with your earliest memory, what did you really like doing and did well?" Then push that through grade school, junior high, high school, university and work assignments afterward, until you start to see a real pattern of where people's real talents and strengths are—where their real voice is. You'll also see patterns of dependency, independency or interdependency, and you'll see a pattern of working with things, people or simply ideas. You must also be willing to share the strategically developed criteria of the roles you expect people to play.

Q: What happens when codependency (passivity and compliance) gets rewarded?

A: It will only be temporarily rewarded—the marketplace will slap it down; it cannot succeed in the long run because a passive, codependent person will not serve customers well with creativity, ingenuity and anticipation. In the long run, if you have transparency in, and good feedback from, the marketplace, neither codependent people nor cultures can survive. Lean, empowered, nimble, creative, innovative cultures are what is needed in today's global economy, particularly if your competition is global, not local.

Q: What about the whole process of building a team?

A: Team building is fundamental, particularly in developing complementary teams where people's strengths are made productive and their weaknesses are made irrelevant by the strengths of others—where the unifying force is a common vision and value system. But I'll tell you, it takes a lot of aligned systems and structures to reinforce team building. If you say to one flower, "Grow," but you water another, the first one won't grow. If you say let's work as a team, but then think independently and authoritatively and make a lot of unilateral, arbitrary decisions, you won't build a team. Team building is an extremely important and desirable activity if it is reinforced by team building principles inside the structures, systems and processes of the organization; otherwise, it will become a buzzword and sideshow and will not come under the main tent.

Q: How do you get a united, cohesive culture when you have so many different visions and goals throughout an entire organization?

A: Induce pain. As long as people are contented and happy, they're not going to do much. You don't want to wait until the market induces pain so you have to induce it in other ways. A balanced Scoreboard approach does it, particularly if people are accountable to it and if rewards are based on it.

Chapter 13

THE EMPOWERING VOICE—
RELEASING PASSION
AND TALENT

The best way to inspire people to a superior performance is to convince them by everything you do and by your everyday attitude that you are wholeheartedly supporting them.

HAROLD S. GRENEEN, FORMER CHAIRMAN OF ITT

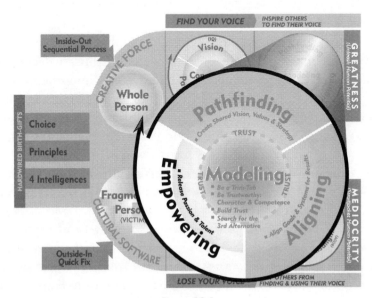

Figure 13.1

M Y T H	'Carrot and sticking'—the Jackass theory—is the best form of motivation. *(Old Paradigm)*
R E A L I T Y	'Carrot and stick' motivation is animal psychology. People have the power to choose. You can buy someone's back, but not their heart and mind. You can buy their hands, but not their spirit. *(New Paradigm)*

Figure 13.2

*T*HE FIRST ALTERNATIVE to the empowering role of leadership is trying to get results by controlling people.

The second alternative would be to set them loose, to abandon them. In other words, preach empowerment when, in fact, you're really into abdication and ignoring accountability.

The third alternative is both tougher and kinder; it's directed autonomy through win-win agreements around cascading line-of-sight goals and accountability for results.

I mentioned earlier that I believe most organizations, including our homes, are overmanaged and underled. Because the friction in our relationships with our children is a painful reminder of this reality, as is the rebellion that often ensues, and because the family setting is so universal, I'm going to begin our discussion of the challenge of empowerment with the true story of a friend and partner of mine who, with his wife, worked to overcome a challenge with their children:

I noticed a "dark cloud" forming over my wife one day. So I asked her, "What's wrong?" "I'm so discouraged," she answered. "Mornings with the kids before school are awful. I feel that if I were not here telling them what to do next, nothing would ever happen. They'd never get to school. They'd never get ready. They'd never get out of bed! I don't know what to do."

So I decided to observe the next morning. She went into each room starting at about 6:15, gave each child a gentle nudge and said, "Honey, it's time to get up. Wake up." She returned two or three times until they were all rousted out. Then she turned on the shower for the one who has the toughest time getting up. For the next ten minutes my wife returned to the shower repeatedly, tapped three times on the glass door, and said, "Time to get out." "I will!" came the defensive answer. Our daughter finally turned off the shower, dried off, went to her room, curled up into a little ball on the floor, and covered her body with the towel to warm up.

Ten minutes later, "Honey, you've got to get dressed. Come on."

"I don't have anything to wear!"

"Wear this."

"I don't like those clothes. They're ugly!"

"What do you want to wear?"

"My jeans—but they're dirty."

The emotional scenario continued until all three were called downstairs at 6:45. My wife continued to prod the children from one thing to the next, warning that the car pool would be coming any minute. They finally got out the door with a hug and a kiss, and Mom was exhausted. I was exhausted just having watched her all morning.

I thought, "No wonder she's miserable. These kids don't know they're capable of anything themselves because we're always there reminding them." That tapping on the shower door became a symbol of how we had both unintentionally enabled their irresponsibility.

So I called the family together one evening and suggested a new approach. "I've noticed that we are having quite a time with our mornings." Everyone started laughing knowingly. I said, "Who likes the way things are going?" No one raised a hand. So I said, "I want to tell you something that I want you to really think about. Here it is: You have within you the power to make choices. You can be responsible."

Then I went through a whole series of questions. I asked, "How many of you can set an alarm clock yourself, and then get up on your own each morning?" They all kind of looked at me like, "Dad, what are you doing?" I said, "No, really, how many of you can do this?" Each raised a hand. "How many of you can be aware enough of the time that you can remember how long you have to shower, and then can turn off the water by yourself?" They all raised their hands. "How many of you can go into your room, choose the clothes you want and then get dressed yourself?" It was getting to be fun because they all thought, "I can do that." "If you don't have the clothes you want, how many of you are capable of checking out what clothes you have the night before, and if the clothes you want are dirty, can do a load of your clothes in the washer and dryer?" "I can do that." "How many of you have the power to make your own bed and get your room cleaned up without being asked or reminded?" Everyone raised a hand. "How many of you can be downstairs at 6:45 for our family time and breakfast?" They all raised a hand.

We went on through every single thing. In each case they agreed, "I have the power and capacity to do this." Then I said, "Okay. What we're going to do is write all this down. We're going to create and agree to a plan for our mornings."

They wrote down all the things they wanted to do and worked out a schedule. Our daughter with whom we were having the greatest struggle was the most excited. She wrote a schedule down to the very minute. We became their source of help on some things. There were a few guidelines. We decided on how and when they'd be accountable and what the consequences would be. The positive consequences were that everyone would be a lot happier in the morning—especially Mom. And we all know that a happy Mom means a happy family! The negative consequence to not getting up on time and completing all their responsibilities on their own was that they would go to bed a half an hour earlier for a few days. This seemed fair, since lack of sleep usually makes it more difficult to get up. Each child signed their agreement, ate a bowl of ice cream, and went off to bed. So we thought, "Okay. We'll see what happens."

The next morning at six o'clock my wife and I were lying in bed. We heard an alarm go off and the light click on in one of the kid's rooms. Before we knew it our daughter with whom we had the toughest time ran to the shower, turned on the water, and got in. My wife and I smiled at each other in mild amazement. We had real hopes it would work with her—but fifteen minutes early? Within fifteen or twenty minutes, she had done everything that usually took an hour and a half, and she even had time to get her piano practicing done. We had a great morning. The other kids did the same thing.

After the kids were out the door, my wife said, "I am in heaven. But the real test is, will it continue? I can see them getting really excited about one morning, but will it go on?"

Well, it's been over a year now. Though we haven't always had quite the enthusiasm of that first morning, with only occasional exceptions (which were followed by earlier bedtimes for a few days) they've all gotten up and done everything on their own. We've also found it helpful to come together every few months to evaluate how we're doing and to renew our commitment.

It's been wonderful to see the children grow in their sense of "I can do this. I have the power. I am responsible." We try not to remind. It's been a profound lesson, and it's totally changed the nature of our family life in the mornings.

You can see that the parents were initially trying to work from the mind-set that says the *kids* needed to change, but gradually came to the awareness that *they* needed to change. The mind-set was that kids need reminding. You've got to check up, hover, and follow up. Maybe you've *worked* for someone like that. It's classic management/control thinking.

But then the parents reflected on their children's worth and potential—particularly their potential. They knew the children had tremendous worth, and they loved them unconditionally, but they had fallen into the typical trap of looking at their children through the lens of misbehavior. They had also not yet clearly communicated to the children their potential. They did this by asking some simple questions about whether the children believed—if they had the mind to—that they could do the basic things of getting up, doing their jobs, and getting ready to go to school. Because the children so identified emotionally with the parents, the communication took. Commitments were made and kept; potential was released; responsibility was taken; growth took place; mutual trust and confidence increased; and peace of mind and peace at home resulted. It's a beautiful, powerful example of empowerment.

Even though this is a simple little family problem, most people can identify with it. Sometimes in organizations, as well as families, people believe in the potential of others but not in their worth, so they're not patient, persistent, long-suffering, trust-giving, and self-sacrificing. It's just not worth it to them; it becomes a cost-benefit analysis and they perhaps unwittingly conclude that the cost is too great. In fact, unless people have a sense of their own personal worth, they will not be able to consistently communicate the worth of other people.

MODELING PRINCIPLE-CENTERED trustworthy behavior inspires trust without "talking it." *Pathfinding* creates order without demanding it. *Aligning* nourishes both vision and empowerment without proclaiming them. *Empowerment* is the fruit of the other three. It is the natural result of both personal and organizational trustworthiness, which enables people to identify and unleash their human potential. In other words, empowering enthrones self-control, self-management and self-organizing. If this co-missioning takes place, not just in organizational pathfinding but at the team, project, task, or job level, where the basic needs of the people and organization overlap, it taps into passion, energy and drive—in short, voice.

Passion is the fire, enthusiasm and courage that an individual feels when she is doing something she loves while accomplishing worthy ends, something that satisfies her deepest needs. Again, remember the roots of the word *enthusiasm* mean "God in you." Empowerment is exactly the same thing, only it's in the *organizational* context of employees doing work they love, and doing it in such a way that meets their deepest needs and the essential needs of the organization. Their voices blend.

In the book *Now Discover Your Strengths*, authors Marcus Buckingham and Donald O. Clifton report this key finding of the Gallup Organization: "The great organization must not only accommodate the fact that each employee is different; it must capitalize on these differences."[1] The authors also report Gallup's research findings surrounding the following question asked of 198,000 employees working in 7,939 business units within thirty-six companies:

> At work, do you have the opportunity to do what you do best every day? We then compared the responses to the performance of the business units and discovered the following: When employees answered "strongly agree" to this question, they were 50% more likely to work in business units with lower employee turnover, 38% more likely to work in more productive business units, and 44% more likely to work in business units with higher customer satisfaction scores. And over time those business units that increased the number of employees who strongly agreed saw company increases in productivity, customer loyalty and employee retention.[2]

Just think about your own personal life. What kind of a job do you like? What kind of supervision? What taps into your deepest passion? What if you had a job that tapped into your passion and a job in which your leaders became your servants—where they existed to personally or systematically help you do your job? What if structures and systems were supportive, helpful, and were geared toward enabling, identifying and releasing your potential? What if you were continuously recognized and rewarded, and most importantly, felt the intrinsic satisfaction of contributing significantly to a cause you felt worthy of such heartfelt commitment?

EMPOWERING THE KNOWLEDGE WORKER

We live in an age of the knowledge worker, where intellectual capital is supreme. Product cost used to be 80 percent on materials and 20 percent on knowledge; now it's split 70/30 the other way.[3] Stuart Crainer, in his book *The Management Century*, writes, "The information age places a premium on intellectual work. There is a growing realization that recruiting, retaining, and nurturing talented people is crucial to competitiveness."[4]

Peter Drucker, in his book *Managing for the Future: The 1990s and Beyond*, writes, "From now on, the key is knowledge. The world is not becoming labor intensive, not materials intensive, not energy intensive, but knowledge intensive."[5]

Leadership is today's hottest topic. The new economy is based on knowledge work, and knowledge work is another word for people. Remember, eighty percent of value added to products and services today comes from knowledge work. It's a knowledge worker economy; wealth creation has migrated from money and things to people.

Our greatest financial investment is the knowledge worker. Just consider what has been invested in the knowledge workers in your organization through salary, benefits, possible stock options and what it took to recruit and train them. That often translates into hundreds of thousands of dollars per year per person!

Quality knowledge work is so valuable that unleashing its potential offers organizations an extraordinary opportunity for value creation. Knowledge work leverages all of the other investments that an organization has already made. In fact, knowledge workers are the link to all other organizational investments. They provide focus, creativity, and leverage in utilizing those investments to better achieve the organization's objectives. Intellectual and social capital are key to leveraging and optimizing all other investments.

And so it is absolutely critical that the empowerment of people (aligning voices) is seen as the *fruit* of modeling, aligning and pathfinding. Otherwise, you will see organizations talk and proclaim empowerment but remain unable to walk their talk. They have no common vision, no discipline and definitely no passion.

Empowerment is not a new idea. In fact, during the nineties it became quite a buzzword and movement in the field of management. But frankly, the empowerment movement has created a lot of cynicism and anger—both with management and among the rank and file. Why? Because again, empowering people is the *fruit* of the other three roles, not the root.

We surveyed 3,500 managers and professionals in client organizations and asked the question: What's holding back empowerment? (See figure

13.3). Notice how their answers underscore the importance of *both* personal and organizational trustworthiness (character and competence):

What is holding back EMPOWERMENT?

Survey of 3,500 managers

Manager afraid to let go	97%
Misaligned systems	93%
Manager lacks skills	92%
Employees lack skills	80%
Employees don't want responsibility	76%
Manager too busy	70%
Management too controlling	67%
Lack of company vision	64%
Employees don't trust manager	49%
Employees lack integrity	12%

Figure 13.3

Now that you've soaked deeper in this Whole Person / 4 Roles paradigm of leadership, you can see why people would become frustrated when empowerment efforts are undertaken without the foundational modeling, pathfinding and aligning work being done first.

THE MANAGER'S DILEMMA—DO I GIVE UP CONTROL?

A few years ago I remember interviewing the chief executive of a company who had just received the prestigious Malcolm Baldrige National Quality Award. I asked him, "What was your toughest challenge as CEO in achieving this level of quality in your organization?" With but a moment of thought, he smiled, and said, "Giving up control."

Empowerment will *always* be a cynicism-inducing platitude unless it's rooted in solid modeling, pathfinding and aligning work. The 4 Roles of Leadership break the manager's dilemma of being caught between *control* and *fear of losing control*. When you truly establish the conditions for empowerment, control is not lost: it is simply transformed into *self-control*.

Self-control does not come when you simply abandon people in the name of "empowerment"; it comes when there is a commonly understood end in mind, with agreed-upon guidelines and supportive structures and systems, and when each person is set up as a whole person in a whole job. Training and coaching is provided to those who lack the competence required to be fully entrusted with greater freedom. A track record of consistent performance earns greater and greater trust and latitude in methods. People become accountable for results and have the freedom, within guidelines, to achieve those results in a way that taps into their unique talents.

I call this *directed autonomy*. The manager's role then shifts from controller to enabler—co-missioning with people, removing barriers, and becoming a source of help and support. That's quite a shift.

When we discussed the trim-tabbing leader, who was full of vision, discipline, passion and conscience, we were talking about self-empowerment. Now, in the larger context, we're looking at how to create an official, institutionalized, formalized philosophy of empowerment. Ideally you would like to have both personal and organizational empowerment so that a person doesn't have to swim upstream against disempowering organizational forces.

THE EMPOWERING TOOL:
THE WIN-WIN AGREEMENT PROCESS

Think about the whole win-win process as two volunteers who co-mission together—one representing the organization and the other representing the stakeholders, team, or individual. Max De Pree, who wrote the brilliant book *Leadership is an Art*, describes the spirit of volunteers working together:

> The best people working for organizations are life volunteers. Since they could probably find good jobs in any number of groups, they choose to work somewhere for reasons less tangible than salary or position. Volunteers do not need contracts, they need covenants. . . . Covenantal relationships induce freedom not paralysis. A covenantal relationship rests on shared commitment to ideas, to issues, to values, to goals, and to management process. Words such as love, warmth, personal chemistry, are certainly pertinent. Covenantal relationships . . . fill deep needs and they enable work to have meaning and to be fulfilling.[6]

A win-win agreement is not a formal job description, neither is it a legal contract. It's an open-ended, psychological/social contract that ex-

plicitly defines expectations. It is written first into the hearts and minds
of people, and then put on paper "in pencil" rather than in ink so that
"easy erasing" can take place when both sense it is appropriate and wise.
You can discuss and renegotiate it at will, based on changing circumstances. Whether people use the language "win-win agreements" or not,
the idea is that you have a common understanding and commitment toward your highest mutual priorities.

Win-win agreements enable a much higher level of flexibility, adaptation and creativity than do job descriptions, which focus primarily on
steps and methods. With the win-win agreement we look at the situation, maturity, character and competence of team members and formal
leaders, and other environmental conditions, such as the presence of
aligned structures, systems and processes.

Once a win-win agreement has been developed, the answer to the
question What's my/our top priority? is abundantly clear. Responsibilities are laid out. Mutual expectations are articulated. Accountability to
these expectations in the form of a balanced Scoreboard is established.
People are free to do whatever they need to do to accomplish the goals
within the context of the guidelines. They simply manage themselves.
They become empowered. In chapter 14, The 8th Habit and The Sweet
Spot, much more will be said on how to foster strong, enabling team accountability.

WIN-WIN EMPOWERMENT: MOVING FROM THE
INDUSTRIAL TO THE KNOWLEDGE WORKER AGE

Now what if we were to forget all we've learned about the whole person? What if we lost sight of the fire that is lit inside those individuals
and organizations when they Find Their Voice and Inspire Others to
Find Their Voice, and we kept working through our traditional Industrial Age "lenses" and traditions? Can you see how easy it would be to
apply the win-win agreement process in the classic style of a controlling
manager? You can see that all the efforts simply would not yield the fruit
of empowerment.

Successful empowerment rests in a commitment to work with team
members by "win-win agreement." In an organization, "win-win" means
that there is an explicit overlapping of the four needs of the organization
(financial health, growth and development, synergistic relationships
with key stakeholders and meaning/contribution) with the four needs of

the individual (physical—economic; mental—growth and development; social/emotional—relationships; and spiritual—meaning and contribution).

If someone violates the spirit of the agreement and continues to do so in spite of sincere efforts to heal the breach, then the individuals may simply go for *no deal.* That means you don't deal at all. There is no agreement. You agree to disagree agreeably. People leave. Hires aren't made. New assignments may be made.

There is a really interesting approach to no-deal that is promulgated by the armed services. It's called the doctrine of stubborn refusal. I learned the doctrine of stubborn refusal from interacting with naval officers. It means that when you know something is wrong and that it would result in serious consequences to the overall mission and values of the organization, then you should respectfully push back, no matter what your position or rank. You should speak up and declare yourself in opposition to the momentum of a growing decision that you are absolutely convinced is dead wrong. That's essentially living from your conscience—allowing your inner voice or light to guide your actions rather than giving in to the sway of peer pressure.

It is important for people in high positions to officially endorse the doctrine of stubborn refusal. This legitimizes the right to push back, to call wrong wrong and to call stupid stupid.

EMPOWERMENT AND PERFORMANCE APPRAISAL

When you think about it, who should evaluate a person's progress and achievements? That person should. Traditional performance appraisal is clearly one of the bloodletting management practices of our day. As mentioned before, this is where the boss basically interviews an employee and uses the sandwich technique—say a few nice words, slip in the knife, twist it a few times—"areas for improvement"—and then pat them on their way. When you have a high-trust culture, helpful systems, and people on the same page, then people are in a far better position to evaluate themselves, particularly if they have 360-degree feedback data from sources around them. Good evidence is shown by looking at the 7 Habits Profile data (see figure 13.4), which involve over a half a million people who have engaged in 360-degree feedback.

You can see in almost all cases that self-evaluation is tougher than anyone else's evaluation. The bosses know the least—they are the fur-

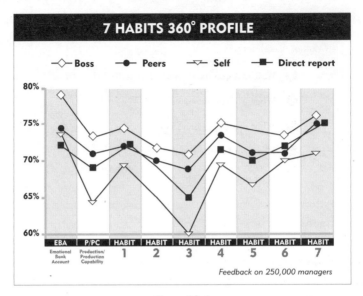

Figure 13.4

thest removed. Codependent people tell them what they like to hear, and they become isolated and insulated from what is in fact going on. The subordinates know next best, and then the peers. Again, in both biblical parables of the pounds and the talents that we mentioned near the beginning of chapter 6, the employee evaluates self, and the master either diminishes or enlarges stewardship.

It would be so misaligned to think that after all this empowerment and honoring of people's power to choose in reaching top-priority goals, you could suddenly set up a so-called boss to be the big judge and evaluator.

The so-called big boss should become the humble servant leader who "runs alongside," asking questions such as (see figure 13.5).

First, *"How is it going?"* The worker knows how it's going far better than any boss does, particularly if feedback systems have been established, including feedback from the boss and from all other stakeholders who are influenced by the work of the person. So the question How is it going? is answered by the person himself or herself according to the terms of the agreed-upon compelling balanced Scoreboard and other 360-degree stakeholder information.

The second question is *"What are you learning?"* A person here may reveal both insights and ignorance, but the point is that they are responsible.

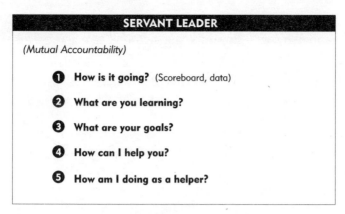

Figure 13.5

The third question is *"What are your goals?"* or *"What are you trying to accomplish?"* It identifies the connection between the vision and the reality. This leads naturally to the fourth question, *"How can I help you?"* clearly communicating that "I am your helper. I am your enabler, your servant." The servant leader might even tap into his or her own experience or awareness to see if that needs to be drawn upon. The key to this exchange is authentic, Indian Talking Stick–type communication. No game playing. No political posturing. No protective, defensive communication. No kissing up. No telling others what they want to hear. The question How am I doing as your helper? communicates open, respectful mutual accountability.

Sometimes facing reality is difficult, especially when hearing it from others. But we demean and insult other people when we treat them as anyone other than accountable, responsible, choice-making individuals. If, in the name of being nice and kind, we start protecting them, we begin the process of the codependency and silent conspiracy that eventually results in the lowest level of initiative—"Wait until told."

It is when the spirit of servant leadership takes hold in a team, and between a manager or team and an associate, that the third form of *trust* mentioned in chapter 9 fully blossoms. Again, it's the trust that one person or team consciously chooses to *give* to another—an act that leads me to *feel* your belief that I can add value. You give me trust and I return it. *Trust* is a verb AND a noun. When it's both a verb and a noun, it's something shared and reciprocated between people. That is the essence of how a person becomes the leader of their boss. They merit trust by giving it. *Trust* the verb comes from the potential trustworthiness of the one receiving the trust and the clear trustworthiness of the one giving the trust. The fourth role—Empowering—embodies making *trust* a verb.

THE CASE OF THE JANITORS (TURNING MANUAL WORKERS INTO KNOWLEDGE WORKERS)

The following is a true story of a whole person in a whole job. It illustrates what can happen in a job that, though honorable, is by nature more menial, unskilled, and low-paid—janitoring. The idea is that if you can have a whole person in a whole job that consists of emptying garbage cans, sweeping and mopping floors, and washing walls and fixtures, etc., you could have it in any job.

A management development instructor was once training a group of first-level supervisors how to enrich a job so that it intrinsically motivates employees. One of the foremen who supervised janitors gave considerable resistance to the theory. It seemed too idealistic and unrelated to most of the work a janitor does—at least the janitors *he* supervised. All the supervisors being trained agreed that there was a problem with the janitors. They agreed with the supervisor that most of their janitors were uneducated, transient, and were there because they couldn't get a better job. Essentially their only desire was to clock in and clock out. Some were even alcoholics.

Because the instructor knew the maintenance foreman was sincere in his belief that motivation and empowerment theory was of no use to him in working with janitors, he abandoned his prepared discussion and began to deal with the janitorial problem directly.

He placed three words on the blackboard: Plan, Do, and Evaluate—three major elements of job enrichment. He then asked the maintenance foreman and the other foremen to list the maintenance duties and activities associated with these three words. Some aspects of the "planning" part of the job were: establishing schedules for maintenance, selecting and purchasing waxes and polishes, and determining which janitor covered which areas of the plant. During the discussion, the maintenance foreman said that he was about to purchase several new floor polishing and scrubbing machines. All of these planning activities were carried out by the maintenance foreman.

Listed under the "doing" section were the normal activities of janitors—sweeping, scrubbing, waxing, and removing the rubbish and refuse. The "evaluating" part of the job included such activities as routine daily checks on the cleanliness of the plant by the maintenance foreman, evaluation of the effectiveness of different soaps, waxes and polishes, reflecting on trial efforts, identifying ways of improving, and ensuring that the cleaning schedules were maintained. Additionally, the maintenance foreman also contacted vendors to determine the type of new machines he could purchase.

When the various activities had been listed, the instructor asked, "Which of these activities could be done by the janitors? For example, why do you, Mr. Foreman, determine which soaps to buy? Why not let your janitors decide? How about having the salesmen give the demonstration of the new machine to the janitors and let them decide which of the machines is best? How about having the janitors identify parts of the job they would be interested in taking on?" (In the actual situation, the wording was not quite so blunt, and the entire group of foremen got involved in the discussion about what additional areas of planning and evaluating could be given to the janitors.)

Over the next five months, the case of the janitors was discussed, at least briefly, in every session held by the instructor. Meanwhile, the maintenance supervisor was engaging more of the minds and hearts of the janitors by steadily giving them more responsibility for the planning, doing and evaluating of their work. They tested out new machines and made the final recommendations for purchase. They experimented with different waxes to determine which stood up the best under normal usage. They began examining the cleaning schedule to determine how much attention should be given to each area. For example, one area that had been wet-mopped daily was mopped only as needed after visual inspection. The janitors developed their own criteria for determining plant cleanliness and began to exert peer pressure on janitors who did not meet the norms.

Little by little, these janitors took over all three tasks so that their best thinking was tapped—body, heart, mind and spirit. The net effect, to the surprise of most, was that quality went up, job turnover and discipline problems went way down, social norms developed around initiative, cooperation, diligence and quality, and job satisfaction increased significantly. In short, they had a turned-on group of janitors—all because the supervisors allowed or empowered the whole person to do the whole job. They had directed autonomy. The janitors no longer needed supervision or management because they supervised and managed themselves according to the criteria they helped develop.

Perhaps more importantly, other foremen began thinking about how they could apply the same principles in their own areas, especially since they could begin to see for themselves the results of the maintenance foreman's work with the janitors.

Service and Meaning

If we put this "plan, do, evaluate" idea into our whole-person model of leadership, here is what it looks like (see figure 13.6):

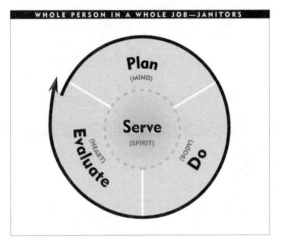

Figure 13.6

The fourth element, "serve," is added at the center to acknowledge the need of the spirit for meaning and contribution. You can see that even the janitors in this case began to experience great meaning in their work. They developed deep pride of workmanship, and it began to lift the level of quality in the entire plant. They found their voice. Again notice the arrow on the outside edge of the diagram. That indicates that this is a cycle, a process. Once the evaluating work is done, new plans are developed that incorporate recent learnings; those plans are executed; and the cycle of improvement repeats itself.

You might ask, "Well, if you empower people to this extent, why do you need supervisors at all?" The simple answer is to set up the *conditions of empowerment* and then to get out of people's way, clear their path and become a source of help as requested. This is servant leadership. After all, your job is not about getting your ego stroked. It's about getting the job done.

Only 45 percent of xQ respondents say they feel their contributions at work are recognized and appreciated.

CHOICES REVISITED

The case of the janitors is a good reminder that people make choices in their work based upon how well the four areas of their nature are respected and engaged. As you can see in the left-hand column in the figure below, each choice is made in response to a deeper motivation that ranges from anger, fear and reward to duty, love and meaning (see figure 13.7):

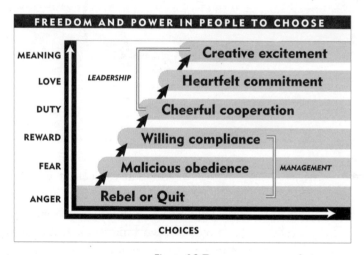

Figure 13.7

Duty, love and meaning are the highest sources of human motivation and will always produce the greatest and most enduring achievements. Leadership draws on the highest of all human impulses. Managing people like things reduces human beings to their lowest instincts. It is modern-day management bloodletting.

This story also illustrates an extremely important point: It's the *leadership beliefs and style of the manager*, not the nature of the job or economic era, that defines whether a person is a knowledge worker or not.

If he is not perceived as a knowledge worker, that is, if a janitor is not seen as the local expert on janitorial work, then he is a manual worker and not a knowledge worker.

FILM: *The Nature of Leadership**

This next little film that I recommend is very much like the opening film in the book. It will give you an opportunity to personally reflect on the underlying principles of this leadership framework, and it will challenge you to internalize and act on them. Nature is the backdrop and the teacher. I believe it will inspire you, as it has me. Again, you will find this film and all the others on the book's companion DVD.

LET'S MOVE NOW to putting it all together by demonstrating how the 4 Roles of Leadership are a framework for focus and execution.

QUESTION & ANSWER

Q: You talk about a complementary team. I'm a loner with no staff or direct reports and have to wear all the hats—how do I develop a complementary team to compensate for my weaknesses?

A: Until you have other people to whom you can delegate, so that your strength can be made productive and your weaknesses made irrelevant by their strengths, you will need to either reach at least a threshold level of competence on your weaknesses or outsource to advisors or suppliers who can compensate.

Q: How do you empower employees in an environment that is highly regulated, with the constant intrusion of new mandates, policies and regulations?

---

* The magnificent photography in this film was taken by Dewitt Jones and Roger Merrill, and is drawn from the book *The Nature of Leadership*.

A: I would turn to the employees and ask them that question: What do you suggest; what is your opinion? I mean it; I would lay it right on their platter. People are amazingly creative and resilient, and no matter how oppressive a regulatory environment may be, if the work is meaningful, you'll always be able to find some areas of creative opportunity where people can exercise their own judgment. In terms of establishing agreements, the regulations are to be clearly indicated as guidelines, even rules to be followed.

I lived in England one time and saw the railroad people become disgusted because of the extreme regulatory environment. They decided, "Okay, we're going to follow the rules to the hilt," and it literally brought all of England to a standstill. None of the trains arrived on time. It was totally chaotic, simply because they strictly followed the checklist of rules. The only way they'd succeeded before had been through their creativity, initiative and resourcefulness. Once this became clearly evident, the administrators began to put more value on human judgment than on rules, and it began to work again.

You may be able to set up a pilot or experimental program that will produce better results at lower costs and without violating any jugular rules. The risk is less and the learning potential is great. And you may begin to discriminate more carefully between rules that are jugular and those that are peripheral or purely cultural artifacts.

I once worked with the highly regulated nuclear power industry. The level of cooperation and communication, even between competitors, was astounding because they all knew that if they had one more Three Mile Island incident, it could shut down the entire industry. On their own they shared every incident or situation that produced any element of risk or breach of safety. The regulatory administrators of the government could not even begin to ratchet up the regulations high enough to compare to what these competitive companies did on their own.

Q: How do you enforce accountability in a win-win way? Doesn't the spirit of win-win tend to go soft on accountability?

A: Absolutely not. The key is to establish accountability against mutually agreed-upon desired results. Use a balanced Scoreboard on these results with both logical and natural consequences that follow the accountability. Without a balanced Scoreboard and agreed-upon desired results and consequences, win-lose will end up becoming lose-win and, in the long run, lose-lose.

Q: How do you deal with the maverick employee—one who just seems to buck at every decision and does his own thing in his own way?

A: A lot of significant progress is made by mavericks. There should always be a place for people who think differently and who are fresh and creative in their thought processes. Learn to appreciate the unique strengths of each person, but if their "maverick-ness" reaches the point where they are poisonous, negative and critical, then I would say set up a feedback system that gives them feedback. Let them soak in others' candid perceptions and the feelings around those perceptions of them until they make their own minds up about what they really want to do. If a maverick is a deviant kind of person who really gets his psychological jollies from violating social norms, and if he adds no real value through creative and innovative contributions, you may need to go into outplacement services. There are a lot of people who are independents—they're not interdependent, but they're also not deviants, and they can play a very important role in independent-oriented kinds of jobs. The real key is to create a culture that embraces diversity within a context of unified purpose and values. As Emile Durkheim put it, "When mores are sufficient, laws are unnecessary; when mores are insufficient, laws are unenforceable."

Q: I personally have a strong need to be in control, and this whole idea of release scares me, even thought it makes sense. Can I change?

A: Absolutely. You're not an animal. Although influenced *by*, you're not a product *of* nature and nurture. You're a product of your choices, but you would have to begin to change at the personal level by using your three unique human endowments—the power of choice, principles and your four intelligences or capacities. Through patience and persistence, you will overcome these control needs, and as you grow in confidence with just a few people closely around you at home and at work, you will come to feel that there is more productivity and peace of mind in teaching principles by both precept and example, as well as in letting others govern themselves. Eventually, you will learn how to institutionalize this kind of moral authority in systems, structures and processes.

The Age of Wisdom

Chapter 14

THE 8TH HABIT AND
THE SWEET SPOT

*The difference between what we are doing and what we're capable of
doing would solve most of the world's problems.*

MAHATMA GANDHI

THE 8TH HABIT—Find Your Voice and Inspire Others to Find Theirs—is an idea whose time has come. "Whose time has come" is a phrase from the famous line by Victor Hugo quoted earlier: "There is nothing so powerful as an idea whose time has come."

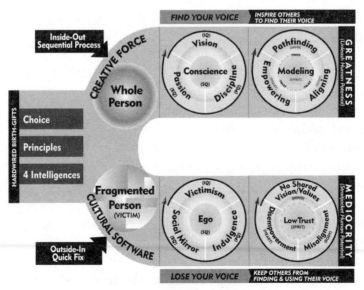

Figure 14.1

The reason why the 8th Habit is such an idea is that it embodies an understanding of the whole person—an understanding that gives its possessors *the* key to crack open the limitless potential of the knowledge worker economy. As is represented on the lower road of figure 14.1, the Industrial Age manual worker economy was based on a part- or fragmented-person paradigm. In today's world, this lower road leads to mediocrity at best. It literally straitjackets human potential. Organizations mired in the mind-set of the Industrial Age continue to have the people at the top making all the important decisions and have the rest "wielding screwdrivers." What an enormous waste! What an enormous loss!

Remember again the statement by author John Gardner: "Most ailing organizations have developed a functional blindness to their own defects. They are not suffering because they cannot resolve their problems but because they cannot *see* their problems." This is *exactly* what has happened.

The 8th Habit gives you a mind-set and a skill-set to constantly look for the potential in people. It's the kind of leadership that communicates to people their worth and potential so clearly they come to see it in themselves. To do this, we must listen to people. We must involve and continually affirm them by our words and through all 4 Roles of Leadership.

Here is a succinct way to remember what each role does. Notice how each role directly or indirectly affirms people's worth as whole people and empowers the unleashing of their potential.

First, *modeling* (individual, team). Modeling inspires trust without expecting it. When people live by the principles embodied in the 8th Habit, trust, the glue of life, flourishes; trust comes only through trustworthiness. In short, modeling produces *personal moral authority*.

Second, *pathfinding*. Pathfinding creates order without demanding it. That means when people identify and are involved in the strategic decisions, particularly on values and high-priority goals, they emotionally connect; the locus of both management and motivation goes from the outside to the inside. Pathfinding produces *visionary moral authority*.

Third, *aligning*. Aligning structures, systems and processes is a form of nourishing the body politic and the spirit of trust, vision and empowerment. Aligning produces *institutionalized moral authority*.

Fourth, *empowering*. Empowering is the fruit of the other three roles—modeling, pathfinding and aligning. It unleashes human poten-

Figure 14.2

tial without external motivation. Empowering produces *cultural moral authority.*

Remember, the most important modeling is done by the leader when he or she *models the other three roles.* In other words, pathfinding is modeling the *courage* to determine a course and the *humility* and *mutual respect* to involve others in deciding what matters most. Aligning is modeling the willingness to set up structures, systems and processes that are congruent with the "what matters most" strategic decisions so that the organization stays constantly focused on its highest-priority goals. Empowering is modeling a bone-deep belief in people's capacity to choose and in the four parts of their nature through co-missioning processes.

FOCUS AND EXECUTION

I suggest that all that we have covered can be essentially summarized in two words: Focus and Execution. In these two words we truly find "simplicity on the far side of complexity." Again, *focus* deals with what matters most, and *execution* deals with making it happen. The cutting-edge bestseller business book by Ram Charan and Larry Bossidy called *Execution: The Discipline of Getting Things Done* has been influential in my thinking behind this two-word summary.

The first two roles of leadership—*modeling* and *pathfinding*—can

> *Leadership without the discipline of execution is incomplete and ineffective. Without the ability to execute, all other attributes of leadership become hollow.*
>
> *No company can deliver on its commitments or adapt well to change unless all leaders practice the discipline of execution at all levels. Execution has to be part of a company strategy in its goals. It is the missing link between aspirations and results.*[1]
>
> RAM CHARAN AND LARRY BOSSIDY

be summarized in one word: *focus.* The next two roles of leadership—*aligning* and *empowering*—can be summarized in one word: *execution.* How is this so? Think about it. Pathfinding is essentially strategic work; it's deciding what the higher-priority goals are—what values are to serve as guidelines in accomplishing and sustaining those goals. But this requires both a clear understanding and a commitment in the culture toward these goals. Such commitment is based upon trust, trustworthiness and synergy—the essence of modeling. Only when there is true personal and interpersonal trustworthiness will trust develop and team synergy be effective. This personal/interpersonal modeling involves mutual respect, mutual understanding and creative cooperation (Habits 4, 5 and 6) in producing a clear, committed set of high-priority goals (Habit 2: Begin With the End in Mind). This personal/interpersonal trustworthiness is in turn based on people living true to their values and goals—in other words, personal focus and execution. This is Habit 3: Put First Things First. The expression "first things first" is another way of describing focus and execution.

The next two roles of leadership, *aligning* and *empowering*, represent the *execution.* This means creating structures, systems and processes (*aligning*) that intentionally enable individuals and teams to translate the organization's larger "line-of-sight" strategic goals or critical priorities (pathfinding) into their actual day-to-day work and team goals. In short, people are *empowered* to get the job done.

Focus and execution are inseparably connected. In other words, until you have people on the same page, they will not execute consistently. If you use the Industrial Age command-and-control transaction model to get focus, you won't be able to use the Knowledge Worker Age empowering transformation model to get execution—simply because without involvement and/or identification, you will not get emotional commitment to the focus. Execution will simply not take place. Likewise, if you use a knowledge worker/involvement/empowerment approach to achieve a common focus, but then an Industrial Age/command-and-control approach for execution, you won't be able to maintain the focus because people will perceive the lack of sincerity and integrity.

On the other hand, if you use the Knowledge Age model on both focus (modeling, pathfinding) and execution (aligning, empowering), you will produce integrity and trustworthiness in the organizational culture. The organization will not only find its voice but it will also use its voice to superbly serve its purposes and stakeholders.

THE GREAT EXECUTION GAP

Early in the book I made the statement, "To know and not to do is really not to know." This is a profound truth. The principles encompassed in the 8th Habit are of little worth until they, by practice and *execution*, become part of our character and skill-set—until they become a *habit*.

Execution is *the* great unaddressed issue in most organizations today.

I am your constant companion. I am your greatest helper or heaviest burden. I will push you onward or drag you down to failure. I am completely at your command. Half the things you do you might just as well turn over to me, and I will be able to do them quickly, correctly. I am easily managed—you must merely be firm with me. Show me exactly how you want something done, and after a few lessons I will do it automatically. I am the servant of all great people; and alas, of all failures as well. Those who are failures, I have made failures. I am not a machine, though I work with all the precision of a machine plus the intelligence of a human being. You may run me for a profit or turn me for ruin—it makes no difference to me. Take me, train me, be firm with me, and I will place the world at your feet. Be easy with me and I will destroy you.

Who am I? I am habit.

—ANONYMOUS

It is one thing to have clear strategy; it is quite another to actually implement and realize the strategy, to execute. In fact, most leaders would agree that they'd be better off having an average strategy with superb execution than a superb strategy with poor execution. Those who execute always have the upper hand. As Louis V. Gerstner, Jr., put it, "All of the great companies in the world *out-execute* their competitors day in and day out in the marketplace, in their manufacturing plants, in their logistics, in their inventory turns—in just about everything they do. Rarely do great companies have a proprietary position that insulates them from the constant hand-to-hand combat of competition."[2]

There are many things that effect execution, but our xQ research shows that there are six core drivers to execution in an organization: *clarity, commitment, translation, enabling, synergy* and *accountability*. It follows, then, that breakdowns in execution typically occur as failures in one or more of these six drivers. We call them *execution gaps:*

- Clarity—people don't clearly know what the goals or priorities of their team or organization are;
- Commitment—people don't buy into the goals;
- Translation—people don't know what they individually need to do to help the team or organization achieve its goals;
- Enabling—people don't have the proper structure, systems or freedom to do their jobs well;
- Synergy—people don't get along or work together well; and
- Accountability—people don't regularly hold each other accountable.

> *So much of what we call management consists of making it difficult for people to work.*
> PETER DRUCKER

The following chart (table 6) identifies these six execution gaps/drivers and gives a very simplified explanation of how the controlling Industrial Age mind-set literally causes these gaps and how the Knowledge Worker/whole-person model, which embodies the 8th Habit, can solve them.

EXECUTION GAPS	INDUSTRIAL AGE CAUSE	KNOWLEDGE WORKER AGE SOLUTION
Clarity	Announcing	Identification and/or Involvement
Commitment	Selling	Whole Person in a Whole Job
Translation	Job description	Aligning Goals for Results
Enabling	Carrot & Stick (people as expense)	Aligning Structures and Culture
Synergy	"Cooperate!"	3rd Alternative Communication
Accountability	Sandwich Technique Performance Appraisal	Frequent, Open, Mutual Accountability re: Compelling Scoreboard

Table 6

1. **Clarity:** The manual worker/Industrial Age approach is simply to announce what the mission, vision, values and high-priority goals are. As we've discussed, these are often the product of top people going to off-site mission statement workshops and then returning to the workforce to announce in smooth language the strategic decisions to guide all other decisions in the organization. Over time, these mission statements become nothing more than PR statements, simply because there is no real involvement; therefore, there is no real identification, which is the essence of the Knowledge Worker Age. Remember that identification is personal moral authority coming from involvement with the admired person, not necessarily from involvement in the strategic decisions.

2. **Commitment:** The Industrial Age approach to getting commitment is to sell—communicate it constantly and frequently, explain it, and try to make sense of it. Sell, sell, sell! But research data show that only one in five have a passionate commitment to the high-priority goals of their team and organization. The 8th Habit approach in the Knowledge Worker Age is to put a whole person in a whole job—body, mind, heart and spirit. Pay me fairly, treat me kindly and respectfully, use my mind creatively in doing work that truly adds value and in doing it in a principle-centered way. It's not just a matter of what we have called The Great Jackass Theory of Human Motivation, where you just throw more money at the workers.

In fact, studies have shown that when you have a Knowledge Worker approach, workers place salary fourth in priority behind trust, respect and pride. Why? Because when people have intrinsic satisfaction in their work, extrinsic, or external, factors are less important. But when there are no intrinsic satisfactions in the work, then money becomes the most important thing. Why? With money you can buy satisfactions off the job. The whole-person 8th Habit unleashes *internal* motivation.

The execution gaps of clarity and commitment are also the primary source of time management problems. There is one simple reason—how people define the high-priority goals, along with mission and values, will govern every other decision. Therefore, when there is a lack of clarity and commitment, you will have nothing but confusion about what is truly important. The end result is that urgency will define importance. That which is popular, pressing, proximate and pleasant—in other words, that which is urgent—becomes important. The net result is that everyone is reading the tea leaves, putting their finger to the political winds, and kissing up to the hierarchy. Then the confusion gets pushed down through the entire organization in a compounded way. So until people develop clarity and commitment toward the mission, vision and values of the organization no amount of time management training will have any sustaining impact, except in people's personal lives. As Charles Hummel once said:

> The important task rarely must be done today, or even this week. . . . But the urgent task calls for instant action. . . . The momentary appeal of these tasks seems irresistible and important, and they devour our energy. But in the light of time's perspective, their deceptive prominence fades; with a sense of loss we recall the vital task we pushed aside. We realize we've become slaves to the tyranny of the urgent.[3]

3. **Translation:** The Industrial Age approach is job descriptions. In the Knowledge Worker Age, you help align people's jobs to their voices (talents and passions), and their jobs have a line of

sight to accomplishing the team's and organization's high-priority goals.

4. **Enabling:** In many ways, enabling is the toughest execution gap to deal with, because it requires you to remove all the dysfunctional structural, systemic and other cultural barriers that we have been discussing throughout the book. These enabling or disabling structures and systems—recruiting, selecting, training and development, compensating, communicating, information, compensation, etc.—are exactly where many people get their sense of security and predictability in their work life. Unless there is genuine involvement in the strategic decision making, particularly regarding values and line-of-sight priorities, you won't get sufficient emotional connection, trust and internal motivation to align deeply embedded structures and systems.

   In the Industrial Age, people are an expense, and things, like equipment and technology, are an investment. Just think about this again! People . . . an expense; things . . . an investment! This is the bottom-line information system. It is sick bloodletting. With the 8th Habit approach to the Knowledge Worker Age, people can become involved in setting up a very powerful visual, compelling, real-time Scoreboard on both result and capability that reflects how well the systems and structures are aligned, to enable key goals to be accomplished.

5. **Synergy:** The Industrial Age is a compromise approach at best, and win-lose or lose-win at worst. Synergy in the Knowledge Worker Age enables Third Alternatives to be created. It's an 8th Habit kind of communication, where people's voices are identified and aligned with the organization's voice so that the voices of different teams or departments harmonize together.

6. **Accountability:** The Industrial Age practices of "carrot-and-stick" motivation and "sandwich technique" performance appraisal are replaced by mutual accountability and open sharing of information against the top-priority goals that everyone understands. It's almost like going into a soccer stadium or a football or baseball arena where the scoreboard displays information so that everyone in the entire arena knows exactly what's happening.

THE SWEET SPOT

Let's tie all this together. Early in the book, I introduced the idea that everyone chooses one of two roads in life—one is the well-traveled road to mediocrity, the other the road to greatness. We've explored how the path to mediocrity straitjackets human potential and how the path to greatness unleashes and realizes human potential. The 8th Habit is the pathway to greatness, and greatness lies in Finding Your Voice and Inspiring Others to Find Theirs.

Together we've explored what could be called three kinds of greatness: *personal* greatness, *leadership* greatness and *organizational* greatness.*

Personal greatness is found as we discover our three birth-gifts—choice, principles and the four human intelligences. When we develop these gifts and intelligences, we cultivate a magnificent character full of vision, discipline and passion that is guided by conscience—one that is simultaneously courageous and kind. This kind of character is driven to make significant contributions that not only serve mankind but also reach and are focused on "the one." Such character I would term *primary greatness*, whereas secondary greatness would include such things as talent, reputation, prestige, wealth and recognition.

Leadership greatness is achieved by people who, regardless of their position, choose to inspire others to find their voice. This is achieved through living the 4 Roles of Leadership.

Organizational greatness is achieved as the organization tackles the final challenge of translating their leadership roles and work (including mission, vision and values) into the principles or drivers of execution in an organization—clarity, commitment, translation, enabling, synergy and accountability. These drivers are also universal, timeless, self-evident principles—for organizations.

THE DIAGRAM THAT FOLLOWS summarizes the relationship between personal greatness, leadership greatness and organizational greatness. Organizations that govern and discipline themselves by all three truly hit what you might call the *sweet spot*. The sweet spot is the nexus where all three circles overlap. This is where the greatest expression of power

---

* For more information on achieving sustained superior performance through developing all three forms of greatness, see Appendix 8.

and potential is found. When you hit the "sweet spot" of a racquet while playing tennis, or of the golf club when connecting with that little white ball, you know when you've hit it. It is exhilarating! It resonates. It just feels right. With no more effort than usual, that connection with the center releases a burst of power and the ball is sent soaring much farther and faster than usual. It is another way of referring to the power that is released when you "Find Your Voice" as an individual, team and organization.

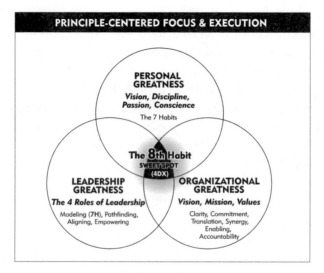

Figure 14.3

THE 4 DISCIPLINES OF EXECUTION (4DX)

There are four disciplines that, if practiced consistently, can close these execution gaps and vastly improve teams' and organizations' ability to focus on and execute their top priorities. We call them *The 4 Disciplines of Execution*. Of course, there are dozens of factors that influence execution. However, our research suggests that these four disciplines represent the 20 percent of activities that produce 80 percent of results, as they pertain to executing consistently with excellence on top priorities. You will notice that these four disciplines are consistent with, and flow out of, the three areas of greatness. They are the Sweet Spot (see 4DX at the center of the diagram), the power-releasing contact point, the set of next-step, actionable, "rubber meets the road," laser-focused practices that will enable a team and organization to consistently get results.

Below is a summary of these four disciplines (4DX):

Discipline 1: Focus on the Wildly Important

There's a key principle that many fail to understand about focusing an organization: **People are naturally wired to focus on only one thing at a time (or at best very few)** with **excellence.**

Suppose you have an 80 percent chance of achieving any particular goal with excellence. Add a second goal to that first goal, and research shows your chances of achieving both goals drop to 64 percent. Keep adding goals and the probability of achieving them plunges steeply. Juggle five goals at once, for example, and you only have a 33 percent chance of actually getting excellent results on all of them.

How vital it is, then, to focus diligently and intensely on only a few crucial goals.

Some objectives are clearly more critical than others. We must learn to distinguish between what is "merely important" and what is "wildly important." A "wildly important goal" carries serious consequences. Failure to achieve these goals renders all other achievements relatively inconsequential.

Consider the situation of the air traffic controller. At any moment, hundreds of airplanes are in the air, and all of them are important—especially if you happen to be on one of them! But the controller cannot focus on them all at once. Her job is to *land them one at a time*, and to do so flawlessly. Every organization is in a similar position. Few can afford the luxury of "divided attention"; some goals simply *must* be landed right now.

So how do we know which goals are "wildly important" and will best help us execute our strategic plan? Sometimes it is immediately clear and obvious. At other times, analysis is needed. The Importance Screen is a valuable strategic planning tool that will help you prioritize your goals by running them through the economic, strategic, and stakeholder screens. In other words, it will help you assess which of all the potential goals would bring the most leverage in terms of economic, strategic, and stakeholder benefits. You may wish to use the Importance Screen when determining your top goals. This is *pathfinding* at the cutting edge of action.

THE IMPORTANCE SCREEN				
Instructions	**Stakeholder Screen**	**Strategic Screen**	**Economic Screen**	
1. List your team's potential goals.	SCALE -1 to 4	SCALE -1 to 4	SCALE -1 to 4	
2. For each screen rate each on a scale of -1 to 4 where: **4= HIGH POSITIVE IMPACT** **0= NO IMPACT** **-1= NEGATIVE IMPACT**	**Stakeholder criteria to consider:** ■ Increases customer loyalty ■ Ignites the passion and energy of our people	**Strategic criteria to consider:** ■ Directly supports the organizational goals ■ Leverages core competencies	**Economic criteria to consider:** ■ Grows revenue ■ Reduces costs ■ Improves cash flow	
3. Total your score. 4. Do a gut check. "Are we facing the brutal realities?" 5. Using the score totals and your gut check, place a check mark by the goals that are truly most important.	■ Has a favorable impact on suppliers/vendors, partners, investors ■ Other stakeholder criteria	■ Increases market strength ■ Increases competitieve advantage ■ Other strategic criteria	■ Improves profitability ■ Other economic criteria	
Potential Goals:				**TOTAL SCORE**

Figure 14.4

The Stakeholder Screen. What are the most important things you should do to fulfill the needs of your stakeholders? Customers, employees, suppliers, investors and others all have a stake in these goals. Consider how the potential goals:

- increase customer loyalty.
- ignite the passion and energy of your people.
- favorably impact suppliers, vendors, business partners and investors.

The Strategic Screen. Consider how the potential goals affect the strategy of the organization, including whether or not the goal:

- directly supports the organization's mission or purpose.
- leverages core competencies.
- increases market strength.
- increases competitive advantage.

Ask yourself: What is the most consequential thing we can do to advance our strategy?

The Economic Screen. A wildly important goal must contribute to the overall economics of the organization in some direct or indirect way. Ask yourself: Of all your potential goals, which few would bring you the most significant economic return? Consider the following:

- Revenue growth
- Cost reduction
- Improved cash flow
- Profitability

Even in a nonprofit organization, economics are still crucial, since every organization must have cash flow to survive.

PUTTING THE GOALS through the stakeholder strategic and economic screens positions a clear "why" behind the "what" of each goal.

In my estimation, a strategic plan will remain vague and lofty unless it is broken down into the two or three top priorities or "wildly important" goals (WIGs). Stakeholders at all levels of the organization should be involved in the identification of these crucial goals so that they have a greater level of commitment and understand the rationale behind each one.

To achieve results with excellence, you must focus on a few wildly important goals and set aside the merely important. Since human beings are wired to do only one thing at a time with excellence (or at best just a few), we must learn to narrow our focus. The reality is, far too many of us try to do far too many things. Like an air traffic controller, we need to learn to land one plane at a time—to do fewer things with excellence rather than many with mediocrity.

To practice this discipline you must clarify your team's top two or three "wildly important" goals and carefully craft them to be in alignment with the organization's top priorities.

FILM: *It's Not Just Important, It's Wildly Important!*

To illustrate the underlying need for focus on "the vital few," I invite you to watch a little film called *It's Not Just Important, It's Wildly Important!* This film is based upon actual interviews we conducted with our own clients, not with actors. It illustrates the misalignment and lack of goal clarity that pervades most organizations. It is humorous but all too indicative of the focus and execution problems most organizations face. Just slip the DVD into your DVD player, select this title, and sit back and see if you don't recognize a little of the organization *you* work for.

Discipline 2: Create a Compelling Scoreboard

A Scoreboard allows you to leverage a basic principle: **People play differently when they're keeping score.**

Have you ever watched a street game of some kind—basketball, hockey, football—when the players were not keeping score? Players tend to do whatever they want, the game stops for a few jokes, and the playing is not very focused. But when they start keeping score, things change. There's a new intensity. Huddles happen. Plays are improvised. Players adapt quickly to each new challenge. And the speed and tempo build dramatically.

The same thing happens at work. Without crystal-clear measures of success, people are never sure what the goal truly is. Without measures, the same goal is understood by a hundred different people in a hundred different ways. As a result, team members get off track doing things that might be urgent but less important. They work at an uncertain pace. Motivation flags.

That is why it's so crucial to have a compelling, visible, accessible Scoreboard for your strategic plan and crucial goals. Most work groups have no clear measures of success, nor do they have any way to see how they are doing on their key priorities.

According to our xQ studies, only about one in three workers can refer to clear, accurate measures to gauge their progress or success on key goals. And only about three in 10 believe that rewards or consequences have anything to do with performance on measurable goals. Obviously, few workers have the feedback system they need to execute with precision.

Think of the tremendous motivating power of the Scoreboard. It is an inescapable picture of *reality*. Strategic success depends on it. Plans must adapt to it. Timing must adjust to it. Unless you can see the score, your strategies and plans are simply abstractions. So you must build a compelling Scoreboard and consistently update it. This is combining *pathfinding* and *aligning* at the cutting edge of action.

HOW TO CREATE A COMPELLING SCOREBOARD?

Through involvement and synergy (*modeling* the 7 Habits), identify the key measures for your organizational or team goals and make a visual representation of them. The Scoreboard should make three things absolutely clear: *From what? To what? By when?*

1. List your top priorities or "wildly important goals"—those your team simply must achieve.

2. Create a scoreboard for each one with these elements:

   • The current result (where we are now)
   • The target result (where we need to be)
   • The deadline (by when)

   The Scoreboard might take the form of a bar graph, a trend line, a pie chart or a Gantt chart. Or it might look like a thermometer or a speedometer or a scale. You decide—but make it visible, dynamic and accessible. Remember also that because ends preexist in the means, you might consider including measures in the Scoreboard regarding principle-centered values.

3. Post the Scoreboard and ask people to review it every day, every week, as appropriate. Meet over it, discuss it, and resolve issues as they come up.

   All team members should be able to see the Scoreboard and watch it change moment by moment, day by day, or week by week. They should be discussing it all the time. They should never really take their minds off it. The compelling Scoreboard has the effect of keeping score in a street game. All of a sudden, the tempo changes. People work faster, conversations change,

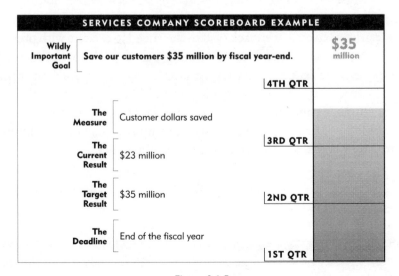

Figure 14.5

people adapt quickly to new issues. And you get to the goal more precisely and rapidly.

Discipline 3: Translate Lofty Goals into Specific Actions

It's one thing to come up with a new goal or strategy. It's quite another to actually turn that goal into action, to break it down into new behaviors and activities at all levels, including the front line. There is a vast difference between the stated strategy and the real strategy. The stated strategy is what is communicated; the real strategy is what people do every day. To achieve goals you've never achieved before, you need to start doing things you've never done before. Just because the leaders may know what the goals are doesn't mean that the people on the front line, where the real action takes place, know what to do. Goals will never be achieved until everyone on the team knows exactly what *they're supposed to do* about them. In the last analysis, the front line produces the bottom line. They are the creative knowledge workers. Leadership, remember, is a choice, not a position; it can be distributed everywhere—at all levels of the organization. Also remember, you cannot hold people responsible for results if you supervise their methods. *You* then become responsible for results and rules replace human judgment, creativity and responsibility.

To practice this discipline, your team must get creative, must identify the *new* and *better* behaviors needed to achieve your goals, then translate them into weekly and daily tasks at all levels of the organization. This is *empowering* at the cutting edge of action.

Discipline 4: Hold Each Other Accountable—All of the Time

In the most effective teams, people meet frequently—monthly, weekly, or even daily—to account for their commitments, examine the Scoreboard, resolve issues, and decide how to support one another. Unless everyone on a team holds everyone else accountable—*all of the time*—the process will be dead on arrival. Mayor Rudolph Giuliani, widely credited with the renaissance of New York City, held regular "morning meetings" with his staff. The idea was to account for progress on key goals every single day. Reengaging less than weekly allows the team to drift off course and lose focus.

A self-empowering team, then, will focus and refocus in frequent accountability sessions. Such meetings are *not* like the typical staff meeting, where people talk about everything under the sun and can't wait for the meeting to end so they can get back to their real work. The purpose of an effective accountability session is to move the key goals forward.

Three key practices are characteristic of effective accountability sessions:

- Triage Reporting
- Finding Third Alternatives
- Clearing the Path

Triage Reporting. In a hospital emergency room, you will often see a large notice posted that goes something like this: PATIENTS ARE TREATED IN ORDER OF SERIOUSNESS, NOT ARRIVAL. The medical staff conducts a process called "triage," in which casualties are sorted and treated based on the severity of their condition. This is why your broken arm has to wait while the doctors work on a patient with a brain injury, even though you might have arrived first.

In triage reporting, everyone reports quickly on the vital few issues, leaving the less important issues for another time. They focus on key results, major problems, and high-level issues. This doesn't mean that only "urgent" issues are discussed. It means that only "important" issues are discussed, even if some of these issues are not "urgent." This table contrasts the typical staff meeting with an effective accountability session:

EFFECTIVE ACCOUNTABILITY SESSIONS (TRIAGE REPORTING)	TYPICAL STAFF MEETINGS
Quick reporting of vital few issues	"Death March" around the room where people feel pressure to talk while everyone else checks out.
Review of scoreboard	No measures of progress
Follow-up	No follow-up
Mutual accountability	Only manager holds people accountable
People openly report struggles and failures	People hide their struggles and failures
Celebration of successes	Focusing only on problems

Table 7

Finding Third Alternatives: In effective accountability sessions, there is intense focus on how to achieve the key goals. The principle here is that a new goal that we've never achieved before requires doing things we've never done before. That means we're constantly looking for the new and better behavior that will get us to the goal. That's why we must find "Third Alternatives"—courses of action that are better than my way or your way, but that are the product of *our* best thinking. Remember again, we produce synergy by honoring diversity or differences—that is, individual differences in the context of *unity* on mission, values, vision, and WIGs.

In such sessions you'll see a lot of brainstorming going on, time allocated for creative dialogue. This table contrasts the typical staff meeting with an effective accountability session:

EFFECTIVE ACCOUNTABILITY SESSIONS (FINDING THIRD ALTERNATIVES)	TYPICAL STAFF MEETINGS
Energetic, synergistic problem solving	All talk, no action
New and better ideas are created (1+1=3, 10, 100 or more)	No time or environment for creative dialogue; forced consensus and compromise
Wisdom of the group	The "lone genius"

Table 8

Clearing the Path: To a great extent, effective leadership consists of clearing the path of barriers and aligning goals and systems so that others can achieve their goals. In a true "win-win agreement" process, the manager agrees to clear the path, to do things only he or she can do, to enable the worker to achieve. Of course, it's not just the manager who clears the path for others. It's everyone's job.

Thus, in an effective accountability session, you'll hear people ask, "How can I clear the path for you?" or "I'm struggling with this issue and need some help." or "What can we do for you to help you get that done?" This table contrasts the typical staff meeting with an effective accountability session:

EFFECTIVE ACCOUNTABILITY SESSIONS (CLEARING THE PATH)	TYPICAL STAFF MEETINGS
A stroke of the pen for me eliminates hours of work for you	Getting stuck because of barriers you can't get over by yourself
We're in this together	You are on your own
Admitting you need help and asking for it	Being afraid to admit when you need help

Table 9

This is *aligning* at the cutting edge of action.

INSTITUTIONALIZING EXECUTION

As you can see, the 4 Disciplines represent a methodology for taking something that is usually considered a variable factor practiced by a few high performers—consistent execution—and turning it into something that is predictable, teachable and replicable. We've learned by research and experience that when these four disciplines are practiced by teams, units or organizations, they demonstrate a much greater ability to execute top priorities, again and again.* Execution then becomes institutionalized and is not a matter of luck or the influence of a few key leaders. Further, the key to institutionalizing a culture of execution is regularly measuring it.

THE EXECUTION QUOTIENT (XQ)

Organizations need a new way to express and measure their collective ability to "focus and execute." Again, we call it xQ—The "Execution Quotient." Just as an IQ test uncovers gaps in intelligence, an xQ evaluation measures the "execution gap"—the gap between setting a goal and actually achieving it. The xQ score is a leading indicator of an organization's ability to execute its most important goals. It's no longer necessary to wait for the lagging indicators to tell you whether you've succeeded or not. By asking workers twenty-seven carefully crafted questions that take around fifteen minutes to answer, you can get at that leading indicator.†

Can you imagine the power of doing an xQ test from the grass roots up every three to six months, one that gives an accurate picture of the degree of focus and execution of the organization? It could be done formally and informally. In fact, the more mature the culture becomes, the narrower the difference will be between formal and informal information gathering. Then based on the xQ Questionnaire, strong grassroots cultural impetus would be given to aligning goals between departments and divisions so that the strategic critical priorities would be constantly

---

* For more information on how to institutionalize The 4 Disciplines of Execution in your team or organization, see Appendix 5: Implementing the 4 Disciplines of Execution.

† For a more detailed summary of the results of the Harris Interactive study of 23,000 workers, managers and executives who took the xQ Questionnaire, see Appendix 6: xQ Results.

focused on and executed. This would drive the Knowledge Worker Age model into the Age of Wisdom.*

HOPEFULLY YOU'RE BEGINNING to see how the 8th Habit—Find Your Voice and Inspire Others to Find Theirs—is another way of saying, "Use the empowering knowledge worker, whole-person model. Apply the 7 Habits (personal greatness), the 4 Roles of Leadership (leadership greatness) and the 6 principles or drivers to execution (organizational greatness) to that model."

We move now to the pinnacle of the 8th Habit: Using Our Voices Wisely to Serve Others.

QUESTION & ANSWER

Q What is the difference between what you have traditionally taught as the 5 elements of a good win-win agreement and the 4 Disciplines of Execution?

A: At the basic principle level, there is no difference. The difference lies in semantics (how words are being used and defined), and in the overall context in which the 4 Disciplines are placed. Let me explain more fully. The 5 elements of a good win-win agreement are:

1. Desired Results
2. Guidelines
3. Resources
4. Accountability
5. Consequences

---

* If you are interested in taking the xQ Questionnaire without charge to personally assess *your individual team's, and organization's ability to focus and execute on top priorities*, go to www.The8thHabit.com/offers. You will receive directions on how to take the test. After completing the test, you will be given an xQ Report that summarizes *your* assessment and compares it to a composite average score of the many thousands of respondents. Further information will be given on how you can measure your entire team or organization.

Desired results and *guidelines* are basically embodied in the first two disciplines of execution—establishing WIGs (Wildly Important Goals) and a compelling Scoreboard. As discussed earlier in the book, ends and means are inseparable; therefore, the accomplishment of desired results with the achievement of the WIGs can be interwoven when done in principle-centered ways.

The third element of a win-win agreement, *resources*, is implicitly involved in the third discipline of execution—translate lofty goals into specific actions. The fourth and fifth elements of a win-win performance agreement—*accountability* and *consequences*—are explicitly involved in the fourth discipline: You hold each other accountable, all of the time. Since consequences are the natural result of the accountability being given, they are also implicitly involved.

The great advantage of the 4 Disciplines approach to execution and team empowerment is that it comes out of a research-based study of execution gaps, the larger context of how the Industrial Age model produces those gaps, and how the Knowledge Worker Age model fills them.

Chapter 15

USING OUR VOICES WISELY TO SERVE OTHERS

I am no longer a young man filled with energy and vitality. I'm given to meditation and prayer. I would enjoy sitting in a rocker, swallowing prescriptions, listening to soft music, and contemplating the things of the universe. But such activity offers no challenge and makes no contribution. I wish to be up and doing. I wish to face each day with resolution and purpose. I wish to use every waking hour to give encouragement, to bless those whose burdens are heavy, to build faith and strength of testimony. It is the presence of wonderful people which stimulates the adrenaline. It is the look of love in their eyes which gives me energy.[1]

GORDON B. HINCKLEY, AGE NINETY-TWO

I slept and dreamed that life was joy.
I awoke and saw that life was service.
I acted, and behold, service was joy.

RABINDRANATH TAGORE

I believe that the rendering of useful service is the common duty of mankind and that only in the purifying fire of sacrifice is the dross of selfishness consumed and the greatness of the human soul set free.[2]

JOHN D. ROCKEFELLER, JR.

T HE INNER DRIVE TO 1) Find Your Own Voice, and 2) Inspire Others to Find Theirs is fueled by one great overarching purpose: serving human needs. It is also the best means of achieving both: Without reaching out and meeting human needs, we really don't expand and develop our freedom to choose as we otherwise could. We grow more personally when we are giving ourselves to others. Our relationships improve and deepen when together we attempt to serve our family, another family, an organization, a community, or some other human need.

> *At first, as a student, I wanted freedom only for myself, the transitory freedoms of being able to stay out at night, read what I pleased, and go where I chose. Later as a young man in Johannesburg, I yearned for the basic and honorable freedoms of achieving my potential, of earning my keep, of marrying and having a family—the freedom not to be obstructed in a lawful life. But I then slowly saw that not only was I not free, but my brothers and sisters were not free . . . that is when the hunger for my own freedom became the greater hunger for the freedom of my people.*
>
> *It was this desire for the freedom of my people to live their lives with dignity and self-respect that animated my life, that transformed a frightened young man into a bold one, that drove a law-abiding attorney to become a criminal, that turned a family-loving husband into a man without a home. . . . I am no more virtuous or self-sacrificing than the next man, but I found that I could not even enjoy the poor and limited freedoms I was allowed when I knew my people were not free.*[3]
>
> NELSON MANDELA

Organizations are established to serve human needs. There is no other reason for their existence. Robert Greenleaf wrote a beautiful essay, "The Institution As Servant," which applied the whole concept of stewardship to an organization.

> Service is the rent we pay for living in this world of ours.[4]
>
> NATHAN ELDON TANNER

Willis Harmon, the cofounder of the World Business Academy, expressed his conviction about the institution of business itself in these words:

> Business has become the most powerful institution on the planet. The dominant institution in any society needs to take responsibility for the whole. But business has not had such a tradition. This is a new role, not well understood or accepted. Built on the concept of capitalism and free enterprise from the beginning was the assumption that the actions of many units of individual enterprise, responding to market forces and guided by the "invisible hand" of Adam Smith, would somehow add up to desirable outcomes. But in the last decade of the 20th century, it has become clear that the "invisible hand" is faltering. It depended on over-arching meanings and values that are no longer present. So business has to adopt a tradition it has never had throughout the entire history of capitalism: to share the responsibility of the whole. Every decision that is made, every action that is taken, must be viewed in light of that responsibility.

THE AGE OF WISDOM

I believe that this millennium *will* become the Age of Wisdom. It will come about either through the force of circumstance that humbles people, or through the force of conscience—or perhaps both.

Remember the Five Ages of Civilization's Voice. The technology for the Hunter-Gatherer Age was symbolized by the bow and arrow; the Agricultural Age, by farm equipment; the Industrial Age, by the factory, the Information/Knowledge Worker Age, by a human being; the Age of Wisdom, by a compass, which signifies the power to choose our direction and purpose and obey the natural laws or principles (magnetic north) that never change and that are universal, timeless, and self-evident.

Remember that with each infrastructure shift, over 90 percent of the people were eventually downsized. I believe this is now happening as we move from the Industrial to the Information/Knowledge Worker Age. People are either losing their jobs or gradually being transformed by the new demands of their new jobs. I personally believe that over 20 percent of the present workforce is becoming obsolete, and that unless they rededicate and reinvent themselves, within a few years, another 20 percent will become obsolete.

This Information Age is transforming so rapidly into the Knowledge Worker Age that it is going to take continual investment in our own education and training to stay abreast. Much of this will be done by the school of hard knocks, but people who see what is happening and who are disciplined will systematically continue their education until they acquire the new mind-set and the new skill-set required to anticipate and accommodate the realities of the new age. Hopefully, this will gradually morph into an Age of Wisdom, when information and knowledge are impregnated with purpose and principles.

WHERE IS WISDOM?

We know that information is not wisdom. We also know that knowledge is not wisdom.

Many years ago, when I was teaching at a university and working on my doctorate, I went to see a friend, who was also my senior professor. I told him, "I'd like to do a dissertation on the subject of motivation and leadership—a philosophical document rather than an empirical study."

He basically said to me, "Stephen, you don't know enough to even ask the right questions." In other words, my knowledge was at one level, but my knowledge would have to be way beyond its current level if I was to deal with the kinds of questions I would need to deal with. This was very emotionally traumatic for me because my heart and mind were really set on taking a philosophical approach rather than the scientific approach that I eventually ended up taking. I believed that the combination of informal philosophical training I'd received during my undergraduate and graduate studies in business would be sufficient. I didn't realize until years later how right he was. It was a humbling experience.

That lesson in humility was the mother of many precious learnings and insights that would come in the years that followed. Eventually we learn that *the more you know, the more you know you don't know.* Look at it this way (see figure 15.1). Here is a circle, which represents your knowledge. Your ignorance is on the outside edge of that circle.

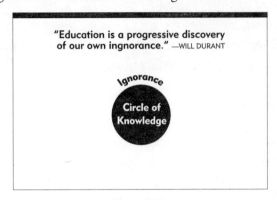

Figure 15.1

Figure 15.2

As your knowledge increases, what happens to your ignorance? It obviously becomes larger, or at least your awareness of your ignorance becomes larger (see figure 15.2). So the more you know, the more you realize you don't know. What if you were trying to serve purposes greater than your knowledge—greater than your comfort zone? This would create genuine humility and a desire to draw upon help from others—from a partnership or team. Successfully working with others makes one's knowledge and abilities productive and necessitates the creation of a complementary team of people who possess knowledge and abilities that can compensate for and make irrelevant one's individual ignorance and weaknesses. That is as it should be.

This awareness should increase our commitment to continual mentored learning, particularly in subjects as critical as personal growth, relationships and leadership. I believe that when information and

> *In a sense, knowledge shrinks as wisdom grows, for details are swallowed up in principles. The details for knowledge, which are important, will be picked up ad hoc in each avocation of life, but the habit of the active utilization of well-understood principles is the final possession of wisdom.*[5]
>
> ALFRED NORTH WHITEHEAD

knowledge are impregnated with worthy purposes and principles, you have wisdom.

Another way of putting this would be that wisdom is the child of integrity—being integrated around principles. And integrity is the child of humility and courage. In fact you could say that humility is the mother of all the virtues because humility acknowledges that there are natural laws or principles that govern the universe. They are in charge. We are not. Pride teaches us that *we* are in charge. Humility teaches us to understand and live by *principles*, because they ultimately govern the consequences of our actions. If humility is the mother, courage is the father of wisdom. Because to truly live by these principles when they are contrary to social mores, norms and values takes enormous courage.

> *Courage is not the absence of fear, but rather the judgment that something else is more important than fear.*
>
> AMBROSE REDMOON

The following chart visually describes these three generations—notice also their opposites in all three generations (see figure 15.3).

You notice that integrity has two children—wisdom and the abundance mentality. Wisdom comes to people who educate and obey their conscience. The abundance mentality is cultivated because integrity breeds inner security. When a person is not dependent upon external judgments and comparisons for his sense of personal worth, he can be genuinely happy for the successes of others. But those with a comparison-based identity simply cannot be happy when others succeed because they operate out of an emotional deficiency. Wisdom and an abundance mentality produce the kinds of paradigms spoken of in this book—paradigms that lead one to believe in people, affirm their worth and potential, and

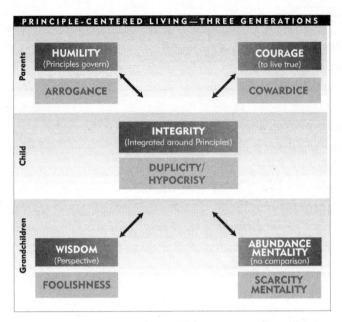

Figure 15.3

think in terms of release rather than control. Such a combination of wisdom and abundance mentality respects the power and capacity people have to choose. That combination also respects the fact that motivation is internal, and therefore people who have that combination make no attempt to manage, control or motivate others. Such leaders inspire rather than require. They control things, but they lead (empower) people. They don't think zero-sum; they think Third Alternatives—higher middle ways. They are filled with gratitude, reverence and respect for all people. They see life as a cornucopia of resources—particularly human resources of opportunity and continuing growth.

MORAL AUTHORITY AND SERVANT LEADERSHIP

> You have not done enough, you have never done enough so long as it is still possible that you have something of value to contribute.[6]
>
> DAG HAMMARSKJÖLD

Wisdom is the beneficial use of knowledge; wisdom is information and knowledge impregnated with higher purposes and principles. Wisdom teaches us to respect all people, to celebrate their differences, to be

> *When I look back on my life nowadays, which I sometimes do,*
> *what strikes me most forcibly about it is that what seemed at the*
> *time significant and seductive, seems now most futile and absurd.*
> *For instance, success in all of its various guises; being known and*
> *being praised; ostensible pleasures, like acquiring money or*
> *seducing women, or traveling, going to and fro in the world*
> *and up and down in it like Satan, explaining and experiencing*
> *whatever Vanity Fair has to offer. In retrospect, all these*
> *exercises in self-gratification seem like pure fantasy,*
> *what Pascal called, "licking the earth."*[7]
>
> MALCOLM MUGGERIDGE

guided by a single ethic—*service above self.* Moral authority is *primary greatness* (character strengths); formal authority is *secondary greatness* (position, wealth, talent, reputation, popularity).

The interesting thing about moral authority is what a paradox it is. The dictionary discusses authority in terms of command, control, power, sway, rule, supremacy, domination, dominion, strength, might. But the antonym is civility, servitude, weakness, follower. Moral authority is the gaining of influence through following principles. Moral dominion is achieved through servanthood, service, and contribution. Power and moral supremacy emerge from humility, where the greatest becomes the servant of all. Moral authority or primary greatness is achieved through sacrifice. Robert K. Greenleaf, the modern founder of the servant leadership movement, put it this way:

A new moral principle is emerging which holds that the only authority deserving one's allegiance is that which is freely and knowingly granted by the led to the leader in response to, and in proportion to, the clearly evident servant stature of the leader. Those who choose to follow this principle will not casually accept the authority of existing institutions. Rather, they will freely respond only to individuals who are chosen as leaders because they are proven and trusted as servants. To the extent that this principle prevails in the future, the only truly viable institutions will be those that are predominantly servant-led.[8]

It has generally been my experience that the very top people of truly great organizations are servant-leaders. They are the most humble, the most reverent, the most open, the most teachable, the most respectful, the most caring. As mentioned earlier in the chapter, Jim Collins, one of the authors of the highly influential book *Built to Last* and author of the more recent *Good to Great*, conducted a five-year research project around the question What catapults an organization from merely good to truly great? His profound conclusion ought to change the way we think about leadership. Here is how he describes "Level 5 Leadership":

> The most powerfully transformative executives possess a paradoxical mixture of personal humility and professional will. They are timid and ferocious. Shy and fearless. They are rare—and unstoppable . . . good to great transformations don't happen without level five leaders at the helm, they just don't.[9]

THE LEVEL 5 HIERARCHY

Good to Great — Jim Collins

LEVEL 5
Level 5 Executive
Builds enduring greatness through a paradoxical combination of personal humility plus professional will.

LEVEL 4
Effective Leader
Catalyzes commitment to and vigorous pursuit of a clear and compelling vision; stimulates the group to high performance standards.

LEVEL 3
Competent Manager
Organizes people and resources toward effective and efficient pursuit of predetermined objectives.

LEVEL 2
Contributing Team Member
Contributes to the achievement of group objectives; works effectively with others in a group setting.

LEVEL 1
Highly Capable Individual
Makes productive contributions through talent, knowledge, skills, and good work habits.

Figure 15.4[10]

When people with the formal authority or position power (secondary greatness) refuse to use that authority and power except as a last resort, their moral authority increases because it is obvious that they have subordinated their ego and position power and use reasoning, persuasion, kindness, empathy, and, in short, trustworthiness instead. In the book *Leading Beyond the Walls*, Jim Collins puts this principle in the context of the broader organizational environment:

First, the executives must define the inside and the outside of the organization by reference to core values and purpose, not by traditional
boundaries. Second, executives must build mechanisms of connection
and commitment rooted in freedom of choice, rather than relying on
systems of coercion and control. Third, executives must accept the fact
that the exercise of true leadership is inversely proportional to the exercise of power. Fourth, executives must embrace the reality that traditional walls are dissolving and that this trend will accelerate.[11]

There are times of great chaos, confusion and survival when the
strong hand of formal authority needs to be used to get things back on
track, to a new level of order and stability or to a new vision. However,
in most cases when people use their formal authority early on, their
moral authority will be lessened. Again, remember that when you borrow strength from position, you build weakness in three places: in self,
because you are not developing moral authority; in the other, because
they become codependent with your use of formal authority; and in the
quality of the relationship, because authentic openness and trust never
develops.

> *The surest way to reveal one's character is not*
> *through adversity but by giving them power.*
> ABRAHAM LINCOLN

Generally you'll find those with high moral authority are eventually
given formal authority—like Mandela, the father of the new South
Africa. But not always—like Gandhi, the father of the new India.

You'll also find, almost always, that those who have formal authority
and use it in principle-centered ways will find their influence increasing
exponentially—like George Washington, the father of the United States
of America.

Why does moral authority exponentially increase the effectiveness of
formal authority and power? Dependent people are super-sensitive to
even the slightest nuance of either "throwing one's weight around" or
the use of patience, kindness, gentleness, empathy and gentle persuasion. Such character strength activates others' consciences and creates
emotional identification with the leader and the cause or principles he
or she stands for. Then when formal authority or positional power is

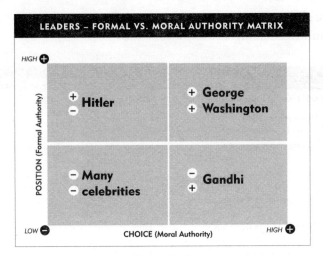

Figure 15.5

also used, people follow for the right reasons, out of genuine commitment rather than out of fear. This is another form of the Third Alternative.

This is the real key to parenting, probably our highest "voice" responsibility in mortality—combining high standards and strong values and consistent discipline with unconditional love, deep empathy and a lot of fun. This is why the greatest test of parenthood—and the key to building a healthy, nurturing family culture—is how we treat the ones who test us the most.

Also, in difficult and troubling economic times, the natural tendency is to revert back to the Industrial Age command-and-control model, because people are fearful for their economic security. It feels safer. People also have the tendency to become more dependent and to respond to the command-and-control style. But it is in this very time that the knowledge worker model has its greatest effect and power—for it is in difficult times that we must produce more for less.

The capacity to produce more for less is based on unleashing the human potential throughout an *entire* organization, rather than again falling into the traditional trap of having people at the top make all the important decisions and having the rest wield the screwdrivers. This approach simply does not work in modern, tough times.

In short, in a bad economy, we may go back to the carrot-and-stick, great jackass theory of human motivation because it works. But though it may enable survival, it will not optimize results.

Notice the contrast between Leadership as a Position (Formal Authority) and Leadership as a Choice (Moral Authority):

LEADERSHIP AS A...	
POSITION (Formal Authority)	**CHOICE (Moral Authority)**
Might makes right	Right makes might
Loyalty above integrity	Integrity is loyalty
To get along, go along	Stubborn refusal
The "wrong" is in getting caught	The "wrong" is in doing wrong
The top people don't buy it	Ethos, Pathos, Logos
The top people don't live it	Be a model, not a critic
Image is everything	"To be rather than to seem"
"No one told me"	Ask; recommend
I did what you told me to; it didn't work. Now what?	"I intend to"
There is only so much	There is enough and to spare

Table 10

Let's explore practical illustrations of how communities and individuals—some *without* formal authority, some with only moral authority, and some with *both* moral *and* formal authority, including a great military leader and other world leaders and heads of state—exercise their wise "voices" in serving human needs.

COMMUNITY POLICING

All around the United States and in other places throughout the world, many communities have reduced crime up to 60 percent through civil society—the Third Alternative. The first alternative is for police to enforce the law. The second alternative is to lower behavior standards and just live with the "weakening of the moral fiber of society." The Third Alternative is to use moral authority to embolden and empower citizens (civil society) to take an active part in the prevention of crime and in finding and prosecuting criminals. Who provides this kind of leadership? The police officer on the beat.

Unless these officers are "convincingly good people" (as L.A. County Sheriff Baca describes their higher recruiting selection criteria), why would neighbors, fathers, mothers, teachers and other ordinary citizens partner with the police in the *prevention* of crime and in the identification of criminals? How are you going to get the social norms and mores in the ghettos and projects to surround zero tolerance of law breaking (even jaywalking) if people in their hearts do not emotionally connect with the trusted flatfoot cops? Remember the brilliant insight of the great sociologist Emile Durkheim: "When mores are sufficient, laws are unnecessary. When mores are insufficient, laws are unenforceable."

A colleague of mine who trains in the law enforcement area full-time frequently asks his audiences, who are made up primarily of the formal leadership (sheriffs, captains, lieutenants), "Who are the real leaders in community policing?" It becomes obvious that the real leaders are the police officers on the beat. They are the ones who have to involve and build relationships of trust with families to prevent crimes and "blow the whistle"—often at great risk to themselves—in neighborhoods full of gangs, drug pushers and users, and frequent violent outbursts. In such situations, formal authority won't work—in fact, it would be counterproductive and further polarize the cultures. Only moral authority produces prevention and crime-identification norms. Like the parable of the shepherd, they must know the sheep and be likewise known (authentic communication). The shepherds care so much they are willing to lay down their lives for the sheep. That's why they walk in front and the sheep follow. Hired sheepherders claim to care but are only there for "what's in it for them" (their wage) and desert the sheep when the "wolf" comes around. That's why the hirelings have to drive from behind using the carrot and stick.

The formal leaders are really managers or, better put, servant leaders. They can help use COMSTAT or other computer technology to identify potential problems so the real leaders—police officers on the beat—can nip things in the bud.

What a concept this is! What a comeuppance for those thinking position confers leadership! This new model sees the police officers, with moral authority, as the real leaders and the rest of the "higher-ups" as managers of aligned systems, servant leaders to those at the bottom. Is this a paradigm shift or not, particularly in a traditional, highly authoritarian, hierarchical, command-and-control field?

When you think about it, this community policing illustration is ex-

> *The basic mission of Police is to PREVENT*
> *crime and disorder. The public are the police and*
> *the police are the public, and both share the*
> *same responsibility for community safety.*[12]
>
> SIR ROBERT PEEL, FOUNDER OF MODERN POLICING

actly that—it is an illustration of what is true and valid in every field of human behavior: People who are at the cutting edge of the chisel, where the tire meets the pavement, have to exercise influence with their customers, their clients, or whomever. They are the ones who really have to exercise leadership by building relationships of trust and becoming creative problem solvers.

JOSHUA LAWRENCE CHAMBERLAIN

The annals of military history have no more inspiring story of a man with moral authority than that of Civil War hero Joshua Lawrence Chamberlain, commander of the Union's 20th Maine Company of volunteers. Chamberlain, a college professor at Bowdoin College, was granted a sabbatical leave from his teaching to answer Abraham Lincoln's call for much-needed additional volunteers to the Union forces. A man of deep character and moral conviction, his letter to the governor of Maine was accepted, and Chamberlain was enlisted. Though he knew little of soldiering, he was quickly promoted up through the ranks.

Chamberlain is probably best known for his bravery and leadership on Little Round Top in the Battle of Gettysburg. His orders were to anchor the extreme left of the Union line and to refuse to allow the attacking Confederate forces to flank him. He and his troops held the line until, at last, his troops ran out of ammunition. Refusing to give way, he ordered the regiment to "fix bayonets." In Chamberlain's own words:

> At that crisis, I ordered the bayonet. The word was enough. It ran like fire along the line, from man to man, and rose into a shout, with which they sprang forward on the enemy, now not 30 yards away. The effect was surprising; many of the enemy's first line threw down their arms and surrendered. An officer fired his pistol at my head with one hand, while he handed me his sword with the other. Holding fast by our right,

and swinging forward our left, we made an extended "right wheel," before which the enemy's second line broke and fell back, fighting from tree to tree, many being captured, until we had swept the valley and cleared the front of nearly our entire brigade.[13]

Many claim that it was this victory of raw courage on Little Round Top that turned the Battle of Gettysburg and the Civil War. Chamberlain was given the honor of receiving the arms of the first Confederate unit to surrender at Appomattox. By the end of the war he had been promoted to major general and was later presented with the Congressional Medal of Honor for his performance on Little Round Top.

Years later, in appreciation for all he had done, friends and former comrades-in-arms presented him with a gift—a magnificent stone gray stallion, dappled white. In characteristic humility and self-deprecation he graciously accepted the gift, but then added, "No sacrifice or service of mine requires any other reward than that which conscience gives to every man who does his duty."[14]

PRESIDENT KIM DAE-JUNG

I had the privilege of teaching former President Kim of South Korea and some of his advisors in the Blue House in Seoul, Korea. Near the end President Kim asked me, "Dr. Covey, do you really believe the things you teach?" I was taken aback by this question and sobered by it. After a short pause I said, "Yes I do." He then asked me, "How do you know you do?" I answered, "I try to live by these teachings. I know I fall short, falter a lot, but I keep coming back to them. I believe in them and am inspired by them and I keep returning to them."

He responded, "That's not good enough for me." I said, "I better listen to you." He asked, "Are you prepared to die for them?" I said, "I sense you're trying to tell me something." He *was* trying to tell me something. He went on to tell his story of many, many years of banishment, of being exiled, of being imprisoned and of several assassination attempts, including being put into a sack with rocks in the bottom, being thrown into the China Sea, and being rescued by a CIA helicopter. He told me of the pressure put upon him to cooperate with the military junta in the north. He was even offered the presidency but declined, knowing he would simply end up being a puppet to a dictatorship. They threatened to kill him if he didn't go along with them. He said, "Then kill me, because if you kill me I'll only die once, but if I cooperate with you, I will die 100 times every day for the rest of my life."

> *I know this now. Every man gives his life to what he believes. Every woman gives her life for what she believes. Sometimes people believe in little or nothing, and so they give their lives to little or nothing . . .*[15]
>
> JOAN OF ARC

He told me the story of the faithfulness and support of his family during his long, torturous ordeals and of his faith as a Christian convert and of his deep belief in people and in the magnificent power of democracy. He communicated his belief in the value and potential of every person, and in the right of self-expression. He gave to me a very privately held book of letters he wrote to his loved ones from prison, containing his deep beliefs, convictions and commitments.

MORAL AUTHORITY AS AN ECOSYSTEM

I worked once with the president of a Third World nation filled with corruption, violence, insurgency and warfare that has gone on for years and years. The new president was a person of great courage. He boldly championed the importance of the rule of law and the constitution, and he was courageous in his unwillingness to negotiate with terrorists and terrorist organizations. He was becoming increasingly trusted and very popular. I asked him what legacy he wanted to leave so that his work would go on and on and become institutionalized. As we spoke it became increasingly clear to him that personal moral authority was not enough. He could see the significant need for both *visionary* moral authority and *institutionalized* moral authority so that his people would identify with his vision of peace through the rule of law and prosperity through Third Alternative/synergistic communication, and that the underlying principles would be embedded in the structures and systems of the government. Then gradually, a civil society could develop with its own *cultural* moral authority—where the norms and mores of society would sustain the rule of law, promote preventative thinking and community policing, and meet the welfare and education needs of the general populace. He could sense how the basic model underlying the 8th Habit of Finding Your Voice and Inspiring Others to Find Theirs illustrates these four forms of moral authority.

Cultural moral authority always develops very, very slowly, as has been the case all around the world, including in the United States. Nevertheless, it's useful to see what an ecosystem the four kinds of moral authority are—how, like a physical ecosystem, they are all interrelated and interdependent. The essence of wisdom is to see the connectedness of all things.

FILM: *Gandhi*

I would like you now to watch a marvelous scene from the movie *Gandhi*. In this scene, which you'll find on the DVD in the back of your book, you'll observe a person of weakness and pride, but also a person who used his birth-gifts to develop humility, courage, integrity, discipline and vision. You will see a person who subordinated all his intelligences to his conscience, his spiritual intelligence. You will see a person who had to win a relationship victory with his wife before he could develop the freedom, power and moral authority to lift a large gathering of angry Indian people to a Third Alternative, even to the point that they were willing to lay down their lives for the cause they jointly espoused. You will see a person whose life exemplifies that power of the sequence in the ancient Greek wisdom, "Know thyself, control thyself, give thyself."

Though imperfect, Gandhi is a beautiful example of a person who developed enormous moral authority through vision, discipline and passion governed by conscience—and the world is different because of him. India, the second largest nation in the world, with over a billion people, is an independent democracy because of him. Isn't it truly amazing that he was never elected and had no formal authority? He, himself, said that any ordinary person who used his or her powers could do the same thing.

As you watch this scene from the movie *Gandhi*, which eventually won an Academy Award for Best Picture of the Year, study the nuances of words and facial expressions, of initiatives and reactions, of the development of mores, norms, values, goals, and vision. This is a video worth buying or renting and studying with your loved ones and fellow workers. Please enjoy the film now.

BIRTH-GIFTS, OUR CULTURAL OVERLAY, AND WISDOM

The thread that weaves itself through both Finding Your Own Voice and Inspiring Others to Find Theirs reveals how, little by little, in spite of our supernal birthday gifts, a cultural overlay is introduced that we, using the computer metaphor, could call software. Just as a tremendously powerful computer cannot operate outside its software, individuals, organizations, and societies cannot operate outside their cultural mores, norms and beliefs—unless you are a Muhammad Yunus (see chapter 1), whose vision of people, discipline, and passion were informed and driven by his conscience until eventually the old software was replaced—not only in individual heads but also in rigid, limiting notions inside the collective heads of families, institutions and society. This is a beautiful illustration of overcoming prejudice or prejudgment. You can feel how Yunus's humility, and courage are the parents of his integrity, and the grandparents of his wisdom and abundance mentality.

You, too, can do the same thing. You can make Finding Your Voice and Inspiring Others to Find Theirs a deeply engrained habit of KNOWLEDGE, ATTITUDE and SKILL. Just listen to your own conscience, your own source of wisdom, and watch how you can see through the flawed cultural overlay or software under the various levels of human need mentioned below. Each will come in the form of a dilemma.

At the personal level, would you not agree that *people want peace of mind and good relationships*, but would you not also agree that *people want to keep their habits and lifestyle*? What would conscience, saturated in *wisdom*, say? Would you not agree that a person, in some way, would need to win a private victory by sacrificing what he wants for a higher, more important purpose, for what is right?

Take the dilemma at a relationship level. Would you not agree that relationships are *built on trust*? Would you not also agree that *most individuals think more in terms of "me"*—my wants, my needs, my rights? What would *wisdom* dictate—would it not direct us to focus on trust-building principles and sacrificing "me" for "we"?

Let's look at two dilemmas at an organizational level. Is it not common that *management wants more for less*, that is, more productivity for less cost, and that *employees want more of what's in it for them for less time and effort?* Is this not a common phenomenon? What would *wisdom* dictate? What about co-missioning, that is, developing Third Alternative win-win performance agreements through sacrificing control or abdication for empowerment, so that management and employees are on the same page of unleashing human potential and producing more for less?

Take another very common organizational dilemma—think carefully about this—are not *businesses run by the economic rules of the marketplace*? But think also about this—are not *organizations run by the cultural rules of the workplace*? In other words, there are two different sets of rules operating—economic and cultural rules. What would *wisdom* dictate? What if you could bring the marketplace into the culture of the workplace so that every person and team, using principle-centered criteria, would have access to 360-degree and/or balanced Scoreboard information? Wouldn't this information, combined with *both* extrinsic and intrinsic compensation, create a natural incentive for them to completely focus on meeting human needs in the marketplace and the needs of *all* stakeholders?

You could even apply this *wisdom* thinking to society itself in dealing with its fundamental dilemma. Briefly put, would you not agree that *society operates by its dominant social values*? But also, would you not agree that *society has to live with the consequences of the inviolate operation of natural laws and principles*? What if you could align social values, mores, and laws with principles by sacrificing special interest for the general welfare?

Can you see how the larger context of *wisdom* in serving human needs resolves these kinds of dilemmas? Can you see also why sacrifice is such an imperative? Sacrifice means to give up something good for something better, so that in a very real sense, when your vision is strong about meeting a particular need, you would not call it sacrifice, even though an outside observer would. This kind of heartfelt sacrifice is the essence of moral authority.

PROBLEM SOLVING THROUGH A PRINCIPLE-CENTERED MODEL

I said early in the book that if the Whole-Person Paradigm of human nature is accurate, it should give you an uncommon ability to explain, predict and diagnose the greatest problems in your organization. I meant what I said. I really believe that the simple, whole-person model and the simple, developmental process *are* simplicity on the far side of complexity.

Over the years I've asked hundreds of thousands of people all over the world to identify their single greatest *personal* challenge—the kind that keeps them up at night. Then I asked people to identify their single greatest *professional* or *organizational* problem. Here is a summary of the responses given most often (notice the similarity with the pain and challenges mentioned at the beginning of the book):

PERSONAL CHALLENGES	PROFESSIONAL/ORGANIZATIONAL CHALLENGES
1. Finances, money	1. Workload, deadlines — inability to reach goals
2. Life balance, not enough time	2. Insufficient time and resources
3. Health	3. Financial survival
4. Relationships –spouse, child/teen, friend	4. Low trust
5. Raising and disciplining children	5. Disempowerment
6. Self-doubt	6. Change and uncertainty
7. Uncertainty, change	7. Staying current with technology
8. Lack of skills, education	8. Confusion — lack of shared vision and values
9. Lack of meaning	9. Job satisfaction — don't enjoy work
10. Lack of peace	10. Lack of integrity in boss / top management

Table 11

Again, I'm confident that you could take any one of these personal or organizational challenges and, with the framework of principles in this book embodied in the three models of greatness, you would know how to begin to solve the problem. Simply take any challenge you face and think about what you could do through *vision, discipline, passion, conscience* and *The 7 Habits* on the personal side, through *modeling, pathfinding, aligning,* and *empowering* as a leader, and through *clarity, commitment, translation, synergy, enabling* and *accountability* in the context of *mission, vision* and *values* in an organization. Like the ecological relationship between the four dimensions of moral authority, you will find a profound ecology and sequence between the models of greatness and their various elements in solving your challenges. See again the model of principle-centered focus and execution that follows (figure 15.6)

You may also be interested to see how practical the leadership framework of this book is by going back to *Max & Max* and thinking like a trim-tabber. Appendix 7—*Max & Max* Revisited—shows how Max and Mr. Harold can use the problem-solving lens of the 4 Roles of Leadership to transform the way they work and solve their toughest challenges.

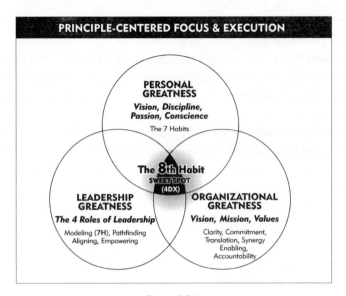

Figure 15.6

Consider further the comprehensive power of this whole person (body, mind, heart and spirit) model. It deals with the four intelligences/ capacities—IQ, EQ, PQ and SQ. It represents the four basic motivations/needs of life—to live, to love, to learn, to leave a legacy. It represents the four attributes of personal leadership—vision, discipline, passion, governed by conscience. Finally, it represents these four attributes at large for organizations (including families) in the form of the four roles—modeling, pathfinding, aligning, and empowering (see figure 15.7).

Finding Your Voice is a synergistic concept of the whole being greater than the sum of the parts, so that when you respect, develop, in-

	4 INTELLIGENCES	4 ATTRIBUTES	4 ROLES	
BODY (TO LIVE)	Physical Intelligence	Vision	Modeling	FOCUS
MIND (TO LEARN)	Mental Intelligence	Discipline	Pathfinding	
HEART (TO LOVE)	Emotional Intelligence	Passion	Aligning	EXECUTION
SPIRIT (TO LEAVE A LEGACY)	Spiritual Intelligence	Conscience	Empowering	

Figure 15.7

tegrate and balance the four parts of your nature, you're led to realize your full potential and lasting fulfillment.

Open your heart. Take the whole-person approach—body, mind, heart and spirit—and see what a powerful expression "open your heart" is. *Physically*, keep your arteries clean through proper diet and exercise so that your heart is strong and healthy. Open your heart *emotionally* so that you are willing to involve people in the problem and work out solutions together, and listen deeply for understanding. Open your heart *mentally* so that you are constantly learning, see people as whole people, and free yourself of "quick-fix" thinking, so that leadership indeed becomes *your* choice. Open your heart *spiritually* so that your life is driven by a higher wisdom, by a divine conscience whose ethic is finding yourself through losing yourself in the service of others—doing well by doing good.

Bring together all of your intelligence and resolve, and go to work in the spirit of Winston Churchill: "To every man there comes in his lifetime that special moment when he is figuratively tapped on the shoulder and offered a chance to do a very special thing, unique to him and fitted to his talents. What a tragedy if that moment finds him unprepared or unqualified for the work which would be his finest hour."

CONCLUSION

This book has primarily attempted to teach one basic paradigm: that people are *whole people*—body, mind, heart and spirit. As a person engages in the *sequential 8th Habit process* of finding one's own voice, making the choice to expand her influence by inspiring others to find their voice, she increases her freedom and power of choice to solve her greatest challenges and serve human needs; she learns how *leadership can eventually become a choice* not a position, so that leadership, the enabling art, is widely distributed throughout organizations and society, and therefore, while we manage or control things, we lead (empower) people.

Regarding the people paradigm, we have learned that every human being is precious in his or her own right, endowed with enormous, almost infinite potential and capacity. We've learned that the pathway to enlarging that capacity is magnifying our present gifts and talents. Then, almost like a flower blooming in the spring, additional gifts and talents are given or opened up to us and our "hardwired" capacities in all four areas are unleashed to lead a balanced, integrated, powerful life. The opposite is also the case. If we neglect our gifts and talents, they, like an unused muscle, will atrophy and waste away.

We've also learned that the culture we live and work in has "soft-wared" us for mediocrity, or in other words, to fall far short of our potential. Anything less than a whole person is a thing, and things have to be controlled or managed. This command-and-control Industrial Age software has driven the workplace to believe that the greatest source of wealth lies in capital and equipment, not in people. We've also learned that we have the hardwired power to rewrite that software, and that this power inspires us to *lead* (empower) people, who have the power of choice, and *manage* things, which do not.

The developmental process paradigm answers the "how" and "when" questions and teaches us to conquer ourselves first by subordinating what we want *now* for what we want *later.* The process is increasingly exciting because it is increasingly powerful in expanding our choices and capacities. If we follow principles (symbolized by a compass) that always point north, we gradually develop moral authority; people trust us, and if we truly respect them, see their worth and potential, and involve them, we can come to share a common vision. If, through our moral authority (primary greatness), we earn formal authority, or position (secondary greatness), we can together institutionalize these principles so that body and spirit are being constantly nourished, leading to unbelievable kinds of freedom and power to expand and deepen our service. In short, the kind of leadership that inspires followership comes only when we put service above self.

Organizations, both private and public, learn that they are only sustainable when they serve human needs. Again, service above self. This is the true DNA of success. It is not about "what's in it for me," but about "what can I contribute?"

> *I sought my God and my God I could not find.*
> *I sought my soul and my soul eluded me.*
> *I sought my brother to serve him in his need,*
> *and I found all three—my God, my soul and thee.*
>
> ANONYMOUS

A FEW FINAL WORDS

To you as the reader, I affirm your worth and potential. My sincere hope is that the principles in this book have been communicated clearly enough so that you have not only come to see that worth and potential in yourself, but so that you will Find Your Voice and live a life of greatness by inspiring many other people, organizations and communities to find theirs.

Even if you live in horrible circumstances, it is in those circumstances that you will find your call to choose your own response. It is then that "life calls out to us" to serve those around us whose needs we become aware of. It is in so doing that we find our true "voice" in life. Haddon Klingberg, Jr., author of the insightful biography of Viktor and Elly Frankl, *When Life Calls Out to Us* (one of the two projects he worked on prior to his passing), articulated this central theme of Frankl's life in this way:

> For Frankl, since spirituality is in its essence self-transcendence, it brings with it human freedom. But it is not freedom *from* as much as freedom *to*. We are not free from our biological nature, whether instinctual drives, genetic legacies, or the functions and malfunctions of our brains and bodies. Nor are we free from the grasp of social, developmental, and environmental influences. But we are free to take a stand toward these, even against them. We are free to do what we will with the cards we are dealt, to choose what response we will make to fateful events, to decide what cause or persons will receive our devotion.
>
> And this *freedom to* carries an *obligation to*. Each of us is responsible for something, to someone. By using our freedom to act responsibly in the world, we uncover meaning in our lives. It is only when our will to meaning is frustrated that we settle for the pursuit of personal pleasure (Freud), or for financial and social success (Adler).
>
> When a person exercises spiritual freedom and responsibility, there follows a host of effects: peace of mind, good conscience, and contentment. But these occur naturally—as by-products, so to speak. But pursuing any of these directly makes their attainment improbable or impossible, he said. There is nothing quite like striving for peace of mind to keep one edgy. To center one's effort on achieving a good conscience may lead to hypocrisy or guilt—or both. To make health one's

chief aim may bring on something akin to hypochondria. For Frankl, these are not ends to be pursued for their own sake or even for one's own good. Instead, they ensue naturally for persons who live for something else, for something greater.[16]

With my deepest conviction, I affirm you with the words of General Joshua Lawrence Chamberlain:

The inspiration of a noble cause involving human interests wide and far, enables men to do things they did not dream themselves capable of before, and which they were not capable of alone. The consciousness of belonging, vitally, to something beyond individuality; of being part of a personality that reaches we know not where, in space and time, greatens the heart to the limit of the souls ideal, and builds out the supreme of character.[17]

MY GRANDFATHER, Stephen L Richards, was one of my most influential mentors. My love and respect and admiration for him is boundless. His life was totally dedicated to serving others. Those who knew him considered him to be one of the wisest people they had ever known. I close in gratitude for the life motto he shared with me:

Life is a mission and not a career, and the purpose of all our education and knowledge is so that we can better represent Him and serve that mission of life in His name and toward His purposes.

QUESTION & ANSWER

Q: Why is sacrifice so central to moral authority?

A: Sacrifice really means giving up something good for something better. It could really even be called up-leveling. When a person has a vision that transcends himself, that focuses on an important cause or project that he is emotionally connected to, then the real course of least resistance is to put service above self. To such a person it is no sacrifice.

To an outside observer it would appear to be a sacrifice because he is denying some present good. Happiness is essentially a by-product of subordinating what we want now for what we want eventually. Rather than being the course of most resistance, sacrifice is the course of least resistance to one who is deeply, spiritually and emotionally connected to a cause or a calling or the serving of another. Service above self is the ethic of all great religions and of all philosophy and psychology that has endured. Albert Schweitzer said, "I know not what your destiny will be, but one thing I know: the only ones among you who will be truly happy are those who have sought and found how to serve."

Q: The buzz used to be about TQM and quality; then it became empowerment; the new buzzword today is innovation. What will it be tomorrow?

A: I suggest it will be wisdom. Unless you have principles at the center of a person's heart and soul and in the relationships and culture of an organization, you cannot build high trust. And without high trust you cannot have empowerment. When rules take the place of human judgment, you can't nurture a climate of innovation and creativity; instead you will nurture a kiss-up culture. Without high trust and aligned structures and systems based on an abundance paradigm, you cannot get TQM or quality. Of necessity, the Age of Wisdom, in my opinion, will follow the Age of Information, where the essence of leadership will be to be a servant leader.

Q: I like the concept of a principle-centered organization. Is it possible to take this to a community?

A: Absolutely. If you can get together enough caring people who are the natural and formal leaders in education, business, government and other professions, and even people without formal authority who have a lot of moral authority but a strong interest, and you get them involved in the process of teaching the 7 Habits and the four roles to organizations and families throughout the community, it's amazing what good can come from it. We have done this in many, many communities around the world.

TWENTY MOST COMMONLY
ASKED QUESTIONS

Q1: I find it's almost impossible for me to change my habits. Is this realistic? Am I unique?

A: You are not alone. Let me explain why.

Perhaps you remember—or have seen in a more recent video or movie—the film clips showing the lunar voyage of Apollo 11. Those of us who witnessed it were absolutely transfixed. We could hardly believe our eyes when we saw men walking on the moon.

Where do you think the most power and energy was expended on that journey into space? Going a quarter of a million miles to the moon? Returning to Earth? Orbiting the moon? Separating and redocking the lunar and command modules? Lifting off the moon?

No, not any of these. Not even in all of these together. It was lifting off from Earth. More energy was spent in the first few minutes of liftoff from Earth—in the first few miles of travel—than was used in half a million miles for several days.

The gravity pull of those first few miles was enormous. It took an internal thrust greater than both the pull of gravity and atmosphere resistance to finally break out into orbit. But once they did break out, it took almost no power to do all those other things. In fact, when one of the astronauts was asked how much power was expended when the lunar module separated from the command module to go down and survey the moon, he answered, "Less than the breath of a baby."

This lunar voyage provides a powerful metaphor for describing what it takes to break out of old habits and create new ones. The gravity force of Earth could be compared to deeply embedded habits, tendencies programmed by genetics, environment, parents and other significant figures. The weight of Earth's atmosphere could be compared to the wider societal and organizational cultures we are part of. These are two powerful forces, and you must have an internal will that is stronger than both of these forces in order to make liftoff happen.

But once it does happen, you will be amazed at the freedom it gives you. During liftoff, astronauts have very little freedom or power; all they can do is carry out the program. But as soon as they pull away from the gravity of Earth and the atmosphere surrounding it, they experience an unbelievable surge of freedom. And they have many, many options and alternatives.

If you will simply start down the pathway of Finding Your Voice and Inspiring Others to Find Theirs and stick with it, you will develop the power of this new habit to grow and change in today's world of tremendous challenge, complexity and opportunity.

Q2: In one sense I'm very excited and intrigued by what you're teaching. But in another sense, I question whether I can really do it.

A: That is very honest, but I suggest you ask two other questions first before attempting to deal with the competency question. The first one is, *Should* I do it? That is a value question. The second one is, Do I *want* to do it? That is a motivation question and deals with your unique voice and passion. If you can answer yes to those two questions, then look at the question Can I do it? That's a competency question, and that deals with getting the proper training and education. Do not confuse the three questions. Don't try to answer a value question with a training answer, a motivation question with a value answer, or a competency question with a motivation answer. Think clearly and carefully about the three questions: Can I do it? Do I want to do it? Should I do it? Keep them separate so you can identify the best starting point.

Q3: Why is leadership such a hot topic today?

A: The new economy is based primarily on knowledge work. That means that wealth has migrated from money and things to people— both intellectual and social capital. In fact, our greatest financial investment is in knowledge workers. Knowledge work has gravitated from arithmetic to both exponential and geometric contribution potential, and this kind of intellectual and social capital is the key to leveraging or optimizing all other investments. Furthermore, the Industrial Age management control style and "people as expense" systems are becoming increasingly obsolete and/or dysfunctional because of the competitive forces of the marketplace. There is also a growing awareness that the human dimension, particularly the trust level, is the root source of all problems. The soft stuff is the hard stuff and everyone is coming to know it. That is why leadership is the highest of all arts; it is the *enabling* art.

Q4: This all seems so idealistic and moralistic to me. With conditions the way they are, I don't know if any of this is really possible.

A: The deeper question you need to ask is, Is there a space between stimulus and response? In other words, Do we really, truly have the power of choice, regardless of circumstances? If you can honestly say yes to that question, you will come to see that idealism is realism. You can't "see" electronic marvels of today, yet you rely upon them and know that they are real. Before they were discovered or invented, they were not "real," they were only idealistic. When you say that these things are too moralistic, this implies right and wrong. In your heart of hearts, you know there is a difference between right and wrong, and if you choose the right, different consequences follow than if you choose the wrong. That's why these ideas are idealistic and moralistic, both of which are very realistic.

Q5: You say that cultural moral authority is the most advanced form of moral authority—what do you mean?

A: Take, for example, the Declaration of Independence of the United States. The sentiments in that document represent visionary moral authority. The Constitution attempted to *institutionalize* the values that "all Men are created equal" and that they are "endowed by their Creator with certain unalienable Rights that among these are Life, Liberty and the Pursuit of Happiness."

The Constitution was in alignment with the vision and value system of the Declaration of Independence. The Declaration said "all" men, yet women didn't have the right to vote for decades, many of the founders were slaveholders, the Emancipation Proclamation did not pass for over eighty years, and still today there are profound pockets of racial prejudice. *Cultural* moral authority always develops slower than institutionalized or visionary moral authority. But ultimately, it is the key to developing a harmonious society. The key lies not in government, which represents force or law, nor in private individuals or private business organizations, which represent freedom. It lies within individuals and groups adopting common meanings and values that are truly connected to their hearts and minds. This level of volunteerism creates a *civil* society, which is the higher Third Alternative between law and freedom. This is the underlying assumption behind the thinking and writing of Adam Smith, author of *The Wealth of Nations*. Long before he wrote this classic he wrote a book called *The Theory of Moral Sentiments*. This work, which was foundational to his later works, including *The Wealth of Nations*, was based on the idea that intentional virtue and goodwill are the foundation of both an economic system of free enterprise and a political system of a representative democracy. He acknowledged that if individual virtue deteriorated, neither the free market nor a democracy could ultimately survive.

Q6: You say that one of the basic problems is that we are using the industrial model in a Knowledge Worker Age, but aren't we still an industrialized nation? Everywhere we look there is industry.

A: That's true, but the nature of the *value-added* work done in these various industries is more and more being done by knowledge workers, not manual workers. So, we are not talking about doing away with industry. We are talking about using a different leadership paradigm inside those industries. In fact, this paradigm can go back to the agrarian or farming era. Outside cities, farms are everywhere. They add increased value through the strengths of the Industrial and Information Ages. We are talking more about a mental framework than a physical environment.

Q7: How do authoritarian cultures create codependency?

A: Think about it. If you have an authoritarian leader who controls, what do the followers do? Most passively obey; they wait until told and do what they're told. The behavior confirms the perception of the authoritarian leader to continue to command and control, which, in turn, justifies the passivity of the followers. In other words, it becomes a self-fulfilling prophecy. All of this disempowers people's capacities and intelligences. It underutilizes them. It turns people into things to be managed or controlled. The cycle of codependency eventually nurtures a politicized kiss-up culture where right is defined by compliance or by loyalty, and where wrong lies in getting caught.

This dynamic also spawns dysfunctional agreement where people say yes when they really mean no. It eliminates healthy conflict and spawns resentment, anger, malicious obedience, low trust, low quality and low performance. Such unexpressed feelings never really die— they're buried alive and come forth later in uglier ways.

The authoritarian then carries the responsibility for results and focuses upon efficiency—that is, methods, process and steps so that rules begin to take the place of human judgment. All this reinforces leadership as a position, not a choice; it becomes part of the cultural DNA. Little by little you see the truth of Lord Acton's statement that "power corrupts and absolute power corrupts absolutely." Everyone then becomes self-serving and subordinates their integrity to pleasing the boss.

The problem is, in the new economy, institutionalized codependent cultures can only survive through market ignorance, artificial subsidization, terror, or by heavy tradition that is sustainable only because the competition is also codependent.

The whole cycle can be broken by one person who sees leadership as a choice, who begins to trim-tab a larger Circle of Influence, and who relies upon the pragmatics of a competitive marketplace to break the self-fulfilling downward spiral. This leadership represents moral authority, which comes from choosing to live by principles and which almost always involves some form of sacrifice. But in a free market economy, it will come out on top simply because it is pragmatic—it works; it produces more for less.

Q8: How does all of this apply in a bad economy, or, let's say, in a good economy but a declining industry?

A: It applies all the more, simply because the greatest resource is the creative capacity of people who come up with Third Alternative solutions in bad times. However, the natural tendency is for people to go back to the command-and-control transactional industrial model, which is not sustainable in the long run. In a short-run crisis situation, where the culture has a common purpose of survival, the authoritarian approach may turn the corner. As Eisenhower once put it, "You don't speak democracy to the man in the foxhole." But, eventually, you need deep involvement of everyone to make significant changes sustainable. This takes trusted moral authority leadership.

Q9: How do the 7 Habits tie in to *The 4 Roles of Leadership*? We've invested significant amounts of time and money in 7 Habits training.

A: Remember, the 7 Habits are based on principles. The 7 Habits are character principles that shape *who and what you are;* the four roles are *what you do* to exert leadership influence in an organization. When you put the 7 Habits in the context of the four roles, they are the modeling role. This makes the 7 Habits strategic because they are the modeling you do while doing the other three roles. The principles underlying the 7 Habits are like a deep well or an aquifer that feeds all other subsurface wells, such as TQM, team building empowerment, innovation, etc.

Q10: Corporate scandals frequently make all business "guilty by association." This brings into sharp focus the topic of character. How do you develop personal and cultural character; how do you avoid these kinds of problems?

A: I had the opportunity of working on the aftermath of the Three Mile Island situation, the Rodney King riots and the Exxon Valdez situation, and I basically found that all of these disasters were acute manifestations of a deep cultural phenomenon, the tip of the iceberg of people doing wrong things, closing up, shredding stuff, ignoring bad things, getting caught, then having the media broadcast it.

I think it's a valuable lesson for all organizations. Revisit what matters most to you—your vision and value systems. Reexamine all your procedures and practices, structures and systems, to see if they have institutionalized those visions and values. Feedback should reflect the honest judgments of advisors, suppliers, customers and the entire value chain. You cannot talk yourself out of problems you have behaved your way into. Eventually, the hens will come home to roost. Loyalty must not be a higher value than integrity; in fact, integrity is loyalty. You want your doctor to tell you the truth even if you don't want to hear it. You want the doctor to be true to his or her profession as the highest form of being true to you. So also with your organization—see yourself as a professional whose highest loyalty is to moral and professional principles, not to your institution. This is the clearest way of being loyal to your institution.

The best way I know of to develop character in an organization is not to put it on some checklist where people judge others, but rather to hold people responsible for results, measured by a balanced Scoreboard, that require a higher level of character development. This way you're not judging someone's character; you're only giving them responsibility that requires character growth.

Q11: How do you maintain a positive, high-trust culture after downsizing?

A: You know why cultures deteriorate after downsizing? Because principles are not followed, people are not involved, people are not informed, and people do not know when the next shoe is going to drop. They don't understand the criteria for the decisions that are going to be made; they may not be economically literate about the industry, the economy, and the company. I have personally seen many organizations go through very, very difficult times requiring tough decisions but manage in a remarkably principled way. Through transparent and open communication, through sincere and meaningful involvement and participation, through adhering to a set of fixed principle-based values and by going the second mile, the people who were negatively affected and their families knew the organization went the extra mile in their behalf, and goodwill in the community actually increased.

Q12: We often have leadership development academies, off-sites, special sessions, outside resource people come in to the organization. They are very helpful, uplifting and inspiring, but within a few days, it's business as usual. What do you recommend?

A: To know and not to do is not to know. You can be temporarily inspired and emboldened with new and important knowledge and skills, but unless you apply them, you don't really know them. If the structures and the systems of the environment do not give you the incentive to apply them, you *won't* apply them and you won't *know* them. Eventually, these kinds of experiences take a toll and breed cynicism throughout a culture. Change efforts and all the new management buzzwords will get to be like cotton candy, which tastes good for a second and then evaporates. The key is to take the material, teach it, discuss it, and try to institutionalize it by building the fundamental principles right into the daily processes of how the daily work gets done and how people get rewarded. Then it will take. No longer will it be a sideshow; it will be under the main tent.

Q13: What if this approach simply doesn't work?

A: If people won't apply it, it won't work. There is no silver bullet. It takes deep commitment, patience and persistence, particularly in making changes or transitions from one mind- and skill-set to another mind- and skill-set. The associated tool-set will help enormously, but, in the last analysis, people must be committed to go to work.

Q14: What is the best way to initiate these changes, assuming you have made them inside yourself?

A: If you were driving a car with your foot on the brake, what would be the fastest way to move forward—to floor it or to release the brake? Obviously, to release the brake. Similarly, with cultures in organizations, there are driving forces and restraining forces. Driving forces are usually the logical, economic realities, which would be equivalent to flooring it, pushing the gas pedal down. Restraining forces are usually cultural and emotional and would represent the brake. Through Third Alternatives and synergistic communication, restraining forces are converted into driving forces. Not only do you make significant advancements but also they are culturally sustained because of this involvement and commitment. Kirk Lewin's force field theory is embodied in this answer.

Q15: Is all this material that new? I have heard these ideas from my youth. I see them everywhere in our history.

A: That's true. In fact, to further make your point, it's because of a principle-centered constitution and a free market that we see the unleashing of human potential inside the United States, where 4.5 percent of the world's population produces almost a third of the world's goods. The evidence of the power of these paradigms and principles drive dramatic results. Remember, principles are universal and timeless. The significant principles are probably best learned, or, better, *earned* by farmers, simply because they are so close to nature and to natural laws or principles. They know you can't cram on the farm like people attempt to do in socially organized institutions such as schools. Competitive, top-level athletics is another excellent metaphor because, again, there is no cramming. The price has to be paid to become a contender.

What is common sense is not common practice. That's why there is a need for renewal and recommitment and a restoration of the character ethic and of principle-centered leadership.

Q16: Is this material based on research?

A: If you mean double-blind, empirical studies, no—that is, with the exception of our scientific execution gap studies. If you mean historical analysis, literature review and drawing upon extensive action research, yes.

Q17: What organizations are models of these kinds of ideas?

A: You will find such models in every field of endeavor. They are all around you: organizations like the A. B. Combs School and the USS *Santa Fe* submarine are all around you. The litmus test is, How empowered is the workforce? How much do they focus on and execute the organization's highest priorities? Companies that were researched in Jim Collins's work *Good to Great* are empowered organizations with humble, fiercely determined leaders and high levels of empowerment. Empowerment, of course, is not the whole answer. Most of the top organizations have moved or are moving toward a balanced report card. Aligning operations with strategy, with the market, requires great judgment. Many organizations that were once very successful have gone into decline. It takes constant vigilance in attracting and developing the best people, building the leadership ethic into the cultural DNA, as well as a great deal of personal, visionary, institutional and cultural moral authority to keep sustaining the road to greatness.

Q18: Is this basically religious material?

A: Principles definitely have a moral and spiritual foundation, but they are not unique to any particular religion. I have personally taught them all around the world in the context of different religions, and have quoted their different scriptural texts. Principles are truly universal and timeless. I used to be shocked, but I am no longer, to see what happens when you get people anywhere in the world at any level in an organization significantly involved in developing their value systems. When the spirit of genuine openness and synergy is present, and when the people are truly informed, all of the selected values become essentially the same. Different words are used, different practices reflecting those values come out, but the underlying sense always deals with the four dimensions spoken about throughout this material—the physical/economic, the relationship or the social, the mental or the talent development, and the spiritual, having to do with both meaning and integrity. If you want to have an interesting experience yourself, just study the mission statements of a few organizations that have produced those mission statements through involvement and identification over time. Different words will be used, but you will find they are basically saying the same things, even though they may not be living them.

Q19: I am both discouraged and impatient. Is it ever too late for me to change?

A: Great question. In fact, I find that the fundamental problem that people have in doubting the validity of these ideas is not the ideas. They make eminent sense to most everybody. It's that they doubt themselves. All I can say is, start slow, and, in small ways, make and keep promises to yourself. Let your conscience be your guide regarding what promises to make. Once you make them, however small, keep them. Little by little, your sense of honor will become greater than your moods. As you acquire an increasing sense of self-control, self-mastery, security and competence, you will be able to make larger promises and keep them, go into new fields, leave your comfort zone and take more initiative. Remember, again, the story of the Chinese bamboo tree. There is a certain species of the Chinese bamboo tree that, when you plant it, you see nothing for four years. Just a little shoot out of the ground and that's it. You weed, water, cultivate, nurture and do everything you can to make it successful, but you see nothing. In the fifth year, this particular species of the Chinese bamboo tree grows up to eighty feet. In its initial stages, all of the growth went underground in the root. Then, once it had its roots in place, all of the growth went above the ground and was visible, giving evidence to the cynics of the growth that had been occurring all along. This is why the personal level of character development always precedes the trust building in interpersonal relationships, which precedes the creation of a culture in an organization that truly executes on its highest priorities. It is never too late. Life is a mission, not a career.

Q20: How do you know this works?

A: You only really know by working it. To know and not to do is really not to know. Another confirming source of evidence will be getting the pragmatic results that come from those that are being served—clients, owners, employees, citizens or customers—and with getting good information on the entire supply team and your own culture. In the last analysis, I put more faith in *discernment* through the conscience, combined with *observation* and *measurement*, than I do in observation and measurement without discernment. I find that most people intimately ("in-to-me-see") know many things they should be doing and many things they should not be doing. If they will simply act on that knowledge, their other questions will be simply academic. Eventually, those questions will also be answered, not just from learning the answers but also from *earning* the answers.

APPENDICES

Appendix 1

DEVELOPING THE 4 INTELLIGENCES/ CAPACITIES—A PRACTICAL GUIDE TO ACTION

DEVELOPING PHYSICAL INTELLIGENCE—PQ

Let's start with the body, with Physical Intelligence (PQ), because the body is the instrument of the mind, heart and spirit. If we can subordinate the body to the spirit—that is, our appetites and passions to our conscience—we become masters of ourselves. People whose lives are a function of their appetites and passions rather than their conscience cannot give of themselves. Their space between stimulus and response is narrowed—they lose personal freedom, thinking all the while that they are exercising it. The body is a good servant but a bad master.

The Greek expression of the self-mastery formula for life—"know thyself, control thyself, give thyself"—is a magnificent sequence. I suggest there are three fundamental ways to develop our physical intelli-

> *Research is now clear that the inability to manage*
> *oneself efficiently leads to premature aging, diminished*
> *mental clarity, and even blocked access to our innate intelligence.*
> *The converse is also true: Increasing internal coherence*
> *leads to more efficiency in all physiological systems and*
> *greater creativity, adaptability, and flexibility.*[1]
>
> DOC CHILDRE AND BRUCE CRYER

331

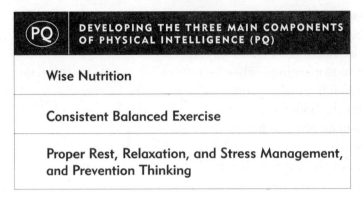

Figure A1.1

gence. First, *wise nutrition;* second, *consistent balanced exercise;* third, *proper rest, relaxation, stress management,* and *prevention thinking.*

These three ways are widely understood and accepted by most people in the civilized world. They're really common sense. But common sense is not common practice. Very few people practice all three of them.

In their book, *The Power of Full Engagement,* Jim Loehr and Tony Schwartz emphasize that managing energy, not time, is the key to high performance and personal renewal. They certainly respect time management, but they suggest that the highest criterion to be used in the management of one's time is how you manage your energy. By studying nature and the natural laws that govern all humanity, they emphasize the importance of respecting the cycle that oscillates between activity/performance and rest/renewal. They use the whole-person approach: body, mind, heart and spirit. They focus on the importance of habits, which they call rituals, to increase our energy and performance capability.

Wise Nutrition

Most of us know what we should and shouldn't eat. The key is balance. I readily admit I am not an expert nutritionist, but I, like most of us, have been educated to know that our bodies and systems, including the immune system, are strengthened most when we eat more whole grains, vegetables, fruits and lower-fat protein. Meats, when eaten (better sparingly), should be lean. Research also increasingly shows the benefits of eating fish regularly. Foods (including many fast foods, processed foods and sweets) high in saturated fat and high in sugar should be eaten very sparingly or avoided. But remember again, the key is balance and moderation. Learn not to indulge yourself and pig out. In other words, learn when to stop eating—when you are satisfied and short of being uncomfortably full. Finally, drink a lot of water—six to ten glasses a day. It optimizes the body's functions and *significantly* contributes to one's efforts to maintain physical fitness and a healthy weight through diet and regular exercise.

I have also come to believe in the efficacy and wisdom of occasional fasting, wherein you miss a meal or two for the purposes of providing rest to the whole digestive process and also for cleansing. From my own experience, the main benefit, however, has not been physical—it has been more mental and spiritual. The principle of fasting is taught in almost all major world religions as a means of developing a higher level of self-mastery and self-control, and also a deeper awareness of how really dependent we are.

I strongly believe that when you properly control your appetites, your ability to control your passions and to purify your desires increases. It gives you a real feeling of humility and enables you to gain greater perspective about what is really important in life.

I have also experienced the negative fruits of overeating, extreme dieting and mindless eating of junk food.

My biggest temptation comes when I'm on the road, exhausted at the end of the day, and I go to the hotel and order room service. I find when I'm unwise and indulge myself, it affects my mind and my spirit, and even the quality of my sleep. The legendary coach Vince Lombardi used to say, "Fatigue makes cowards of us all." This is surely true in my case, because when I get really tired I tend to slip into a self-indulging pattern, and it really does affect my mind and my spirit for a day or two. When you subordinate your body to your mind and your spirit, the peace and confidence that flow from that kind of discipline and self-mastery is enormous. In fact, for myself, when I feel hunger pains that aren't really associated with true hunger but are more a function of the withdrawal of a sugar addiction, I say to myself: "Nothing tastes as good as thin feels." I also visualize those so-called hunger pains gobbling up the fat stores. When we subordinate taste to nutrition, gradually we reeducate our taste buds to give voice to the trillions of cells that are screaming for proper nutrition.

But really, all this is a personal matter, and everyone must decide what is wise nutrition for him or her. I do believe, however, that almost everyone can experience the tremendous benefits of winning the private victory over the body. Such a victory also impacts our ability to produce public victories in our relationships with others and on reorienting ourselves to a life of service and contribution.

Consistent, Balanced Exercise

Regular exercise—cardiovascular, strength and flexibility—significantly increases both the quality of life and life expectancy. Again, the key is balance. Our society has adopted increasingly sedentary, inactive lifestyles. But there are so many ways to get regular exercise. Start small, in ways you can sustain. Do something daily, or at least three to five times a week. Choose something you enjoy and that fits your specific needs and conditions. Consult with your physician. Vary the kinds of exercises you do so that you strengthen different parts of your body and avoid becoming bored or burned out on one thing. Many people love to walk, vigorously, if possible. Others run, swim, garden or bike. Many take advantage of equipment in gyms designed to give you an aerobic/cardiovascular workout, such as treadmills, stationary bicycles, stair climbers, elliptical machines, rowing machines, etc.

Weight lifting, as well as other strength training, has many significant benefits for people of all ages, including improving one's strength, posture, energy, slowing and stopping the deterioration of the bones and increasing the body's ability to burn calories.

I cannot say enough personally about the inevitable fruits that I experience from consistent, balanced exercise. For me, the greatest benefit is mental and spiritual, rather than physical, even though I'm impressed by the overwhelming research that shows the physical benefits that come from regular exercise. Aerobic exercise, wherein you use the big muscles of the leg to strengthen the heart and the circulatory systems so that you can process oxygen in the most efficient way, has always been the basic foundation of my exercise program.

My preferred aerobic exercise is running, but I have messed up my knees in various sports activities and need now to use a stationary bike. But I have found that while I'm on the bike I can also do other things. I can talk to people on the phone and conduct business even though I am breathing like a frantic Darth Vader. I can watch either educational or entertainment television. I can have meaningful conversations with my wife or children or friends who are also exercising at the same time. We encourage each other or share our best ideas with each other on what works and doesn't.

I have also come to believe strongly in the importance of muscle toning and flexibility exercises. I remember once a trainer spotting me in a bench press exercise. He basically told me to go as far as I could go and then to do one more. I asked him why, and he said that most of the benefit comes at the very end of the exercise when the muscle fiber is exhausted and breaks (pain), and within about forty-eight hours is renewed and strengthened. This was a fascinating learning experience for me, because I wanted to quit when I was tired and hurting. But he stood above me and said, "I'll take the bar as soon as you cannot go any further." This is a great metaphor for the other three dimensions of life as well. As we go to the end of our tether, our capacity to do increases. Emerson put it this way: "That which we persist in doing becomes easier, not that the nature of the thing has changed, but our ability to do has increased."

My particular commitment is to exercise five to six days a week aerobically, three days a week in muscle toning, and six days a week in some kind of stretching and/or yoga for flexibility. I have also benefited from Pilates in strengthening the inner core. Everyone has to study his or her own situation and determine that which is most wise. But again, I am convinced that exercise increases our own sense of self-control and self-mastery, which enhances the totality of our lives and truly enlarges the space between stimulus and response.

When I was teaching at the university in full semesters, I encouraged the students to develop their own particular goals they wanted to achieve for that semester. The overwhelming majority of the students selected proper eating and regular exercise as one of their goals. This is what I would call a "win-win agreement" with the students, and once it was approved, they were responsible and accountable. They also were to share their insights and learnings from these experiences and to evaluate themselves against the goals they had selected. Because this evaluation became a significant portion of the grade they received for the course, they had both external and internal motivation. Some students didn't want to deal with this physical side, which was fine—they would set and be accountable for other goals they felt they should accomplish.

You would not believe the fruits that came from those who conquered their sugar or junk food addiction and who exercised a minimum of thirty minutes at least three times a week. Cultivating these new habits and breaking old ones became so enormously impactful that it affected all their relationships. It affected their energy, their mental acumen, their studies, and their sense of self-mastery. At the end of the semester, those who hadn't selected physical goals wished they had when they heard the testimonies of those who had selected and achieved their physical mastery goals.

Just think about it for a moment. There are 168 hours in every person's week. But if you will physically sharpen the saw through regular and balanced exercise for, let's say, only two or three of those 168 hours, you will experience such a positive effect of those two or three on the other 166, including the depth and quality of your sleep, that you will begin to see the tremendous leverage and power that comes in your life from this kind of self-mastery.

Mind over mattress.

Proper Rest, Relaxation, Stress Management and Prevention Thinking

The work of the great pioneer and leader in the field of stress, Dr. Hans Selye, suggests that there are two kinds of stress: distress and eustress. *Distress* comes from hating your work, resenting the multiplied pressures of life, and feeling you are a victim. *Eustress* comes from the positive tension between where we are now and where we want to go—some meaningful goal or project or cause that really turns us on and taps into our talents and passion; in short, our voice. Through good empirical research, Dr. Selye taught how eustress braces the immune system and increases longevity and enjoyment of life. In short, we shouldn't avoid stress if it's the right kind of stress—eustress: It will strengthen us and enlarge our capacity. Of course, it must all be balanced and tempered by the proper rest and relaxation, or what is called "stress management," or more properly, "eustress management." Selye explained that women live roughly seven years longer than men for psychological/spiritual reasons, not physiological reasons. "A woman's work is never done."

In professional circles, it is widely accepted that at least two-thirds of all diseases are caused by lifestyle choices that people make. These choices relate to nutrition, to smoking, to insufficient rest and relaxation, to attempting to burn the candle at both ends, and many other abuses of the body. Many attribute various diseases to genetic factors, but as we have mentioned before, there is always a space between stimulus and response, and when people are aware of this space and aware of their own capacity to make choices based on principles, they don't necessarily get the diseases of their genetic predisposition. Even most cancers can be cured if they are detected in the first or second stage before they become aggressive.

Modern Western medicine is primarily focused on treatment rather than prevention, and the treatment usually comes under the two categories of chemistry or surgery. I would like to see the medical paradigm become broader, deeper and more complementary, with empirically validated alternative therapies.

I think it's very important to have frequent checkups, at least annually, so that various disease tendencies or symptoms can yield to wise choices. I myself have a treatment doctor and a prevention doctor and respect both of them enormously. I have learned that the most fundamental principle is that we must take responsibility for our own health. We must ask questions, get very involved, study, check second opinions, and look at alternative forms of therapy, rather than just throw the responsibility for our health and wellness to an outside person or profession.

Neglecting the Development and Health of the Body

Just think about what happens to the other three dimensions when the body is neglected. We can lose not only our health but *mentally* we can also lose our focus, our creativity, our endurance, our toughness, our courage, our learning capacity, our retention. And to the contrary, when we exercise, rest and eat properly, we retain our mental focus and toughness, as well as our thirst for learning.

What happens to our *emotional* intelligence, to our heart, when we neglect our bodies—when we become a function of appetites and passions? Patience, love, understanding, empathy, the ability to listen and compassion are themselves subordinated—they become buzzwords without flesh and blood to drive them.

I have learned for myself that if I make a commitment or a promise to myself regarding diet or exercise (or anything else), and I don't keep it, I definitely become less sensitive to the needs and feelings of others. I feel more upset and angry with myself, and I can feel integrity lessening. It's not until I go back, recommit, make up my mind, and then keep my

> *A man who gives in to temptation after five minutes simply*
> *does not know what it would have been like an hour later.*
> *That is why bad people, in a sense, know very little about badness.*
> *They have lived a sheltered life by always giving in.*[2]
>
> C.S. LEWIS

promises that I can basically forget myself and genuinely empathize with other people.

What happens to our *spirit*, to our peace of mind? It affects our desire to serve, to contribute, our willingness to sacrifice, to subordinate ourselves for a higher good; our conscience becomes dulled, yielding to almost any temptation. Any loss of personal integrity makes me more self-oriented, more selfish. However, I find that when I make up my mind to live by principles and by conscience, my resolve to serve and to contribute in meaningful ways returns.

Physical self-mastery and development is foundational. It is also very concrete, something we can immediately do something about. We have more direct access to it; we can control it. As we master the body's appetites and strengthen its intelligence, we'll begin to see the space enlarging between stimulus and response, with all the attending positive mental, emotional, and spiritual spin-offs.

I find most people acknowledge they get off the track from time to time. But if they will sincerely listen to the feedback of their body, mind, heart and spirit and make the necessary changes, they can get back on track. It's just like the flight of an airplane. Most airplanes are off track almost the entire time, but because the pilot receives constant feedback from various instruments to help him get back on the flight path, almost all flights arrive at the destination established in the submitted flight plans.

A person's conscience, if he will listen to it, will direct him in all three of these areas. And the more he follows it, the stronger it becomes, so that he can move more and more toward giving of himself. By eating wisely, exercising, resting and relaxing, we deepen our capacities and strengthen the body's immune system and ability to rebuild itself; most importantly, we release the other three intelligences contained in the mind, the heart and the spirit.

DEVELOPING MENTAL INTELLIGENCE—IQ

I suggest three ways to develop IQ, or mental capacity: First, *systematic, disciplined study and education,* including study outside of one's own field; second, the *cultivation of self-awareness* so that one can make assumptions explicit and think "outside the box" and outside the comfort zone; third, *learning by teaching and by doing.*

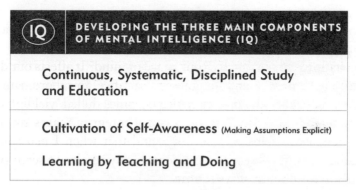

(IQ)	DEVELOPING THE THREE MAIN COMPONENTS OF MENTAL INTELLIGENCE (IQ)
	Continuous, Systematic, Disciplined Study and Education
	Cultivation of Self-Awareness (Making Assumptions Explicit)
	Learning by Teaching and Doing

Figure A1.2

Continuous, Systematic, Disciplined Study and Education

People who have made a commitment to continual learning, growth and improvement are those who have the ability to change, adapt, flex with the changing realities of life, and become fundamentally equipped to produce in any area of life. Our only real economic security lies in our power to meet human needs. So the worse conditions become, the more evident human needs become. Our security does not lie in our organizations or our jobs; disruptive technologies may simply make them irrelevant. But if we have strong, active, alert, growing, learning minds we will be able to "land on all fours." The concept that mental IQ is a fixed commodity has long since been disproved. The more the mind is used, the stronger it becomes; the more responsive the mind is to the conscience, the wiser it becomes.

I strongly believe that we should turn the TV way down in our lives and get back to reading—reading broadly, deeply, outside our comfort zones and outside our professional fields. For instance, among other magazines, I like to read *Scientific American, The Economist, Psychology Today, Harvard Business Review, Fortune,* and *Business Week.* My wife constantly encourages me to read more fiction, biographies and autobiographies, which are where her main interests lie. I think she counsels wisely. I am also sent many books for endorsement purposes, and I have learned to read conceptually by studying the table of contents and learning the style of the writer in order to discover where the main ideas are expressed or summarized. In this way I can capture the essence of many books in a day or so.

Another very interesting and helpful learning style is to break down the presentations you hear or books you read into four areas: first, *purpose*; second, *main point*; third, *validation*—in other words, evidence; and fourth, *application*—in other words, examples and stories. I have found that by training your mind to think in this way while you listen or read, it is amazing how well and accurately you can capture and understand the material—almost to the point of being able to make the presentation that you just listened to as if you had spent many times that time acquiring such understanding.

Fundamentally, everyone has to decide for himself or herself the best way to maintain continued education. In a Knowledge Worker Age world it is so vital. People have to look carefully at where they are spending their time and how much time they are wasting, then become very mentally disciplined. The page pays huge dividends. Most people say that because they are so busy, they don't have much time for reading—or even time for their children. The evidence is overwhelming, however, that people spend about half their time doing things that are not important, even though they are urgent. But the more disciplined a person becomes about *focusing* on the vitally important things, the more she has a strong feeling of "Yes" burning inside her heart, it's very easy to smilingly, happily and cheerfully say "No" to all the many distractions that inevitably come.

Cultivation of Self-Awareness (Making Assumptions Explicit)

Self-awareness involves all four intelligences and is a unique human endowment. It's essentially another word for the space between stimulus and response—the space where you can pause and then make a choice or decision.

Cultivating self-awareness by trying to understand and make explicit our underlying assumptions, theories and paradigms is without any question one of the highest leverage activities we can be involved in. Because we are always making assumptions and because they are very *implicit* (we are unaware that we are making them), by making them *explicit*, we can make huge quantum leaps. We can learn to think outside the box.

Let me give you an experience as illustration. It's called the 9-Dot Exercise. Even if you have participated in this exercise before, I encourage you to take it again now to reinforce the importance of making assumptions explicit and thinking outside the box.

Using the nine dots below and without lifting your pen or pencil from the paper, draw four straight, connected lines that go through all nine dots (see figure A1.3).

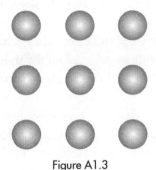

Figure A1.3

Having trouble? If so, try again, but this time, think outside the box. You've probably assumed that your lines have to stay inside the box. (That's where the expression "think outside the box," originates.) Notice what you're doing right now. You're thinking about your own thinking. No animal can do that. That's why no animal can reinvent itself. You and I can. Why? We can examine our assumptions. Now try it again.

LET'S LOOK AT what happens when you think outside the box. See— draw the first line so it goes outside the box (see figure A1.4).

Then the second, third, and fourth (see figure A1.5).

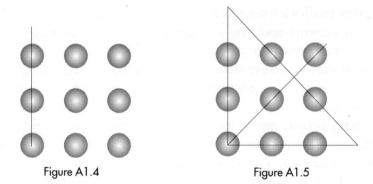

Figure A1.4   Figure A1.5

Okay. I'll give you another one. Draw one straight line through all nine dots. Now examine your mind. What are you assuming? One straight line through all nine dots. You can't rearrange the dots. They have to go through the same nine dots. What are you assuming?

The width of the line (see figure A1.6 on page 344).

Self-awareness involves all four intelligences and is a unique human endowment. It's essentially another word for the space between stimulus and response—the space where you can pause and then make a choice or decision.

Let me suggest several other approaches to nurture self-awareness. My daughter, Colleen, probably has seventy different journals filled with her thoughts written for her eyes only. Journal writing has enabled her to be an observer of her own involvements in life, and also to make choices based on those observations. She has developed the capacity to reinvent herself almost on a moment's notice, simply because her self-awareness is so deep and strong. I've seen her make important decisions based on the direction of conscience, or spiritual intelligence, subordinating both IQ and EQ, and then later finding all three to be in harmony.

The discipline of putting thoughts into writing is grueling, but powerful and clarifying. A failure learned from becomes a success. So in this sense, there need be no real failures, only learning experiences put to good use in life.

Another powerful way to develop awareness of self and others and to make assumptions explicit is seeking feedback from other people. We all have blind spots. Some of them are literally crippling to our effectiveness. But if we will cultivate the habit, either informally or formally, of seeking feedback from other people—people we care about and around whom we work and live—we will fast-track our growth and development. It's analogous to people doing market research and benchmarking against world-class excellence, rather than local or regional competitors. This often gives us information on blind spots that are also blind to other people.

Many people, myself included, see sincere prayer, pondering prayer, listening prayer, as a way to sense the direction of conscience and to see life as a mission, a stewardship and contribution opportunity. Prayer also can give strength and courage to step back, admit mistakes to others, apologize, recommit, and then get back on track.

Learning by Teaching and Doing

See again chapter 3. To review, almost everyone acknowledges you learn best when you teach another and that your learning is internalized when you live it. To know and not to do is really not to know. To learn and not to do is not to learn. In other words, to understand something but not apply it is really not to understand it. It is only in the doing, the applying, that knowledge and understanding are internalized.

Neglecting the Development of the Mind

We live in a world of compounding complexity and digital speed. Markets and technology are becoming globalized. A new kind of terrorism—one with potentially worldwide devastating consequences—is creating fear in most every heart. Whole communities are experiencing confusion and vertigo in values. Families are being stressed as never before. Our engine to meet these challenges is the mind, the power to think. When it is neglected, the *body* itself will suffer. As someone put it, "If you think education is expensive, just try ignorance." The moral imperative of life is grow or die. The half-life of many professions is just a few years. If we transfer responsibility for our mental development to our employing organization, we become increasingly codependent and may become professionally obsolete. It reduces our capacity to earn; we might lose our jobs. The body deteriorates more rapidly; we die earlier.

What is the impact on the *heart*, on relationships, when we neglect the mind and its constant development? We're governed more and more by ignorance, by prejudice, by stereotyping and labeling. It can lead to very provincial thinking, even narcissism and paranoia; our whole view of life becomes myopic, narrow, and self-focused.

What is the impact on the *spirit* when we stop learning? The conscience first becomes numbed, then dulled, and finally silenced, because it constantly tells us to learn and to grow. We lose both a sense of vision in life and the struggle to find our voice, both of which are primary sources of our passion in life. We find the wisdom literature boring and uninspiring, even irrelevant.

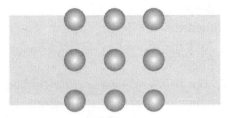

Figure A1.6

DEVELOPING EMOTIONAL INTELLIGENCE—EQ

Interestingly, if you carefully study the emotional intelligence literature, it suggests first the transcending importance of EQ in long-term effectiveness, and second, that EQ *can* be developed. But interestingly, there is relatively little out there on *how* it can be developed.

The five commonly accepted primary components of emotional in-

(EQ) THE FIVE MAIN COMPONENTS OF EMOTIONAL INTELLIGENCE (EQ)
Self-Awareness
Personal Motivation
Self-Regulation
Empathy
Social Skills

Figure A1.7

telligence are first, *self-awareness,* the ability to reflect on one's own life, grow in self-knowledge, and use that knowledge to improve oneself and either overcome or compensate for weaknesses; second, *personal motivation,* which deals with what really excites people—the vision, values, goals, hopes, desires and passions that make up their priorities; third, *self-regulation,* or the ability to manage oneself toward achieving one's vision and values; fourth, *empathy,* the ability to see how other people see and feel about things; and fifth, *social and communication skills,* which deal with how people resolve differences, solve problems, produce creative solutions, and interact optimally to further their joint purposes.

I have become deeply convinced that the best, systematic way to develop these five dimensions of EQ is through The 7 Habits of Highly Effective People. As I mentioned in chapter 8, the Habits cannot be adequately covered here in a way that truly impacts—that is best experienced in the book. But below you'll find a chart indicating the underlying principle or essence of each of the 7 Habits. You may also review again the brief summary of the 7 Habits in chapter 8.

PRINCIPLES EMBODIED IN THE 7 HABITS	
Habit	*Principle*
❶ Be Proactive	Responsibility/Initiative
❷ Begin with the End in Mind	Vision/Values
❸ Put First Things First	Integrity/Execution
❹ Think Win-Win	Mutual Respect/Benefit
❺ Seek First to Understand, Then to be Understood	Mutual Understanding
❻ Synergize	Creative Cooperation
❼ Sharpen the Saw	Renewal

Figure A1.8

Developing the 4 Dimensions of EQ Through the 7 Habits

Let's consider the five elements of emotional intelligence in relation to these 7 Habits:

EQ DEVELOPING THE FIVE MAIN COMPONENTS OF EMOTIONAL INTELLIGENCE (EQ) THROUGH THE 7 HABITS	
Self-Awareness	❶ Be Proactive
Personal Motivation	❷ Begin with the End in Mind
Self-Regulation	❸ Put First Things First ❼ Sharpen the Saw
Empathy	❺ Seek First to Understand, Then to be Understood
Social Skills	❹ Think Win-Win ❺ Seek First to Understand, Then to be Understood ❻ Synergize

Figure A1.9

Self-Awareness

An *awareness of self*, of our freedom and power to choose, is the heart of Habit—Be Proactive—in other words, you are aware of the space between stimulus and response, you're aware of your genetic, biological inheritance, your upbringing, and of the environmental forces around you. Unlike animals, you can make wise choices regarding these things. You sense you are or can become the creative force of your own life. This is your most *fundamental* decision.

Personal Motivation

Personal motivation is the basis of those choices—that is, you decide what your highest priorities, goals and values are; that's essentially what Habit 2 is about—Begin with the End in Mind. This decision to direct your own life is your *primary* decision.

Self-Regulation

Self-regulation is another way of expressing Put First Things First— Habit 3 and Sharpen the Saw—Habit 7. In other words, once you decide what your priorities are, then you *live* by them; it is the habit of integrity, the habit of self-mastery, of doing what you intend to do; of living by your values. Then constantly renew yourself. Execution strategies and tactical decisions are your *secondary* decisions.

Empathy

Empathy is the first half of Habit 5—Seek First to Understand. Then to Be Understood. It's learning to transcend your own autobiography and get into the head and hearts of other people. It's becoming socially very sensitive and aware of the situation before attempting to be understood, influence others, or make decisions or judgments.

Social Communication Skills

The combination of Habits 4, 5 and 6 represents *social communication skills.* You think in terms of mutual benefit and mutual respect (Habit 4—Think Win-Win), you strive for mutual understanding (Habit 5—Seek First to Understand, then to be Understood) in order to have creative cooperation (Habit 6—Synergize).

I acknowledge again that I have made connections between the 7 Habits and the development of these five dimensions of emotional intelligence in a summary fashion only. If you have a serious interest in developing greater EQ, I commend to you a sincere study and effort to apply the principles contained in *The 7 Habits of Highly Effective People.* I do so without any desire to promote my own work, but rather with a conviction of the power of the universal, timeless, self-evident principles it contains—principles I cannot take credit for, for they belong to all humanity and are present in every nation, society, religion or community that has endured and prospered.

Neglecting Emotional Intelligence

Authors Doc Childre and Bruce Cryer describe the impact that ignoring the intelligent voice of the heart has on the *body.* "Intelligence capacity is diminished when frustration, anxiety, or inner turmoil operate. Such emotional states cause incoherence in the rhythmic and electrical output of the heart, diminishing neurological efficiency. It's one of the reasons smart people can do stupid things. When you make internal coherence a daily priority, you save time and energy." They also explain, "Our immune system is weakened when we act counter to our deeper values and conscience, which grows in strength when we feel and express heartfelt love or care. The HeartMath organization has scientifically demonstrated this connection both at the level of personal immunity—did you ever become sick after a major argument or upon hearing a key initiative you worked on for months had been cancelled—and even at the organizational level, which they refer to as an emotional virus sapping the organizational spirit, vitality, and morale."[3]

If we neglect developing our emotional intelligence by failing in our self-discipline to win the private victories that lead to public victories, we will experience emotional traumas, stresses, and such negative and disruptive emotions as anger, envy, covetousness, jealousy, and irrational guilt. When a core relationship is stressed, broken or violated, it impacts the body and weakens the immune system. People experience headaches and psychosomatic illnesses of many kinds. Their *minds* often become depressed, unfocused, and distracted, and they lose the ability to think abstractly, carefully, analytically and creatively. The *spirit* also becomes depressed and discouraged. People often begin feeling helpless, hopeless, victimized, and sometimes so despairing that they become suicidal. That is why it is so important to constantly nourish relationships with other people and with ourselves.

DEVELOPING SPIRITUAL INTELLIGENCE—SQ

> *The end of education is to see men made whole,*
> *both in competence and in conscience. For to create*
> *the power of competence without creating a*
> *corresponding direction to guide the use of that*
> *power is bad education. Furthermore, competence*
> *will finally disintegrate apart from conscience.*
>
> JOHN SLOAN DICKEY

I suggest three ways to develop spiritual intelligence: first, *integrity*—being true to one's highest values, convictions and conscience, and having a connection with the Infinite; second, *meaning*—having a sense of

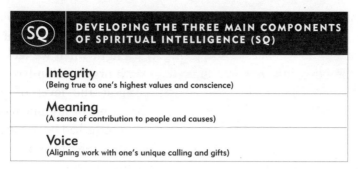

Figure A1.10

contribution to people and to causes; and third, *voice*—aligning our work with our unique talents or gifts, and our sense of calling.

Integrity—Making and Keeping Promises

The best way to develop integrity is to start small, and to make and keep promises. Make a promise that may seem so small and insignificant to others but to you represents a sincere effort—exercising for ten minutes, not eating that dessert, watching one less hour of television a day and instead reading one chapter of a book, expressing thanks in a letter to someone, expressing thanks in person, praying daily, asking forgiveness, or reading sacred literature for ten minutes a day.

The point is that when you make a promise and keep it, your capacity to make and keep a larger promise increases. Continue to do this, and soon your sense of honor will become stronger than your moods. You will develop personal integrity—meaning you are integrated—which will be a great source of power to you. This is truly *igniting* a small fire until it becomes a large fire within.

Integrity—Educating and Obeying Your Conscience

Perhaps the most compelling way to develop spiritual intelligence is to educate and obey your conscience. Madame de Stael put it this way: "The voice of Conscience is so delicate that it is easy to stifle it but it is also so clear that it is impossible to mistake it." As you begin to study the wisdom literature of your own tradition, or as you study the lives of people who have inspired and lifted yours, you'll sense the voice of conscience guiding and directing you; it's a still, small voice. And what C.S. Lewis says will literally come to pass: "The more you obey your conscience, the more your conscience demands of you." It not only makes demands upon you but it also enlarges your capacities, your intelligences, and your contributions. Your talents double when you wisely use those given you.

Finding Meaning and Your Voice

This subject, of course, is the main thrust of this book and overlaps everything else. But one simple way to find one's voice, as mentioned before, is to simply ask the question What does my life situation ask of me now; what should I do in my present responsibilities, duties, stewardships; what would be the wise action to take? When we live true to the answers our conscience gives, the space becomes larger and the conscience louder.

> *My object in living is to unite*
> *My avocation and my vocation*
> *As my two eyes make one in sight.*
> *Only where love and need are one*
> *And the work is play for mortal stakes,*
> *Is the deed ever really done*
> *For Heaven and the future's sakes.*[4]
>
> ROBERT FROST

Another very significant way of finding your sense of voice or calling is when you are selecting a career, job or cause to give yourself to. Remember to ask fundamental questions representing the four intelligences—body, mind, heart and spirit. What do I really like doing that I do well? Should I do it? Can I make a living at it? Can I learn to get better at it? Do I want to pay the price of learning? Jim Collins, in his compelling book *Good to Great*, encourages people, as well as organizations, to ask the question What can I be best in the world at? I know at least one correct answer to this question that applies to all of us who are parents. If we make up our minds, we can be best in the world at raising our own children. No one cares like we do.

> *One hundred years from now, it will not matter what*
> *kind of car I drove, what kind of house I lived in, how*
> *much money I had in my bank account nor what my*
> *clothes looked like. But the world may be a little better*
> *because I was important in the life of a child.*
>
> ANONYMOUS

Neglecting, Ignoring, or Violating Our Spiritual Intelligence

What happens to the *body* when our conscience and our integrity are violated? You can usually see it in the countenance of people, in their eyes. Usually they neglect their bodies; they often are burned out if they're not already worn out. Their *minds* are usually full of rationalization, which really means telling oneself rational lies. They feel guilty, which is a very healthy emotion when there is a genuine violation of integrity and conscience. They lack peace; they have impaired judgment. The University of California at Berkeley summarized some of their research in a newsletter with this expression: "Doing well by doing good."

What happens to the *heart?* Those same people lose control over their emotions, their ability to understand others, to empathize with others. Their ability to have compassion and love for others is significantly diminished.

> *When a man is getting better he understands more and more*
> *clearly the evil that is still left in him. When a man is getting*
> *worse, he understands his own badness less and less. A moderately*
> *bad man knows he is not very good; a thoroughly bad man thinks*
> *he is all right. This is common sense, really. You understand sleep*
> *when you are awake, not while you are sleeping. You can see*
> *mistakes in arithmetic when your mind is working properly; while*
> *you are making them you cannot see them. Good people know*
> *about both bad and evil; bad people do not know about either.*[5]
>
> C.S. LEWIS

Appendix 2

LITERATURE REVIEW OF
LEADERSHIP THEORIES

Five broad approaches in leadership theories have emerged in the twentieth century; approaches include trait, behavioral, power-influence, situational, and integrative. Great-man theories of leadership, which dominated any discussion of leadership prior to 1900, gave rise to trait theories of leadership. In response, theorists began to place a strong emphasis on situational and environmental factors. Finally, theories of integration have been developed around persons and situations, psychoanalysis, role attainment, change, goals and contingencies. Leadership theories since 1970 have developed around one of these fundamental theories.

LEADERSHIP THEORIES: REVIEW OF LITERATURE

Theory	Representative Authors/Year	Summary
Great-Man Theories	Dowd (1936)	History and social institutions shaped by the leadership of great men and women (e.g. Moses, Mohammed, Jeanne d'Arc, Washington, Gandhi, Churchill, etc.). Dowd (1936) maintained that "there is no such thing as leadership by the masses. The individuals in every society possess different degrees of intelligence, energy, and moral force, and in whatever direction the masses may be influenced to go, they are always led by the superior few."

LEADERSHIP THEORIES: REVIEW OF LITERATURE (*continued*)

Theory	Representative Authors/Year	Summary
Trait Theories	L. L. Barnard (1926); Bingham (1927); Kilbourne (1935); Kirkpatrick & Locke (1991); Kohs & Irle (1920); Page (1935); Tead (1929)	The leader is endowed with superior traits and characteristics that differentiate him from his followers. Research of trait theories addressed the following two questions: What traits distinguish leaders from other people? What is the extent of those differences?
Situational Theories	Bogardus (1918); Hersey & Blanchard (1972); Hocking (1924); Person (1928); H. Spencer	Leadership is the product of situational demands: Situational factors determine who will emerge as a leader rather than a person's heritage. The emergence of a great leader is the result of time, place and circumstance.
Personal-Situational Theories	Barnard (1938); Bass (1960); J. F. Brown (1936); Case (1933); C. A. Gibb (1947, 1954); Jenkins (1947); Lapiere (1938); Murphy (1941); Westburgh (1931)	Personal-situational theories represent a combination of great-man, trait, and situational leadership. Research suggested that the study of leadership must include affective, intellectual, and action traits, as well as the specific conditions under which the individual operates. Conditions included: (1) personality traits, (2) nature of group and its members, and (3) events confronting the group.
Psychoanalysis Theories	Erikson (1964); Frank (1939); Freud (1913, 1922); Fromm (1941); H. Levison (1970); Wolman (1971)	The leader functions as a father figure: a source of love or fear, as the embodiment of the superego, the emotional outlet for followers' frustrations and destructive aggression.
Humanistic Theories	Argyris (1957, 1962, 1964); Blake & Mouton (1964, 1965); Hersey & Blanchard (1969, 1972); Likert (1961, 1967); Maslow (1965); McGregor (1960, 1966)	Humanistic theories deal with the development of the individual in effective and cohesive organizations. Those holding this theoretical perspective assume that human beings are by nature motivated beings, and that organizations are by nature structured and controlled. According to them, leadership is to modify organizational constraints to provide freedom for individuals in order to realize their full potential and contribute to the organization.
Leader-Role Theory	Homans (1950); Kahn & Quinn (1970); Kerr & Jermier (1978); Mintzberg (1973); Osborn & Hunt (1975)	Characteristics of the individual and the demands of the situation interact in a way to allow one or a few individuals to emerge as leaders. Groups are structured based upon the interactions of the members of the group, and the group

LEADERSHIP THEORIES: REVIEW OF LITERATURE (*continued*)

Theory	Representative Authors/Year	Summary
		becomes organized according to different roles and positions. Leadership is one of the differentiated roles, and the person in that position is expected to behave in a way that differs from others in the group. Leaders behave according to how they perceive their role and what others expect them to do. Mintzberg articulated the following leadership roles: figurehead, leader, liaison, monitor, disseminator, spokesman, entrepreneur, disturbance handler, resource allocator, and negotiator.
Path-Goal Theory	M. G. Evans (1970); Georgopoulos, Mahoney, & Jones (1957); House (1971); House & Dessler (1974)	Leaders reinforce change in followers by showing followers the behaviors (paths) through which rewards may be obtained. Leaders also clarify followers' goals and encourage them to perform well. Situational factors will determine the way leaders will achieve these path-goal purposes.
Contingency Theory	Fiedler (1967); Fiedler, Chemers, & Mahar (1976)	The effectiveness of a task- or relations-oriented leader is contingent upon the situation. Leadership-training programs modeled after this theory help a leader identify his or her orientation and to adjust better to the favorability or unfavorability of the situation.
Cognitive Leadership: Twentieth-Century Great-Man	H. Gardner (1995); J. Collins (2001)	Leaders are "persons who, by word and/or personal example, markedly influence behaviors, thoughts, and/or feelings of a significant number of their fellow human beings." Gaining an understanding of the nature of the human minds, both of the leader and followers, provides insight into the nature of leadership. The research of Collins concludes that the difference between organizations that produce *sustained* great results and those that don't are that the great organizations are led by what he calls Level 5 Leaders—those with a paradoxical combination of humility and fierce resolve.

LEADERSHIP THEORIES: REVIEW OF LITERATURE (*continued*)

Theory	Representative Authors/Year	Summary
Theories and Models of Interactive Processes: Multiple-Linkage Model, Multiple-Screen Model, Vertical-Dyad Linkage, Exchange Theories, Behavior Theories, and Communication Theories	Davis & Luthans (1979); Fiedler & Leister (1977); Fulk & Wendler (1982); Graen (1976); Greene (1975); Yuki (1971)	Leadership is an interactive process. Examples include theories regarding leaders' initiation structure, the relationship between a leader's intelligence and his or her group's performance, the relationship between the leader and each individual rather than the group, and social interaction as a form of exchange or behavioral contingency.
Power-Influence: Participative Leadership, Rationale-Deductive	Coch & French (1948); J. Gardner (1990); Lewin, Lippitt, & White (1939); Vroom & Yetton (1974)	The power-influence approach to leadership includes participative leadership. Power-influence research examines how much power the leader possesses and exerts. The approach also assumes unidirectional causality. Participative leadership deals with power sharing and empowerment of followers. Vroom & Yetton proposed a prescriptive theory of leadership that assumes leaders are directive and subordinates are passive followers. When subordinates possess more knowledge, however, their role should be more participative. Gardner believes that "leadership is the process of persuasion or example by which an individual (or leadership team) induces a group to pursue objectives held by the leader or shared by the leader and his or her followers." He indicates that leadership is a role to be filled and therefore, leaders play an integral role in the system over which they preside.
Attribution, Information Processing, and Open Systems	Bryon & Kelley (1978); Katz & Kahn (1966); Lord (1976, 1985); Lord, Binning, Rush, & Thomas (1978); Mitchell, Larsen & Green (1977); Newell & Simon (1972); H. M. Weiss (1977)	Leadership is a socially constructed reality. According to Mitchell et al., "Attributions of leadership by observers and group members are biased by their individual social realities." Furthermore, individual, processual, structural, and environmental variables are mutually causal phenomena in leadership studies; that is, delineating cause and effect among these variables is difficult.
Integrative: Transformational, Values-Based	Bass; Bennis (1984, 1992, 1993); Burns (1978); Downton (1973); Fairholm (1991); O'Toole (1995); DePree (1992); Tichy & Devanna; Renesch	According to Burns, transformational leadership is a process wherein "leaders and followers raise one another to higher levels of morality and motivation." Followers are assumed to transcend self-interest for the good of the

LEADERSHIP THEORIES: REVIEW OF LITERATURE (*continued*)

Theory	Representative Authors/Year	Summary
		group, consider long-term objectives, and develop an awareness of what is important. According to Bennis, effective leaders perform the three functions: align, create, and empower. Leaders transform organizations by aligning human and other resources, creating an organizational culture that fosters the free expression of ideas, and empowering others to contribute to the organization. Bennis is known for the distinction he makes between management and leadership; his view, summarized best in his own words, is: "Leaders are people who do the right thing; managers are people who do things right."
Charismatic Leadership	Conger & Kanungu (1987); House (1977); Kets se Vries (1988); J. Maxwell (1999); Meindl (1990); Shamir, House & Arthur (1993); Weber (1947)	Charismatic leadership, on the other hand, assumes that leaders possess exceptional qualities as perceived by subordinates. A leader's influence is not based upon authority or tradition but upon the perceptions of his or her followers. Explanations of charismatic leadership include attribution, objective observations, self-concept theory, psychoanalytic, and social contagion.
Competency-Based Leadership	Bennis (1993); Boyatizis; Cameron; Quinn	One can learn and improve critical competencies that tend to predict the differences between outstanding performers (leaders) and average performers.
Aspirational and Visionary Leadership	Burns; Kouzes & Posner (1995); Peters; Waterman (1990); Richards & Engle (1986)	According to Kouzes and Posner, leaders "ignite" subordinates' passions and serve as a compass by which to guide followers. They define leadership "as the art of mobilizing others to want to struggle for shared aspirations." The emphasis lies in the follower's desire to contribute and the leader's ability to motivate others to action. Leaders respond to customers, create vision, energize employees, and thrive in fast-paced "chaotic" environments. Leadership is about articulating visions, embodying values, and creating the environment within which things can be accomplished.

LEADERSHIP THEORIES: REVIEW OF LITERATURE (*continued*)

Theory	Representative Authors/Year	Summary
Managerial and Strategic Leadership	Drucker (1999); Jacobs & Jaques (1990); Jaques & Clement (1991); Kotter (1998, 1999); Buckingham & Coffman (1999); Buckingham & Clifton (2001)	Leadership represents integration between external and internal partnerships. Drucker highlights three components of that integration: financial, performance and personal. He believes leaders are responsible for performance of their organizations and for the community as a whole. Leaders fill roles and possess special characteristics. According to Kotter, leaders communicate vision and direction, align people, motivate, inspire, and energize followers. In addition, leaders are change agents and empowerers of their people. Leadership is the process of giving purpose (meaningful direction) to collective effort, and causing willing effort to be expended to achieve purpose. Further, effective managerial leadership spawns effective managerial work. These authors favor requisite leadership that is dependent upon time and place, and the individual and situations.
Results-Based Leadership	Ulrich, Zenger, & Smallwood (1999); Nohria, Joyce & Robertson (2003)	Ulrich et al. propose a leadership brand which "describes the distinct results leaders deliver" and links results with character. Leaders possess moral character, integrity and energy, in addition to technical knowledge and strategic thinking. Moreover, leaders demonstrate effective behaviors that further organizational success. Furthermore, since leadership results are measurable, they also may be taught and learned. In what they call the Evergreen Project, Nohria, et al., examine more than 200 management practices over a ten-year period to determine which produce truly superior results. The four primary practices are strategy, execution, culture and structure. Companies with superior results also embrace two of the following four secondary practices: talent, innovation, leadership and mergers and acquisitions.
Leader as Teacher	DePree (1992); Tichy (1998)	Leaders are teachers. Leaders establish the "teachable point of view." Leadership is about motivating others by teaching stories. Tichy contends that effective leadership equates with effective teaching.

LEADERSHIP THEORIES: REVIEW OF LITERATURE (*continued*)

Theory	Representative Authors/Year	Summary
Leadership as a Performing Art	DePree (1992); Mintzberg (1998); Vaill (1989)	Leadership is covert in the sense that leaders do not outwardly perform leadership actions (e.g., motivating, coaching, etc.) but perform unobtrusive actions that encompass all the things a leader or manager does. A common metaphor for leadership as a performing art are orchestra conductors and jazz ensembles.
Cultural and Holistic Leadership	Fairholm (1994); Senge (1990); Schein (1992); Wheatley (1992)	Leadership is the ability to step outside the culture to start evolutionary change processes that are more adaptive. Leadership is the ability to include important stakeholders, evoke followership, and empower others. Wheatley's holistic approach assumes that leadership is contextual and systemic. Leaders create synergistic relationships between individuals, organizations, and the environment. Leaders promote learning organizations through adherence to the five disciplines. According to Senge, leaders play three roles: designers, stewards and teachers.
Servant Leadership	Greenleaf (1996); Spears & Frick (1992)	Servant leadership implies that leaders primarily lead by serving others— employees, customers and community. Characteristics of a servant leader include listening, empathy, healing, awareness, persuasion, conceptualization, foresight, stewardship, commitment to others' growth, and community building.
Spiritual Leadership	DePree (1989); Etzioni (1993); Fairholm (1997); Greenleaf (1977); Hawley (1993); Keifer (1992); J. Maxwell; Vaill (1989)	Leadership involves influencing people's souls rather than controlling action. Fairholm believes that leadership involves connecting with others. Furthermore, "as leaders commit to the care of the whole person, they must include spiritual care into their practice. . . . Leaders in the new century must consider and actively engage in making for themselves and then helping their followers make these connections." A leader's influence stems from his or her knowledge of the organizational culture, customs, values and traditions.

References Consulted

Bass, B.M. *Bass and Stogdill's Handbook of Leadership: Theory, Research, and Managerial Applications*, 3d ed. London: Collier Macmillan, 1990.

Bennis, W.G. *An Invented Life: Reflections on Leadership and Change*. Reading, Mass.: Addison-Wesley, 1993.

Buckingham, M., and D.O. Clifton. *Discover Your Strengths*. New York: Free Press, 2001.

Buckingham, M., and C. Coffman. *First, Break All the Rules: What the World's Greatest Managers Do Differently*. New York: Simon & Schuster, 1999.

Collins, J.C. *Good to Great: Why Some Companies Make the Leap . . . and Others Don't*. New York: HarperCollins Publishers, 2001.

Fairholm, G.W. *Capturing the Heart of Leadership: Spirituality and Community in the New American Workplace*. Westport, Conn.: Praeger, 1997.

Fairholm, G.W. *Perspectives on Leadership: From the Science of Management to Its Spiritual Heart*. Westport, Conn.: Quorum Books, 1998.

Gardner, H. *Leading Minds: An Anatomy of Leadership*. New York: BasicBooks, 1995.

Gardner, J.W. *On Leadership*. New York: Collier Macmillan, 1990.

Jaques, E., and S.D. Clement. *Executive Leadership: A Practical Guide to Managing Complexity*. Arlington, Va.: Cason Hall, 1991.

Kouzes, J.M., and B.Z. Posner. *The Leadership Challenge: How to Keep Getting Extraordinary Things Done in Organizations*. San Francisco: Jossey-Bass, 1995.

Renesch, J., ed. *Leadership in a New Era: Visionary Approaches to the Biggest Crisis of Our Time*. San Francisco: New Leaders Press, 1994.

Senge, P.M. *The Fifth Discipline: The Art and Practice of the Learning Organization*. New York: Currency Doubleday, 1990.

Ulrich, D., J. Zenger, and N. Smallwood. *Results-Based Leadership: How Leaders Build the Business and Improve the Bottom Line*. Boston: Harvard Business School Press, 1999.

Vaill, P.B. *Managing as a Performing Art: New Ideas for a World of Chaotic Change*. San Francisco: Jossey-Bass, 1989.

Wheatley, M.J. *Leadership and the New Science: Learning about Organization from an Orderly Universe*. San Francisco: Berrett-Koehler, 1992.

Wren, J.T. *Leader's Companion: Insights on Leadership through the Ages*. New York: The Free Press, 1995.

Yuki, G. *Leadership in Organizations*, 4th ed. Upper Saddle River, N.J.: Prentice-Hall, 1998.

Appendix 3

REPRESENTATIVE STATEMENTS ON
LEADERSHIP AND MANAGEMENT

Authors and References	Statements: Management versus Leadership
Warren Bennis Bennis, W. G. (1994). "Leading Change: The Leader as the Chief Transformation Officer." In J. Renesch (Ed.), *Leadership in a New Era: Visionary Approaches to the Biggest Crisis of Our Time* (pp. 102–110). San Francisco: New Leaders Press.	"Management is getting people to do what needs to be done. Leadership is getting people to *want* to do what needs to be done. Managers push. Leaders pull. Managers command. Leaders communicate."
Bennis, W. G. (1993). *An Invented Life: Reflections on Leadership and Change*. Reading, MA: Addison-Wesley.	"Leaders are people who do the right thing; managers are people who do things right."
In Carter-Scott, C. (1994). "The Differences Between Management and Leadership." *Manage*, 10+.	"Leaders conquer the context—the volatile, turbulent, ambiguous surroundings that sometimes seem to conspire against us and will surely suffocate us if we let them— while managers surrender to it. The manager administers; the leader innovates. The manager is a copy; the leader is an original. The manager maintains; the leader develops. The manager focuses on systems and structure; the leader focuses on people. The manager relies on control; the leader inspires trust. The manager has a short-range view; the leader has a long-range perspective. The manager asks how and when; the leader asks what and why. The manager has his eye on the bottom line; the leader has his eye on the horizon. The manager imitates; the leader originates. The manager accepts the status quo; the leader challenges it. The manager is the classic good soldier; the leader is his own person. Managers do things right; leaders do the right thing."

Authors and References	Statements: Management versus Leadership
John W. Gardner Gardner, J. W. (1990). *On Leadership*. New York: Collier Macmillan.	"Leaders and leader/managers distinguish themselves from the general run of managers in at least six respects: 1. They think longer term . . . 2. In thinking about the unit they are heading they grasp its relationships to larger realities . . . 3. They reach and influence constituents beyond their jurisdictions, beyond boundaries . . . 4. They put heavy emphasis on the intangibles of vision, values, and motivation and understand intuitively the nonrational and unconscious elements in leader-constituent interaction. 5. They have the political skill to cope with the conflicting requirements of multiple constituencies. 6. They think in terms of renewal . . ." "The manager is more tightly linked to an organization than is the leader. Indeed, the leader may have no organization at all."
James Kouzes and Barry Posner Kouzes, J. M. & Posner, B. Z. (1995). *The Leadership Challenge: How to keep Getting Extraordinary Things Done in Organizations.* San Francisco: Jossey-Bass.	". . . [T]he word *lead,* at its root, means 'go, travel, guide.' Leadership has about it a kinesthetic feel, a sense of movement . . . [Leaders] begin the quest for a new order. They venture into unexplored territory and guide us to new and unfamiliar destinations. In contrast, the root origin of *manage* is a word meaning 'hand.' At its core, managing is about 'handling' things, about maintaining order, about organization and control. The critical difference between management and leadership is reflected in the root meanings of the two words—the difference between what it means to handle things and what it means to go places."
In Carter-Scott, C. (1994). "The Differences between Management and Leadership." *Manage,* 10+.	Kouzes: "A major difference between management and leadership can be found in the root meanings of the two words, the difference between what it means to handle things and what it means to go places."
Abraham Zaleznik Zaleznik, A. (1977). "Managers and Leaders: Are They Different?" *Harvard Business Review,* 55(5), 67–78.	Managers are concerned about how things get done, and leaders are concerned with what the things mean to people. "Leaders and managers differ in their conceptions. Managers tend to view work as an enabling process involving some combination of people and ideas interacting to establish strategy and make decisions. ". . . Where managers act to limit choices, leaders work in the opposite direction, to develop fresh approaches to longstanding problems and to open issues for new options . . . Leaders create excitement in work."

Authors and References	Statements: Management versus Leadership
John Kotter Kotter, J. (1990). "What Leaders Really Do." *Harvard Business Review, 68,* 103+.	"Management is about coping with complexity. Its practices and procedures are largely a response to one of the most significant developments of the twentieth century: the emergence of large organizations. Without good management, complex enterprises tend to become chaotic in ways that threaten their very existence. Good management brings a degree of order and consistency to key dimensions like the quality and profitability of products. "Leadership, by contrast, is about coping with change. Part of the reason it has become so important in recent years is that the business world has become more competitive and more volatile. Faster technological change, greater international competition, the deregulation of markets, overcapacity in capital-intensive industries, an unstable oil cartel, raiders with junk bonds, and the changing demographics of the work force are among the many factors that have contributed to this shift. The net result is that doing what was done yesterday, or doing it 5% better, is no longer a formula for success. Major changes are more and more necessary to survive and compete effectively in this new environment. More change always demands more leadership."
James M. Burns Burns, J. M. (1978). *Leadership.* New York: Harper and Row.	Transactional (management) versus Transformational (leadership) Transactional leadership: Such leadership occurs when one person takes the initiative in making contact with others for the purpose of an exchange of valued things. Transforming leadership: Such leadership occurs when one or more persons engage with others in such a way that leaders and followers raise one another to higher levels of motivation and morality. Their purposes, which might have started out as separate but related, as in transactional leadership, become fused.
Peter Drucker In Galagan, P. A. (1998). *Peter Drucker: Training & Development,* 52, 22–27.	"The test of any leader is not what he or she accomplishes. It is what happens when they leave the scene. It is the succession that is the test. If the enterprise collapses the moment these wonderful, charismatic leaders leave, that is not leadership. That is—very bluntly—deception. ". . . I have always stressed that leadership is responsibility. Leadership is accountability. Leadership is doing . . . ". . . [As] for separating management from leadership, that is nonsense—as much nonsense as separating management from entrepreneurship. Those are part and parcel of the same job. They are different to be sure, but only as different as the right hand from the left or the nose from the mouth. They belong to the same body."

Authors and References	Statements: Management versus Leadership
Richard Pascale In Johnson, M. (1996). "Taking the Lid Off Leadership." *Management Review*, 59–61.	"Management is the exercise of authority and influence to achieve levels of performance consistent with previously demonstrated levels. . . . Leadership is making happen what wouldn't happen anyway . . . [and will] always entail working at the edge of what is acceptable."
George Weathersby Weathersby, G. B. (1999). "Leadership versus Management." *Management Review*, 88, 5+.	"Management is the allocation of scarce resources against an organization's objective, the setting of priorities, the design of work and the achievement of results. Most important, it's about controlling. Leadership, on the other hand, focuses on the creation of a common vision. It means motivating people to contribute to the vision and encouraging them to align their self-interest with that of the organization. It means persuading, not commanding."
John Mariotti Mariotti, J. (1998). "Leadership Matters." *Industry Week*, 247, 70+.	"People who are 'managed' well may lack the inclination to put forth the kind of effort necessary for success—unless they have good leaders. Great leaders get extraordinary results from ordinary people. Great managers simply get well-planned and sometimes well-executed outcomes, but seldom the huge successes that arise from the passion and enthusiastic commitment inspired by true leadership. Leaders are the architects. Managers are the builders. Both are necessary, but without the architect, there is nothing special to build."
Rosabeth Moss Kanter Kanter, R. M. (1989). "The New Managerial Work." *Harvard Business Review*, 85+.	"The old bases of managerial authority are eroding, and new tools of leadership are taking their place. Managers whose power derived from hierarchy and who were accustomed to a limited area of personal control are learning to shift their perspectives and widen their horizons. The new managerial work consists of looking outside a defined area of responsibility to sense opportunities and of forming project teams drawn from any relevant sphere to address them. It involves communication and collaboration across functions, across divisions, and across companies whose activities and resources overlap. Thus rank, title, or official charter will be less important factors in success at the new managerial work than having the knowledge, skills, and sensitivity to mobilize people and motivate them to do their best."
Tom Peters Peters, T. (1994). *Thriving on Chaos*. New York: Alfred A. Knopf.	Peters draws from Bennis's and Kouzes and Posner's conceptions of leadership and management outlined above. Peters believes that "Developing a vision and, more important, living it vigorously are essential elements of leadership. . . . Vision occupies an equally important place of honor in the supervisor's or middle manager's world."

I've been reminded in this project that we often learn best by seeing contrasts. Consider here a summary of the differences between leadership and management (figure A3.1):

Leadership	Management
People	Things
Spontaneity, serendipity	Structure
Release, empowerment	Control
Effectiveness	Efficiency
Programmer	Program
Investment	Expense
Principles	Techniques
Transformation	Transaction
Principle-centered power	Utility
Discernment	Measurement
Doing the right things	Doing things right
Direction	Speed
Top line	Bottom line
Purposes	Methods
Principles	Practices
On the systems	In the systems
"Is the ladder against the right wall?"	Climbing the ladder fast

Figure A3.1

Appendix 4

THE HIGH COST OF LOW TRUST

AUTHOR, COLLEAGUE and consultant Mahan Khalsa has devised one of the most humbling ways to get a team of corporate executives to want to change. If you want an organization humbled so that its people are capable of initiating and sustaining change, they need the force of circumstances brought to bear upon them. You can use a series of questions to create the force of circumstances in order to prepare people's minds for change.

The process involves asking two kinds of questions that get to the heart of the problem: 1) *evidence questions* (how, what, where, which, who, and when . . . specifically) that provide needed facts about a situation, even if they are peripheral, and 2) *impact questions* that get to the heart of the matter—one of the strongest such questions being "And then what happens?"

The following hypothetical conversation between you and a fellow professional, manager or executive is an example of how to use this diagnostic tool to get at the high cost of low trust (the same process could be used by people at any level who have access to the needed information):

Colleague: "Our people just don't trust each other."

At this point, you could ask additional evidence questions such as, "Which people specifically don't trust each other? When is not trusting each other really showing up? What lets you know trust is low?" Eventually, if you desire to discover the impact of low trust in the organization, you will have to ask an impact question.

You: "And when people don't trust each other, then what happens?"

Colleague: "People won't share information."

Again, you could ask more evidence questions such as, "Which people specifically don't/won't share information? What information are they not sharing? How do you know they're not sharing information?" At some point, however, you will want to go down a level closer to impact, and so you ask:

You: "And when people won't share information, then what happens?"

Colleague: "Their projects and activities aren't aligned with the business objectives of the company."

Once again, you could ask evidence questions such as, "Which objectives specifically are they not aligned with? Which projects and activities specifically? What lets you know they're not aligned?" Then you ask another impact question.

You: "And when people aren't aligned with the business objectives of the company, then what happens?"

Colleague: "It raises the cost of new product development."

Now your colleague has given you something you can actually measure as it relates to low trust—the rising cost of new product development. When you see or hear a measurable perception, you then ask five golden questions:

1. How do you measure it?
2. What is it now?
3. What would you like it to be?
4. What's the value of the difference?
5. Over time (the appropriate management timeline)?

So when your colleague said, "It's raising the cost of new product development" you can ask those five questions.

You: "How do you measure the cost of new product development?"

Colleague: "Project dollars spent per new product launched."

You: "What is that amount now?"

Colleague: "$500,000."

You: "What would you like it to be?"

Colleague: "We think it should be closer to $350,000."

You: "So a $150,000 difference. How many new products per year are you producing?"

Colleague: "Twenty."

Now you do the math with your colleague or team.

You: "So that's $150,000 per new product multiplied by 20 new products . . . that looks roughly like it's 3 million per year. Does that sound right to you?"

Colleague: "If anything it's low."

You: "So, assuming costs don't get better and they don't get worse, over the next three years are we looking at a nine-million-dollar problem?"

Colleague: "I think we are."

By asking impact questions, you've discovered that just one dimension of "low trust" may actually be costing the company nine million dollars over the next three years. You would need to do more work to verify that number, but at least you have something measurable to look at, and your looking will be focused on something specific. When your colleagues see the problem in terms of dollar-amount costs, they will realize there is a need for change.

Notice that you ask a mixture of evidence and impact questions until the questioning process has brought the two people to the very core of the problem. Then impact questions are used. All the time, the other person or extended team is the intelligence force. You act only as the guiding force, the mentor. In effect, you provide nonthreatening mentored learning to your colleagues, who remain the central force. This is a very powerful, penetrating set of questions that allows people to objectively arrive at the personal and organizational costs associated with organizational challenges that are of deep concern to you.

Most significantly, this process will not only establish a culture of openness within your team and organization but it will also strengthen the bonds of trust among you.

For more information see www.franklincovey.com/letsgetreal.

Appendix 5

IMPLEMENTING THE 4 DISCIPLINES OF EXECUTION

THE 4 DISCIPLINES OF EXECUTION is a one- to three-day work session for everyone inside an organization. These work sessions can be held with senior leadership teams, operating teams, managers, or individual contributors. They are facilitated by FranklinCovey consultants, or alternatively, clients can be licensed and certified to lead these discussions themselves. In these work sessions, participants are guided through a process of clarifying their top goals, building measures and a Scoreboard for those goals, breaking down the goals into new activities and behaviors, and learning an accountability process for maintaining commitment to the goals. We assist organizations in their efforts to implement strategy and rapidly cascade goals throughout the organization, creating greater understanding of and commitment to the key goals and strategies. We help organizations of all shapes and sizes implement this methodology, including Fortune 100 organizations. For more information on The 4 Disciplines of Execution, please call +44 (0)870 870 7600 or visit our website at www.franklincoveyweurope.com.

Appendix 6

XQ RESULTS

T HE XQ TEST gauges an organization's ability to execute key goals. Just as an IQ test uncovers gaps in intelligence, an xQ evaluation measures the "execution gap"—the gap between setting a goal and actually achieving it. The term "xQ" is an abbreviation for "execution quotient."

After surveying around 2.5 million people on the effectiveness of their managers, and in association with Harris Interactive (the originators of the Harris Poll), FranklinCovey has developed a method for measuring execution capability.

The results of the xQ study are striking and troubling; there is indeed a serious execution gap, as these percentages reveal:

Execution Issue	Percent who agree
ORGANIZATIONAL LINE OF SIGHT: Are all workers focused on organizational goals?	22%
TEAM GOALS QUALITY: Do work teams have clear, measurable goals?	9%
TEAM PLANNING: Do work teams plan together how to achieve their goals?	16%
TEAM COMMUNICATION: Do work teams have mutual understanding and creative dialogue?	17%
TEAM TRUST: Do work teams function in a safe, "win-win" work environment?	15%
TEAM EMPOWERMENT: Do teams have adequate resources and freedom to do the job?	15%
TEAM ACCOUNTABILITY: Do team members hold each other accountable for their commitments?	10%

Execution Issue	Percent who agree
TEAM MEASURES—QUALITY: Are success measures tracked accurately and openly?	10%
INDIVIDUAL WORK GOALS: Do people have clear, measurable, deadline-driven work goals?	10%
INDIVIDUAL ENGAGEMENT: Are workers motivated? Do they feel valued?	22%
INDIVIDUAL PLANNING: Do people systematically schedule their priorities?	8%
INDIVIDUAL INITIATIVE: Do people take individual initiative and responsibility for results?	13%
ORGANIZATIONAL DIRECTION: Are organizational strategy and goals precisely understood by everyone?	23%
ORGANIZATIONAL COLLABORATION: Do teams work smoothly across functions?	13%
ORGANIZATIONAL TRUSTWORTHINESS: Does the organization honor its own values and commitments?	20%
ORGANIZATIONAL PERFORMANCE IMPROVEMENT: Is there a consistent, systematic approach?	13%
INDIVIDUAL COMMITMENT: Are people committed to the organization's direction?	39% very highly or highly
ORGANIZATIONAL SUPPORT: Does upper management actively support the goals of work teams?	45% say high or very high
TEAM FOCUS: Is my work group totally and diligently focused on its top goals?	14%
INDIVIDUAL TIME ALLOCATION: How much time do our people actually spend on key goals?	60%

Table 14

Highlights of the FranklinCovey xQ Study

Key Findings	How Calculated
Only about a third say they have a clear understanding of what their companies are trying to achieve.	37% selected the option "I clearly understand the reasons for my organization's strategic direction."
Only about 1 in 6 is diligently focused on the most important goals.	14% selected the option "We stay diligently focused on our most important goals."
Do leaders communicate their most important goals?	44% say that their organizations have clearly communicated their most important goals.
Do workers have clear "line of sight" between their own tasks and their company's goals? About 1 in 10 thinks so.	22% report they have clear "line of sight" between their own goals and the organization's goals.
Are people totally energized and committed to their company's goals? About 1 in 10 says so.	9% selected the option "Very highly energized and committed."
Only 1 in 3 has clearly defined work goals.	33% report having work goals that are "written down."
Workers spend 1 hour in 4 on urgent but irrelevant tasks.	Respondents estimate 23% of their time is spent on activities that have little relevance to key goals but demand immediate attention.
Workers waste about 1 hour in 5 dealing with politics and bureaucracy.	Respondents estimate 17% of their time is spent on counterproductive activities like dealing with internal bureaucracies, infighting, covering up, etc.
Only about half of workers feel their jobs allow them to apply all they have to give.	48% agree with this statement: *The majority of people in my organization possess far more talent, intelligence capability, and creativity than their present jobs require or even allow.*
Only 3 in 5 feel they can express themselves openly at work.	58% agree with this statement: *I feel safe in expressing my opinions openly without fear of retribution.*
About 2 in 5 say that they work in a "win-win" atmosphere.	43% agree that "we live by the principle that 'my success is your success.' "
Fewer than half meet with their managers at least monthly to review progress on their work goals.	48% say so.
Only half say they are held accountable for their budgets.	50% agree or strongly agree with this statement: *We hold ourselves accountable for staying on budget.*

Key Findings	How Calculated
Overwhelming workloads, lack of resources, and unclear work priorities are the three biggest barriers to execution.	When asked what are the top 3 barriers to execution, 31% selected "overwhelming workload," 30% selected "lack of resources," and 27% selected "unclear or shifting work priorities."
About 3 in 5 don't trust their employers to keep commitments to employees.	43% say that their employer "consistently honors commitments to its people."
Teams work in silos; very little active cross-functional cooperation happens	When asked about other groups within the organization, 28% agree with the statement: *We actively help each other to achieve our respective goals.*
Only about a third say they have clear measures of success on their goals.	35% agree with the statement: *The measures are clear.*

Table 15

If you are interested in experiencing the xQ Survey to personally assess *your individual, team's, and organization's ability to focus and execute on top priorities*, go to www.The8thHabit.com/offers. Just follow the on-line instructions. You will be enabled to take the test without charge. After completing the survey, you will be given an xQ Report that summarizes your assessment and compares it to a composite average score of the many thousands of organizations measured. Further information will be given on how you can measure the entire team or organization.

Appendix 7

MAX & MAX REVISITED

Let's demonstrate how practical the leadership framework of this book is by going back to *Max & Max* and thinking like a trim-tabber. *You may want to view the film again at this point* to experience it through the problem-solving lens of the 4 Roles of Leadership.

WHAT REALISTICALLY can Max do? His boss, Mr. Harold, is a control freak. He is scarcity minded, is running scared of his boss, and knows no way to change things except through the Industrial Age boss-centered model of control, rules, and carrot-and-stick motivation.

Max is a broken spirit—frustrated and disempowered. He could remain codependent—that would be the first alternative. He could fight or even organize resistance or he could flight (quit)—the second alternative. Or he could wisely exercise initiative inside his own circle of influence—the Third Alternative.

One Third Alternative approach would be to use the trim-tabbing *ethos-pathos-logos* approach with Mr. Harold (recommend—fourth level of initiative). If you remember in the film, Max used only *logos* (logic) in his recommendation and did it at the worst possible moment—shortly after Mr. Harold was "chewed out" by his boss. In short, Max was far outside his Circle of Influence, so he was similarly chewed out by Mr. Harold, even after his creative proactive "saving" of a customer. This really broke Max's spirit, and the reactive codependent cycle accelerated.

His circle of influence was reduced. (See figure A7.1.)

How then could Max practice *ethos-pathos-logos? Ethos* would involve proactively and cheerfully doing his own job superbly well and helping others in every way possible. Admittedly, he's straitjacketed by unfriendly customer guidelines, but he can get as positive and creative as

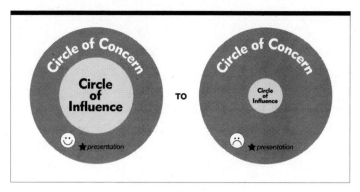

Figure A7.1

possible to produce business. No bad-mouthing Mr. Harold. He would just do the best he could in the circumstances and be seen as a source of help to others—*within* his Circle of Influence and *outside* his job. Instead of criticizing, he complements.

Then he can request another visit with Mr. Harold and this time listen, really listen, and be influenced by what he comes to understand. For instance, perhaps Mr. Harold has been burned by some creative, inexperienced loose cannon whose "overpromising and underdelivering" resulted in a performance suit against the company—a mess for which Mr. Harold has been getting all the heat. To avoid more loose cannons doing dumb things, he establishes new inflexible rules, micromanages everybody, and disempowers the whole culture.

Once Mr. Harold feels understood, much of the defensive, negative energy will dissipate. You cannot fight someone who is sincerely trying to understand. This is the fruit of *pathos*, or emotional alignment. After accurately restating Mr. Harold's objections and concerns, Max could then use *logos*—perhaps suggesting that an experimental pilot program of one person (Max) be set up for three months, with the opportunity to do new creative things to get new customers and upsell present customers. Feeling understood and with increased confidence in Max because of his cooperative attitude and diligence *(ethos)* and empathy *(pathos)*, Mr. Harold is willing to go along with the pilot idea *(logos)*, which has very little downside and a lot of upside potential.

Let's say Max increases his sales 25 percent in three months. He returns to Mr. Harold and suggests the pilot program continue and include three other salespeople in whom Max has high confidence. Mr. Harold agrees. They also increase their production 25 percent. Then all

four people return, suggesting for all salespeople a training program
with tough certification criteria that would screen out unwise loose cannons. Mr. Harold approves—thrilled with the significant new sales. His
boss congratulates Mr. Harold, saying, "That party really worked, didn't
it?" Mr. Harold courageously responds, "I'll tell you what's working . . ."

In short, through this process of ethos-pathos-logos (recommendation—fourth level of initiative), Max became the leader of his boss and a
great source of influence in the entire company.

Admittedly, this scenario was fictional, and Mr. Harold's problem
may have been entirely different. If so, Max's response would have reflected that difference and increased his production and influence in another way.

The point is, Max found his job voice through vision, discipline and
passion governed by conscience.

I've also learned most "bad bosses" are usually part of codependent
cultures and are modeling behavior modeled to them. The cycle can be
broken by one who is the creative force of his or her own life.

Now let's ask what Mr. Harold—an enlightened Mr. Harold—could
do with broken-spirited Max. The first alternative would be to "stay the
course"—just keep pressing, cajoling, threatening, throwing parties,
catching Max doing things right and praising him—in short, carrot-
and-sticking him (the Industrial Age model).

The second alternative would be to "give in," sell out, capitulate by
permissively letting Max have his way. However, unintended consequences could follow. Mr. Harold could be fired or reprimanded by his
boss for not stepping in and for such weak, permissive leadership. Furthermore, this approach could encourage "loose cannons" to make
more unilateral, unrealistic promises in order to "get their numbers."

The Third Alternative would be to fully acknowledge his overreach-
ing mistake in punishing Max's creative saving of a customer relationship—and sincerely apologizing for it. Max—still codependent—may
not trust this "soft" approach and continue to "kiss up." Mr. Harold
would need to authentically share what he's been going through and essentially say in sincerity and with specifics, "Look, Max, I took my own
frustrations out on you. You did great work going the second mile with
that customer. But I've been feeling so pressured to produce 'more for
less' and also so anxious about other 'loose cannons' doing dumb things
and getting me in more trouble, that I didn't know what to do other
than ride herd on the rules. But Max, with you it was wrong. At the time

I didn't know any better. Now I've had time to pause and reflect and would really like to explore your suggestion. I just hope we can do something that won't open up another Pandora's box. Can you help me better understand how you see it?"

The depth of sincerity and authenticity of Mr. Harold may encourage Max to be more authentic himself. Real communication—horizontal rather than vertical—between two human beings struggling with the same problem, may lead to the synergistic Third Alternative described before when we were looking at the question What realistically can Max do?

In both cases, notice the sequential process, the inside-out approach and the whole person foundation. Notice the movement from *personal* to an authentic trusting *relationship* and finally to formalizing an *organizational* arrangement (pilot program, which expanded as trust and trustworthiness grew).

This is truly a Third Alternative solution no one would have imagined at the beginning. It emerged from creative communication and will be bonding in the relationship. It would also create an "immune system" that can handle other difficult, even blindsiding, problems in the future.

Again, I fully know I manufactured these scenarios and that things may go in completely opposite directions. But I'm not trying to teach *practices*—what to do—but rather *principles*—universally applicable principles that would underlie many different possible practices. I'm only using *Max & Max* as an illustration of possible principle-based practices that may work.

Now let's stand back and theorize. First, let's look at Max. In the process of Max's becoming the leader of Mr. Harold, notice the four roles he participated in. These four roles would have taken place in any scenario that worked. First, *modeling*. Max modeled proactive initiative and achieving *ethos*. He modeled empathy in achieving *pathos* and courage in achieving *logos*. As the two genuinely interacted, synergistic communication took place in coming up with a Third Alternative, far better than Mr. Harold's past win-lose command-and-control approach and infinitely better than Max's simply doing nothing by numbing out and "kissing up."

Again, the essence of modeling, either as an individual or a team, is found in The 7 Habits of Highly Effective People.

The second role—*pathfinding*—represented the win-win pilot program and put both Max and Mr. Harold on the same page of securing more business through creative second-mile customer service within the guidelines of honest values and good judgment. Modeling trustworthiness and authentic communication produced the trust necessary for pathfinding. Thus, Max's voice overlapped the organization's voice for this pilot program.

The third role—*aligning*—took place when Mr. Harold formally approved the pathfinding pilot program agreement, first with Max, then with three others, then with the entire sales force. Aligning means to set up the structure, systems and processes necessary to accomplish the pathfinding purposes within the guidelines agreed-upon. The overlapping voices are being nourished, enabled.

The three roles of modeling, pathfinding and aligning enabled *empowering* to take place so that initially Max, and later others, could use their own trained judgment and creativity to do whatever was necessary to get and keep customers consistent with the agreed-upon guidelines. In this way, rules no longer took the place of judgment. You simply cannot hold people responsible for results if you supervise their methods and ride hard on rules. Empowering enabled *directed autonomy* so that each person's voice was respected and expressed.

Now let's look at the enlightened knowledge worker response from Mr. Harold. He exercised the same four roles of leadership—using the Third Alternative to either staying the control course or permissively caving in.

It all started inside out with *modeling*. Mr. Harold genuinely acknowledged his mistake and began a synergistic communication. As trust built and became "more real," the *pathfinding* solution was created (limited pilot program). Mr. Harold's formal authority joined the evolved moral authority, and he formalized or institutionalized the one-person pilot program. This *aligning* made it legitimate in the culture and enabled Max to have autonomy and use his creativity and flexibility to get new business. In short, the *empowering* role.

As things progressed successfully (*modeling* a complementary team), others were involved in the new path (*pathfinding*), were nurtured by *aligning* structures, systems and processes, eventually enabling all who met the criteria to be *empowered*.

Appendix 8

THE FRANKLINCOVEY APPROACH

S USTAINABLE, SUPERIOR PERFORMANCE . . .

That's the tough part about business and most any organization. Sure, almost anyone can deliver results for a quarter or two. But the real challenge is to create an organizational culture that can deliver consistent results year after year.

Amazingly, few organizations can do it. Consider the following statistics from leading business publications:

- *Profit from the Core:* only 111 of 1,854 companies (13 percent) were able to generate sustained profitable growth for a ten-year period.
- *Good to Great:* only 126 of 1,435 companies (9 percent) managed to outperform the equity market averages for a decade or more. Further, only 11 of 1,435 companies (less than 1 percent) met the study's criteria for sustained superior performance.
- *Creative Destruction:* only 160 of 1,008 companies (16 percent) studied over a thirty-year period managed to remain in existence at all.
- *Stall Points:* only 5 percent of the Fortune 50 successfully sustained their growth.

Delivering superior performance while building the capability to do it again and again is the definition of a great organization. Yet most organizations and their leaders fail to achieve this. The roots of their failure lie in their approach.

AESOP'S FABLE

One day a poor farmer discovers in the nest of his pet goose a glittering golden egg. At first, he thinks it must be some kind of trick. But on second thought, he decides to take the egg and have it appraised.

The farmer can't believe his good fortune. The egg is pure gold! He becomes even more excited the next day when the goose lays another golden egg. Day after day, he awakens to rush to the nest and find another golden egg. Soon he becomes fabulously wealthy.

But with wealth comes greed and impatience. Unable to wait day after day for the golden eggs, the farmer decides to kill the goose and get them all at once. But when he opens the goose, he finds it empty. There are no golden eggs—and now there is no way to get any more. The farmer has destroyed the very thing that produced them.

Within this fable is a key principle of organizational performance. Sustained, superior performance is a function of two things: what is produced (the golden eggs) and the capacity to produce (the goose).

If organizations focus only on producing golden eggs (achieving results today) and neglect the goose (building capability for tomorrow) they will soon be without the asset that produces golden eggs. On the other hand, if organizations only take care of the goose with no aim toward the golden eggs, they soon won't have the wherewithal to feed the goose. The key lies in the balance.

Maybe your organization is like this:

When confronted with pressure to deliver results, we pull out all the stops. We create a program to marshal the troops and push everyone to achieve the urgent objective. One time it may be a sales goal. The next crisis may be a cost-cutting goal. The next time it will be something else. We're constantly reactive, lurching from one "critical objective" or "emergency initiative" to the next. The problem is that we always seem to underinvest in the people, processes or equipment we need to really improve our business. As a result, we can never get into a rhythm of consistent performance.

Or, maybe your organization is like this:

We invested heavily in people and culture for many years. Our theory was that great, talented people with the best systems and technologies, would automatically generate sustained superior performance. It was a great place to work, but then the hard times hit. We found that we really didn't have the hard-coded ability to execute in the face of tough competition and an unfavorable economic environment. We were forced to cut back on all the investments people were used to during the golden years. People have become disillusioned, morale has tanked and many of our best people are leaving.

FranklinCovey has learned this lesson the hard way because we, too, have vacillated on this performance–performance capability pendulum. It has therefore become an "earned" learning and our approach has more than theoretical conviction behind it.

At FranklinCovey we approach the goal of sustained superior performance from both sides of the equation. We help organizations focus on and deliver specific results. We also help them build more capability—leaders and individual contributors that can have the capability to perform at new levels.

Under these two areas (Achieving Results and Building Capability) FranklinCovey works with clients in three distinct "jobs to be done." They represent the three core areas of greatness embodied in The 8th Habit: *organizational greatness*, *leadership greatness* and *personal greatness*.

Achieving Results

Job 1. Execution on Key Priorities. We help clients achieve specific results—such as increasing sales, implementing specific initiatives or improving quality—by increasing commitment and clarity to top priorities and building execution processes around those priorities. This builds *organizational greatness*.

Building Capability

Job 2. Leadership and Management Development. We help clients build enduring leadership capability based on character, team building and the ability to achieve results with excellence. This builds *leadership greatness*.

Job 3. Individual Effectiveness. We help organizations increase the knowledge, skills and personal performance of their workforce, achieving greater results as individuals and teams. This builds *personal greatness*.

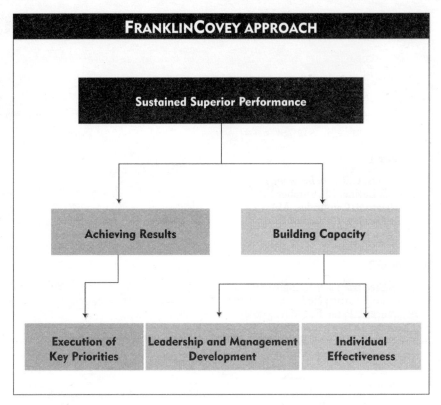

Figure A8.1

Consider for a moment how you might build a championship sports team. By investing in the quality and conditioning of the athletes, your team will improve—better players make better teams. At the same time, no matter how good the individual players, the team only wins if they can work together against specific objectives and "execute the play" again and again with excellence.

What you want is great players and great execution. A team that can perform consistently season after season—a winning franchise. This is the essence of the FranklinCovey approach: translating organizational capabilities into specific results again and again, resulting in a winning organization.

NOTES

Chapter 1

1. Rogers, C.R., *On Becoming a Person* (Boston: Houghton Mifflin, 1961), p. 26.
2. Rick Levine, Christopher Locke, Doc Searls and David Weinberger, *The Cluetrain Manifesto* (Cambridge, MA: Perseus Books Publishing, 2000), pp. 36, 39.
3. Antony Jay, *The Oxford Dictionary of Political Quotations* (Oxford: Oxford University Press, 1996), p. 68.

Chapter 2

1. Quoted from a speech given by Stanley M. Davis at a conference in Asia in which we both participated.
2. Drucker, Peter F., "Managing Knowledge Means Managing Oneself," *Leader to Leader*, 16 (Spring 2000), pp. 8–10.
3. Drucker, Peter F., *Management Challenges for the 21st Century* (New York: Harper Business, 1999), p. 135.

Chapter 3

1. Henry David Thoreau, *Walden* (Boston: Beacon Press, 1997), p. 70.
2. Robert Frost, Elizabeth Knowles, ed., *The Oxford Dictionary of Quotations*, 5th ed. "The Road Not Taken," (1916) (Oxford: Oxford University Press, 1999).

Chapter 4

1. Daniel Ladinsky, *The Gift:* Poems by Hafiz the Great Sufi Master (New York: Penguin Compass, 1999), pp. 67–68.
2. Marianne Williamson, *A Return to Love: Reflections on the Principles of a Course in Miracles* (New York: Harper Collins, 1992), pp. 190–191.
3. Michael C. Thomsett, speech, Oct. 9, 1956, in *War and Conflict Quotations* (North Carolina: McFarland & Company, 1997), p. 50.
4. *Munsey's Magazine* (February 1897), 554. Found on the Ella Wheeler Wilcox Society web site visited on May 15, 2004: http://www.ellawheelerwilcox.org.
5. C.S. Lewis, *Mere Christianity* (New York: Simon & Schuster, 1980), pp. 19–21.
6. Doc Childre and Bruce Cryer, *From Chaos to Coherence* (Boston: Butterworth-Heinemann, 1999), p. 23.
7. Ibid., p. 29.
8. Daniel Goleman, *Working with Emotional Intelligence* (New York: Bantam Books, 1998), p. 31.
9. Richard Wolman, *Thinking with Your Soul* (New York: Harmony Books, 2001), p. 26.
10. *The Holy Bible*, King James Version.
11. Danah Zohar and Ian Marshall, *SQ: Connecting with Our Spiritual Intelligence* (New York and London: Bloomsbury, 2000).

12. William Bloom, *The Endorphin Effect* (United Kingdom: Judy Piatkus Publishers Ltd., 2001), p. 12.
13. Anwar el-Sadat, *In Search of Identity: An Autobiography* (New York: Harper and Row Publishers, 1978), p. 303.
14. "The Speaker's Electronic Reference Collection," AApex Software, 1994.
15. YMCA of the USA, Dartmouth Medical School, The Institute for American Values, *Hardwired to Connect: The New Scientific Case for Authoritative Communities*, A Report to the Nation from the Commission on Children at Risk (2003), p. 6.
16. Dee Hock, "The Art of Chaordic Leadership," *Leader to Leader*, 15 (Winter 2000), pp. 20–26.
17. Warren G. Bennis and Robert J. Thomas, *Geeks and Geezers: How Era, Values, and Defining Moments Shape Leaders* (Boston: Harvard Business School Publishing, 2002).
18. Jim Loehr and Tony Schwartz, *The Power of Full Engagement* (New York: Simon & Schuster, 2003).

Chapter 5

1. Philip Massinger, Timoleon, in *The Bondman*, act 1, sc. 3 (1624), *Poems of Philip Massinger*, P. Edwards and C. Gibson, eds. (1976).
2. Susana Wesley, letter to her son dated June 8, 1725. Found on the Wesleyan Church website www.wesleyan.org. visited on 5/14/04.
3. Polly LaBarre, "Do You Have the Will to Lead?," *Fast Company Magazine* 32 (March 2000), p. 222. Found on website visited on May 27, 2004: http://www.fast-company.com/online/32/koestenbaum.html.
4. Lucinda Vardey. A Simple Path, introduction to Mother Teresa, Lucinda Vardey, ed. (New York: Ballantine, 1995), p. xxxviii.
5. Josef Hell, *Aufzeichnung*, (Institut für Zeitgeschichte, 1922) ZS 640, p. 5.
6. Dag Hammarskjöld, *Markings* (New York: Alfred A Knopf, 2001), p. 124.
7. Albert E. N. Gray Essay *"The common denominator of success"* (Philadelphia: NALU annual convention, 1940).
8. Harold B. Lee, *Teachings of Harold B. Lee*. Clyde J. Williams, ed. (Salt Lake City: Bookcraft, 1996), p. 606.
9. Charles Moore, introduction to *Washington's School Exercises: Rules of Civility and Decent Behavior in Company and conversation*, Charles Moore, ed. (Boston: Houghton Mifflin Company, 1926), pp. xi–xv.
10. Elizabeth Knowles, ed., *The Oxford Dictionary of Quotations*, 5th ed. (Oxford: Oxford University Press, 1999.), p. 396.
11. JoAnn C. Jones, "Brockville," *Ontario-Guide Posts*, January 1996.
12. David O. McKay, *Conference Report*, The Church of Jesus Christ of Latter-day Saints, April 1964, p. 5.
13. John G. Whittier, *Maud Muller* (Boston: Riverside Press, 1866), p. 12.

Chapter 6

1. Peter F. Drucker, *Management Challenges for the 21st Century* (New York: Harper Collins, 1999), p. 8.
2. Philip Evans and Thomas S. Wurster, *Blown to Bits* (Boston: Harvard Business School Press), p. 13.
3. Dave Ulrich, Jack Zenger and Norm Smallwood, *Results Based Leadership* (Boston: Harvard Business School Press, 1999), p. 7.

Chapter 7

1. Del Jones, "What would Attila the Hun do?" *USA Today* (April 6, 2003). Found on *USA Today* website visited on May 27, 2004: http://www.usatoday.com/money/companies/management/2003-04-06-warleaders_x.htm.
2. Tom Peters, *The Project 50* (New York: Alfred A. Knopf, 1999), pp. 48–49.

Chapter 8

1. American Museum of Natural History, found on web site visited on May 15, 2004: http://www.amnh.org/common/faq/quotes.html.
2. Eknath Easwaran, *Gandhi, the Man*, 2nd ed. (Nilgin Press, 1978), p. 145.
3. Lieutenant General Dave R. Palmer '56 (retired) "Competence and Character: Schwarzkopf's Message to the Corps." *Assembly Magazine*, May 1992.

Chapter 9

1. Gordon B. Hinckley, "The True Strength of the Church," *Ensign Magazine*, July 1973, p. 48.
2. Rick Pitino, *Lead to Succeed* (New York: Broadway Books, 2000), p. 64.
3. Elizabeth Knowles, ed., *The Oxford Dictionary of Quotations*, 5th ed. (Oxford: Oxford University Press, 1999), p. 503.
4. Dag Hammarskjöld, *Markings* (New York: Alfred A Knopf, 2001), p. 197.
5. C.S. Lewis, *Mere Christianity* (New York: Simon & Schuster, 1980), pp. 165–166.

Chapter 10

1. Warren Bennis, *Why Leaders Can't Lead* (San Francisco, Jossey-Bass Publishers 1989), p. 158.
2. Arun Gandhi, "Reflections of Peace," *BYU Magazine*, vol. 54, no. 1 (Spring 2000) pp. 1–6. Found on web site visited on May 14, 2004: http://magazine.byu.edu/bym/2000sp/pages/peace1.shtml#.
3. Ralph Roughton, M.D., used with permission.

Chapter 11

1. J.A. Belasco, *Teaching the Elephant to Dance: The Manager's Guide to Empowering Change* (New York: Plume, 1991), p. 11.
2. Clayton M. Christensen, *The Innovators Dilemma* (Boston: Harvard Business School Press, 1997), pp. xviii–xix.
3. Jim Collins, *Good to Great* (New York: HarperCollins, 2001), p. 96.

Chapter 12

1. Martin H. Manser, *The Westminister Collections of Christian Quotations* (Louisville: Westminister John Knox Press, 2001), p. 76.
2. Randall Rothenberg and Noel M. Tichy: "The Thought Leader Interview," *Strategy + Business Magazine* (Spring 2002), pp. 91–92.

Chapter 13

1. Marcus Buckingham and Donald O. Clifton, *Now Discover Your Strengths* (New York: Simon & Schuster, 2001), p. 5.
2. Ibid.

3. Thomas Stewart, *Intellectual Capital: The New Wealth of Organizations* (New York: Doubleday Books, 1997).
4. Stuart Crainer, *The Management Century* (San Francisco: Jossey-Bass Publishers, 2000), p. 207.
5. Peter F. Drucker, *Managing for the Future: The 1990's and Beyond* (New York: Truman Tally Books, Dutton, 1992), p. 334.
6. Max De Pree, *Leadership Is an Art* (New York: Dell Publishing, 1989), pp. 28, 38.

Chapter 14

1. Larry Bossidy and Ram Charan, *Execution: The Discipline of Getting Things Done* (New York: Crown Business, 2002), pp. 19, 34.
2. Louis V. Gerstner, *Who Says Elephants Can't Dance?* (New York: HarperCollins Publishers, 2002), p. 230.
3. Charles Hummel, *Tyranny of the Urgent* (Downers Grove, IL: Inter Varsity Christian Fellowship of the United States of America, 1967), pp. 9–10.

Chapter 15

1. Gordon B. Hinckley, "Testimony," *Ensign Magazine* (May 1998), p. 69.
2. Engraved in a monument at Rockefeller Center, New York City, New York.
3. Nelson Mandela, *Long Walk to Freedom* (Boston: Little, Brown and Company, 1994), pp. 543–544.
4. Engraved in a monument at the entrance of the Nathan Eldon Tanner Building, Marriott School of Management, Brigham Young University, Provo, Utah.
5. Alfred North Whitehead, "The Rhythmic Claims of Freedom and Discipline," *The Aims of Education and Other Essays* (New York: New American Library, 1929), p. 46.
6. Dag Hammarskjöld, *Markings* (New York: Alfred A Knopf, 2001), p. 158.
7. Muggeridge, Malcolm, "A Twentieth Century Testimony" *Malcolm Muggeridge,* Thomas Howard, ed. (London: Collins, 1979).
8. Robert K. Greenleaf, "The Servant as Leader," *Servant Leadership: A Journey into the Nature of Legitimate Power and Greatness,* 25th anniversary ed. (Mahwah, New Jersey: Paulist Press, 2002), pp. 23–24.
9. Jim Collins, "Level Five Leadership: The Triumph of Humility and Fierce Resolve," *Harvard Business Review,* vol. 79, no. 1 (January 2001), p. 67.
10. Jim Collins, *Good to Great* (New York: HarperCollins Publishers, 2001), p. 20.
11. Jim Collins, "And the Walls Came Tumbling Down," *Leading Beyond the Walls,* The Peter F. Drucker Foundation for Nonprofit Management; Frances Hesselbein, Marshall Goldsmith and Iain Somerville, ed. (Jossey-Bass Publishers, 1999).
12. *Peel's Principles of Modern Policing,* 1829.
13. Report of Col. Joshua L. Chamberlain, Twentieth Maine Infantry Field Near Emmitsburg—July 6, 1863.
14. Alice Rains Trulock, *In the Hands of Providence: Joshua L. Chamberlain and the American Civil War* (Chapel Hill: The University of North Carolina Press, 1992), p. 5.
15. Maxwell Anderson, *Joan of Lorraine,* (Washington, D.C.: Anderson House, 1947).
16. Haddon Klingberg Jr., *When Life Calls Out to Us* (New York: Doubleday 2001), p. 8.
17. Trulock, p. 154. Excerpt from the dedication of the Maine Monuments at Gettysburg on the evening of October 3, 1889.

Appendix 1

1. Doc Childre and Bruce Cryer, *From Chaos to Coherence* (Boston: Butterworth-Heinemann, 1999), p. 23.
2. C.S. Lewis, *Mere Christianity* (New York: Simon & Schuster, 1980), pp. 124–125.
3. Childre and Cryer, p. 69.
4. Robert Frost, "Two Tramps in Mud Time," *The Poetry of Robert Frost*, Edward Connery Lathem, ed. (New York: Henry Holt and Co., 1969).
5. Lewis, p. 88.

INDEX

Page numbers in *italics* refer to figures and tables.

ABOUT FRANKLINCOVEY

MISSION STATEMENT

We enable greatness in people and organizations everywhere.

FOUNDATIONAL BELIEFS

We believe:

1. **People** are inherently capable, aspire to greatness and have the power to choose.
2. **Principles** are timeless and universal, and are the foundation for lasting effectiveness.
3. **Leadership** is a choice, built inside out on a foundation of character. Great leaders unleash the collective talent and passion of people toward the right goal.
4. **Habits of effectiveness** come only from the committed use of integrated processes and tools.
5. **Sustained superior performance** requires P/PC Balance®—a focus on achieving results and on building capability.

VALUES

1. **Commitment to Principles.** We are passionate about our content, and strive to be models of the principles and practices we teach.
2. **Lasting Customer Impact.** We are relentless about delivering on our promises to our customers. Our success comes only with their success.

3. **Respect for the Whole Person.** We value each other and treat each person with whom we work as true partners.
4. **Profitable Growth.** We embrace profitability and growth as the lifeblood of our organization; they give us the freedom to fulfill our mission and vision.

FranklinCovey (NYSE:FC) is the global leader in effectiveness training, productivity tools and assessment services for organizations, teams and individuals. Clients include 90 percent of the Fortune 100, more than 75 percent of the Fortune 500, thousands of small and midsized businesses, as well as numerous government entities and educational institutions. Organizations and individuals access FranklinCovey products and services through corporate training, licensed client facilitators, one-on-one coaching, public workshops, catalogs, more than 140 retail stores and www.franklincovey.com.

FranklinCovey has 2,000 associates providing professional services, products and materials in twenty-eight languages, in thirty-nine offices and in ninety-five countries worldwide.

Programs and Services

- xQ Survey and Debrief *(to help leaders assess their organization's "Execution Quotient")*
- The 7 Habits of Highly Effective People workshop
- The 4 Disciplines of Execution worksession
- FOCUS: Achieving Your Highest Priorities workshop
- The 4 Roles of Leadership workshop
- The FranklinCovey Planning System

To learn more about FranklinCovey products and services,
please call +44 (0)870 870 7600,
or go to www.franklincoveyeurope.com.

ABOUT THE AUTHOR

Stephen R. Covey is an internationally respected leadership authority, family expert, teacher, organizational consultant and author who has dedicated his life to teaching principle-centered living and leadership to build both families and organizations. He holds an M.B.A. from Harvard University and a doctorate from Brigham Young University, where he was a professor of organizational behavior and business management and also served as director of university relations and assistant to the president.

Dr. Covey is the author of several acclaimed books, including the international bestseller, *The 7 Habits of Highly Effective People*, which was named the #1 Most Influential Business Book of the Twentieth Century and one of the top-ten most influential management books ever. It has sold more than 15 million copies in thirty-eight languages throughout the world. Other bestsellers include *First Things First, Principle-Centered Leadership* and *The 7 Habits of Highly Effective Families*, bringing the combined total to more than 20 million books sold.

As a father of nine and grandfather of forty-three, he received the 2003 Fatherhood Award from the National Fatherhood Initiative, which he says is the most meaningful award he has ever received. Other awards given to Dr. Covey include the Thomas More College Medallion for continuing service to humanity, Speaker of the Year in 1999, the Sikh's 1998 International Man of Peace Award, the 1994 International Entrepreneur of the Year Award and the National Entrepreneur of the Year Lifetime Achievement Award for Entrepreneurial Leadership. Dr. Covey has also been recognized as one of *Time* magazine's 25 Most Influential Americans and has received seven honorary doctorate degrees.

Dr. Covey is the cofounder and vice chairman of FranklinCovey Company, the leading global professional services firm with offices in 123 countries. They share Dr. Covey's vision, discipline and passion to inspire, lift and provide tools for change and growth of individuals and organizations throughout the world.

⑧ The 8th Habit Challenge

ONE: Read the chapter
TWO: Teach the chapter to at least two people, including work colleagues, family members, friends, etc.
THREE: Make a sincere, concerted effort to live the principles included in the chapter for one month.
FOUR: Report the results and your learnings from seeking to live the ideas in the chapter to a trusted colleague, family member or friend.

Find your voice and inspire others to find theirs.

	① READ	② TEACH TWO		③ LIVE PRINCIPLES	④ REPORT RESULTS
	☐	☐	☐	☐ 30 days	☐
	☐	☐	☐	☐ 30 days	☐
	☐	☐	☐	☐ 30 days	☐
	☐	☐	☐	☐ 30 days	☐
	☐	☐	☐	☐ 30 days	☐
	☐	☐	☐	☐ 30 days	☐
	☐	☐	☐	☐ 30 days	☐
	☐	☐	☐	☐ 30 days	☐
	☐	☐	☐	☐ 30 days	☐
	☐	☐	☐	☐ 30 days	☐
	☐	☐	☐	☐ 30 days	☐
esults	☐	☐	☐	☐ 30 days	☐
	☐	☐	☐	☐ 30 days	☐
	☐	☐	☐	☐ 30 days	☐
	☐	☐	☐	☐ 30 days	☐
	☐	☐	☐	☐ 30 days	☐

THE DVD FOUND ON THE INSIDE BACK COVER FEATURES:

16 Inspirational Companion Films

1. Legacy
2. Max & Max
3. Discovery of a Character
4. Law of the Harvest
5. AB Combs
6. Stone
7. Permanent Whitewater
8. Mauritius
9. Big Rocks
10. Teacher
11. Street Hawkers
12. Goal!
13. Berlin Wall
14. The Nature of Leadership
15. It's Not Just Important, It's *Wildly* Important
16. Gandhi

www.the8thhabit.com

Not to Be Sold or Distributed Separately